Thomas Keneally

Thomas Keneally began his writing career in 1964 and has published thirty-three novels since. They include *The Chant Of Jimmie Blacksmith*, *Confederates* and *Gossip From The Forest*, each of which was shortlisted for the Booker Prize, before he won it with *Schindler's Ark* in 1982. In 1993 the novel was made by Steven Spielberg into the internationally acclaimed film *Schindler's List*, which went on to win seven Academy Awards, including Best Picture and Best Director. His recent novels include *The Daughters Of Mars*, which was shortlisted for the Walter Scott Prize in 2013, *Napoleon's Last Island*, *Crimes of the Father* and *The Book of Science and Antiquities*. He has also written several works of non-fiction, including his memoir *Homebush Boy*, *Searching for Schindler* and *Australians*. He is married with two daughters and lives in Sydney.

'A magnificent book, powerful, harrowing and beautifully written.'

SUNDAY EXPRESS

'Brilliantly detailed, moving, powerful and gripping.'

THE TIMES

'Keneally is a superb storyteller. With *Schindler's Ark* he has given us his best book yet, a magnificent novel which held me from the first page to the last.'

ALAN SILLITOE

'This remarkable book has the immediacy and the almost unbearable detail of a thousand eye witnesses who forgot nothing.'

NEW YORK TIMES BOOK REVIEW

'Thomas Keneally has done marvellous justice to a marvellous story.'

THE SUNDAY TIMES

'An extraordinary achievement.'
GRAHAM GREENE

'A fine and moving story'
EVENING STANDARD

'An astounding story . . . in this case the truth is far more powerful than anything the imagination can invent'
NEWSWEEK

'Fascinating, expertly told and impossible to put down.'
BOOKSELLER

'Extraordinary . . . A notable achievement.'
NEW YORK REVIEW OF BOOKS

'Magnificent . . . Beautifully written'
MAIL ON SUNDAY

OTHER NOVELS BY THOMAS KENEALLY
PUBLISHED BY SCEPTRE

Blood Red, Sister Rose
Gossip from the Forest
A Victim of the Aurora
Confederates
A Family Madness
The Playmaker
Towards Asmara
By the Line
Flying Hero Class
Woman of the Inner Sea
Jacko: The Great Intruder
A River Town
Bettany's Book
The Office of Innocence
The Tyrant's Novel
The Widow and Her Hero
The People's Train
The Daughters of Mars
Shame and the Captives
Napoleon's Last Island
Crimes of the Father
The Book of Science and Antiquities

SCHINDLER'S ARK

Thomas Keneally

SCEPTRE

First published in Great Britain in 1982 by Hodder & Stoughton

This edition published in 2019

The authorised representative in the EEA is Hachette Ireland, 8 Castlecourt Centre, Dublin 15, D15 XTP3, Ireland (email: info@hbgi.ie)

Copyright © 1982, Serpentine Publishing Co. Pty. Ltd.

The right of Thomas Keneally to be identified as the Author of the Work has been asserted by him in accordance with the Copyright, Designs and Patents Act 1988

All rights reserved. No part of this publication may be reproduced, stored in a retrieval system, or transmitted, in any form or by any means without the prior written permission of the publisher, nor be otherwise circulated in any form of binding or cover other than that in which it is published and without a similar condition being imposed on the subsequent purchaser.

All characters in this publication are fictitious and any resemblance to real persons, living or dead, is purely coincidental.

A CIP catalogue record for this title is available from the British Library

ISBN 9781529324976

Printed and bound in Great Britain by Clays Ltd, Elcograf S.p.A.

Hodder & Stoughton policy is to use papers that are natural, renewable and recyclable products and made from wood grown in sustainable forests. The logging and manufacturing processes are expected to conform to the environmental regulations of the country of origin.

Hodder & Stoughton Ltd
Carmelite House
50 Victoria Embankment
London EC4Y 0DZ

www.sceptrebooks.co.uk

To the memory of Oskar Schindler, and to Leopold Pfefferberg, who by zeal and persistence caused this book to be written

Glossary

SS Ranks and Their Army Equivalents

Commissioned Ranks

Oberst-gruppenführer	general
Obergruppenführer	lieutenant general
Gruppenführer	major general
Brigadeführer	brigadier general
Oberführer	(no army equivalent)
Standartenführer	colonel
Obersturmbannführer	lieutenant colonel
Sturmbannführer	major
Hauptsturmführer	captain
Obersturmführer	first lieutenant
Untersturmführer	second lieutenant

Non-commissioned Ranks

Oberscharführer	a senior noncommissioned rank
Unterscharführer	equivalent to sergeant
Rottenführer	equivalent to corporal

Author's Note

In 1980 I visited a luggage store in Beverly Hills, California, and inquired the prices of briefcases. The store belonged to Leopold Pfefferberg, a Schindler survivor. It was beneath Pfefferberg's shelves of imported Italian leather goods that I first heard of Oskar Schindler, the German *bon vivant*, speculator, charmer, and sign of contradiction, and of his salvage of a cross section of a condemned race during those years now known by the generic name Holocaust.

This account of Oskar's astonishing history is based in the first place on interviews with 50 Schindler survivors from seven nations – Australia, Israel, West Germany, Austria, the United States, Argentina, and Brazil. It is enriched by a visit, in the company of Leopold Pfefferberg, to locations that prominently figure in the book: Cracow, Oskar's adopted city; Płaszów, the scene of Amon Goeth's foul labour camp; Lipowa Street, Zablocie, where Oskar's factory still stands; Auschwitz-Birkenau, from which Oskar extracted his women prisoners. But the narration depends also on documentary and other information supplied by those few wartime associates of Oskar's who can still be reached, as well as by the large body of his postwar friends. Many of the plentiful testimonies regarding Oskar deposited by Schindler Jews at *Yad Vashem*, The Martyrs' and Heroes' Remembrance Authority, further enriched the record, as did written testimonies from private sources and a body of Schindler papers and letters, some supplied by *Yad Vashem*, some by Oskar's friends.

To use the texture and devices of a novel to tell a true story is a course that has frequently been followed in modern writing. It is the one I chose to follow here – both because the novelist's craft is the only one I can lay claim to, and because the novel's techniques seem suited for a character of such ambiguity and magnitude as Oskar. I have attempted, however, to avoid all fiction, since fiction would debase the record, and to distinguish between reality and the myths which are likely to attach themselves to a man of Oskar's stature. It has sometimes been necessary to make reasonable constructs of conversations of which Oskar and others have left only the briefest record. But most exchanges and conversations, and all events, are based on the detailed recollections of the *Schindlerjuden* (Schindler Jews), of Schindler himself, and of other witnesses to Oskar's acts of outrageous rescue.

I would like to thank first three Schindler survivors – Leopold Pfefferberg, Justice Moshe Bejski of the Israeli Supreme Court, and Mieczyslaw Pemper – who not only passed on their memories of Oskar to the author and gave him certain documents which have contributed to the accuracy of the narrative, but also read the early draft of the book and suggested corrections. Many others, whether Schindler survivors or Oskar's postwar associates, gave interviews and generously contributed information through letters and documents. These include Frau Emilie Schindler, Mrs. Ludmila Pfefferberg, Dr. Sophia Stern, Mrs. Helen Horowitz, Dr. Jonas Dresner, Mr. and Mrs. Henry and Mariana Rosner, Leopold Rosner, Dr. Alex Rosner, Dr. Idek Schindel, Dr. Danuta Schindel, Mrs. Regina Horowitz, Mrs. Bronislawa Karakulska, Mr. Richard Horowitz, Mr. Shmuel Springmann, the late Mr. Jakob Sternberg, Mr. Jerzy Sternberg, Mr. and Mrs. Lewis Fagen, Mr. Henry Kinstlinger, Mrs. Rebecca Bau, Mr. Edward Heuberger, Mr. and Mrs. M. Hirschfeld, Mr. and Mrs. Irving Glovin, and many others. In my home city, Mr. and Mrs. E. Korn not only gave of their memories of Oskar but were a constant support. At *Yad Vashem*, Dr. Josef Kermisz, Dr. Shmuel Krakowski, Vera Prausnitz, Chana Abells, and Hadassah Mödlinger provided generous access to the testimonies of Schindler survivors and to video and photographic material.

Lastly, I would like to honour the efforts which the late Mr. Martin Gosch expended on bringing the name of Oskar Schindler to the world's notice, and to signify my thanks to his widow, Mrs. Lucille Gaynes, for her cooperation with this project.

Through the assistance of all these people, Oskar Schindler's astonishing history appears for the first time in extended form.

TOM KENEALLY

Prologue

Autumn, 1943

In Poland's deepest autumn, a tall young man in an expensive overcoat, double-breasted dinner jacket beneath it and – in the lapel of the dinner jacket – a large ornamental gold-on-black-enamel *Hakenkreuz* (swastika) emerged from a fashionable apartment building in Straszewskiego Street, on the edge of the ancient centre of Cracow, and saw his chauffeur waiting with fuming breath by the open door of an enormous and, even in this blackened world, lustrous Adler limousine.

'Watch the pavement, Herr Schindler,' said the chauffeur. 'It's as icy as a widow's heart.'

In observing this small winter scene, we are on safe ground. The tall young man would to the end of his days wear double-breasted suits, would – being something of an engineer – always be gratified by large dazzling vehicles, would – though a German and at this point in history a German of some influence – always be the sort of man with whom a Polish chauffeur could safely crack a lame, comradely joke.

But it will not be possible to see the whole story under such easy character headings. For this is the story of the pragmatic triumph of good over evil, a triumph in eminently measurable, statistical, unsubtle terms. When you work from the other end of the beast – when you chronicle the predictable and measurable success evil generally achieves – it is easy to be wise, wry, piercing, to avoid bathos. It is easy to show the inevitability by which evil acquires all of what you could call the *real estate* of the story, even though good might finish up with a few imponderables like dignity and self-knowledge. Fatal human malice is the staple of narrators, original sin the mother-fluid of historians. But it is a risky enterprise to have to write of virtue.

'Virtue' in fact is such a dangerous word that we have to rush to explain; Herr Oskar Schindler, risking his glimmering shoes on the icy pavement in this old and elegant quarter of Cracow, was not a virtuous young man in the customary sense. In this city he kept house with his German mistress and maintained a long affair with his Polish secretary. His wife, Emilie, chose to live most of the time at home in Moravia, though she sometimes came to Poland to visit him. There's this to be said for him: that to all his women he was a well-mannered and generous lover. But under the normal interpretation of 'virtue,' that's no excuse.

Likewise, he was a drinker. Some of the time he drank for the pure glow of it, at other times with associates, bureaucrats, SS men for more palpable results. Like few others, he was capable of staying canny while drinking, of keeping his head. That again, though – under the narrow interpretation of morality – has never been an excuse for carousing. And although Herr Schindler's merit is well documented, it is a feature of his ambiguity that he worked within or, at least, on the strength of a corrupt and savage scheme, one that filled Europe with camps of varying but consistent inhumanity and created a submerged, unspoken-of nation of prisoners. The best thing, therefore, may be to begin with a tentative instance of Herr Schindler's strange virtue and of the places and associates to which it brought him.

At the end of Straszewskiego Street, the car moved beneath the black bulk of Wawel Castle, from which the National Socialist Party's darling lawyer Hans Frank ruled the Government General of Poland. As from the palace of any evil giant, no light showed. Neither Herr Schindler nor the driver glanced up at the ramparts as the car turned southeast toward the river. At the Podgórze Bridge, the guards, placed above the freezing Vistula to prevent the transit of partisans and other curfew-breakers between Podgórze and Cracow, were used to the vehicle, to Herr Schindler's face, to the *Passierschein* presented by the chauffeur. Herr Schindler passed this checkpoint frequently, travelling either from his factory (where he also had an apartment) to the city on business, or else from his Straszewskiego Street apartment to his plant in the suburb of Zablocie. They were used to seeing him after dark too, attired formally or semiformally, passing one way or another to a dinner, a party, a bedroom; perhaps, as was the case tonight, on his way ten kilometres out of town to the forced-labour camp at Płaszów, to dine there with SS *Hauptsturmführer* Amon Goeth, that highly placed sensualist. Herr Schindler had a reputation for being generous with gifts of liquor at Christmas, and so the car was permitted to pass over into the suburb of Podgórze without much delay.

It is certain that by this stage of his history, in spite of his liking for good food and wine, Herr Schindler approached tonight's dinner at Commandant Goeth's more with loathing than with anticipation. There had in fact never been a time when to sit and drink with Amon had not been a repellent business. Yet the revulsion Herr Schindler felt was of a piquant kind, an ancient, exultant sense of abomination – of the same sort as, in a mediaeval painting, the just show for the damned. An emotion, that is, which stung Oskar rather than unmanned him.

In the black leather interior of the Adler as it raced along the trolley tracks in what had been until recently the Jewish ghetto, Herr Schindler – as always – chain-smoked. But it was composed chain smoking. There was never tension in the hands; he was stylish. His manner implied that he knew where the next cigarette was coming from and the next bottle of cognac. Only he could have told us whether he had to succour himself from a flask as he passed by the mute, black village of Prokocim and saw, on the line to Lwów, a string of stalled cattle cars, which might hold infantry or prisoners or even – though the odds were against it – cattle.

Out in the countryside, perhaps ten kilometres from the centre of town, the Adler turned right at a street named – by an irony

– Jerozolimska. This night of sharp frosty outlines, Herr Schindler saw beneath the hill first a ruined synagogue, and then the bare shapes of what passed these days as the city of Jerusalem, Forced Labour Camp Płaszów, barracks town of 20,000 unquiet Jews. The Ukrainian and *Waffen* SS men at the gate greeted Herr Schindler courteously, for he was known at least as well here as on the Podgórze Bridge.

When level with the Administration Building, the Adler moved onto a prison road paved with Jewish gravestones. The campsite had been till two years before a Jewish cemetery. Commandant Goeth, who claimed to be a poet, had used in the construction of his camp whatever metaphors were to hand. This metaphor of shattered gravestones ran the length of the camp, splitting it in two, but did not extend eastward to the villa occupied by Commandant Goeth himself.

On the right, past the guard barracks, stood a former Jewish mortuary building. It seemed to declare that here all death was natural and by attrition, that all the dead were laid out. In fact the place was now used as the Commandant's stables. Though Herr Schindler was used to the sight, it is possible that he still reacted with a small ironic cough. Admittedly, if you reacted to every little irony of the new Europe, you took it into you, it became part of your baggage. But Herr Schindler possessed an immense capacity for carrying that sort of luggage.

A prisoner named Poldek Pfefferberg was also on his way to the Commandant's villa that evening. Lisiek, the Commandant's nineteen-year-old orderly, had come to Pfefferberg's barracks with passes signed by an SS NCO. The boy's problem was that the Commandant's bathtub had a stubborn ring around it, and Lisiek feared that he would be beaten for it when Commandant Goeth came to take his morning bath. Pfefferberg, who had been Lisiek's teacher in high school in Podgórze, worked in the camp garage and had access to solvents. So in company with Lisiek he went to the garage and picked up a stick with a swab on the end and a can of cleaning fluid. To approach the Commandant's villa was always a dubious business, but involved the chance that you would be given food by Helen Hirsch, Goeth's mistreated Jewish maid, a generous girl who had also been a student of Pfefferberg's.

When Herr Schindler's Adler was still 100 metres from the villa, it set the dogs barking – the Great Dane, the wolfhound and all the others Amon kept in the kennels beyond the house. The villa itself was square-built, with an attic. The upper windows gave onto a balcony. All around the walls was a terraced patio with a balustrade. Amon Goeth liked sitting out of doors in the summer. Since he'd come to Płaszów, he'd put on weight. Next summer he'd make a fat sun-worshipper. But in this particular version of Jerusalem, he'd be safe from mockery.

An SS *Unterscharführer* (sergeant) in white gloves had been put on the door tonight. Saluting, he admitted Herr Schindler to the house. In the hallway, the Ukrainian orderly Ivan took Herr Schindler's coat and homburg. Schindler patted the breast pocket of his suit to be sure he had the gift for his host: a gold-plated cigarette case, black-market. Amon was doing so well on the side, especially with confiscated jewellery, that he would be offended by anything less than gold plate.

At the double doors opening onto the dining room, the Rosner brothers were playing, Henry on violin, Leo on accordion. At Goeth's demand, they had put aside the tattered clothing of the camp paint shop where they worked in the daytime and adopted the evening clothes they kept in their barracks for such events. Oskar Schindler knew that although the Commandant admired their music, the Rosners never played at ease in the villa. They had seen too much of Amon. They knew he was erratic and given to *ex tempore* executions. They played studiously and hoped that their music would not suddenly, inexplicably, give offence.

At Goeth's table that night there would be seven men. Apart from Schindler himself and the host, the guests included Julian Schemer, head of the SS for the Cracow region, and Rolf Czurda, chief of the Cracow branch of the SD, the late Heydrich's Security Service. Schemer was an *Oberführer* – an SS rank between colonel and brigadier general, for which there is no army equivalent; Czurda, an *Obersturmbannführer*, equivalent to lieutenant colonel. Goeth himself held the rank of *Hauptsturmführer*, or captain. Schemer and Czurda were the guests of highest honour, for this camp was under their authority. They were years older than Commandant Goeth, and SS police chief Schemer looked definitely middle-aged with his glasses and bald head and slight obesity. Even so, in view of his protégé's profligate living habits, the age difference between himself and Amon didn't seem so great.

The oldest of the company was Herr Franz Bosch, a veteran of the first war, manager of various workshops, legal and illegal, inside Płaszów. He was also an 'economic adviser' to Julian Scherner and had business interests in the city.

Oskar despised Bosch and the two police chiefs, Schemer and Czurda. Their cooperation, however, was essential to the existence of his own peculiar plant in Zablocie, and so he regularly sent them gifts. The only guests with whom Oskar shared any fellow feeling were Julius Madritsch, owner of the Madritsch uniform factory inside this camp of Płaszów, and Madritsch's manager, Raimund Titsch. Madritsch was a year or so younger than Oskar and Herr Commandant Goeth. He was an enterprising but humane man, and if asked to justify the existence of his profitable factory inside the camp, would have argued that it kept nearly four thousand prisoners employed and therefore safe from the death mills. Raimund Titsch, a man in his early forties, slight and private and likely to leave the party early, was Madritsch's manager, smuggled in truckloads of food for his prisoners (an enterprise that could have earned him a fatal stay in Montelupich prison, the SS jail, or else Auschwitz) and agreed with Madritsch.

Such was the regular roster of dinner companions at Herr Commandant Goeth's villa.

The four women guests, their hair elaborately coiffed and their gowns expensive, were younger than any of the men. They were better-class whores, German and Polish, from Cracow. Some of them were regular dinner guests here. Their number permitted a range of gentlemanly choice for the two field-grade officers. Goeth's German mistress, Majola, usually stayed at her apartment in the city during these feasts of Amon's. She looked on Goeth's dinners as male occasions and thus offensive to her sensibilities.

There is no doubt that in their fashion the police chiefs and the Commandant liked Oskar. There was, however, something odd about him. They might have been willing to write it off in part as stemming from his origins. He was Sudeten German – Arkansas to their Manhattan, Liverpool to their Cambridge. There were signs that he wasn't *right-minded*, though he paid well, was a good source of scarce commodities, could hold his liquor and had a slow and sometimes rowdy sense of humour. He was the sort of man you smiled and nodded at across the room, but it was not necessary or even wise to jump up and make a fuss over him.

It is most likely that the SS men noticed Oskar Schindler's entrance because of a *frisson* among the four girls. Those who knew Oskar in those years speak of his easy magnetic charm, exercised particularly over women, with whom he was unremittingly and improperly successful. The two police chiefs, Czurda and Scherner, now probably paid attention to Herr Schindler as a means of keeping the attention of the women. Goeth also came forward to take his hand. The Commandant was as tall as Schindler, and the impression that he was abnormally fat for a man in his early thirties was enhanced by this height, an athletic height onto which the obesity seemed unnaturally grafted. The face seemed scarcely flawed at all, except that there was a vinous light in the eyes. The Commandant drank indecent quantities of the local brandy.

He was not, however, as far gone as Herr Bosch, Płaszów's and the SS's economic genius. Herr Bosch was purple-nosed; the oxygen which by rights belonged to the veins of his face had for years gone to feed the sharp blue flame of all that liquor. Schindler, nodding to the man, knew that tonight Bosch would, as usual, put in an order for goods.

'A welcome to our industrialist,' boomed Goeth, and then he made a formal introduction to the girls around the room. The Rosner brothers played Strauss melodies through this, Henry's eyes wandering only between his strings and the emptiest corner of the room, Leo smiling down at his accordion keys.

Herr Schindler was now introduced to the women. While Herr Schindler kissed the proffered hands, he felt some pity for these Cracow working girls, since he knew that later – when the slap-and-tickle began – the slap might leave welts and the tickle gouge the flesh. But for the present, *Hauptsturmführer* Amon Goeth, a sadist when drunk, was an exemplary Viennese gentleman.

The predinner conversation was unexceptional. There was talk of the war, and while SD chief Czurda took it upon himself to assure a tall German girl that the Crimea was securely held, SS chief Schemer informed one of the other women that a boy he knew from Hamburg days, a decent chap, *Oberscharführer* in the SS, had had his legs blown off when the partisans bombed a restaurant in Czestochowa. Schindler talked factory business with Madritsch and his manager Titsch. There was a genuine friendship between these three entrepreneurs. Herr Schindler knew that little Titsch procured illegal quantities of black-market bread for the prisoners of the Madritsch uniform factory, and that much of the money for the purpose was put up by Madritsch. This was the merest humanity, since the profits in Poland were large enough, in Herr Schindler's opinion, to satisfy the most inveterate capitalist and justify some illegal outlay for extra bread. In Schindler's case, the contracts of the *Rustungsinspektion*, the Armaments Inspectorate – the body that solicited bids and awarded contracts for the manufacture of every commodity the German forces needed – had been so rich that he had exceeded his desire to be successful in the eyes of his father. Unhappily, Madritsch and Titsch and he, Oskar Schindler, were the only ones he knew who regularly spent money on black-market bread.

Near the time when Goeth would call them to the dinner table, Herr Bosch approached Schindler, predictably took him by the elbow and led him over by the door where the musicians played, as if he expected the Rosners' impeccable melodies to cover the conversation.

'Business good, I see,' said Bosch.

Schindler smiled at the man. 'You *see* that, do you, Herr Bosch?'

'I do,' said Bosch. And of course Bosch would have read the official bulletins of the Main Armaments Board, announcing contracts awarded to the Schindler factory.

'I was wondering,' said Bosch, inclining his head, 'if in view of the present boom, founded, after all, on our general successes on a series of Fronts . . . I was wondering if you might wish to make a generous gesture. Nothing big. Just a gesture.'

'Of course,' said Schindler. He felt the nausea that goes with being used, and at the same time a sensation close to joy. The office of police chief Schemer had twice used its influence to get Oskar Schindler out of jail. His staff were willing now to build up the obligation of having to do it again.

'My aunt in Bremen's been bombed out, poor old dear,' said Bosch. 'Everything! The marriage bed. The sideboards – all her Meissen and crockery. I wondered could you spare some kitchenware for her. And perhaps a pot or two – those big tureen things you turn out at DEF.'

Deutsche Emailwaren Fabrik (German Enamelware Factory) was the name of Herr Schindler's booming business. Germans called it DEF for short, but the Poles and the Jews had a different sort of shorthand, calling it Emalia.

Herr Schindler said, 'I think that can be managed. Do you want the goods consigned direct to her or through you?'

Bosch did not even smile. 'Through me, Oskar. I'd like to enclose a little card.'

'Of course.'

'So it's settled. We'll say half a gross of everything – soup bowls, plates, coffee mugs. And half a dozen of those stewpots.'

Herr Schindler, raising his jaw, laughed frankly, though with weariness. But when he spoke he sounded complaisant. As indeed he was. He was always reckless with gifts. It was simply that Bosch seemed to suffer constantly from bombed-out kinfolk.

Oskar murmured, 'Does your aunt run an orphanage?'

Bosch looked him in the eye again; nothing furtive about this drunk. 'She's an old woman with no resources. She can barter what she doesn't need.'

'I'll tell my secretary to see to it.'

'That Polish girl?' said Bosch. 'The looker?'

'The looker,' Schindler agreed.

Bosch tried to whistle, but the tension of his lips had been destroyed by the overproof brandy and the sound emerged as a low raspberry. 'Your wife,' he said, man to man, 'must be a saint.'

'She is,' Herr Schindler admitted curtly. Bosch was welcome to his kitchenware, but Schindler didn't want him talking about his wife.

'Tell me,' said Bosch. 'How do you keep her off your back? She must *know* . . . yet you seem to be able to control her very well.'

All the humour left Schindler's face now. Anyone could have seen frank distaste there. The small potent growl that arose from him, however, was not unlike Schindler's normal voice.

'I never discuss private matters,' he said.

Bosch rushed in. 'Forgive me. I didn't . . .' He went on incoherently begging pardon. Herr Schindler did not like Herr Bosch enough to explain to him at this advanced night of his life that it wasn't a matter of controlling anyone, that the Schindler marital disaster was instead a case of an ascetic temperament – Frau Emilie Schindler's – and a hedonistic temperament – Herr Oskar Schindler's – willingly and against good advice binding themselves together. But Oskar's anger at Bosch was more profound than even he would have admitted. Emilie was very like Oskar's late mother, Frau Louisa Schindler. Herr Schindler senior had left Louisa in 1935. So Oskar had a visceral feeling that in making light of the Emilie-Oskar marriage, Bosch was also demeaning the marriage of the Schindlers senior.

The man was still rushing out apologies. Bosch, a hand in every till in Cracow, was now in a sweating panic at the chance of losing six dozen sets of kitchen ware.

The guests were summoned to the table. An onion soup was carried in and served by the maid. While the guests ate and chatted, the Rosner brothers continued to play, moving in closer to the diners, but not so close as to impede the movements of the maid or of Ivan and Petr, Goeth's two Ukrainian orderlies. Herr Schindler, sitting between the tall girl whom Schemer had appropriated and a sweet-faced, small-boned Pole who spoke German, saw that both girls watched this maid. She wore the traditional domestic uniform, black dress and white apron. She bore no Jewish star on her arm, no stripe of yellow paint on her back. She was Jewish just the same. What drew the attention of the other women was the condition of her face. There was bruising along the jawline, and you would have thought that Goeth had too much shame to display a servant in that condition in front of the guests from Cracow. Both the women and Herr Schindler could see, as well as the injury to her face, a more alarming purple, not always covered by her collar, at the junction where her thin neck met her shoulder.

Not only did Amon Goeth refuse to leave the girl unexplained in the background, but he turned his chair toward her, gesturing at her with a hand, displaying her to the assembled company. Herr Schindler had not been at this house for six weeks now, but his informants told him the relationship between Goeth and the girl had taken this twisted path. When with friends, he used her as a conversation piece. He hid her only when senior officers from beyond the Cracow region were visiting.

'Ladies and gentlemen,' he called, mimicking the tones of a mock-drunken cabaret master of ceremonies, 'may I introduce Lena. After five months with me she is now doing well in cuisine and deportment.'

'I can see from her face,' said the tall girl, 'that she's had a collision with the kitchen furniture.'

'And the bitch could have another,' said Goeth with a genial gurgle. 'Yes. Another. Couldn't you, Lena?'

'He's hard on women,' the SS chief boasted, winking at his tall consort. Schemer's intention might not have been unkind, since he did not refer to *Jewish* women but to women in general. It was when Goeth was reminded of Lena's Jewishness that she took more punishment, either publicly, in front of dinner guests, or later when the Commandant's friends had gone home. Schemer, being Goeth's superior, could have ordered the Commandant to stop beating the girl. But that would have been bad form, would have soured the friendly parties at Amon's villa. Schemer came here not as a superior, but as a friend, an associate, a carouser, a savourer of women. Amon was a strange fellow, but no one could produce parties the way he could.

Next there was herring in sauce, then pork knuckles, superbly cooked and garnished by Lena. They were drinking a heavy Hungarian red wine with the meat, the Rosner brothers moved in with a torrid czardas, and the air in the dining room thickened, all the officers removing their uniform jackets. There was more gossip about war contracts. Madritsch, the uniform manufacturer, was asked about his Tarnow factory. Was it doing as well with Armaments Inspectorate contracts as was his factory inside Płaszów? Madritsch referred to Titsch, his lean, ascetic manager. Goeth seemed suddenly preoccupied, like a man who has remembered in the middle of dinner some urgent business detail he should have cleared up that afternoon and which now calls out to him from the darkness of his office.

The girls from Cracow were bored, the small-boned Pole, glossy-lipped, perhaps twenty, probably eighteen, placing a hand on Herr Schindler's right sleeve. 'You're not a soldier?' she murmured. 'You'd look dashing in uniform.' Everyone began to chuckle – Madritsch too. He'd spent a while in uniform in 1940 until released because his managerial talents were so essential to the war effort. But Herr Schindler was so influential that he had never been threatened with the *Wehrmacht*. Madritsch laughed knowingly.

'Did you hear that?' *Oberführer* Schemer asked the table at large. 'The little lady's got a picture of our industrialist as a soldier. Private Schindler, eh? Eating out of one of his own mess kits with a blanket around his shoulders. Over in Kharkov.'

In view of Herr Schindler's well-tailored elegance it *did* make a strange picture, and Schindler himself laughed at it.

'Happened to . . .' said Bosch, trying to snap his fingers; 'happened to . . . what's his name up in Warsaw?'

'Toebbens,' said Goeth, reviving without warning. 'Happened to Toebbens. Almost.'

The SD chief, Czurda, said, 'Oh, yes. Near thing for Toebbens.' Toebbens was a Warsaw industrialist. Bigger than Schindler, bigger than Madritsch. Quite a success. 'Heini,' said Czurda (Heini being Heinrich Himmler), 'went to Warsaw and told the armaments man up there, Get the fucking Jews out of Toebbens' factory and put Toebbens in the Army *and* . . . *and* send him to the Front. I mean, the *Front*! And then Heini told my associate up there, he said, Go over his books with a microscope!'

Toebbens was a darling of the Armaments Inspectorate, which had favoured him with war contracts and which he had favoured in return with gifts. The Armaments Inspectorate's protests had managed to save Toebbens, Schemer told the table solemnly, and then leaned over his plate to wink broadly at Schindler. 'Never happen in Cracow, Oskar. We all love you too much.'

All at once, perhaps to indicate the warmth the whole table felt for Herr Schindler the industrialist, Goeth climbed to his feet and sang a wordless tune in unison with the theme from *Madame Butterfly* which the dapper brothers Rosner were working on as industriously as any artisan in any threatened factory in any threatened ghetto.

By now Pfefferberg and Lisiek, the orderly, were upstairs in Goeth's bathroom, scrubbing away at the heavy bathtub ring. They could hear the Rosners' music and the bursts of laughter and conversation. It was coffee time down there, and the battered girl Lena had brought the tray in to the dinner guests and retreated unmolested back to the kitchen.

Madritsch and Titsch drank their coffee quickly and excused themselves. Schindler prepared to do the same. The little Polish girl seemed to protest, but this was the wrong house for him. Anything was permitted at the *Goethhaus*, but Oskar found that his inside knowledge of the limits of SS behavior in Poland threw sickening light on every word you spoke here, every glass you drank, not to mention any proposed sexual exchange. Even if you took a girl upstairs, you could not forget that Bosch and Schemer and Goeth were your brothers in pleasure, were – on the stairs or in a bathroom or bedroom – going through the same motions. Herr Schindler, no monk, would rather *be* a monk than have a woman at *chez* Goeth.

He spoke across the girl to Schemer, talking about war news, Polish bandits, the likelihood of a bad winter. Letting the girl know that Schemer was a brother and that he would never take a girl from a brother. Saying good night, though, he kissed her on the hand. He saw that Goeth, in his shirt sleeves, was disappearing out the dining-room door, heading for the stairwell, supported by one of the girls who had flanked him at dinner. Oskar excused himself and caught up with the Commandant. He reached out and laid a hand on Goeth's shoulder. The eyes Goeth turned on him struggled for focus. 'Oh,' he muttered. 'Going, Oskar?'

'I have to be home,' said Oskar. At home was Ingrid, his German mistress.

'You're a bloody stallion,' said Goeth.

'Not in your class,' said Schindler.

'No, you're right. I'm a frigging Olympian. We're going . . . where're we going?' He turned his head to the girl but answered the question himself. 'We're going to the kitchen to see that Lena's clearing up properly.'

'No,' said the girl, laughing. 'We aren't doing that.' She steered him to the stairs. It was decent of her – the sorority in operation – to protect the thin, bruised girl in the kitchen.

Schindler watched them – the hulking officer, the slight, supporting girl – staggering crookedly up the staircase. Goeth looked like a man who would have to sleep at least till lunchtime, but Oskar knew the Commandant's amazing constitution and the clock that ran in him. By 3 A.M. Goeth might even decide to rise and write a letter to his father in Vienna. By seven, after only an hour's sleep, he'd be on the balcony, infantry rifle in hand, ready to shoot any dilatory prisoners.

When the girl and Goeth reached the first landing, Schindler sidled down the hallway toward the back of the house.

Pfefferberg and Lisiek heard the Commandant, considerably earlier than they had expected him, entering the bedroom and mumbling to the girl he'd brought upstairs. In silence they picked up their cleaning equipment, crept into the bedroom and tried to slip out a side door. Still standing and able to see them on their line of escape, Goeth recoiled at the sight of the cleaning stick, suspecting the two men might be assassins. When Lisiek stepped forward, however, and began a tremulous report, the Commandant understood that they were merely prisoners.

'Herr Commandant,' said Lisiek, panting with justified fear, 'I wish to report that there has been a ring in your bathtub . . . .'

'Oh,' said Amon. 'So you called in an expert.' He beckoned to the boy. 'Come here, darling.'

Lisiek edged forward and was struck so savagely that he went sprawling halfway under the bed. Amon again uttered his invitation, as if it might amuse the girl to see him speaking endearments to prisoners. Young Lisiek rose and tottered toward the Commandant again for another round. As the boy picked himself up the second time, Pfefferberg, an experienced prisoner, expected anything – that they'd be marched down to the garden and summarily shot by Ivan. Instead the Commandant simply raged at them to leave, which they did at once.

When Pfefferberg heard a few days later that Lisiek was dead, shot by Amon, he presumed it was over the bathroom incident. In fact it was for a different matter altogether – Lisiek's offence had been to harness a horse and buggy for Herr Bosch without first asking the Commandant's permission.

*

In the kitchen of the villa, the maid, whose real name was Helen Hirsch (Goeth called her Lena out of laziness, she would always say), looked up to see one of the dinner guests in the doorway. She put down the dish of meat scraps she'd been holding and stood at attention with a jerky suddenness. '*Herr* . . .' She looked at his dinner jacket and sought the word for him. '*Herr Direktor*, I was just putting aside the bones for the Herr Commandant's dogs.'

'Please, please,' said Herr Schindler. 'You don't have to report to me, Fraulein Hirsch.'

He moved around the table. He did not seem to be stalking her, but she feared his intentions. Even though Amon enjoyed beating her, her Jewishness always saved her from overt sexual attack. But there were Germans who were not as fastidious on racial matters as Amon. This one's tone of voice, however, was one to which she was not accustomed, even from the SS officers and NCOs who came to the kitchen to complain about Amon.

'Don't you know me?' he asked, just like a man – a football star or a violinist – whose sense of his own celebrity has been hurt by a stranger's failure to recognise him. 'I'm Schindler.'

She bowed her head. '*Herr Direktor*,' she said. 'Of course, I've heard . . . and you've been here before. I remember . . .'

He put his arm around her. He could surely feel the tensing of her body as he touched her cheek with his lips.

He murmured, 'It's not that sort of kiss. I'm kissing you out of pity, if you must know.'

She couldn't avoid weeping. *Herr Direktor* Schindler kissed her hard now in the middle of the forehead, in the manner of Polish farewells in railway stations, a resounding Eastern European smack of the lips. She saw that he had begun to weep too. 'That kiss is something I bring you from . . .' He waved his hand, indicating some honest tribe of men out in the dark, sleeping in tiered bunks or hiding in forests, people for whom – by absorbing punishment from *Hauptsturmführer* Goeth – she was in part a buffer.

Herr Schindler released her and reached into his side pocket, bringing out a large candy bar. In its substance it too seemed prewar.

'Keep that somewhere,' he advised her.

'I get extra food here,' she told him, as if it were a matter of pride that he not assume she was starving. Food, in fact, was the least of her worries. She knew she would not survive Amon's house, but it wouldn't be for lack of food.

'If you don't want to eat it, trade it,' Herr Schindler told her. 'Or why not build yourself up?' He stood back and surveyed her. 'Itzhak Stern told me about you.'

'Herr Schindler,' murmured the girl. She put her head down and wept neatly, economically for a few seconds. 'Herr Schindler, he likes to beat me in front of *those* women. On my first day here, he beat me because I threw out the bones from dinner. He came down to the basement at midnight and asked me where they were. For his dogs, you understand. That was the first beating. I said to him . . . I don't know why I said it; I'd never say it now . . . Why are you beating me? He said, The reason I'm beating you now is you asked me why I'm beating you.'

She shook her head and shrugged, as if reproving herself for talking so much. She didn't want to say any more; she couldn't convey the history of her punishments, her repeated experience of the *Hauptsturmführer*'s fists.

Herr Schindler bent his head to her confidingly. 'Your circumstances are appalling, Helen,' he told her.

'It doesn't matter,' she said. 'I've accepted it.'

'Accepted it?'

'One day he'll shoot me.'

Schindler shook his head, and she thought it was too glib an encouragement to her to hope. Suddenly, the good cloth and the pampered flesh of Herr Schindler were a provocation. 'For God's sake, *Herr Direktor*, I *see* things. We were up on the roof on Monday, chipping off the ice, young Lisiek and I. And we saw the Herr Commandant come out of the front door and down the steps by the patio, right below us. And there on the steps, he drew his gun and shot a woman who was passing. A woman carrying a bundle. Through the throat. Just a woman on her way somewhere. You know. She didn't seem fatter or thinner or slower or faster than anyone else. I couldn't guess what she'd done. The more you see of the Herr Commandant, the more you see that there's no set of rules you can keep to. You can't say to yourself, If I follow *these* rules, I'll be safe . . . .'

Schindler took her hand and wrung it for emphasis. 'Listen, my dear Fraulein Helen Hirsch, in spite of all that, it's still better than Majdanek or Auschwitz. If you can keep your health . . .'

She said, 'I thought it would be easy to do that in the Commandant's kitchen. When I was assigned here, from the camp kitchen, the other girls were jealous.'

A pitiful smile spread on her lips.

Schindler raised his voice now. He was like a man enunciating a principle of physics. 'He won't kill you, because he enjoys you too much, my dear Helen. He enjoys you so much he won't even let you wear the Star. He doesn't want anyone to know it's a Jew he's enjoying. He shot the woman from the steps because she meant nothing to him, she was one of a series, she neither offended nor pleased him. You understand that. But *you* . . . it's not decent, Helen. But it's life.'

Someone else had said that to her. Leo John, the Commandant's deputy. John was an SS *Untersturmführer* – equivalent to second lieutenant. 'He won't kill you,' John had said, 'till the end, Lena, because he gets too much of a kick out of you.' Coming from John, it hadn't had the same effect. Herr Schindler had just condemned her to a painful survival.

He seemed to understand that she was stunned. He murmured encouragement. He'd see her again. He'd try to get her out. Out? she asked. Out of the villa, he explained; into my factory, he said. Surely you have heard of my factory. I have an enamelware factory.

'Oh, yes,' she said like a slum child speaking of the Riviera. '"Schindler's Emalia." I've heard of it.'

'Keep your health,' he said again. He seemed to know it would be the key. He seemed to draw on a knowledge of future intentions – Himmler's, Frank's – when he said it.

'All right,' she conceded.

She turned her back on him and went to a china closet, dragging it forward from the wall, an exercise of strength which in such a diminished girl amazed Herr Schindler. She removed a brick from the section of wall the closet had previously covered. She brought out a wad of money – Occupation złoty.

'I have a sister in the camp kitchen,' she said. 'She's younger than I am. I want you to spend this buying her back if ever she's put on the cattle cars. I believe you often find out about these things beforehand.'

'I'll make it my business,' Schindler told her, but with ease, not like a solemn promise. 'How much is it?'

'Four thousand złoty.'

He took it negligently, her nest egg, and shoved it into a side pocket. It was still safer with him than in a niche behind Amon Goeth's china closet.

So the story of Oskar Schindler is begun perilously, with Gothic Nazis, with SS hedonism, with a thin and brutalised girl, and with a figure of the imagination somehow as popular as the golden-hearted whore: the good German.

On one hand, Oskar has made it his business to know the full face of the system, the rabid face behind the veil of bureaucratic decency. He knows, that is, earlier than most would dare know it, what *Sonderbehandlung* means; that though it says 'Special Treatment,' it means pyramids of cyanotic corpses in Bełżec, Sobibor, Treblinka, and in that complex west of Cracow known to the Poles as Oświęcim-Brzezinka but which will be known to the West by its German name, Auschwitz-Birkenau.

On the other hand, he is a businessman, a dealer by temperament, and he does not openly spit in the system's eye. He has already reduced the pyramids, and though he does not know how this year and next they will grow in size and number and overtop the Matterhorn, he knows the mountain is coming. Though he cannot predict what bureaucratic shifts will occur in its construction, he still presumes there will always be room and need for Jewish labour. Therefore, during his visit to Helen Hirsch, he insists, 'Keep your health.' He is sure, and out in the darkened *Arbeitslager* (work camp) of Płaszów, wakeful Jews stir and promise themselves, that no regime – the tide set against it – can afford to do away with a plentiful source of free labour. It's the ones who break down, spit blood, fall to dysentery who are put on the Auschwitz transports. Herr Schindler himself has heard prisoners, out on the *Appellplatz* of the Płaszów labour camp, summoned for morning roll call, murmur, 'At least I still have my health,' in a tone which in normal life only the aged use.

So, this winter night, it is both early days and late days for Herr Schindler's practical engagement in the salvage of certain human lives. He is in deep; he has broken Reich laws to an extent that would earn him a multiplicity of hangings, beheadings, consignments to the draughty huts of Auschwitz or Gröss-Rosen. But he does not know yet how much it will really cost. Though he has spent a fortune already, he does not know the extent of payments still to be made.

Not to stretch belief so early, the story begins with a quotidian act of kindness – a kiss, a soft voice, a bar of chocolate. Helen Hirsch would never see her 4,000 zloty again – not in a form in which they could be counted and held in the hand. But to this day she considers it a matter of small importance that Oskar was so inexact with sums of money.

I

General Sigmund list's armoured divisions, driving north from the Sudetenland, had taken the sweet south Polish jewel of Cracow from both flanks on September 6, 1939. And it was in their wake that Oskar Schindler entered the city which, for the next five years, would be his oyster. Though within the month he would show that he was disaffected from National Socialism, he could still see that Cracow, with its railroad junction and its as yet modest industries, would be a boomtown of the new regime. He wasn't going to be a salesman anymore. Now he was going to be a tycoon.

It is not immediately easy to find in Oskar's family's history the origins of his impulse toward rescue. He was born on April 28, 1908, into the Austrian Empire of Franz Josef, into the hilly Moravian province of that ancient Austrian realm. His hometown was the industrial city of Zwittau, to which some commercial opening had brought the Schindler ancestors from Vienna at the beginning of the sixteenth century.

Herr Hans Schindler, Oskar's father, approved of the imperial arrangement, considered himself culturally an Austrian, and spoke German at the table, on the telephone, in business, in moments of tenderness. Yet when in 1918 Herr Schindler and the members of his family found themselves citizens of the Czechoslovak republic of Masaryk and Beneš, it did not seem to cause any fundamental distress to the father, and even less still to his ten-year-old son. The child Hitler, according to the man Hitler, was tormented even as a boy by the gulf between the mystical unity of Austria and Germany and their political separation. No such neurosis of disinheritance soured Oskar Schindler's childhood. Czechoslovakia was such a bosky, unravished little dumpling of a republic that the German-speakers took their minority stature with some grace, even if the Depression and some minor governmental follies would later put a certain strain on the relationship.

Zwittau, Oskar's hometown, was a small, coal-dusted city in the southern reaches of the mountain range known as the Jeseniks. Its surrounding hills stood partly ravaged by industry and partly forested with larch and spruce and fir. Because of its community of German-speaking *Sudetendeutschen*, it maintained a German grammar school, which Oskar attended. There he took the *Realgymnasium* Course which was meant to produce engineers – mining, mechanical, civil – to suit the area's industrial landscape. Herr Schindler himself owned a farm-machinery plant, and Oskar's education was a preparation for this inheritance.

The family Schindler was Catholic. So too was the family of young Amon Goeth, by this time also completing the Science Course and sitting for the Matura examinations in Vienna.

Oskar's mother, Louisa, practiced her faith with energy, her clothes redolent all Sunday of the incense burned in clouds at High Mass in the Church of St. Maurice. Hans Schindler was the sort of husband who drives a woman to religion. He liked cognac; he liked coffeehouses. A redolence of brandy-warm breath, good tobacco, and confirmed earthiness came from the direction of that good monarchist, Mr. Hans Schindler.

The family lived in a modern villa, set in its own gardens, across the city from the industrial section. There were two children, Oskar and his sister, Elfriede. But there are not witnesses left to the dynamics of that household, except in the most general terms. We know, for example, that it distressed Frau Schindler that her son, like his father, was a negligent Catholic.

But it cannot have been too bitter a household. From the little that Oskar would say of his childhood, there was no darkness there. Sunlight shines among the fir trees in the garden. There are ripe plums in the corner of those early summers. If he spends a part of some June morning at Mass, he does not bring back to the villa much of a sense of sin. He runs his father's car out into the sun in front of the garage and begins tinkering inside its motor. Or else he sits on a side step of the house, filing away at the carburetor of the motorcycle he is building.

Oskar had a few middle-class Jewish friends, whose parents also sent them to the German grammar school. These children were not village Ashkenazim – quirky, Yiddish-speaking, Orthodox – but multilingual and not-so-ritual sons of Jewish businessmen. Across the Hana Plain and in the Beskidy Hills, Sigmund Freud had been born of just such a Jewish family, and that not so long before Hans Schindler himself was born to solid German stock in Zwittau.

Oskar's later history seems to call out for some set piece in his childhood. The young Oskar should defend some bullied Jewish boy on the way home from school. It is a safe bet it didn't happen, and we are happier not knowing, since the event would seem too pat. Besides, one Jewish child saved from a bloody nose proves nothing. For Himmler himself would complain, in a speech to one of his *Einsatzgruppen*, that every German had a Jewish friend. '"The Jewish people are going to be annihilated," says every Party member. "Sure, it's in our programme: elimination of the Jews, annihilation – we'll take care of it." And then they all come trudging, eighty million worthy Germans, and each one has his one decent Jew. Sure, the others are swine, but this one is an A-One Jew.'

Trying still to find, in the shadow of Himmler, some hint of Oskar's later enthusiasms, we encounter the Schindlers' next-door neighbor, a liberal rabbi named Dr. Felix Kantor. Rabbi Kantor was a disciple of Abraham Geiger, the German liberaliser of Judaism who claimed that it was no crime, in fact was praiseworthy, to be a German as well as a Jew. Rabbi Kantor was no rigid village scholar. He dressed in the modern mode and spoke German in the house. He called his place of worship a 'temple' and not by that older name, 'synagogue.' His temple was attended by Jewish doctors, engineers, and proprietors of textile mills in Zwittau. When they travelled, they told other businessmen, 'Our rabbi is Dr. Kantor – he writes articles not only for the Jewish journals in Prague and Brno, but for the dailies as well.'

Rabbi Kantor's two sons went to the same school as the son of his German neighbor Schindler. Both boys were bright enough eventually, perhaps, to become two of the rare Jewish professors at the German University of Prague. These crew-cut German-speaking prodigies raced in knee pants around the summer gardens. Chasing the Schindler children and being chased. And Kantor, watching them flash in and out among the yew hedges, might have thought it was all working as Geiger and Graetz and Lazarus and all those other nineteenth-century German-Jewish liberals had predicted. We lead enlightened lives, we are greeted by German neighbors – Mr. Schindler will even make snide remarks about Czech statesmen in our hearing. We are secular scholars as well as sensible interpreters of the Talmud. We belong both to the twentieth century *and* to an ancient tribal race. We are neither offensive nor offended against.

Later, in the mid-1930s, the rabbi would revise this happy estimation and make up his mind in the end that his sons could never buy off the National Socialists with a German-language Ph.D. – that there was no outcrop of twentieth-century technology or secular scholarship behind which a Jew could find sanctuary, any more than there could ever be a species of rabbi acceptable to the new German legislators. In 1936 all the Kantors moved to Belgium. The Schindlers never heard of them again.

Race, blood, and soil meant little to the adolescent Oskar. He was one of those boys for whom a motorcycle is the most compelling model of the universe. And his father – a mechanic by temperament – seems to have encouraged the boy's zeal for red-hot machinery. In the last year of high school, Oskar was riding around Zwittau on a red 500cc Galloni. A school friend, Erwin Tragatsch, watched with unspeakable desire as the red Galloni farted its way down the streets of the town and arrested the attention of promenaders on the square. Like the Kantor boys, it too was a prodigy – not only the sole Galloni in Zwittau, not only the only 500cc Italian Galloni in Moravia, but probably a unique machine in all Czechoslovakia.

In the spring of 1928, the last months of Oskar's adolescence and prelude to a summer in which he would fall in love and decide to marry, he appeared in the town square on a 250cc Moto-Guzzi, of which there were only four others on the Continent outside Italy, and those four owned by international racers – Giessler, Hans Winkler, the Hungarian Joo and the Pole Kolaczkowski. There must have been townspeople who shook their heads and said that Herr Schindler was spoiling the boy.

But it would be Oskar's sweetest and most innocent summer. An apolitical boy in a skull-fitting leather helmet revving the motor of the Moto-Guzzi, racing against the local factory teams in the mountains of Moravia, son of a family for whom the height of political sophistication was to burn a candle for Franz Josef. Just around the pine-clad curve, an ambiguous marriage, an economic slump, seventeen years of fatal politics. But on the rider's face no knowledge, just the wind-flattened grimace of a high-speed biker who – because he is new, because he is no pro, because all his records are as yet unset – can afford the price better than the older ones, the pros, the racers with times to beat.

His first contest was in May, the mountain race between Brno and Sobeslav. It was high-class competition, so that at least the expensive toy prosperous Herr Hans Schindler had given his son was not rusting in a garage. He came in third on his red Moto-Guzzi, behind two Terrots which had been souped up with English Blackburne motors.

For his next challenge he moved farther from home to the Altvater circuit, in the hills on the Saxon border. The German 250cc champion Walfried Winkler was there for the race, and his veteran rival Kurt Henkelmann, on a water-cooled DKW. All the Saxon hotshots – Horowitz, Kocher, and Kliwar – had entered; the Terrot-Blackburnes were back and some Coventry Eagles. There were three Moto-Guzzis, including Oskar Schindler's, as well as the big guns from the 350cc class and a BMW 500cc team.

It was nearly Oskar's best, most unalloyed day. He kept within touch of the leaders during the first laps and watched to see what might happen. After an hour, Winkler, Henkelmann, and Oskar had left the Saxons behind, and the other Moto-Guzzis fell away with some mechanical flaw. In what Oskar believed was the second-to-last lap he passed Winkler and must have felt, as palpably as the tar itself and the blur of pines, his imminent career as a factory-team rider, and the travel-obsessed life it would permit him to lead.

In what then he assumed was the last lap, Oskar passed Henkelmann and both the DKWs, crossed the line and slowed. There must have been some deceptive sign from officials, because the crowd also believed the race was over. By the time Oskar knew it wasn't – that he had made some amateur mistake – Walfried Winkler and Mita Vychodil had passed him, and even the exhausted Henkelmann was able to nudge him out of third place.

He was feted home. Except for a technicality, he'd beaten Europe's best.

Tragatsch surmised that the reasons Oskar's career as a motorcycle racer ended there were economic. It was a fair guess. For that summer, after a courtship of only six weeks, he hurried into marriage with a farmer's daughter, and so fell out of favour with his father, who happened also to be his employer.

The girl he married was from a village to the east of Zwittau in the Hana Plain. She was convent-schooled and had the sort of reserve he admired in his mother. Her widowed father was no peasant but a gentleman farmer. In the Thirty Years War, her Austrian ancestors had survived the recurrent campaigns and famines which had swept that fertile plain. Three centuries later, in a new era of risk, their daughter entered an ill-advised marriage with an unformed boy from Zwittau. Her father disapproved of it as deeply as Oskar's.

Hans didn't like it because he could see that Oskar had married in the pattern of his, Hans's, own uneasy marriage. A sensual husband, a boy with a wild streak, looking too early in his life for some sort of peace from a nunlike, gracious, unsophisticated girl.

Oskar had met Emilie at a party in Zwittau. She was visiting friends from her village of Alt-Molstein. Oskar knew the place, of course; he'd sold tractors in the area.

When the banns were announced in the parish churches of Zwittau, some people thought the couple so ill-matched that they began to look for motives other than love. It is possible that even that summer the Schindler farm-machinery factory was in trouble, for it was geared to the manufacture of steam-driven tractors of a type already going out of style with farmers. Oskar was pouring a large part of his wages back into the business, and now – with Emilie – came a dowry of half a million Reichsmarks, an honest and alleviating lump of capital in anyone's language. The suspicion of the gossips was unfounded, though, for that summer Oskar was infatuated. And since Emilie's father would never find grounds to believe the boy would settle down and be a good husband, only a fraction of the half-million was ever paid.

Emilie herself was delighted to escape stultifying Alt-Molstein by marrying handsome Oskar Schindler. Her father's closest friend had always been the dull parish priest, and Emilie had grown up pouring the two of them tea and listening to their naive opinions on politics and theology. If we are still seeking significant Jewish connections, there had been some in Emilie's girlhood – the village doctor who treated her grandmother, and Rita, granddaughter of the storekeeper Reif. During one of his visits to the farmhouse, the parish priest told Emilie's father that it was not good on principle for a Catholic child to have a particular friendship with a Jew. Out of the almost glandular stubbornness of girlhood, Emilie resisted the priest's edict. The friendship with Rita Reif would survive till the day in 1942 when local Nazi officials executed Rita in front of the store.

*

After the marriage, Oskar and Emilie settled in an apartment in Zwittau. For Oskar, the Thirties must have seemed a mere epilogue to his glorious mistake on the Altvater circuit in the summer of '28. He did his military service in the Czechoslovak Army and, although it gave him the chance to drive a truck, found that he abhorred the military life – not on pacifist grounds but on grounds of discomfort. Home again in Zwittau, he neglected Emilie in the evenings, staying late in cafés like a single man, talking to girls neither nunlike nor gracious. The family business went bankrupt in 1935, and that same year his father left Frau Louisa Schindler and took an apartment of his own. Oskar hated him for that and went and drank tea with his aunts and denounced Hans to them and, even in cafés, made speeches about his father's treachery to a good woman. He seems to have been blind to the resemblance between his own faltering marriage and his parents' broken one.

Because of his good business contacts, his conviviality, his gifts of salesmanship, his ability to hold his liquor, he got a job even in the midst of the Depression as sales manager of Moravian Electrotechnic. Its head office was located in the grim provincial capital of Brno, and Oskar commuted between Brno and Zwittau. He liked the travelling life. It was half the destiny he'd promised himself when he'd passed Winkler on the Altvater circuit.

When his mother died, he rushed back to Zwittau and stood beside his aunts; his sister, Elfriede; and his wife, Emilie, on one side of the grave, while treacherous Hans stood solitary – except, of course, for the parish priest – at the head of the coffin. Louisa's death had consecrated the enmity between Oskar and Hans. Oskar couldn't see it – only the women could – that Hans and Oskar were in fact two brothers separated by the accident of paternity.

By the time of that funeral, Oskar was wearing the *Hakenkreuz* emblem of Konrad Henlein's Sudeten German Party. Neither Emilie nor the aunts approved, but they did not take it too hard – it was something young Czech Germans were wearing that season. Only the Social Democrats and the Communists did not sport the badge or subscribe to Henlein's Party, and God knew

Oskar was neither a Communist nor a Social Democrat. Oskar was a salesman. All things being equal, when you went in to a German company manager wearing the badge, you got the order.

Yet even with his order book wide open and his pencil flying, Oskar also – in the months in 1938 before the German divisions entered the Sudetenland – felt a sense of a grand shift in history, and was seduced by the itch to be party to it.

Whatever his motives for running with Henlein, it seems that as soon as the divisions entered Moravia he suffered an instant disillusionment with National Socialism, as thorough and as quick as the disillusionment that had set in after marriage. He seems to have expected that the invading power would allow some brotherly Sudeten Republic to be founded. In a later statement, he said he was appalled by the new regime's bullying of the Czech population, by the seizure of Czech property. His first documented acts of rebellion would occur very early in the coming world conflict, and there is no need to doubt that the Protectorate of Bohemia and Moravia, proclaimed by Hitler from Hradschin Castle in March 1939, surprised him with its early showing of tyranny.

Besides that, the two people whose opinions he most respected – Emilie, and his estranged father – were not taken in by the grand Teutonic hour and both claimed to know Hitler could not succeed. Their opinions were not sophisticated, but neither were Oskar's. Emilie believed simply that the man would be punished for making himself God. Herr Schindler senior, as his position was relayed to Oskar by an aunt, fell back on basic historical principles. Just outside Brno was the stretch of river where Napoleon had won the battle of Austerlitz. And what had befallen this triumphant Napoleon? He'd become a nobody, growing potatoes on an island in the mid-Atlantic. The same would happen to this fellow. Destiny, said Herr Schindler senior, was not a limitless rope. It was a piece of elastic. The harder you went forward, the more fiercely you were jerked back to your starting point. That was what life, a failed marriage, and the economic slump had taught Herr Hans Schindler.

But perhaps his son, Oskar, was not yet a clear enemy of the new system. One evening that autumn, young Herr Schindler attended a party at a sanitarium in the hills outside Ostrava, up near the Polish border. The hostess was the sanitarium manager, a client and friend Oskar had acquired on the road. She introduced him to a personable German named Eberhard Gebauer. They talked about business and what moves France and Britain and Russia might make. Then they went off with a bottle to a spare room so that, as Gebauer suggested, they could talk more frankly. There Gebauer identified himself as an officer of Admiral Canaris' *Abwehr* intelligence and offered his new drinking companion the chance to work for the Foreign Section of the *Abwehr*. Oskar had accounts across the border in Poland, throughout Galicia and Upper Silesia. Would he agree to supply the *Abwehr* with military intelligence from that region? Gebauer said he knew from his friend the hostess that Oskar was intelligent and gregarious. With these gifts, he could make use not only of his own observations of industrial and military installations in the area but of those of any German Poles he might happen to recruit in restaurants or bars, or during business meetings.

Again, apologists for the young Oskar would say that he agreed to work for Canaris because, as an *Abwehr* agent, he was exempt from army service. That was a large part of the proposal's charm. But he must also have believed that a German advance into Poland would be appropriate. Like the slim officer sitting drinking on the bed with him, he must still have approved of the national business, though he did not like the management. For Oskar, Gebauer may have possessed a moral allure, for he and his *Abwehr* colleagues considered themselves a decent Christian elite. Though it did not prevent their planning for a military intrusion into Poland, it gave them a contempt for Himmler and the SS, with whom, they believed high-handedly, they were in competition for the control of Germany's soul.

Later, a very different intelligence-gathering body would find Oskar's reports to be full and praiseworthy. On his Polish journeys for the *Abwehr*, he showed a gift for charming news out of people, especially in a social setting – at the dinner table, over cocktails. We do not know the exact nature or importance of what he found out for Gebauer and Canaris, but he came to like the city of Cracow very well, and to discover that though it was no great industrial metropolis, it was an exquisite mediaeval city surrounded with a fringe of metal, textile, and chemical plants.

As for the unmotorised Polish Army, its secrets were all too apparent.

2

In late October 1939, two young German NCOs entered the showroom of J. C. Buchheister & Company in Stradom Street, Cracow, and insisted on buying some expensive bolts of cloth to send home. The Jewish clerk behind the counter, a yellow star sewn to his breast, explained that Buchheister's did not sell direct to the public but supplied garment factories and retail outlets. The soldiers would not be dissuaded. When it was time to settle their bill, they did it whimsically with a Bavarian banknote of 1858 and a piece of German Army Occupation scrip dated 1914. 'Perfectly good currency,' one of them told the Jewish bookkeeper. They were healthy-looking young men who had spent all spring and summer on manoeuvres, the early autumn yielding them an easy triumph and, later, all the latitude of conquerors in a sweet city. The bookkeeper agreed to the transaction and got them out of the shop before ringing up a sale on the cash register.

Later in the day, a young German accounts manager, an official appointed by the deftly named East Trust Agency to take over and run Jewish businesses, visited the showroom. He was one of two German officials assigned to Buchheister. The first was Sepp Aue, the supervisor, a middle-aged, unambitious man, and the second, this young go-getter. The young man inspected the books and the till. He took out the valueless currency. What did it mean, this comic-opera money?

The Jewish bookkeeper told his story; the accounts manager accused him of substituting the antique notes for hard złoty. Later in the day, in Buchheister's warehouse upstairs, the go-getter reported to Sepp Aue and said they should call in the *Schutzpolizei*.

Herr Aue and the young accountant both knew that such an act would lead to the imprisonment of the bookkeeper in the SS jail in Montelupich Street. The accountant thought that this would set an excellent example for Buchheister's remaining Jewish staff. But the idea distressed Aue, who had a secret liability of his own, his grandmother having been Jewish, though no one had yet found that out.

Aue sent an office boy with a message to the company's original accountant, a Polish Jew named Itzhak Stern, who was at home with influenza. Aue was a political appointee with little accounting experience. He wanted Stern to come into the office and resolve the impasse over the bolts of linen. He had just sent the message off to Stern's house in Podgórze when his secretary came into the office and announced that a Herr Oskar Schindler was waiting outside, claiming to have an appointment. Aue went into the outer room and saw a tall young man, placid as a large dog, tranquilly smoking. The two had met at a party the night before. Oskar had been there with a Sudeten German girl named Ingrid, *Treuhänder*, or supervisor, of a Jewish hardware company, just as Aue was *Treuhänder* of Buchheister's. They were a glamorous couple, Oskar and this Ingrid, frankly in love, stylish, with lots of friends in the *Abwehr*.

Herr Schindler was looking for a career in Cracow. Textiles? Aue had suggested. 'It isn't just uniforms. The Polish domestic market itself is large enough and inflated enough to support us all. You're welcome to look Buchheister's over,' he'd urged Oskar, not knowing how he might regret his tipsy camaraderie at 2 P.M. the next day.

Schindler could see that Herr Aue had possible second thoughts about his invitation. If it's not convenient, *Herr Treuhänder*, Oskar suggested . . .

Herr Aue said not at all and took Schindler through the warehouse and across a yard to the spinning division, where great rolls of golden fabric were running off the machines. Schindler asked if the *Treuhänder* had had trouble with the Poles. No, said Sepp, they're cooperative. Stunned, if anything. After all, it's not exactly a munitions factory.

Schindler so obviously had the air of a man with connections that Aue could not resist the temptation to test the point. Did Oskar know the people at the Main Armaments Board? Did he know General Julius Schindler, for example. Perhaps General Schindler was a relative.

That makes no difference, said Herr Schindler disarmingly. (In fact General Schindler was unrelated to him.) The General wasn't such a bad fellow, compared with some, said Oskar.

Aue agreed. But he himself would never dine with General Schindler or meet him for drinks; that was the difference.

They returned to the office, encountering on the way Itzhak Stern, Buchheister's Jewish accountant, waiting on a chair provided by Aue's secretary, blowing his nose and coughing harshly. He stood up, joined his hands one on top of the other in front of his chest, and with immense eyes watched both conquerors approach, pass him, and enter the office. There Aue offered Schindler a drink and then, excusing himself, left Oskar by the fire and went out to interview Stern.

He was so thin, and there was a scholarly dryness to him. He had the manners of a Talmudic scholar, but also of a European intellectual. Aue told him the story of the bookkeeper and the NCOs and the assumptions the young German accountant had made. He produced from the safe the currency: the 1858 Bavarian, the 1914 Occupation. 'I thought you might have instituted an accounting procedure to deal with just this situation,' said Aue. 'It must be happening a great deal in Cracow just now.'

Itzhak Stern took the notes and studied them. He had indeed developed a procedure, he told the *Herr Treuhänder*. Without a smile or a wink, he moved to the open fire at the end of the room and dropped both notes into it.

'I write these transactions off to profit and loss, under "free samples,"' he said. There had been a lot of free samples since September.

Aue liked Stern's dry, effective style with the legal evidence. He began to laugh, seeing in the accountant's lean features the complexities of Cracow itself, the parochial canniness of a small city. Only a local knew the ropes. In the inner office Herr Schindler sat in need of local information.

Aue led Stern through into the manager's office to meet Herr Schindler, who stood staring at the fire, an unstoppered hip flask held absently in one hand. The first thing Itzhak Stern thought was, *This isn't a manageable German*. Aue wore the badge of his *Führer*, a miniature *Hakenkreuz*, as negligently as a man might wear the badge of a cycling club. But big Schindler's coin-sized emblem took the light from the fire in its black enamel. It, and the young man's general affluence, were all the more the symbols of Stern's autumn griefs as a Polish Jew with a cold.

Aue made the introductions. According to the edict already issued by Governor Frank, Stern made his statement: 'I have to tell you, sir, that I am a Jew.'

'Well,' Herr Schindler growled at him. 'I'm a German. So there we are!'

All very well, Stern almost intoned privately behind his sodden handkerchief. *In that case, lift the edict*.

For Itzhak Stern was a man – even now, in only the seventh week of the New Order in Poland – not under one edict but already under many. Hans Frank, Governor General of Poland, had already initiated and signed six restrictive edicts, leaving others to his district governor, Dr. Otto Wächter, an SS *Gruppenführer* (equivalent to major general), to implement. Stern, besides declaring his origins, had also to carry a distinctive registration card marked by a yellow stripe. The Orders-in-Council forbidding kosher preparation of meats and commanding forced labour for Jews were three weeks old when Stern stood coughing in Schindler's presence. And Stern's official ration as an *Untermensch* (subhuman) was little more than half that of a non-Jewish Pole, the latter being tainted by *Untermensch*-hood himself.

Finally, by an edict of November 8, a general registration of all Cracovian Jews had begun and was required to be completed by the 24th.

Stern, with his calm and abstract cast of mind, knew that the edicts would continue, would circumscribe his living and breathing further still. Most Cracow Jews expected such a rash of edicts. There would be some disruption of life – Jews from the *shtetls* being brought to town to shovel coal, intellectuals being sent into the countryside to hoe beets. There would also be sporadic slaughters for a time, like the one over at Tursk where an SS artillery unit had kept people working on a bridge all day and then driven them into the village synagogue in the evening and shot them. There would always be such intermittent instances. But the situation would settle; the race would survive by petitioning, by buying off the authorities – it was the old method, it had been working since the Roman Empire, it would work again. In the end the civil authorities needed Jews, especially in a nation where they were one in every eleven.

Stern, however, wasn't one of the sanguine ones. He didn't presume that the legislation would soon achieve a plateau of negotiable severity. For these were the worst of times. So though he did not know that the coming fire would be different in substance as well as degree, he was already resentful enough of the future to think, *All very well for you, Herr Schindler, to make generous little gestures of equality*.

This man, said Aue, introducing Itzhak Stern, was Buchheister's right-hand man. He had good connections in the business community here in Cracow.

It was not Stern's place to argue with Aue about that. Even so, he wondered if the *Treuhänder* wasn't gilding the lily for the distinguished visitor.

Aue excused himself.

Left alone with Stern, Schindler murmured that he'd be grateful if the accountant could tell him what he knew about some of the local businesses. Testing Oskar, Stern suggested that perhaps Herr Schindler should speak to the officials of the Trust Agency.

'They're thieves,' said Herr Schindler genially. 'They're bureaucrats too. I would like some latitude.' He shrugged. 'I am a capitalist by temperament and I don't like being regulated.'

So Stern and the self-declared capitalist began to talk. And Stern was quite a source; he seemed to have friends or relatives in every factory in Cracow – textiles, garments, confectionery, cabinet-making, metalwork. Herr Schindler was impressed and took an envelope from the breast pocket of his suit. 'Do you know a company called Rekord?' he asked.

Itzhak Stern did. It was in bankruptcy, he said. It had made enamelware. Since it had gone bankrupt some of the metal-press machinery had been confiscated, and now it was largely a shell, producing – under the management of one of the former owners' relatives – a mere fraction of its capacity. His own brother, said Stern, represented a Swiss company that was one of Rekord's major creditors. Stern knew that it was permitted to reveal a small degree of fraternal pride and then to deprecate it. 'The place was very badly managed,' said Stern.

Schindler dropped the envelope into Stern's lap. 'This is their balance sheet. Tell me what you think.'

Itzhak said that Herr Schindler should of course ask others as well as himself. Of course, Oskar told him. But I would value your opinion.

Stern read the balance sheets quickly; then, after some three minutes of study, all at once felt the strange silence of the office and looked up, finding Herr Oskar Schindler's eyes full on him.

There was, of course, in men like Stern an ancestral gift for sniffing out the just Goy, who could be used as buffer or partial refuge against the savageries of the others. It was a sense for where a safe house might be, a potential zone of shelter. And from now on the possibility of Herr Schindler as sanctuary would colour the conversation as might a half-glimpsed, intangible sexual promise colour the talk between a man and a woman at a party. It was a suggestion Stern was more aware of than Schindler, and nothing explicit would be said for fear of damaging the tender connection.

'It's a perfectly good business,' said Stern. 'You could speak to my brother. And, of course, now there's the possibility of military contracts . . . .'

'Exactly,' murmured Herr Schindler.

For almost instantly after the fall of Cracow, even before Warsaw's siege ended, an Armaments Inspectorate had been set up in the Government General of Poland, its mandate being to enter into contracts with suitable manufacturers for the supply of army equipment. In a plant like Rekord, mess kits and field kitchenware could be turned out. The Armaments Inspectorate, Stern knew, was headed by a Major General Julius Schindler of the *Wehrmacht*. Was the general a relative of Herr Oskar Schindler's? Stern asked. No, I'm afraid not, said Schindler, but as if he wanted Stern to keep his nonrelationship a secret.

In any case, said Stern, even the skeleton production at Rekord was grossing more than a half-million złoty a year, and new metal-pressing plant and furnaces could be acquired relatively easily. It depended on Herr Schindler's access to credit.

Enamelware, said Schindler, was closer to his line than textiles. His background was in farm machinery, and he understood steam presses and so forth.

It did not any longer occur to Stern to ask why an elegant German entrepreneur wished to talk to him about business options. Meetings like this one had occurred throughout the history of his tribe, and the normal exchanges of business did not quite explain them. He talked on at some length, explaining how the Commercial Court would set the fee for the leasing of the bankrupt estate. Leasing with an option to buy – it was better than being a *Treuhänder*. As a *Treuhänder*, only a supervisor, you were completely under the control of the Economics Ministry.

Stern lowered his voice then and risked saying it: 'You will find you are restricted in the people you'll be allowed to employ . . . .'

Schindler was amused. 'How do you know all this? About ultimate intentions?'

'I read it in a copy of the *Berliner Tageblatt*. A Jew is still permitted to read German newspapers.'

Schindler continued to laugh, reached out a hand, and let it fall on Stern's shoulder. 'Is that so?' he asked.

In fact, Stern knew these things because Aue had received a directive from Reich Secretary of State Eberhard von Jagwitz of the Economics Ministry outlining the policies to be adopted in Aryanising businesses. Aue had left it to Stern to make a digest of the memorandum. Von Jagwitz had indicated, more in sadness than in anger, that there would be pressure from other government and Party agencies, such as Heydrich's RHSA, the Reich Security Main Office, to Aryanise not just the ownership of companies, but also the management and work force. The sooner *Treuhänders* filtered out the skilled Jewish employees the better – always, of course, bearing in mind the maintenance of production at an acceptable level.

At last Herr Schindler put the accounts of Rekord back into his breast pocket, stood up, and led Itzhak Stern out into the main office. They stood there for a time, among the typists and clerks, growing philosophical, as Oskar liked to do. It was here that Oskar brought up the matter of Christianity's having its base in Judaism, a subject which for some reason, perhaps even because of his boyhood friendship with the Kantors in Zwittau, interested him. Stern spoke softly, at length, learnedly. He had published articles in journals of comparative religion. Oskar, who wrongly fancied himself a philosopher, had found an expert. The scholar himself, Stern, whom some thought a pedant, found Oskar's understanding shallow, a mind genial by nature but without much conceptual deftness. Not that Stern was about to complain. An ill-assorted friendship was firmly established. So that Stern found himself drawing an analogy, as Oskar's own father had, from previous empires and giving his own reasons why Adolf Hitler could not succeed.

The opinion slipped out before Stern could withdraw it. The other Jews in the office bowed their heads and stared fixedly at their worksheets. Schindler did not seem disturbed.

Near the end of their talk, Oskar did say something that had novelty. In times like these, he said, it must be hard for the churches to go on telling people that their Heavenly Father cared about the death of even a single sparrow. He'd hate to be a priest, Herr Schindler said, in an era like this, when life did not have the value of a pack of cigarettes. Stern agreed but suggested, in the spirit of the discussion, that the Biblical reference Herr Schindler had made could be summed up by a Talmudic verse which said that he who saves the life of one man saves the entire world.

'Of course, of course,' said Oskar Schindler.

Itzhak, rightly or wrongly, always believed that it was at that moment that he had dropped the right seed in the furrow.

3

There is another Cracow Jew who gives an account of meeting Schindler that autumn – and of coming close to killing him. This man's name was Leopold (Poldek) Pfefferberg. He had been a company commander in the Polish Army during the recent tragic campaign. After suffering a leg wound during the battle for the river San, he'd limped around the Polish hospital in Przemyśl, helping with the other wounded. He was no doctor, but a high school physical-education teacher who had graduated from the Jagiellonian University of Cracow and so had some knowledge of anatomy. He was resilient; he was self-confident, twenty-seven years old, and built like a wedge.

With some hundreds of other captured Polish officers from Przemyśl, Pfefferberg was on his way to Germany when his train drew into his home city of Cracow and the prisoners were herded into the first-class waiting room, to remain there until new transport could be provided. His home was ten blocks away. To a practical young man, it seemed outrageous that he could not go out into Pawia Street and catch a No. 1 trolley home. The bucolic-looking *Wehrmacht* guard at the door seemed a provocation.

Pfefferberg had in his breast pocket a document signed by the German hospital authority of Przemyśl indicating that he was free to move about the city with ambulance details tending to the wounded of both armies. It was spectacularly formal, stamped and signed. He took it out now and, going up to the guard, thrust it at him.

'Can you read German?' Pfefferberg demanded.

This sort of ploy had to be done right, of course. You had to be young; you had to be persuasive; you had to have retained, undiminished by summary defeat, a confident bearing of a particularly Polish nature – something disseminated to the Polish officer corps, even to those rare members of it who were Jewish, by its plentiful aristocrats.

The man had blinked. 'Of course I can read German,' he said. But after he'd taken the document he held it like a man who couldn't read at all – held it like a slice of bread. Pfefferberg explained in German how the document declared his right to go out and attend to the ill. All the guard could see was a proliferation of official stamps. Quite a document. With a wave of the head, he indicated the door.

Pfefferberg was the only passenger on the No. 1 trolley that morning. It was not even 6 A.M. The conductor took his fare without a fuss, for in the city there were still many Polish troops not yet processed by the *Wehrmacht*. The officers had to register, that was all.

The trolley swung around the Barbakan, through the gate in the ancient wall, down Floriańska to the Church of St. Mary, across the central square, and so within five minutes into Grodzka Street. Nearing his parents' apartment at No. 48, as he had as a boy he jumped from the car before the air brakes went on and let the momentum of the jump, enhanced by that of the trolley, bring him up with a soft thud against the doorjamb.

After his escape, he had lived not too uncomfortably in the apartments of friends, visiting Grodzka 48 now and then. The Jewish schools opened briefly – they would be closed again within six weeks – and he even returned to his teaching job. He was sure the Gestapo would take some time to come looking for him, and so he applied for ration books. He began to dispose of jewellery – as an agent and in his own right – on the black market that operated in Cracow's central square, in the arcades of the Sukiennice and beneath the two unequal spires of St. Mary's Church. Trade was brisk, among the Poles themselves but more so for the Polish Jews. Their ration books, full of precancelled coupons, entitled them to only two-thirds of the meat and half of the butter allowance that went to Aryan citizens, while *all* the cocoa and rice coupons were cancelled. And so the black market which had operated through centuries of occupation and the few decades of Polish autonomy became the food and income source and the readiest means of resistance for respectable bourgeois citizens, especially those who, like Leopold Pfefferberg, were streetwise.

He presumed that he would soon be travelling over the ski routes around Zakopane in the Tatras, across Slovakia's slender neck into Hungary or Rumania. He was equipped for the journey: he had been a member of the Polish national ski team. On one of the high shelves of the porcelain stove in his mother's apartment he kept an elegant little .22 pistol – armoury both for the proposed escape and in case he was ever trapped inside the apartment by the Gestapo.

With this pearl-handled semitoy, Pfefferberg came close to killing Oskar Schindler one chilly day in November. Schindler, in double-breasted suit, Party badge on the lapel, decided to call on Mrs. Mina Pfefferberg, Poldek's mother, to offer her a commission. He had been given by the Reich housing authorities a fine modern apartment in Straszewskiego Street. It had previously been the property of a Jewish family by the name of Nussbaum. Such allocations were carried out without any compensation to the previous occupant. On the day Oskar came calling, Mrs. Mina Pfefferberg herself was worried that it would happen to her apartment in Grodzka.

A number of Schindler's friends would claim later – though it is not possible to prove it – that Oskar had gone looking for the dispossessed Nussbaums at their lodgings in Podgórze and had given them a sum close to 50,000 złoty in compensation. With this sum, it is said, the Nussbaums bought themselves an escape to Yugoslavia. Fifty thousand złoty signified substantial dissent; but there would be other similar acts of dissent by Oskar before Christmas. Some friends would in fact come to say that generosity was a disease in Oskar, a frantic thing, one of his passions. He would tip taxi drivers twice the fare on the metre. But this has to be said too – that he thought the Reich housing authorities were unjust and told Stern so, not when the regime got into trouble but even in that, its sweetest autumn.

In any case, Mrs. Pfefferberg had no idea what the tall, well-tailored German was doing at her door. He could have been there to ask for her son, who happened to be in the kitchen just then. He could have been there to commandeer her apartment, and her decorating business, and her antiques, and her French tapestry.

In fact, by the December feast of Hanukkah the German police would, on the orders of the housing office, get around to the Pfefferbergs, arriving at their door and then ordering them, shivering in the cold, downstairs onto the pavement of Grodzka. When Mrs. Pfefferberg asked to go back for a coat, she would be refused; when Mr. Pfefferberg made for a bureau to get an ancestral gold watch, he would be punched in the jaw. 'I have witnessed terrible things in the past,' Hermann Göring had said; 'little chauffeurs and Gauleiters have profited so much from these transactions that they now have about half a million.' The effect of such easy pickings as Mr. Pfefferberg's gold watch on the moral fibre of the Party might distress Göring. But in Poland that year, it was the style of the Gestapo to be unaccountable for the contents of apartments.

When Schindler first came to the Pfefferbergs' second-floor apartment, however, the family were still in tenuous occupation. Mrs. Pfefferberg and her son were talking among the samples and bolts of fabric and wallpaper when Herr Schindler knocked. Leopold was not worried. There were two front entrances to the apartment – the business door and the kitchen door faced each other across a landing. Leopold retreated to the kitchen and looked through the crack in the door at the visitor. He saw the formidable size of the man, the fashionable cut of his suit. He returned to his mother in the living room. He had the feeling, he said, that the man was Gestapo. When you let him in at the office door, I can always slip out through the kitchen.

Mrs. Mina Pfefferberg was trembling. She opened the office door. She was, of course, listening for sounds along the corridor. Pfefferberg had in fact picked up the pistol and put it into his belt and intended to wed the sound of his exit to the sound of Herr Schindler's entry. But it seemed folly to go without knowing what the German official wanted. There was a chance the man would have to be killed, and then there would need to be a concerted family flight into Rumania.

If the magnetic drift to the event had drawn Pfefferberg to take out his pistol and fire, the death, the flight, the reprisals would have been considered unexceptional and appropriate to the history of the month. Herr Schindler would have been briefly mourned and summarily avenged. And this would have been, of course, the brisk ending to all Oskar's potentialities. And back in Zwittau they would have said, 'Was it someone's husband?'

The voice surprised the Pfefferbergs. It was calm, quiet, suited to the doing of business, even to the asking of favours. They had got used in past weeks to the tone of decree and summary expropriation. This man sounded fraternal. That was somehow worse. But it intrigued you too.

Pfefferberg had slipped from the kitchen and concealed himself behind the double doors of the dining room. He could see a sliver of the German. You're Mrs. Pfefferberg? the German asked. You were recommended to me by Herr Nussbaum. I have just taken over an apartment in Straszewskiego Street, and I would like to have it redecorated.

Mina Pfefferberg kept the man at the door. She spoke so incoherently that the son took pity on her and appeared in the doorway, his jacket buttoned up over the weapon. He asked the visitor in and at the same time whispered assurances in Polish to his mother.

Now Oskar Schindler gave his name. There was some measuring up, for Schindler could tell that Pfefferberg had appeared to perform an act of primal protection. Schindler showed his respect by talking now through the son as through an interpreter.

'My wife is coming up from Czechoslovakia,' he said, 'and I'd like the place redone in her style.' He said the Nussbaums had maintained the place excellently, but they went in for heavy furniture and sombre colours. Mrs. Schindler's tastes were livelier – a little French, a little Swedish.

Mrs. Pfefferberg had recovered enough to say that she didn't know – it was a busy time with Christmas coming up. Leopold could tell there might be an instinctive resistance in her to developing a German clientele; but the Germans might be the only race this season with enough confidence in the future to go in for interior design. And Mrs. Pfefferberg needed a good contract – her husband had been removed from his job and worked now for a pittance in the housing office of the Gemeinde, the Jewish welfare bureau.

Within two minutes the men were chatting like friends. The pistol in Pfefferberg's belt had now been relegated to the status of armament for some future, remote emergency. There was no doubt that Mrs. Pfefferberg was going to do the Schindler apartment, no expense spared, and when that was settled, Schindler mentioned that Leopold Pfefferberg might like to come around to the apartment to discuss other business. 'There is the possibility that you can advise me on acquiring local merchandise,' Herr Schindler said. 'For example, your very elegant blue shirt . . . I don't know where to begin to look for that kind of thing myself.' His ingenuousness was a ploy, but Pfefferberg appreciated it. 'The stores, as you know, are empty,' murmured Oskar like a hint.

Leopold Pfefferberg was the sort of young man who survived by raising the stakes. 'Herr Schindler, these shirts are extremely expensive, I hope you understand. They cost twenty-five złoty each.'

He had multiplied the price by five. There was all at once an amused knowingness in Herr Schindler – not enough, though, to imperil the tenuous friendship or remind Pfefferberg that he was armed.

'I could probably get you some,' said Pfefferberg, 'if you give me your size. But I'm afraid my contacts will require money in advance.'

Herr Schindler, still with that knowingness in his eyes, took out his wallet and handed Pfefferberg 200 Reichsmarks. The sum was flamboyantly too much and even at Pfefferberg's inflated price would have bought shirts for a dozen tycoons. But Pfefferberg knew the game and did not blink. 'You must give me your measurements,' he said.

A week later, Pfefferberg brought a dozen silk shirts to Schindler's apartment on Straszewskiego Street. There was a pretty German woman in the apartment who was introduced to Pfefferberg as *Treuhänder* of a Cracow hardware business. Then, one evening, Pfefferberg saw Oskar in the company of a blond and large-eyed Polish beauty. If there was a Frau Schindler, she did not appear even after Mrs. Pfefferberg had redecorated the place. Pfefferberg himself became one of Schindler's most regular connections to that market in luxuries – silk, furnishings, jewellery – which flourished in the ancient town of Cracow.

4

The next time Itzhak Stern met Oskar Schindler was on a morning in early December. Schindler's application to the Polish Commercial Court of Cracow had already been filed, yet Oskar had the leisure to visit the offices of Buchheister and, after conferring with Aue, to stand near Stern's desk in the outer office, clap his hands, and announce in a voice that sounded already tipsy, 'Tomorrow, it's going to start. Józefa and Izaaka Streets are going to know all about it!'

There *were* in Kazimierz a Józefa Street and an Izaaka Street. There were in every ghetto, and Kazimierz was the site of the old ghetto of Cracow, once an island ceded to the Jewish community by Kazimier the Great, now a near suburb nestled in an elbow of the Vistula River.

Herr Schindler bent over Stern, and Stern felt his brandy-warm breath and considered this question: *Did Herr Schindler know something would happen in Józefa Street and Izaaka Street? Or was he just brandishing the names?* In any case, Stern suffered a nauseating sense of disappointment. Herr Schindler was whistling up a pogrom, boasting inexactly about it, as if to put Stern in his place.

It was December 3. When Oskar said 'tomorrow,' Stern presumed he was using the term not in the sense of December 4, but in the terms in which drunks and prophets always used it, as something that either would or damn well should happen soon. Only a few of those who heard, or heard about, Herr Schindler's boozy warning took it literally. Some packed an overnight bag and moved their families across the river to Podgórze.

As for Oskar, he felt he had passed on hard news at some risk. He had got it from at least two sources, new friends of his. One, an officer attached to the SS police chief's staff, was a policeman named *Wachtmeister* (sergeant) Herman Toffel. The other, Dieter Reeder, belonged to the staff of SD chief Czurda. Both these contacts were characteristic of the sympathetic officers Oskar always managed to sniff out.

He was never good, though, at explaining his motives for speaking to Stern that December. He would say later that in the period of the German Occupation of Bohemia and Moravia he had seen enough seizure of Jewish and Czech property, and forcible removal of Jews and Czechs from those Sudeten areas considered German, to cure him of any zeal for the New Order. His leaking of the news to Stern, far more than the unconfirmed Nussbaum story, goes some way toward proving his case.

He must have hoped also, as the Jews of Cracow did, that after its initial fury the regime would relax and let people breathe. If the SS raids and incursions of the next few months could be mitigated by the leaking of advance information, then perhaps sanity would reassert itself in the spring. After all, both Oskar and the Jews told themselves, the Germans were a *civilised* nation.

The SS invasion of Kazimierz would, however, arouse in Oskar a fundamental disgust – not one that impinged too directly yet on the level at which he made his money, entertained women or dined with friends, but one that would, the clearer the intentions of the reigning power became, lead, obsess, imperil, and exalt him. The operation was meant in part to be a raid for jewellery and furs. There'd be some evictions from houses and apartments in the wealthier borderland between Cracow and Kazimierz. But beyond these practical results, that first *Aktion* was also meant to serve dramatic notice to the dismayed people of the old Jewish quarter. For that purpose, Reeder told Oskar, a small detachment of *Einsatzgruppe* men would drive down Stradom and into Kazimierz in the same trucks as the boys of the local SS and the Field Police.

Six *Einsatzgruppen* had come to Poland with the invading army. Their name had subtle meanings. 'Special-duty groups' is a close translation. But the amorphous word *Einsatz* was also rich with a nuance – of challenge, of picking up a gauntlet, of knightliness. These squads were recruited from Heydrich's *Sicherheitsdienst* (SD; Security Service). They already knew their mandate was broad. Their supreme leader had six weeks ago told General Wilhelm Keitel that 'in the Government General of Poland there will have to be a tough struggle for national existence which will permit of no legal restraints.' In the high rhetoric of their leaders, the *Einsatz* soldiers knew, a struggle for national existence meant race warfare, just as *Einsatz* itself, Special Chivalrous Duty, meant the hot barrel of a gun.

The *Einsatz* squad destined for action in Kazimierz that evening were an elite. They would leave to the pieceworkers of the Cracow SS the sordid task of searching the tenements for diamond rings and fur-trimmed coats. They themselves would take part in some more radically symbolic activity to do with the very instruments of Jewish culture – that is, with the ancient synagogues of Cracow.

They had for some weeks been waiting to exercise *Einsatz*, as had the local SS *Sonderkommandos* (or Special Squads), also assigned to this first Cracow *Aktion*, and the Security Police of SD chief Czurda. The Army had negotiated with Heydrich and the higher police chiefs a stay of operations until Poland passed from military to civil rule. This passage of authority had now taken place, and throughout the country the Knights of *Einsatz* and the *Sonderkommandos* were unleashed to advance with an appropriate sense of racial history and professional detachment into the old Judaic ghettos.

At the end of the street where Oskar's apartment stood rose the fortified rock outcrop of Wawel Castle from which Hans Frank ruled. And if Oskar's Polish future is to be understood, there is a need to look at the linkage between Frank and the young field operatives of SS and SD, and then between Frank and the Jews of Cracow.

In the first place, Hans Frank had no direct kingship over these special squads moving into Kazimierz. Heinrich Himmler's police forces, wherever they worked, would always be their own lawmakers.

As well as resenting their independent power, Frank also disagreed with them on practical grounds. He had as refined an abomination of the Jewish population as anyone in the Party and found the sweet city of Cracow intolerable because of its manifold Jews. In past weeks he'd complained when the authorities tried to use the Government General, and especially Cracow with its railway junction, as a dumping ground for Jews from the cities of the Wartheland, from Łódź and Poznan. But he did not believe the *Einsatzgruppen* or the *Sonderkommandos*, using current methods, could really make a dent in the problem. It was Frank's belief, shared with Himmler in some stages of 'Heini's' mental vagaries, that there should be a single vast concentration camp for Jews, that it should at least be the city of Lublin and the surrounding countryside, or even more desirably, the island of Madagascar.

The Poles themselves had always believed in Madagascar. In 1937 the Polish Government had sent a commission to study that high-spined island so far from the coasts of their European sensibilities. The French Colonial Office, to which Madagascar belonged, was willing to make a deal, government to government, on such a resettlement, for a Madagascar crowded with Europe's Jews would make a grand export market. The South African Defense Minister, Oswald Pirow, had acted for a time as negotiator between Hitler and France in the matter of the island. Therefore Madagascar, as a solution, had an honourable pedigree. Hans Frank had his money on it and not on the *Einsatzgruppen*. For their sporadic raids and massacres could not cut down the subhuman population of Eastern Europe. During the time of the campaign around Warsaw, the *Einsatzgruppen* had hung Jews up in the synagogues of Silesia, ruptured their systems with water torture, raided their homes on Sabbath evenings or feast days, cut off their prayer locks, set their prayer shawls afire, stood them against a wall. It had barely counted. There were many indications from history, Frank proposed, that threatened races generally outbred the genocides. The phallus was faster than the gun.

What no one knew – neither the parties to the debate, the

well-educated *Einsatzgruppe* boys in the back of one truck, the not-so-refined SS boys in the back of another, the evening worshippers in the synagogues, Herr Oskar Schindler on his way home to Straszewskiego to dress for dinner – what none of them knew and many a Party planner scarce hoped for was that a technological answer would be found – that a disinfectant chemical compound, Zyklon B, would supplant Madagascar as the solution.

There had been an incident involving Hitler's pet actress and director, Leni Riefenstahl. She had come to Łódź with a roving camera crew soon after the city fell and had seen a line of Jews – visible Jews, the prayer-locked variety – executed with automatic weapons. She had gone straight to the *Führer*, who was staying at Southern Army headquarters, and made a scene. That was it – the logistics, the weight of numbers, the considerations of public relations; they made the *Einsatz* boys look silly. But Madagascar too would look ridiculous once means were discovered to make substantial inroads into the subhuman population of Central Europe at fixed sites with adequate disposal facilities which no fashionable moviemaker was likely to stumble upon.

As Oskar had forewarned Stern in the front office of Buchheister's, the SS carried economic warfare from door to door in Jakoba and Izaaka and Józefa. They broke into apartments, dragged out the contents of closets, smashed the locks on desks and dressers. They took valuables off fingers and throats and out of watch fobs. A girl who would not give up her fur coat had her arm broken; a boy from Ciemna Street who wanted to keep his skis was shot.

Some of those whose goods were taken – unaware that the SS were operating outside legal restraint – would tomorrow complain at police stations. Somewhere, history told them, was a senior officer with a little integrity who would be embarrassed and might even discipline some of these unruly fellows. There would have to be an investigation into the business of the boy in Ciemna and the wife whose nose was broken with a truncheon.

While the SS were working the apartment buildings, the

Einsatzgruppe squad moved against the fourteenth-century synagogue of Stara Boznica. As they expected, they found at prayer there a congregation of traditional Jews with beards and sidelocks and prayer shawls. They collected a number of the less Orthodox from surrounding apartments and drove them in as well, as if they wanted to measure the reaction of one group to the other.

Among those pushed across the threshold of Stara Bożnica was the gangster Max Redlicht, who would not otherwise have entered an ancient temple or been invited to do so. They stood in front of the Ark, these two poles of the same tribe who would on a normal day have found each other's company offensive. An *Einsatz* NCO opened the Ark and took out the parchment Torah scroll. The disparate congregation on the synagogue floor were to file past and spit at it. There was to be no faking – the spittle was to be visible on the calligraphy.

The Orthodox Jews were more rational about it than those others, the agnostics, the liberals, the self-styled Europeans. It was apparent to the *Einsatz* men that the modern ones balked in front of the scroll and even tried to catch their eye as if to say, Come on, we're all too sophisticated for this nonsense. The SS men had been told in their training that the European character of liberal Jews was a tissue-thin facade, and in Stara Bożnica the backsliding reluctance of the ones who wore short haircuts and contemporary clothes went to prove it.

Everyone spat in the end except Max Redlicht. The *Einsatzgruppe* men may have seen this as a test worth their time – to make a man who visibly does not believe renounce with spittle a book he views intellectually as antique tribal drivel but which his blood tells him is still sacred. Could a Jew be retrieved from the persuasions of his ridiculous blood? Could he think as clearly as Kant? That was the test.

Redlicht would not pass it. He made a little speech. 'I've done a lot. But I won't do that.' They shot him first, and then shot the rest anyway and set fire to the place, making a shell of the oldest of all Polish synagogues.

5

Victoria Klonowska, a Polish secretary, was the beauty of Oskar's front office, and he immediately began a long affair with her. Ingrid, his German mistress, must have known, as surely as Emilie Schindler knew about Ingrid. For Oskar would never be a surreptitious lover. He had a childlike sexual frankness. It wasn't that he boasted. It was that he never saw any need to lie, to creep into hotels by the back stairs, to knock quietly on any girl's door in the small hours. Since Oskar would not seriously try to tell his women lies, their options were reduced; traditional lovers' arguments were difficult.

Blond hair piled up above her pretty, foxy, vividly made-up face, Victoria Klonowska looked like one of those lighthearted girls to whom the inconveniences of history are a temporary intrusion into the real business of life. This autumn of simple clothes, Klonowska was frivolous in her jacket and frilled blouse and slim skirt. Yet she was hardheaded, efficient, and adroit. She was a nationalist too, in the robust Polish style. She would in the end negotiate with the German dignitaries for her Sudeten lover's release from SS institutions. But for the moment Oskar had a less risky job for her.

He mentioned that he would like to find a good bar or cabaret in Cracow where he could take friends. Not *contacts*, not senior people from the Armaments Inspectorate. Genuine friends. Somewhere lively where middle-aged officials would not turn up.

Did Klonowska know of such a place?

She discovered an excellent jazz cellar in the narrow streets north of the Rynek, the city square. It was a place that had always been popular with the students and younger staff of the university, but Victoria herself had never been there before. The middle-aged men who had pursued her in peacetime would never want to go to a student dive. If you wished to, it was possible to rent an alcove behind a curtain for private parties under cover of the tribal rhythms of the band. For finding this music club, Oskar nicknamed Klonowska 'Columbus.' The Party line on jazz was that it not only was artistically decadent but expressed an African, a subhuman animality. The ump-pa-pa of Viennese waltzes was the preferred beat of the SS and of Party officials, and they earnestly avoided jazz clubs.

Round about Christmas in 1939, Oskar got together a party at the club for a number of his friends. Like any instinctive cultivator of contacts, he would never have any trouble drinking with men he didn't like. But that night the guests were men he *did*. Additionally, of course, they were all useful, junior but not uninfluential members of sundry agencies of Occupation; and all of them more or less double exiles – not only were they away from home, but home or abroad, they were all variously uneasy under the regime.

There was, for example, a young German surveyor from the Government General's Division of the Interior. He had marked out the boundaries of Oskar's enamel factory in Zablocie. At the back of Oskar's plant, Deutsche Email Fabrik (DEF), stood a vacant area where two other manufactories abutted, a box factory and a radiator plant. Schindler had been delighted to find that most of the waste area belonged, according to the surveyor, to DEF. Visions of economic expansion danced in his head. The surveyor had, of course, been invited because he was a decent fellow, because you could talk to him, because he might be handy to know for future building permits.

The policeman Herman Toffel was there also, and the SD man Reeder, as well as a young officer – also a surveyor, named Steinhauser – from the Armaments Inspectorate. Oskar had met and taken to these men while seeking the permits he needed to start his plant. He had already enjoyed drinking bouts with them.

He would always believe that the best way to untie bureaucracy's Gordian knot, short of bribery, was booze.

Finally there were two *Abwehr* men. The first was Eberhard Gebauer, the lieutenant who had recruited Oskar into the *Abwehr* the year before. The second was *Leutnant* Martin Plathe of Canaris' headquarters in Breslau. It had been through his friend Gebauer's recruitment that Herr Oskar Schindler had first discovered what a city of opportunity Cracow was.

There would be a by-product from the presence of Gebauer and Plathe. Oskar was still on the *Abwehr*'s books as an agent and, in his years in Cracow, would keep the staff of Canaris' Breslau office satisfied by passing on to them reports on the behavior of their rivals in the SS. Gebauer and Plathe would consider his bringing along of a more-or-less disaffected gendarme like Toffel, and of Reeder of the SD, as an intelligence favour, a gift quite apart from the good company and the liquor.

Though it is not possible to say exactly what the members of the party talked about that night, it is possible from what Oskar said later of each of these men to make a plausible reconstruction.

It was Gebauer, of course, who would have made the toast, saying he would not give them governments, armies or potentates: instead he would give them the enamel factory of their good friend Oskar Schindler. He did so because if the factory prospered, there would be more parties, parties in the Schindler style, the best parties you could imagine.

But after the toast had been drunk, the talk turned naturally to the subject that bemused or obsessed all levels of the civil bureaucracy. The Jews.

Toffel and Reeder had spent the day at Mogilska Station supervising the unloading of Poles and Jews from eastbound trains. These people had been shipped in from the Incorporated Territories, newly conquered regions which had been German in the past. Toffel wasn't making a point about the comfort of the passengers in the *Ostbahn* cattle cars, although he confessed that the weather had been cold. But the transport of populations in livestock carriages was new to everyone, and the cars were not as yet inhumanly crowded. What confused Toffel was the policy behind it all.

There is a persistent rumor, said Toffel, that we are at war. And in the midst of it the Incorporated Territories are too damn simon-pure to put up with a few Poles and a half-million Jews. 'The whole *Ostbahn* system,' said Toffel, 'has to be turned over to delivering them to *us*.'

The *Abwehr* men listened, slight smiles on their faces. To the SS the enemy within might be the Jew, but to the Canaris the enemy within was the SS.

The SS, Toffel said, had reserved the entire rail system from November 15 on. Across his desk in Pomorska Street, he said, had crossed copies of angry SS memoranda addressed to Army officials and complaining that the Army was welching on its deal, had gone two weeks over schedule in its use of the *Ostbahn*. For Christ's sake, Toffel asked, shouldn't the Army have first use, for as long as it liked, of the railway system? How else is it to deploy east and west? Toffel asked, drinking excitedly. On bicycles?

Oskar was half-amused to see that the *Abwehr* men did not comment. They suspected Toffel might be a plant instead of simply being drunk.

The surveyor and the man from the Armaments Inspectorate asked Toffel some questions about these remarkable trains arriving at Mogilska. Soon such shipments wouldn't be worth talking about: transports of humans would become a cliché of resettlement policy. But on the evening of Oskar's Christmas party, they were still a novelty.

'They call it,' said Toffel, '*concentration*. That's the word you find in the documents. *Concentration*. I call it bloody obsession.'

The owner of the jazz club brought in plates of herring and sauce. The fish went down well with the fiery liquor, and as they wolfed it, Gebauer spoke about the *Judenrats*, the Jewish councils set up in each community on the order of Governor Frank. In cities like Warsaw and Cracow the *Judenrat* had twenty-four elected members personally responsible for the fulfilment of the orders of the regime. The *Judenrat* of Cracow had been in existence for less than a month; Marek Biberstein, a respected municipal authority, had been appointed its president. But, Gebauer remarked, he had heard that it had already approached Wawel Castle with a plan for a roster of Jewish labour. The *Judenrat* would supply the labour details for digging ditches and latrines and clearing snow. Didn't everyone find that excessively cooperative of them?

Not at all, said engineer Steinhauser of the Armaments Inspectorate. They thought that if they supplied the labour squads it would stop random press-ganging. Press-ganging led to beatings and the occasional bullet in the head.

Martin Plathe agreed. They'll be cooperative for the sake of avoiding something worse, he said. It's their method – you have to understand that. They'd always bought the civil authorities off by cooperating with them and then negotiating.

Gebauer seemed to be out to mislead Toffel and Reeder by pushing the point, by seeming more passionately analytic about Jews than he really was. 'I'll tell you what I mean by cooperation,' he said. 'Frank passes an edict demanding that every Jew in the Government General wear a star. *That* edict's only a few weeks old. In Warsaw you've got a Jewish manufacturer churning them out in washable plastic at three złoty each. It's as if they've got no idea what sort of law it is. It's as if the thing were an emblem of a bicycle club.'

It was suggested then that since Schindler was in the enamel business, it might be possible to press a deluxe enamel badge at the Schindler plant and retail it through the hardware outlet his girlfriend Ingrid supervised. Someone remarked that the star was *their* national insigne, the insigne of a state that had been destroyed by the Romans and that now existed only in the minds of Zionists. So perhaps people were proud to wear the star.

'The thing is,' said Gebauer, 'they don't have any organisation for saving themselves. They've got weathering-the-storm sorts of organisations. But this one's going to be different. This storm will be managed by the SS.' Gebauer, again, sounded as if without being too florid about it, he approved of the professional thoroughness of the SS.

'Come on,' said Plathe; 'the worst that can happen to them is that they'll get sent to Madagascar, where the weather is better than it is in Cracow.'

'I don't believe they'll ever *see* Madagascar,' said Gebauer.

Oskar demanded a change of subject. Wasn't it *his* party?

In fact, Oskar had already seen Gebauer hand over forged papers for a flight to Hungary to a Jewish businessman in the bar of the Hotel Cracovia. Maybe Gebauer was taking a fee, though he seemed too morally sensitive to deal in papers, to sell a signature, a rubber stamp. But it was certain, in spite of his act in front of Toffel, that he was no abominator of Jews. Nor was any of them. At Christmas 1939 Oskar found them simply a relief from the orotund official line. Later they would have more positive uses.

6

The *Aktion* of the night of December 4 had convinced Stern that Oskar Schindler was that rarity, the just Goy. There is the Talmudic legend of the *Hasidei Ummot Ha-olam*, the Righteous of the Nations, of whom there are said to be – at any point in the world's history – thirty-six. Stern did not believe literally in the mystical number, but the legend was psychologically true for him, and he believed it a decent and wise course to try to make of Schindler a living and breathing sanctuary.

The German needed capital – the Rekord plant had been partially stripped of machinery, except for one small gallery of metal presses, enamel bins, lathes, and furnaces. While Stern might be a substantial spiritual influence on Oskar, the man who put him in touch with capital on good terms was Abraham Bankier, the office manager of Rekord, whom Oskar had won over.

The two of them – big, sensual Oskar and squat, elfin Bankier – went visiting possible investors. By a decree of November 23, the bank and safe deposits of all Jews were held by the German administration, in fixed trust, without allowing the owner any right of access or interest. Some of the wealthier Jewish businessmen, those who knew anything about history, kept secret funds in hard currencies. But they could tell that for a few years under Governor Hans Frank, currencies would be risky; portable wealth – diamonds, gold, trade goods – would be desirable.

Around Cracow there were a number of men Bankier knew who were willing to put up investment capital in return for a guaranteed quantity of product. The deal might be an investment of 50,000 złoty in return for so many kilos of pots and pans a month, delivery to begin July 1940 and to continue for a year. For a Cracow Jew, given Hans Frank in the Wawel, kitchen ware was safer and more disposable than złoty.

The parties to these contracts – Oskar, the investor, Bankier as middleman – brought away from these arrangements nothing, not even deal memoranda. Full-fledged contracts were of no use and could not be enforced anyhow. Nothing could be enforced. It all depended on Bankier's accurate judgment of this Sudeten manufacturer of enamelware.

The meetings would take place perhaps in the investor's apartment in the Centrum of Cracow, the old inner city. The Polish landscapists the investor's wife adored, the French novels his bright and fragile daughters savoured would glow in the light of the transaction. Or else the investing gentleman had already been thrown out of his apartment and lived in poorer quarters in Podgórze. And he would be a man already in shock – his apartment gone and himself now an employee in his own business – and all this in a few months, the year not over yet.

At first sight, it seems a heroic embellishment of the story to say that Oskar was never accused of welching on these informal contracts. He would in the new year have a fight with one Jewish retailer over the quantity of product the man was entitled to take from DEF's loading dock in Lipowa Street. And the gentleman would be critical of Oskar on those grounds to the end of his life. But that Oskar did not fulfill deals – *that* was never said.

For Oskar was by nature a payer, who somehow gave the impression that he could make limitless repayments out of limitless resources. In any case, Oskar and other German opportunists would make so much in the next four years that only a man consumed by the profit motive would have failed to repay what Oskar's father would have called a debt of honour.

Emilie Schindler came up to Cracow, to visit her husband there for the first time, in the new year. She thought the city was the most delightful she had ever been in, so much more gracious and pleasant and old-fashioned than Brno with its clouds of industrial smoke.

She was impressed with her husband's new apartment. The front windows looked across at the Planty, an elegant ring of parkland that ran right around the city following the route of the ancient walls long since knocked down. At the bottom of the street the great fortress of Wawel rose, and amidst all this antiquity was Oskar's modern apartment. She looked around at Mrs. Pfefferberg's fabrics and wall hangings. His new success was tangible in them.

'You've done very well in Poland,' she said.

Oskar knew that she was really talking about the matter of the dowry, the one her father had refused to pay a dozen years back when travellers from Zwittau had rushed into the village of Alt-Molstein with news that his son-in-law was living and loving like an unmarried man. His daughter's marriage had become exactly the marriage he had feared it would, and he was damned if he'd pay.

And though the absence of the 400,000 RM. had altered Oskar's prospects a little, the gentleman farmer of Alt-Molstein did not know how the nonpayment would pain his daughter, make her even more defensive, nor that twelve years later, when it no longer counted for Oskar, it would be still at the front of Emilie's mind.

'My dear,' Oskar was always growling, 'I never needed the damn money.'

Emilie's intermittent relations with Oskar seem to have been those of a woman who knows her husband is not and will not be faithful, but who nonetheless doesn't want evidence of his affairs thrust under her nose. She must have moved warily in Cracow, going to parties where Oskar's friends would surely know the truth, would know the names of the other women, the names she did not really want to hear.

One day a young Pole – it was Poldek Pfefferberg, who had nearly shot her husband, but she could not know that – arrived at the door of the apartment with a rolled-up rug over his shoulder. It was a black-market rug from Istanbul via Hungary, and Pfefferberg had been given the job of finding it by Ingrid, who had moved out for the duration of Emilie's visit.

'Is Frau Schindler in?' asked Pfefferberg. He always referred to Ingrid as Frau Schindler because he thought it was less offensive.

'*I* am Frau Schindler,' said Emilie, knowing what the question meant.

Pfefferberg showed some sensitivity in covering up. Actually he did not need to see Frau Schindler, though he'd heard so much about her from Herr Schindler. He had to see Herr Schindler about some business matter.

Herr Schindler wasn't in, said Emilie. She offered Pfefferberg a drink, but he hastily refused. Emilie knew what that meant too. That the young man was just a little shocked by Oskar's personal life and thought it indecent to sit and drink with the victim.

The factory Oskar had leased was across the river in Zablocie at No. 4 Lipowa Street. The offices, which faced the street, were modern in design, and Oskar thought it might be possible and convenient for him to move in at some time, to have an apartment on the third floor, even though the surroundings were industrial and not as exhilarating as Straszewskiego Street.

When Oskar took over the Rekord works, renaming it Deutsche Emailwaren Fabrik, there were forty-five employees involved in a modest output of kitchen ware. Early in the new year he received his first Army contracts. They were no surprise. He had cultivated various influential *Wehrmacht* engineers who sat on the Main Armaments Board of General Schindler's Armaments Inspectorate. He had gone to the same parties and taken them to dinner at the Cracovia Hotel. There are photographs of Oskar sitting with them at expensive tables, everyone smiling urbanely at the camera, everyone well fed, generously liquored, and the officers elegantly uniformed. Some of them put the right stamps on his bids, and wrote the crucial letters of recommendation to General Schindler, merely out of friendship and because they believed Oskar had the plant and would deliver. Others were influenced by gifts, the sort of gifts Oskar would always proffer to officials – cognac and carpets, jewellery and furniture and hampers of luxury food. As well as that, it became known that General Schindler was acquainted with and liked very much his enamelware-producing namesake.

Now, with the authority of his lucrative Armaments Inspectorate contracts, Oskar was permitted to expand his plant. There was room. Beyond the lobby and offices of DEF stood two large industrial lofts. Some of the floor space in the building on the left as you emerged from the lobby into the interior of the factory was occupied by present production. The other building was totally empty.

He bought new machinery, some locally, some from the homeland. Apart from the military demand, there was the all-devouring black market to serve. Oskar knew now that he could be a magnate. By midsummer of 1940 he would be employing 250 Poles and would be faced with instituting a night shift. Herr Hans Schindler's farm-machinery plant in Zwittau had at the best of times employed 50. It is a sweet thing to outstrip a father whom you haven't forgiven.

At times throughout the year, Itzhak Stern would call on Schindler to arrange employment for some young Jew – a special case; an orphan from Łódź; the daughter of a clerk in one of the departments of the *Judenrat* (Jewish Council). Within a few months, Oskar was employing 150 Jewish workers and his factory had a minor reputation as a haven.

It was a year, like each succeeding year for the rest of the war, when Jews would be looking for some employment considered essential to the war effort. In April, Governor General Frank had decreed an evacuation of Jews from his capital, Cracow. It was a curious decision, since the Reich authorities were still moving Jews and Poles back into the Government General at the rate of nearly 10,000 a day. Yet conditions in Cracow, Frank told his cabinet, were scandalous. He knew of German divisional commanders who had to live in apartment buildings that contained Jewish tenants. Higher officials were also subjected to the same scandalous indignity. Over the next six months, he promised, he would make Cracow *juden-*

frei (free of Jews). There would be a permitted remnant of 5,000 to 6,000 skilled Jewish workers. All the rest were to be moved into other cities in the Government General, into Warsaw or Radom, Lublin, or Czestochowa. Jews could immigrate voluntarily to the city of their choice as long as they did it before August 15. Those still left in the city after that date would be trucked out with a small amount of luggage to whatever place suited the administration. From November 1, said Hans Frank, it would be possible for the Germans of Cracow to breathe 'good German air,' to walk abroad without seeing the streets and lanes 'crawling with Jews.'

Frank would not manage that year to reduce the Jewish population to quite so low a level; but when his plans were first announced, there was a rush among the Jews of Cracow, especially among the young, to acquire skilled qualifications. Men like Itzhak Stern, official and unofficial agents of the *Judenrat*, had already developed a list of sympathisers, Germans to whom they could appeal. Schindler was on that list; so was Julius Madritsch, a Viennese who had recently managed to get himself released from the *Wehrmacht* and taken up the post of *Treuhänder* of a plant manufacturing military uniforms. Madritsch could see the benefits of Armaments Inspectorate's contracts and now intended to open a uniform factory of his own in the suburb of Podgórze. In the end he would make an even larger fortune than Schindler, but in the *annus mirabilis* of 1940 he was still on a salary. He was known to be humane – that was all.

By November 1, 1940, Frank had managed to move 23,000 Jewish volunteers out of Cracow. Some of them went to the new ghettos in Warsaw and Łódź. The gaps at table, the grieving at railway stations can be imagined, but people took it meekly, thinking, *We'll do this, and that will be the brunt of what they ask*. Oskar knew it was happening, but, like the Jews themselves, hoped it was a temporary excess.

That year would very likely be the most industrious of Oskar's life – a year spent building the place up from a bankrupt manufactory to a company government agencies could take seriously.

As the first snows fell, Schindler noticed and was irritated when, on any given day, 60 or more of his Jewish employees would be absentees. They would have been detained by SS squads on the way to work and employed in clearing snow. Herr Schindler visited his friend Toffel at SS headquarters in Pomorska Street to complain. On one day, he told Toffel, he had 125 absentees.

Toffel confided in him. 'You've got to understand that some of these fellows here don't give a damn about production. To them it's a matter of national priority that Jews be made to shovel snow. I don't understand it myself . . . it's got a ritual significance for them, Jews shovelling snow. And it's not just you, it's happening to everyone.'

Oskar asked if all the others were complaining too. Yes, said Toffel. However, he said, an economic big shot from the SS Budget and Construction Office had come for lunch in Pomorska and said that to believe the Jewish skilled worker had a place in Reich economics was treasonable. 'I think you're going to have to put up with a lot of snow shovelling yet, Oskar.'

Oskar, for the moment, assumed the stance of the outraged patriot, or perhaps of the outraged profiteer. 'If they want to win the war,' said Oskar, 'they'd have to get rid of SS men like that.'

'Get rid of them?' asked Toffel. 'For Christ's sake, they're the bastards who're on top.'

As a result of such conversations, Oskar became an advocate of the principle that a factory owner should have unimpeded access to his own workers, that these workers should have access to the plant, that they should not be detained or tyrannised on their way to and from the factory. It was, in Oskar's eyes, a moral axiom as much as an industrial one. In the end, he would apply it to its limit at Deutsche Email Fabrik.

7

Some people from the big cities – from Warsaw and Łódź with their ghettos and Cracow with Frank's commitment to making it *judenfrei* – went to the countryside to lose themselves among the peasants. The Rosner brothers, Cracovian musicians who would come to know Oskar well, settled in the old village of Tyniec. It was on a pretty bend of the Vistula, and an old Benedictine abbey on a limestone cliff hung above it. It was anonymous enough for the Rosners, though. It had a few Jewish storekeepers and Orthodox artisans, with whom nightclub musicians had little to converse about. But the peasants, busy with the tedium of the harvest, were as pleased as the Rosners could have hoped to find musicians in their midst.

They'd come to Tyniec not from Cracow, not from that great marshalling point outside the botanical gardens in Mogilska Street where young SS men pushed people onto trucks and called out bland and lying promises about the later delivery of all adequately labelled baggage. They had come in fact from Warsaw, where they had been enjoying an engagement at the Basilisk. They had left the day before the Germans sealed up the Warsaw ghetto – Henry and Leopold and Henry's wife, Manci, and five-year-old son, Olek.

The idea of a south Polish village like Tyniec, not far from their native Cracow, appealed to the brothers. It offered the option, should conditions improve, of catching a bus into Cracow and finding work. Manci Rosner, an Austrian girl, had brought with her her sewing machine, and the Rosners set up a little clothing business in Tyniec. In the evenings they played in the taverns and became a sensation in a town like that. Villages welcome and support occasional wonders, even Jewish ones. And the fiddle was, of all instruments, most venerated in Poland.

One evening a travelling *Volksdeutscher* (German-speaking Pole) from Poznan heard the brothers playing outside the inn. The *Volksdeutscher* was a municipal official from Cracow, one of those Polish Germans in whose name Hitler had taken the country in the first place. The *Volksdeutscher* told Henry that the mayor of Cracow, *Obersturmbannführer* Pavlu, and his deputy, the renowned skier Sepp Röhre, would be visiting the countryside at harvest time, and he would like to arrange for them to hear such an accomplished pair as the Rosners.

On an afternoon when the bound sheaves lay drowsing in fields as quiet and as abandoned as on Sunday, a convoy of limousines wound through Tyniec and up a rise to the villa of an absentee Polish aristocrat. On the terrace, the dapper Rosner brothers waited, and when all the ladies and gentlemen had been seated in a room that might once have been used for balls, they were invited to perform. Henry and Leopold felt both exultation and fear at the seriousness with which *Obersturmbannführer* Pavlu's party had geared themselves for their playing. The women wore white dresses and gloves, the military officials full dress, the bureaucrats their winged collars. When people went to such trouble, it was easier to disappoint them. For a Jew, even to impose a cultural disappointment on the regime was a serious crime.

But the audience loved them. They were a characteristically *gemütlich* crowd; they loved Strauss, the confections of Offenbach and Lehar, André Messager and Leo Fall. At request time they grew mawkish.

And as Henry and Leopold performed, the ladies and gentlemen drank champagne from long-stemmed flutes brought in by hamper.

Once the official recital had finished, the brothers were taken down the hill to where the peasants and the soldiers of the escort had been gathered. If there was to be some crude racial demonstration, it would take place here. But again, once the brothers had climbed onto a wagon and looked the crowd in the eye, Henry knew they would be safe. The pride of the peasants, partly a national thing – the Rosners being for the night a credit to Polish culture – all that protected them. It was so like old times that Henry found himself smiling down at Olek and Manci, playing to her, capable of ignoring the rest. It did seem for those seconds that the earth had at last been pacified by music.

When it was finished, a middle-aged SS NCO – a *Rottenführer* (a junior noncommissioned SS rank) perhaps – Henry not being as familiar as he might become with the gradations of SS rank – approached them as they stood by the wagon receiving congratulations. He nodded to them and barely smiled. 'I hope you have a nice harvest holiday,' he said, bowed, and left.

The brothers stared at each other. As soon as the SS man was out of hearing, they gave in to the temptation to discuss his meaning. Leopold was convinced. 'It's a threat,' he said. It went to show what they had feared in their marrow when the *Volksdeutsche* official first spoke to them – that these days it didn't do to stand out, to acquire a distinctive face.

That was life in the country in 1940. The curtailment of a career, the rustic tedium, the scratching out of a trade, the occasional terror, the pull of that bright core called Cracow. To that, the Rosners knew, they would eventually return.

Emilie had returned home in the autumn, and when Stern next came to Schindler's apartment it was Ingrid who brought the coffee. Oskar made no secret of his weaknesses, and never seemed to think that ascetic Itzhak Stern needed any apologia for Ingrid's presence. Similarly, when the coffee was finished, Oskar went to the liquor cabinet and brought back a fresh bottle of brandy, setting it down on the table between his seat and Stern's, as if Stern were really likely to help him drink it.

Stern had come that evening to tell Oskar that a family whom we shall call the Cs* were spreading stories about him, old David

---

*The reason an initial is employed here instead of a fictionalised name is that in Cracow the whole range of Polish Jewish names were found, and that to employ any name other than the Cs' real one might cause offence to the memory of some vanished family or to some living friend of Oskar's.

and young Leon C, saying even on the streets in Kazimierz – let alone in parlors – that Oskar was a German gangster, a thug. When Stern passed on these accusations to Oskar, he didn't use terms quite as vivid as that.

Oskar knew Stern wasn't looking for a response, that he was just passing on intelligence. But of course he felt he had to respond anyway.

'I could spread stories about them,' said Oskar. 'They're robbing me blind. Ask Ingrid if you like.'

Ingrid was the Cs' supervisor. She was a benign *Treuhänder* and, being only in her twenties, commercially inexperienced. The rumor was that Schindler himself had got the girl appointed so that he would have an assured outlet for his kitchenware. The Cs, however, still did pretty well what they wanted with their company. If they resented the idea that it was held in trust by the occupying power, no one could blame them for that.

Stern waved Oskar's suggestion away. Who was he to want to grill Ingrid? It wasn't much use to compare notes with the girl anyhow.

'They run rings around Ingrid,' said Oskar. They turned up at Lipowa Street for delivery of their orders and altered the invoices on the spot and took away more than they had paid for. '*She* says it's all right,' they'd tell the Schindler employees. '*He's* arranged it with Ingrid.'

The son had in fact been gathering crowds and telling them that Schindler had had the SS beat him up. But his story varied – the beating was supposed to have occurred at Schindler's factory, in a storeroom from which young C emerged with a black eye and broken teeth. Then it was supposed to have occurred on Lima-nowskiego, in front of witnesses. A man called F, an employee of Oskar's and a friend of the Cs, had said he'd heard Oskar stamping up and down in his office in Lipowa Street and threatening to kill old David C. Then Oskar was said to have driven around to Stradom and raided the C cash register, to have stuffed his pockets with currency and told them that there was a New Order in Europe, and then to have beaten up old David in his office.

Was it possible that Oskar could let fly at old David C and land him in bed with bruises? Was it likely he would call on friends in the police to assault Leon? On one level Oskar and the Cs were gangsters, selling tons of kitchen ware illegally, without sending records of sales to the *Transferstelle*, without use of the required merchandising coupons called *Bezugschein*. On the black market, the dialogue was primitive and tempers were short. Oskar admitted he'd raged into the Cs' showroom and called father and son thieves and indemnified himself out of the till for the kitchenware the Cs had taken without authorisation. Oskar admitted he'd punched young Leon. But that was the limit of his admissions.

And the Cs, whom Stern had known since childhood – they had one of those reputations. Not exactly criminal, but sharp in dealing and, significant in this case, with a reputation for squealing when caught.

Stern knew Leon C's bruises *did* exist. Leon wore them down the street and was willing to elaborate on them. The SS beating *did* take place somewhere or other, but it could have had a dozen causes. Stern not only did not believe that Oskar had begun asking the SS for *that* sort of favour, but also had the sense that to believe or disbelieve what was said to have happened in this case was irrelevant to his own wider purposes. It would become relevant only when and if Herr Schindler established a brutal pattern. For Stern's purposes, occasional lapses did not count. Had Oskar been without sin, this apartment would not exist in its present form, and neither would Ingrid be waiting in the bedroom.

And it is yet again one of those things which must be said, that Oskar would save all of them – Mr. and Mrs. C, Leon C, Mr. H, Miss M, old C's secretary – and that they would always admit that, but that they would also and always stick to their story of the bruises.

That evening Itzhak Stern also brought news of Marek Biberstein's jail sentence. He had got two years in the prison in

Montelupich Street, this Marek Biberstein who was the president of the *Judenrat*, or who had been until his arrest. In other cities the *Judenrat* was already cursed by the general Jewish population, for its main work had become the drawing up of lists for forced labour, for transfers to camps. The *Judenrats* were regarded by the German administration as organs of its will, but in Cracow, Marek Biberstein and his cabinet still saw themselves as buffers between the office of the military mayor of Cracow, Schmid and later Pavlu, on one hand, and the Jewish inhabitants of the city on the other. In the Cracow German newspaper of March 13, 1940, a Dr. Dietrich Redecker said that on a visit to the *Judenrat* office he was struck by the contrast between its carpet and plush chairs and the poverty and squalor of the Jewish quarter in Kazimierz. But Jewish survivors do not remember the first Cracow *Judenrat* as men who cut themselves off from the people. Hungry for revenue, however, they had made the mistake the *Judenrats* of Łódź and Warsaw had made before them, permitting the affluent to buy their way off forced-labour lists, forcing the poor onto the roster in return for soup and bread. But even later, in 1941, Biberstein and his council still had the respect of the Jews of Cracow.

That first membership of the *Judenrat* consisted of twenty-four men, most of them intellectuals. Each day, on his way to Zablocie, Oskar passed their corner office in Podgórze into which were crowded a number of secretariats. In the manner of a cabinet, each member of the council took care of a different aspect of government. Mr. Schenker had charge of taxes, Mr. Steinberg of buildings – an essential job in a society where people drifted in and out, this week trying the option of refuge in some small village, next week walking back to town surfeited with the narrowness of the peasants. Leon Salpeter, a pharmacist by profession, had charge of one of the social-welfare agencies. There were secretariats for food, cemeteries, health, travel documentation, economic affairs, administrative services, culture, even – in the face of the ban on schooling – of education.

Biberstein and his council believed on principle that the Jews who were expelled from Cracow would end up in worse places, and so they decided to fall back on an ancient stratagem: bribery. The hard-up *Judenrat* treasury allocated 200,000 złoty for the purpose. Biberstein and the Housing Secretary, Chaim Goldfluss, had sought out an intermediary, in this case a *Volksdeutscher* named Reichert, a man who had contacts in the SS and the city administration. Reichert's task was to pass on the money to a series of officials beginning with *Obersturmführer* (an SS rank equivalent to first lieutenant) Seibert, the liaison officer between the *Judenrat* and the city government. In return for the money, the officials were to permit another 10,000 Jews of the Cracow community to remain at home, despite Frank's order. Whether Reichert had insulted officials by retaining too large a percentage for himself and making too low an offer, or whether the gentlemen involved felt that Governor Frank's most cherished ambition to render his city *judenfrei* made the taking of bribes too perilous, no one could tell from the court proceedings. But Biberstein had got two years in Montelupich, Goldfluss six months in Auschwitz. Reichert himself had got eight years. Yet everyone knew he would have a softer time of it than the other two.

Schindler shook his head at the idea of putting 200,000 złoty on such a fragile hope. 'Reichert is a crook,' he murmured. Just ten minutes before, they had been discussing whether he and the Cs were crooks and had let the question stand. But there was no doubt about Reichert. 'I could have told them Reichert was a crook,' he kept insisting.

Stern commented – as a philosophic principle – that there were times when the only people left to do business with were crooks.

Schindler laughed at that – a wide, toothy, almost rustic laugh. 'Thank you very much, my friend,' he told Stern.

8

It wasn't such a bad Christmas that year. But there was a wistfulness, and snow lay like a question in the parkland across from Schindler's apartment, like something posed, watchful and eternal, on the roof of the Wawel up the road and under the ancient facades of Kanonicza Street. No one believed anymore in a quick resolution – neither the soldiery nor the Poles nor the Jews on either side of the river.

For his Polish secretary Klonowska, that Christmas, Schindler bought a poodle, a ridiculous Parisian thing, acquired by Pfefferberg. For Ingrid he bought jewellery and sent some also to gentle Emilie down in Zwittau. Poodles were hard to find, Leopold Pfefferberg reported. But jewellery was a snap. Because of the times, gems were in a high state of movement.

Oskar seems to have pursued his simultaneous attachments to three women and sundry casual friendships with others, all without suffering the normal penalties that beset the womaniser. Visitors to his apartment cannot remember ever finding Ingrid sulking. She seems to have been a generous and complaisant girl. Emilie, with even greater grounds for complaint, had too much dignity to make the scenes Oskar richly deserved. If Klonowska had any resentment, it does not seem to have affected her manner in the front office of DEF nor her loyalty to the *Herr Direktor*. One could expect that in a life like Oskar's, public confrontations between angry women would be commonplace. But no one among Oskar's friends and workers – witnesses willing enough to admit and even in some cases chuckle over his sins of the flesh – remembers such painful confrontations, so often the fate of far more restrained philanderers than Oskar.

To suggest as some have that any woman would be pleased with partial possession of Oskar is to demean the women involved. The problem was, perhaps, that if you wanted to talk to Oskar about fidelity, a look of childlike and authentic bewilderment entered his eyes, as if you were proposing some concept like Relativity which could be understood only if the listener had five hours to sit still and concentrate. Oskar never had five hours and never understood.

Except in his mother's case. That Christmas morning, for his dead mother's sake, Oskar went to Mass at the Church of St. Mary. There was a space above the high altar where Wit Stwosz's wooden tryptych had until weeks ago diverted worshippers with its crowd of jostling divinities. The vacancy, the pallor of the stone where the tryptych's fixings had been, distracted and abashed Herr Schindler. Someone had stolen the tryptych. It had been shipped to Nuremberg. What an improbable world it had become!

Business was wonderful that winter just the same. In the next year his friends in the Armaments Inspectorate began to talk to Oskar about the possibility of opening a munitions division to manufacture antitank shells. Oskar was not as interested in shells as in pots and pans. Pots and pans were easy engineering. You cut out and pressed the metal, dipped it in the tubs, fired it at the right temperature. You didn't have to calibrate instruments; the work was nowhere near as exacting as it would be for arms. There was no under-the-counter trade in shell casings, and Oskar liked under-the-counter – liked the sport of it, the disrepute, the fast returns, the lack of paperwork.

But because it was good politics, he established a munitions section, installing a few immense Hilo machines, for the precision pressing and tooling of shell casings, in one gallery of his No. 2 workshop. The munitions section was so far developmental; it would take some months of planning, measuring, and test production before any shells appeared. The big Hilos, however, gave the Schindler works, as a hedge against the questionable future, at least the *appearance* of essential industry.

*

Before the Hilos had even been properly calibrated, Oskar began to get hints from his SS contacts at Pomorska Street that there was to be a ghetto for Jews. He mentioned the rumor to Stern, not wanting to arouse alarm. Oh, yes, said Stern, the word was out. Some people were even looking forward to it. We'll be inside, the enemy will be outside. We can run our own affairs. No one will envy us, no one stone us in the streets. The walls of the ghetto will be fixed. The walls would be the final, fixed form of the catastrophe.

The edict, 'Gen. Gub. 44/91,' posted on March 3, was published in the Cracow dailies and blared forth from loudspeakers on trucks in Kazimierz. Walking through his munitions department, Oskar heard one of his German technicians comment on the news. 'Won't they be better off in there?' asked the technician. 'The Poles hate them, you know.'

The edict used the same excuse. As a means of reducing racial conflict in the Government General, a closed Jewish quarter would be set up. Enclosure in the ghetto would be compulsory for all Jews, but those with the proper labour card could travel from the ghetto to work, returning in the evening. The ghetto would be located in the suburb of Podgórze just across the river. The deadline for entering it would be March 20. Once in, you would be allocated housing by the *Judenrat*, but Poles presently living in the area of the ghetto and who therefore had to move were to apply to their own housing office for apartments in other parts of town.

A map of the new ghetto was appended to the edict. The north side would be bounded by the river, the east end by the railway line to Lwów, the south side by the hills beyond Rekawka, the west by Podgórze Place. It would be crowded in there.

But there was hope that repression would take definite form now and provide people with a basis on which to plan their restricted futures. For a man like Juda Dresner, a textile wholesaler of Stradom Street who would come to know Oskar, the past year and a half had brought a bewildering succession of decrees, intrusions, and confiscations. He had lost his business to the Trust

Agency, his car, his apartment. His bank account had been frozen. His children's schools had been closed, or else they had been expelled from them. The family's jewellery had been seized, and their radio. He and his family were forbidden entry to the centre of Cracow, denied any travel by train. They could use only segregated trolley cars. His wife and daughter and sons were subject to intermittent roundups for snow shovelling or other compulsory labour. You never knew, when you were forced into the back of a truck, if the absence would be a short or long one, or what sort of hair-trigger madmen might be supervising the work you would be forced to. Under this sort of regimen you felt that life offered no footholds, that you were slithering into a pit which had no bottom. But perhaps the ghetto was the bottom, the point at which it was possible to take organised thought.

Besides, the Jews of Cracow were accustomed — in a way that could best be described as congenital — to the idea of a ghetto. And now that it had been decided, the very word had a soothing, ancestral ring. Their grandfathers had not been permitted to emerge from the ghetto of Kazimierz until 1867, when Franz Josef signed a decree permitting them to live wherever they wished in the city. Cynics said that the Austrians had needed to open up Kazimierz, socketed as it was in the elbow of the river so close to Cracow, so that Polish labourers could find accommodation close to their places of work. But Franz Josef was nonetheless revered by the older people from Kazimierz as energetically as he had been in the childhood household of Oskar Schindler.

Although their liberty had come so late, there was at the same time among the older Cracow Jews a nostalgia for the old ghetto of Kazimierz. A ghetto implied certain squalors, a crowding in tenements, a sharing of bathroom facilities, disputes over drying space on clotheslines. Yet it also consecrated the Jews to their own specialness, to a richness of shared scholarship, to songs and Zionist talk, elbow to elbow, in coffeehouses rich in ideas if not in cream. Evil rumors emanated from the ghettos of Łódź and Warsaw, but the Podgórze ghetto as planned was more generous with space, for if you superimposed it on a map of the Centrum, you found that the ghetto was in area about half the size of the Old City – by no means enough space, but not quite strangulation.

There was also in the edict a sedative clause that promised to protect the Jews from their Polish countrymen. Since the early 1930s, a willfully orchestrated racial contest had prevailed in Poland. When the Depression began and farm prices fell, the Polish government had sanctioned a range of anti-Semitic political groups of the kind that saw the Jews as the base of all their economic troubles. Sanacja, Marshal Pilsudski's Moral Cleansing Party, made an alliance after the old man's death with the Camp of National Unity, a right-wing Jew-baiting group. Prime Minister Sklad-kowski, on the floor of the Parliament in Warsaw, declared, 'Economic war on the Jews? All right!' Rather than give the peasants land reform, Sanacja encouraged them to look at the Jewish stalls on market day as the symbol and total explanation of Polish rural poverty. There were pogroms against the Jewish population in a series of towns, beginning in Grodno in 1935. The Polish legislators also entered the struggle, and Jewish industries were starved under new laws on bank credit. Craft guilds closed their lists to Jewish artisans, and the universities introduced a quota, or what they themselves – strong in the classics – called *numerus clausus aut nullus* (a closed number or nil), on the entry of Jewish students. Faculties gave way to National Unity insistence that Jews be appointed special benches in the quadrangle and be exiled to the left side of the lecture halls. Commonly enough in Polish universities, the pretty and brilliant daughters of city Jewry emerged from lecture halls to have their faces savaged by a quick razor stroke delivered by a lean, serious youth from the Camp of National Unity.

In the first days of the German Occupation, the conquerors had been astounded by the willingness of Poles to point out Jewish households, to hold a prayer-locked Jew still while a German docked the Orthodox beard with scissors or, pinking the facial flesh as well, with an infantry bayonet. In March 1941, therefore, the promise to protect the ghetto dwellers from Polish national excess fell on the ear almost credibly.

Although there was no great spontaneous joy among the Jews of Cracow as they packed for the move to Podgórze, there were strange elements of homecoming to it, as well as that sense of arriving at a limit beyond which, with any luck, you wouldn't be further uprooted or tyrannised. Enough so that even some people from the villages around Cracow, from Wieliczka, from Niepolomice, from Lipnica, Murowana, and Tyniec hurried to town lest they be locked out on March 20 and find themselves in a comfortless landscape. For the ghetto was by its nature, almost by definition, habitable, even if subject to intermittent attack. The ghetto represented *stasis* instead of flux.

The ghetto would introduce a minor inconvenience in Oskar Schindler's life. It was usual for him to leave his luxury apartment in Straszewskiego, pass the limestone lump of the Wawel stuck in the mouth of the city like a cork in a bottle, and so roll down through Kazimierz, over the Kosciuszko bridge and left toward his factory in Zablocie. Now that route would be blocked by the ghetto walls. It was a minor problem, but it made the idea of maintaining an apartment on the top floor of his office building in Lipowa Street more reasonable. It wasn't such a bad place, built in the style of Walter Gropius. Lots of glass and light, fashionable cubic bricks in the entranceway.

Whenever he did travel between the city and Zablocie in those March days before the deadline, he would see the Jews of Kazimierz packing, and on Stradom Street would pass, early in the grace period, families pushing barrows piled with chairs, mattresses, and clocks toward the ghetto. Their families had lived in Kazimierz since the time it was an island separated from the Centrum by a stream called Stara Wisła. Since, in fact, the time Kazimier the Great had invited them to Cracow when, elsewhere, they were footing the blame for the Black Death. Oskar surmised that their ancestors would have turned up in Cracow like that, pushing a barrowful of bedding, more than five hundred years before. Now they were leaving, it seemed, with the same barrowful. Kazimier's invitation had been cancelled.

During those morning journeys across town, Oskar noticed that the plan was for the city trolleys to go on rolling down Lwówska Street, through the middle of the ghetto. All walls facing the trolley line were being bricked up by Polish workmen, and where there had been open spaces, cement walls were raised. As well, the trolleys would have their doors closed as they entered the ghetto and could not stop until they emerged again in the *Umwelt*, the Aryan world, at the corner of Lwówska and ś.w. Kingi Street. Oskar knew people would catch that trolley anyhow. Doors closed, no stops, machine guns on walls – it wouldn't matter. Humans were incurable that way. People would try to get off it, someone's loyal Polish maid with a parcel of sausage. And people would try to get on, some fast-moving athletic young man like Leopold Pfefferberg with a pocketful of diamonds or Occupation złoty or a message in code for the partisans. People responded to any slim chance, even if it was an outside one, its doors locked shut, moving fast between mute walls.

From March 20, Oskar's Jewish workers would not receive any wages and were meant to live entirely by their rations. Instead he would pay a fee to SS headquarters in Cracow. Both Oskar and Madritsch were uneasy about that, for they knew the war would end and the slaveholders, just as in America, would be shamed and stripped naked. The dues he would pay to the police chiefs were the standard SS Main Administrative and Economic Office fees – 7.50 Reichsmarks per day for a skilled worker, 5 RM. for unskilled and women. They were, by a margin, cheaper rates than those which operated on the open labour market. But for Oskar and Julius Madritsch both, the moral discomfort outweighed the economic advantage. The meeting of his wage bill was the least of Oskar's worries that year. Besides, he was never an ideal capitalist. His father had accused him often in his youth of being reckless with money. While he was a mere sales manager, he'd maintained two cars, hoping that Hans would get to hear of it and be shocked. Now, in Cracow, he could afford to keep a stableful – a Belgian Minerva, a Maybach, an Adler cabriolet, a BMW.

To be a prodigal and still be wealthier than your more careful father – that was one of the triumphs Schindler wanted out of life. In boom times the cost of labour was beside the point.

It was that way for Madritsch too. Julius Madritsch's uniform mill stood on the western side of the ghetto, a mile or so from Oskar's enamelworks. He was doing so well that he was negotiating to open a similar plant in Tarnow. He too was a darling of the Armaments Inspectorate, and his credit was so good that he had received a loan of a million złoty from the Bank Emisyjny (Issue Bank).

Whatever ethical queasiness they felt, it is not likely that either entrepreneur, Oskar or Julius, felt a moral obligation to avoid employing additional Jews. That was a stance, and since they were pragmatists, stances weren't their style. In any case, Itzhak Stern as well as Roman Ginter, a businessman and representative of the Relief Office of the *Judenrat*, called on Oskar and Julius both and begged them to employ more Jews, as many as could be fitted in. The objective was to give the ghetto an economic permanence. It was almost axiomatic, Stern and Ginter considered at that stage, that a Jew who had an economic value in a precocious empire hungry for skilled workers was safe from worse things. And Oskar and Madritsch agreed.

So for two weeks the Jews trundled their barrows through Kazimierz and over the bridge into Podgórze. Middle-class families whose Polish servants had come with them to help push the cart. At the bottom of the barrows lay the remaining brooches, the fur coats, under mattresses and kettles and skillets. Crowds of Poles on Stradom and Starovislna Streets jeered and hurled mud. 'The Jews are going, the Jews are going. Goodbye, Jews.'

Beyond the bridge a fancy wooden gate greeted the new citizens of the ghetto. White with scalloped ramparts which gave it an

Arabesque look, it had two wide arches for the trolleys coming from and going to Cracow, and at the side was a white sentry box. Above the arches, a title in Hebrew sought to reassure. JEWISH TOWN, it proclaimed. High barbed-wire fences had been strung along the front of the ghetto, facing the river, and open spaces were sealed with round-topped cement slabs nine feet tall, resembling strings of gravestones for the anonymous.

At the ghetto gate the trundling Jew was met by a representative of the *Judenrat* Housing Office. If he had a wife and large family, a man might be assigned two rooms and have the use of a kitchen. Even so, after the good living of the Twenties and Thirties, it was painful to have to share your private life with families of different rituals, of another, distasteful musk and habits. Mothers screamed, and fathers said things could be worse and sucked on hollow teeth and shook their heads. In the one room, the Orthodox found the liberals an abomination.

On March 20, the movement was complete. Everyone outside the ghetto was forfeit and in jeopardy. Inside, for the moment, there was living space.

Twenty-three-year-old Edith Liebgold was assigned a first-floor room to share with her mother and her baby. The fall of Cracow eighteen months back had put her husband into a mood verging on despair. He'd wandered away from home as if he wanted to look into the courses open to him. He had ideas about the forests, about finding a safe clearing. He had never returned.

From her end window Edith Liebgold could see the Vistula through the barbed-wire barricade, but her path to other parts of the ghetto, especially to the hospital in Wegierska Street, took her through Plac Zgody, Peace Square, the ghetto's only square. Here, on the second day of her life inside the walls, she missed by twenty seconds being ordered into an SS truck and taken to shovel coal or snow in the city. It was not just that work details often, according to rumor, returned to the ghetto with one or more fewer members than when they had left. More than this sort of odds, Edith feared being forced into a truck when, half a minute earlier, you'd thought you were going to Pankiewicz' pharmacy, and your baby was due to be fed in twenty minutes. Therefore she went with friends to the Jewish Employment Office. If she could get shift work, her mother would mind the baby at night.

The office in those first days was crowded. The *Judenrat* had its own police force now, the *Ordnungsdienst* (or OD), expanded and regularised to keep order in the ghetto, and a boy with a cap and an armband organised waiting lines in front of the office.

Edith Liebgold's group were just inside the door, making lots of noise to pass the time, when a small middle-aged man wearing a brown suit and a tie approached her. They could tell that they'd attracted him with their racket, their brightness. At first they thought he intended to pick Edith up.

'Look,' he said, 'rather than wait . . . there is an enamel factory over in Zablocie.'

He let the address have its effect. Zablocie was outside the ghetto, he was telling them. You could barter with the Polish workers there. He needed ten healthy women for the night shift.

The girls made faces, as if they could afford to choose work and might even turn him down. Not heavy, he assured them. And they'll teach you on the job. His name, he said, was Abraham Bankier. He was the manager. There was a German owner, of course. What sort of German? they asked. Bankier grinned as if he suddenly wanted to fulfill all their hopes. Not a bad sort, he told them.

That night Edith Liebgold met the other members of the enamel-factory night shift and marched across the ghetto toward Zablocie under the guard of a Jewish OD. In the column she asked questions about this Deutsche Email Fabrik. They serve a soup with plenty of body, she was told. Beatings? she asked. It's not that sort of place, they said. It's not like Beckmann's razor-blade factory; more like Madritsch. Madritsch is all right, and Schindler too.

At the entrance to the factory, the new night-shift workers were called out of the column by Bankier and taken upstairs and past vacant desks to a door marked HERR DIREKTOR. Edith Liebgold heard a deep voice tell them all to come in. They found the *Herr Direktor* seated on the corner of his desk, smoking a cigarette. His hair, somewhere between blond and light brown, looked freshly brushed; he wore a double-breasted suit and a silk tie. He looked exactly like a man who had a dinner to go to but had waited specially to have a word with them. He was immense; he was still young. From such a Hitlerite dream, Edith expected a lecture on the war effort and increasing production quotas.

'I wanted to welcome you,' he told them in Polish. 'You're part of the expansion of this factory.' He looked away; it was even possible he was thinking, *Don't tell them that – they've got no stake in the place.*

Then, without blinking, without any introduction, any qualifying lift of the shoulders, he told them, 'You'll be safe working here. If you work here, then you'll live through the war.' Then he said good night and left the office with them, allowing Bankier to hold them back at the head of the stairs so that the *Herr Direktor* could go down first and get behind the wheel of his automobile.

The promise had dazed them all. It was a godlike promise. How could a mere man make a promise like that? But Edith Liebgold found herself believing it instantly. Not so much because she wanted to; not because it was a sop, a reckless incentive. It was because in the second Herr Schindler uttered the promise it left no option but belief.

The new women of DEF took their job instruction in a pleasant daze. It was as if some mad old Gypsy with nothing to gain had told them they would marry a count. The promise had forever altered Edith Liebgold's expectation of life. If ever they did shoot her, she would probably stand there protesting, 'But the *Herr Direktor* said this couldn't happen.'

The work made no mental demands. Edith carried the enamel-dipped pots, hanging by hooks from a long stick, to the furnaces. And all the time she pondered Herr Schindler's promise. Only madmen made promises as absolute as that. Without blinking. Yet he wasn't mad. For he was a businessman with a dinner to go to. Therefore, he must *know*. But that meant some second sight, some profound contact with god or devil or the pattern of things. But again, his appearance, his hand with the gold signet ring, wasn't the hand of a visionary. It was a hand that reached for the wine; it was a hand in which you could somehow sense the latent caresses. And so she came back to the idea of his madness again, to drunkenness, to mystical explanations, to the technique by which the *Herr Direktor* had infected her with certainty.

Similar loops of reasoning would be traced this year and in years to come by all those to whom Oskar Schindler made his heady promises. Some would become aware of the unstated corollary. If the man was wrong, if he lightly used his powers of passing on conviction, then there was no God and no humanity, no bread, no succour. There were, of course, only odds, and the odds weren't good.

9

That spring Schindler left his factory in Cracow and drove west in a BMW over the border and through the awakening spring forests to Zwittau. He had Emilie to see, and his aunts and sister. They had all been allies against his father; they were all tenders of the flame of his mother's martyrdom. If there was a parallel between his late mother's misery and his wife's, Oskar Schindler – in his coat with the fur lapels, guiding the custom-made wheel with kid-gloved hands, reaching for another Turkish cigarette on the straight stretches of thawing road in the Jeseniks – did not see it. It was not a child's business to see these things. His father was a god and subject to tougher laws.

He liked visiting the aunts – the way they raised their hands palm upward in admiration of the cut of his suit. His younger sister had married a railway official and lived in a pleasant apartment provided by the rail authorities. Her husband was an important man in Zwittau, for it was a rail-junction town and had large freight yards. Oskar drank tea with his sister and her husband, and then some schnapps. There was a faint sense of mutual congratulation: the Schindler children hadn't turned out so badly.

It was, of course, Oskar's sister who had nursed Frau Schindler in her last illness and who had now been visiting and speaking to their father in secret. She could do no more than make certain hints in the direction of a reconciliation. She did that over the tea and was answered by growls.

Later, Oskar dined at home with Emilie. She was excited to have him there for the holiday. They could attend the Easter ceremonies together like an old-fashioned couple. Ceremonies was right, for they danced around each other ceremoniously all evening, attending to each other at table like polite strangers. And in their hearts and minds, both Emilie and Oskar were amazed by this strange marriage disability – that he could offer and deliver more to strangers, to workers on his factory floor than he could to her.

The question that lay between them was whether Emilie should join him in Cracow. If she gave up the apartment in Zwittau and put in other tenants, she would have no escape at all from Cracow. She believed it her duty to be with Oskar; in the language of Catholic moral theology, his absence from her house was a 'proximate occasion of sin.' Yet life with him in a foreign city would be tolerable only if he was careful and guarded and sensitive to her feelings. The trouble with Oskar was that you could not depend on him to keep his lapses to himself. Careless, half-tipsy, half-smiling, he seemed sometimes to think that if he really liked some girl, *you* had to like her too.

The unresolved question about her going to Cracow lay so oppressively between them that when dinner was finished he excused himself and went to a café in the main square. It was a place frequented by mining engineers, small businessmen, the occasional salesman turned Army officer. Gratefully he saw some of his biker friends there, most of them wearing *Wehrmacht* uniforms. He began drinking cognac with them. Some expressed surprise that a big husky chap like Oskar was not in uniform.

'Essential industry,' he growled. 'Essential industry.'

They reminisced about their motorcycle days. There were jokes about the one he'd put together out of spare parts when he was in high school. Its explosive effects. The explosive effects of his big 500cc Galloni. The noise level in the café mounted; more cognac was being shouted for. From the dining annex old school friends appeared, that look on their faces as if they had recognised a forgotten laugh, as in fact they had.

Then one of them got serious. 'Oskar, listen. Your father's having dinner in there, all by himself.' Oskar Schindler looked into his cognac. His face burned, but he shrugged.

'You ought to talk to him,' said someone. 'He's a shadow, the poor old bastard.'

Oskar said that he had better go home. He began to stand, but their hands were on his shoulders, forcing him down again. 'He knows you're here,' they said. Two of them had already gone through to the annex and were persuading old Hans Schindler over the remnants of his dinner. Oskar, in a panic, was already standing, searching in his pocket for the checkroom disk, when Herr Hans Schindler, his expression pained, appeared from the dining room propelled gently along by two young men. Oskar was halted by the sight. In spite of his anger at his father, he'd always imagined that if any ground was covered between himself and Hans, he'd be the one who'd have to cover it. The old man was so proud. Yet here he was letting himself be dragged to his son.

As the two of them were pushed toward each other, the old man's first gesture was an apologetic half-grin and a sort of shrug of the eyebrows. The gesture, by its familiarity, took Oskar by storm. *I couldn't help it*, Hans was saying. *The marriage and everything, your mother and me, it all went according to laws of its own*. The idea behind the gesture might have been an ordinary one, but Oskar had seen an identical expression on someone's face already that evening – on his own, as he shrugged to himself, facing the mirror in the hallway of Emilie's apartment. *The marriage and everything, it's all going according to laws of its own*. He had shared that look with himself, and here – three cognacs later – his father was sharing it with him.

'How are you, Oskar?' asked Hans Schindler. There was a dangerous wheeze along the edge of the words. His father's health was worse than he remembered it.

So Oskar decided that even Herr Hans Schindler was human – a proposition he had not been able to swallow at teatime at his sister's; and he embraced the old man, kissing him on the cheek three times, feeling the impact of his father's bristles, and beginning to weep as the corps of engineers and soldiers and past motorcyclists applauded the gratifying scene.

10

The councilmen of Artur Rosenzweig's *Judenrat*, who still saw themselves as guardians of the breath and health and bread ration of the internees of the ghetto, impressed upon the Jewish ghetto police that they were also public servants. They tended to sign up young men of compassion and some education. Though at SS headquarters the OD was regarded as just another auxiliary police force which would take orders like any police force, *that* was not the picture most OD men lived by in the summer of '41.

It cannot be denied that as the ghettos grew older, the OD man became increasingly a figure of suspicion, a supposed collaborator. Some OD men fed information to the underground and challenged the system, but perhaps a majority of them found that their existence and that of their families depended increasingly on the cooperation they gave the SS. To honest men, the OD would become a corrupter. To crooks it was an opportunity.

But in its early months in Cracow, it seemed a benign force. Leopold Pfefferberg could stand as a token of the ambiguity of being a member. When all education for Jews, even that organised by the *Judenrat*, was abolished in December 1940, Poldek had been offered a job managing the waiting lines and keeping the appointment book in the *Judenrat* housing office. It was a part-time job, but gave him a cover under which he could travel around Cracow with some freedom. In March 1941, the OD itself was founded with the stated purpose of protecting the Jews entering the Podgórze ghetto from other parts of the city. Poldek accepted the invitation to put on the cap of the OD. He believed he understood its purpose – that it was not only to ensure rational behavior inside the walls but also to achieve that correct degree of grudging tribal obedience which, in the history of European Jewry, has tended to ensure that the oppressors will go away more quickly, will become forgetful so that, in the interstices of their forgetfulness, life may again become feasible.

At the same time Pfefferberg wore his OD cap, he ran illegal goods – leatherwork, jewellery, furs, currency – in and out of the ghetto gate. He knew the *Wachtmeister* at the gate, Oswald Bosko, a policeman who had become so rebellious against the regime that he let raw materials into the ghetto to be made up into goods – garments, wine, hardware – and then let the goods out again to be sold in Cracow, all without even asking for a bribe.

On leaving the ghetto, the officials at the gate, the lounging *schmalzownicks*, or informers, Pfefferberg would take off the Judaic armband in some quiet alley before moving on to business in Kazimierz or the Centrum.

On the city walls, above fellow passengers' heads in the trolleys, he would read the posters of the day: the razor-blade advertisements, the latest Wawel edicts on the harbouring of Polish bandits, the slogan 'JEWS – LICE – TYPHUS,' the billboard depicting a virginal Polish girl handing food to a hook-nosed Jew whose shadow was the shadow of the Devil. 'WHOEVER HELPS A JEW HELPS SATAN.' Outside groceries hung pictures of Jews mincing rats into pies, watering milk, pouring lice into pastry, kneading dough with filthy feet. The fact of the ghetto was being validated in the streets of Cracow by poster art, by copywriters from the Propaganda Ministry. And Pfefferberg, with his Aryan looks, would move calmly beneath the artwork, carrying a suitcase full of garments or jewellery or currency.

Pfefferberg's greatest coup had been last year, when Governor Frank had withdrawn 100- and 500-złoty notes from circulation and demanded that existing notes of those denominations be deposited with the Reich Credit Fund. Since a Jew could exchange only 2,000 zł., it meant that all notes held secretly – in excess of 2,000 and against the regulations – would no longer have any value. Unless you could find someone with Aryan looks and no armband who was willing on your behalf to join the long lines of Poles in front of the Reich Credit Bank. Pfefferberg and a young Zionist friend gathered from ghetto residents some hundreds of thousands of złoty in the proscribed denominations, went off with a suitcase full of notes, and came back with the approved Occupation currency, minus only the bribes they'd had to pay to the Polish Blue Police at the gate.

That was the sort of policeman Pfefferberg was. Excellent by the standards of Chairman Artur Rosenzweig; deplorable by the standards of Pomorska.

Oskar visited the ghetto in April – both from curiosity and to speak to a jeweller he had commissioned to make two rings. He found it crammed beyond what he had imagined – two families to a room unless you were lucky enough to know someone in the *Judenrat*. There was a smell of clogged plumbing, but the women held off typhus by arduous scrubbing and by boiling clothes in courtyards. 'Things are changing,' the jeweller confided in Oskar. 'The OD have been issued truncheons.' As the administration of the ghetto, like that of all ghettos in Poland, had passed from the control of Governor Frank to that of Gestapo Section 4B, the final authority for all Jewish matters in Cracow was now SS *Oberführer* Julian Schemer, a hearty man of somewhere between forty-five and fifty, who in civilian clothes and with his baldness and thick lenses looked like a nondescript bureaucrat. Oskar had met him at German cocktail parties. Schemer talked a great deal – not about the war but about business and investment. He was the sort of functionary who abounded in the middle ranks of the SS, a sport, interested in liquor, women, and confiscated goods. He could sometimes be discovered wearing the smirk of his unexpected power like a childish jam stain in the corner of the mouth. He was always convivial and dependably heartless. Oskar could tell that Scherner favoured working the Jews rather than killing them, that he would bend rules for the sake of profit, but that he would fulfill the general drift of SS policy, however that might develop.

Oskar had remembered the police chief last Christmas, sending him half a dozen bottles of cognac. Now that the man's power had expanded, he would rate more this year.

It was because of this shift of power – the SS becoming not simply the arm of policy but the makers of it as well – that beneath the high June sun the OD was taking on a new nature. Oskar, merely by driving past the ghetto, became familiar with a new figure, a former glazier named Symche Spira, the new force in the OD. Spira was of Orthodox background and by personal history as well as temperament despised the Europeanised Jewish liberals who were still found on the *Judenrat* Council. He took his orders not from Artur Rosenzweig but from *Untersturmführer* Brandt and SS headquarters across the river. From his conferences with Brandt, he returned to the ghetto with increased knowingness and power. Brandt had asked him to set up and lead a Political Section OD, and he recruited various of his friends for it. Their uniform ceased to be the cap and armband and became instead grey shirt, cavalry breeches, Sam Browne belt, and shiny SS boots.

Spira's Political Section would go beyond the demands of grudging cooperation and would be full of venal men, men with complexes, with close-held grudges about the social and intellectual slights they'd received in earlier days from respectable middle-class Jewry. Apart from Spira, there were Szymon Spitz and Marcel Zellinger, Ignacy Diamond, David Gutter the salesman, Forster and Grüner and Landau. They settled in to a career of extortion and of making out for the SS lists of unsatisfactory or seditious ghetto dwellers.

Poldek Pfefferberg now wanted to escape the force. There was a rumor that the Gestapo would make all OD men swear an oath to the *Führer*, after which they would have no grounds for disobedience. Poldek did not want to share a profession with grey-shirted Spira or with Spitz and Zellinger, the makers of lists. He went down the street to the hospital at the corner of Wegierska to speak to a gentle physician named Alexander Biberstein, the official physician to the *Judenrat*. The doctor's brother Marek had been that first president of the Council and was presently doing time in mournful Montelupich prison for currency violations and attempting to bribe officials.

Pfefferberg begged Biberstein to give him a medical certificate so that he could leave the OD. It was difficult, Biberstein said. Pfefferberg did not even look sick. It would be impossible for him to feign high blood pressure. Dr. Biberstein instructed him in the symptoms of a bad back. Pfefferberg took to reporting for duty severely stooped and using a cane.

Spira was outraged. When Pfefferberg had first asked him about leaving the OD, the police chief had pronounced – like a commander of some palace guard – that the only way out was on your shield. Inside the ghetto, Spira and his infantile friends were playing a game of Elite Corps. They were the Foreign Legion; they were the praetorians. 'We'll send you to the Gestapo doctor,' screamed Spira.

Biberstein, who had been aware of the shame in young Pfefferberg, had tutored him well. Poldek survived the Gestapo doctor's inspection and was discharged from the OD as suffering from an ailment likely to inhibit his good performance in crowd control. Spira, saying goodbye to officer Pfefferberg, expressed a contemptuous enmity.

The next day, Germany invaded Russia. Oskar heard the news illicitly on the BBC and knew that the Madagascar Plan was finished now. It would be years before there were ships for a solution like that. Oskar sensed that the event changed the essence of SS planning, for everywhere now the economists, the engineers, the planners of movements of people, the policemen of every stripe put on the mental habits appropriate not only to a long war, but to a more systematic pursuit of a racially impeccable empire.

11

In an alley off Lipowa, its rear pointing toward the workshop of Schindler's enamel plant, stood the German Box Factory. Oskar Schindler, always restless and hungry for company, used to stroll over there sometimes and chat with the *Treuhänder*, Ernst Kuhnpast, or to the former owner and unofficial manager, Szymon Jereth. Jereth's Box Factory had become the German Box Factory two years back according to the usual arrangement – no fees being paid, no documents to which he was signatory having been drawn up.

The injustice of that did not particularly worry Jereth anymore. It had happened to most of the people he knew. What worried him was the ghetto. The fights in the kitchens, the pitiless communality of life there, the stench of bodies, the lice that jumped onto your suit from the greasy jacket of the man whose shoulder you brushed on the stairs. Mrs. Jereth, he told Oskar, was deeply depressed. She'd always been used to nice things; she'd come from a good family in Kleparz, north of Cracow. And when you think, he told Oskar, that with all the pineboard I could build myself a place *there*. He pointed to the wasteland behind his factory. Workers played football there, vast, hard-running games in plentiful space. Most of it belonged to Oskar's factory, the rest to a Polish couple named Bielski. But Oskar did not point that out to poor Jereth, or say either that he too had been preoccupied by that vacant space. Oskar was more interested in the implied offer of lumber. You can 'alienate' as much pineboard as that? You know, said Jereth, it's only a matter of paperwork.

They stood together at Jereth's office window, considering the wasteland. From the workshop came the sound of hammering and whining power saws. I would hate to lose contact with this place, Jereth told Oskar. I would hate just to vanish into some labour camp and have to wonder from a distance what the damn fools were doing here. You can understand that, surely, Herr Schindler?

A man like Jereth could not foresee any deliverance. The German armies seemed to be enjoying limitless success in Russia, and even the BBC was having trouble believing that they were advancing into a fatal salient. The Armament Inspectorate orders for field kitchenware kept turning up on Oskar's desk, sent on with the compliments of General Julius Schindler scribbled at the bottom of the covering letters, accompanied by the telephoned best wishes of sundry junior officers. Oskar accepted the orders and the congratulations in their own right, but took a contradictory joy from the rash letters his father was writing to him to celebrate their reconciliation. It won't last, said Schindler senior. The man [Hitler] isn't meant to last. America will come down on him in the end. And the Russians? My God, did anyone ever take the trouble to point out to the dictator just how many godless barbarians there are over there? Oskar, smiling over the letters, was not troubled by the conflicting pleasures – the commercial exhilaration of the Armaments Inspectorate contracts and the more intimate delight of his father's subversive letters. Oskar sent Hans a monthly bank draft of 1,000 RM. in honour of filial love and sedition, and for the joy of largesse.

It was a fast and, still, almost a painless year. Longer hours than Schindler had ever worked, parties at the Cracovia, drinking bouts at the jazz club, visits to the gorgeous Klonowska's apartment. When the leaves began to fall, he wondered where the year had gone. The impression of vanished time was augmented by the late summer and now by autumn rains earlier than usual. The asymmetric seasons would, by favouring the Soviets, affect the lives of all Europeans. But to Herr Oskar Schindler in Lipowa Street, weather was still simply weather.

*

Then, in the butt end of 1941, Oskar found himself under arrest. Someone – one of the Polish shipping clerks, one of the German technicians in the munitions section, you couldn't tell – had denounced him, had gone to Pomorska Street and given information. Two plainclothes Gestapo men drove up Lipowa Street one morning and blocked the entrance with their Mercedes as if they intended to bring all commerce at Emalia to an end. Upstairs, facing Oskar, they produced warrants entitling them to take all his business records with them. But they did not seem to have any commercial training. 'Exactly what books do you want?' Schindler asked them.

'Cashbooks,' said one.

'Your main ledgers,' said the other.

It was a relaxed arrest; they chatted to Klonowska while Oskar himself went to get his cash journal and accounts ledger. Oskar was permitted time to scribble down a few names on a pad, supposedly the names of associates with whom Oskar had appointments which must now be cancelled. Klonowska understood, though, that they were a list of people to be approached for help in bailing him out.

The first name on the list was that of *Oberführer* Julian Schemer; the second, that of Martin Plathe of the *Abwehr* in Breslau. That would be a long-distance call. The third name belonged to the supervisor of the *Ostfaser* works, the drunken Army veteran Franz Bosch on whom Schindler had settled quantities of illegal kitchen-ware. Leaning over Klonowska's shoulder, over her piled-up flaxen hair, he underlined Bosch's name. A man of influence, Bosch knew and advised every high official who played the black market in Cracow. And Oskar knew that this arrest had to do with the black market, whose danger was that you could always find officials ready to be bribed, but you could never predict the jealousy of one of your employees.

The fourth name on the list was that of the German chairman of Ferrum AG of Sosnowiec, the company from which Herr Schindler bought his steel. These names were a comfort to him as the Gestapo Mercedes carried him to Pomorska Street, a kilometre or so west of the Centrum. They were a guarantee that he would not vanish into the system without a trace. He was not, therefore, as defenseless as the 1,000 ghetto dwellers who had been rounded up according to Symche Spira's lists and marched beneath the frosty stars of Advent to the cattle cars at Prokocim Station. Oskar knew some heavy guns.

The SS complex in Cracow was an immense modern building, humourless, but not as portentous as the Montelupich prison. Yet even if you disbelieved the rumors of torture attached to the place, the building confused the arrestee as soon as he entered by its size, its Kafkaesque corridors, by the numb threat of the departmental names painted on the doors. Here you could find the SS Main Office, the headquarters of the Order Police, of Kripo, Sipo and Gestapo, of SS Economy and Administration, of Personnel, of Jewish Affairs, of Race and Resettlement, of the SS Court, of Operations, of SS Service, of the *Reichskommissariat* for the Strengthening of Germandom, of the Welfare Office for Ethnic Germans.

Somewhere in that hive a middle-aged Gestapo man, who seemed to have a more exact knowledge of accountancy than the arresting officers, began interviewing Oskar. The man's manner was half-amused, like a customs official who finds that a passenger suspected of currency smuggling is really smuggling house plants for an aunt. He told Oskar that all the enterprises involved in war production were under scrutiny. Oskar did not believe it but said nothing. Herr Schindler could understand, the Gestapo man told him, that businesses supplying the war effort had a moral duty to devote all their product to that great enterprise – and to desist from undermining the economy of the Government General by irregular dealings.

Oskar murmured away in that peculiar rumble of his which could at the same time contain threat and bonhomie. 'Do you imply, *Herr Wachtmeister*, that there are reports that my factory does not fulfill its quotas?'

'You live very well,' said the man, but with a concessive smile, and as if that were all right, it was acceptable for important industrialists to live well. And anyone who lives well, he pointed out . . . well, we have to be sure that his standard of living derives entirely from legitimate contracts.

Oskar beamed at the Gestapo man. 'Whoever gave you my name,' he said, 'is a fool and is wasting your time.'

'Who's the plant manager of DEF?' asked the Gestapo man, ignoring this.

'Abraham Bankier.'

'A Jew?'

'Of course. The business used to belong to relatives of his.'

These records might be adequate, said the Gestapo man. But if they wanted more, he presumed Herr Bankier could supply it.

'You mean you're going to detain me?' asked Oskar. He began to laugh. 'I want to tell you now,' he said, 'when *Oberführer* Schemer and I are laughing about all this over a drink, I'll tell him that you treated me with the utmost courtesy.'

The two who had made the arrest took him to the second floor, where he was searched and permitted to keep cigarettes and 100 zł. to buy small luxuries. Then he was locked in a bedroom – one of the best they had, Oskar surmised, equipped with a washbasin and toilet and dusty draperies at the barred window – the sort of room they kept dignitaries in while interrogating them. If the dignitary was released, he could not complain about a room like this, any more than he could enthuse over it. And if he was found to be treacherous, seditious, or an economic criminal, then, as if the floor of this room opened like a trapdoor, he'd find himself waiting in an interrogation cell in the basement, sitting motionless and bleeding in one of the series of stalls they called tramways, looking ahead to Montelupich, where prisoners were hanged in their cells. Oskar considered the door. Whoever lays a hand on me, he promised himself, I'll have him sent to Russia.

He was bad at waiting. After an hour he knocked at the door from the inside and gave the *Waffen* SS man who answered 50 zł.

to buy him a bottle of vodka. It was, of course, three times the price of liquor, but that was Oskar's method. Later in the day, by arrangement between Klonowska and Ingrid, a bag of toiletries, books, and pyjamas arrived. An excellent meal was brought to him with a half-bottle of Hungarian wine, and no one came to disturb him or ask him a question. He presumed that the accountant was still slaving over the Emalia books. He would have enjoyed a radio on which to listen to the BBC news from Russia, the Far East, and the newly combatant United States, and he had the feeling that if he asked his jailers they might bring him one. He hoped the Gestapo had not moved into his apartment on Straszewskiego, to assess the furnishings and Ingrid's jewellery. But by the time he fell asleep, he'd got to the stage where he was looking forward to facing interrogators.

In the morning he was brought a good breakfast – herring, cheese, eggs, rolls, coffee – and still no one bothered him. And then the middle-aged SS auditor, holding both the cash journal and the accounts ledger, came to visit him.

The auditor wished him good morning. He hoped he had had a comfortable night. There had not been time to conduct more than a cursory examination of Herr Schindler's records, but it had been decided that a gentleman who stood so high in the opinion of so many people influential in the war effort need not be too closely looked at for the moment. We have, said the SS man, received certain telephone calls . . . . Oskar was convinced, as he thanked the man, that the acquittal was temporary. He received the ledgers and got his money handed back in full at the reception desk.

Downstairs, Klonowska was waiting for him, radiant. Her liaison work had yielded this result, Schindler coming forth from the death house in his double-breasted suit and without a scratch. She led him to the Adler, which they had let her park inside the gate. Her ridiculous poodle sat on the back seat.

12

The child arrived at the Dresners', on the eastern side of the ghetto, late in the afternoon. She had been returned to Cracow by the Polish couple who had been taking care of her in the country. They had been able to talk the Polish Blue Police at the ghetto gate into allowing them entry on business, and the child passed as theirs.

They were decent people, and shamefaced at having brought her up to Cracow and the ghetto from the countryside. She was a dear girl; they were attached to her. But you couldn't keep a Jewish child in the countryside anymore. The municipal authorities – never mind the SS – were offering sums of 500 zł. and upward for every Jew betrayed. It was one's neighbors. You couldn't trust your neighbors. And then not only would the child be in trouble, we'd all be. My God, there were areas where the peasants went out hunting Jews with scythes and sickles.

The child didn't seem to suffer too much from whatever squalors the ghetto now imposed on her. She sat at a little table among screens of damp clothing and fastidiously ate the heel of bread Mrs. Dresner gave her. She accepted whatever endearments the women sharing the kitchen happened to utter. Mrs. Dresner noticed how strangely guarded the child was in all her answers. She had her vanities, though, and like most three-year-olds a passionately preferred colour. Red. She sat there in red cap, red coat, small red boots. The peasants had indulged her passion.

Mrs. Dresner made conversation by talking about the child's real parents. They too had been living – in fact, *hiding* – in the countryside. But, said Mrs. Dresner, they were going to come and join everyone here in Cracow soon. The child nodded, but it didn't seem to be shyness that kept her quiet.

In January her parents had been rounded up according to a list supplied to the SS by Spira, and while being marched to Prokocim Station had passed a crowd of jeering Poles – 'Bye-bye, Jews.' They had dodged out of the column just like two decent Polish citizens crossing the street to watch the deportation of social enemies, and had joined the crowd, jeered a little themselves, and then strolled off into the countryside around that outer suburb.

Now they too were finding life no safer out there and intended to sneak back into Cracow during the summer. The mother of 'Redcap,' as the Dresner boys nicknamed her as soon as they got home with the work details from the city, was a first cousin of Mrs. Dresner's.

Soon Mrs. Dresner's daughter, young Danka, also got home from her work as a cleaning woman at the *Luftwaffe* air base. Danka was going on fourteen, tall enough to have the *Kennkarte* (labour card) enabling her to work outside the ghetto. She enthused over the noncommittal child. 'Genia, I know your mother, Eva. She and I used to go shopping for dresses together, and she'd buy me cakes at the patisserie in Bracka Street.'

The child kept to her seat, did not smile, looked ahead. 'Madam, you're mistaken. My mother's name is not Eva. It's Jasha.' She went on naming the names in the fictional Polish genealogy in which her parents and the peasants had schooled her in case the Blue Police or the SS ever questioned her. The family frowned at each other, brought to a standstill by the unusual cunning of the child, finding it obscene but not wanting to undermine it, since it might, before the week was out, be essential survival equipment.

At suppertime Idek Schindel, the child's uncle, a young doctor at the ghetto hospital in Wegierska Street, arrived. He was the sort of whimsical, half-teasing, and infatuated uncle a child needs. At the sight of him, Genia *became* a child, getting down off her chair to rush at him. If he were here, calling these people cousins, then they *were* cousins. You could admit now that you had a mother named Eva and that your grandparents weren't really named Ludwik and Sophia.

Then Mr. Juda Dresner, purchasing officer of the Bosch plant, arrived home and the company was complete.

April 28 was Schindler's birthday, and in 1942 he celebrated it like a child of the spring, loudly, profligately. It was a big day at DEF. The *Herr Direktor* brought in rare white bread, regardless of expense, to be served with the noonday soup. The festivity spread into the outer office and to the workshops out back. Oskar Schindler, industrialist, was celebrating the general succulence of life.

This, his thirty-fourth birthday, began early at Emalia. Schindler signalled it by walking through the outer office carrying three bottles of cognac under his arm to share with the engineers, the accountants, the draughtsmen. Office workers in Accounts and Personnel had handfuls of cigarettes thrust at them, and by mid-morning the handouts had spread to the factory floor. A cake was brought in from a patisserie, and Oskar cut it on Klonowska's desk. Delegations of Jewish and Polish workers began to enter the office to congratulate him, and he heartily kissed a girl named Kucharska, whose father had figured in the Polish parliament before the war. And then the Jewish girls came up, and the men shaking hands, even Stern getting there somehow from the Progress Works where he was now employed, to take Oskar's hand formally and find himself wrapped up in a rib-cracking embrace.

That afternoon someone, perhaps the same malcontent as last time, contacted Pomorska and denounced Schindler for his racial improprieties. His ledgers might stand up to scrutiny, but no one could deny he was a 'Jew-kisser.'

The manner of his arrest seemed more professional than the last. On the morning of the 29th, a Mercedes blocked the factory entrance and two Gestapo men, seeming somehow surer of their ground than the last two, met him crossing the factory yard. He was charged, they told him, with breaking the provisions of the Race and Resettlement Act. They wanted him to come with them. And no, there was no need for him to visit his office first.

'Do you have a warrant?' he asked them.

'We don't need one,' they told him.

He smiled at them. The gentlemen should understand that if they took him away without a warrant, they would come to regret it.

He said it lightly, but he could tell by their demeanour that the level of threat in them had firmed and focused since last year's half-comic detention. Last time the conversation at Pomorska had been about economic matters and whether they had been breached. This time you were dealing with grotesque law, the law of the lower guts, edicts from the black side of the brain. Serious stuff.

'We will have to risk regret,' one of the two told him.

He assessed their assurance, their perilous indifference to him, a man of assets, newly turned thirty-four. 'On a spring morning,' he told them, 'I can spare a few hours for driving.'

He comforted himself that he would again be put into one of those urbane cells at Pomorska. But when they turned right up Kolejowa, he knew that this time it would be Montelupich prison.

'I shall wish to speak to a lawyer,' he told them.

'In time,' said the driver.

Oskar had it on the reasonable word of one of his drinking companions that the Jagiellonian Institute of Anatomy received corpses from Montelupich.

The wall of the place stretched a long block, and the ominous sameness of the windows of the third and fourth floors could be seen from the back seat of the Gestapo Mercedes. Inside the front gate and through the archway they came to an office where the SS clerk spoke in whispers, as if raised voices would set up head-splitting echoes along the narrow corridors. They took his cash, but told him it would be given to him during his imprisonment at a rate of 50 zł. a day. No, the arresting officers told him, it was not yet time for him to call a lawyer.

Then they left, and in the corridor, under guard, he listened for the traces of screams which might, in this convent hush, spill out through the cracks of the Judas windows in the walls. He was led down a flight of stairs into a claustrophobic tunnel and past a string of locked cells, one with an open grille. Some half-dozen prisoners in shirt sleeves sat there, each in a separate stall, facing the rear wall so that their features could not be seen. Oskar noticed a torn ear. And someone was sniffling but knew better than to wipe his nose. *Klonowska, Klonowska, are you making your telephone calls, my love?*

They opened a cell for him and he went in. He had felt a minor anxiety that the place might be crowded. But there was only one other prisoner in the cell, a soldier wearing his greatcoat up around his ears for warmth and seated on one of the two low wooden bed frames, each with its pallet. There were no washbasins, of course. A water bucket and a waste bucket. And what proved to be a *Waffen* SS *Standartenführer* (an SS rank equivalent to colonel) wearing a slight stubble, a stale, unbuttoned shirt under the overcoat, and muddy boots.

'Welcome, sir,' said the officer with a crooked grin, raising one hand to Oskar. He was a handsome fellow, a few years older than Oskar. The odds were in favour of his being a plant. But one wondered why they had put him in uniform and provided him with such exalted rank. Oskar looked at his watch, sat, stood, looked up at the high windows. A little light from the exercise yards filtered in, but it was not the sort of window you could lean against and relieve the intimacy of the two close bunks, of sitting hands on knees facing each other.

In the end they began to talk. Oskar was very wary, but the *Standartenführer* chattered wildly. What was his name? Philip was his name. He didn't think gentlemen should give their second names in prison. Besides, it was time people got down to first names. If we'd all got down to first names earlier, we'd be a happier race now.

Oskar concluded that if the man was not a plant, then he had had some sort of breakdown, was perhaps suffering shell shock. He'd been campaigning in southern Russia, and his battalion had helped hang on to Novgorod all winter. Then he had got leave to visit a Polish girlfriend in Cracow and they had, in his words, 'lost themselves in each other,' and he had been arrested in her apartment three days after his leave expired.

'I suppose I decided,' said Philip, 'not to be too damn exact about dates when I saw the way the other bastards' – he waved a hand at the roof, indicating the structure around him, the SS planners, the accountants, the bureaucrats – 'when I saw the way *they* lived. It wasn't as if I deliberately decided to go absent without leave. But I just felt I was owed a certain damn latitude.'

Oskar asked him would he rather be in Pomorska Street. No, said Philip, I'd rather be here. Pomorska looked more like a hotel. But the bastards had a death cell there, full of shining chromium bars. But that aside, what had Herr Oskar done?

'I kissed a Jewish girl,' said Oskar. 'An employee of mine. So it's alleged.'

Philip began to hoot at this. 'Oh, oh! Did your prick drop off?'

All afternoon *Standartenführer* Philip continued to condemn the SS. Thieves and orgiasts, he said. He couldn't believe it. The money some of the bastards made. They started so incorruptible too. They would kill some poor bloody Pole for smuggling a kilo of bacon while they lived like goddamn Hanseatic barons.

Oskar behaved as if it were all news to him, as if the idea of venality among the *Reichführers* was a painful assault on his provincial *Sudetendeutsch* innocence which had caused him to forget himself and caress a Jewish girl. At last Philip, worn out by his outrage, took a nap.

Oskar wanted a drink. A certain measure of liquor would help speed time, make the *Standartenführer* better company if he was not a plant and more fallible if he was. Oskar took out a 10-zł. note and wrote down names on it and telephone numbers; more names than last time: a dozen. He took out another four notes, crumpled them in his hands and went to the door and knocked at the Judas window. An SS NCO turned up – a grave middle-aged face staring in at him. He didn't look like a man who exercised Poles to death or ruptured kidneys with his boots, but of course, that was one of the strengths of torture: you didn't expect it from a man whose features were those of someone's country uncle.

Was it possible to order five bottles of vodka? Oskar asked.

Five bottles, sir? said the NCO. He might have been advising a young, callow drinker uncertain of quantities. He was also pensive, however, as if he were considering reporting Oskar to his superiors. The general and I, said Oskar, would appreciate a bottle apiece to stimulate conversation. You and your colleagues please accept the rest with my compliments. I presume also, said Oskar, that a man of your authority has power to make routine telephone calls on behalf of a prisoner. You'll see the telephone numbers there ... yes, on the note. You don't have to call them all yourself. But give them to my secretary, eh? Yes, she's the first on the list.

These are very influential people, murmured the SS NCO.

You're a damn fool, Philip told Oskar. They'll shoot you for trying to corrupt their guards.

Oskar slumped, apparently casual.

It's as stupid as kissing a Jewess, said Philip.

We'll see, said Oskar. But he was frightened.

At last the NCO came back and brought, together with the two bottles, a parcel of clean shirts and underwear, some books, and a bottle of wine, packed at the apartment in Straszewskiego Street by Ingrid and delivered to the Montelupich gate. Philip and Oskar had a pleasant enough evening together, though at one time a guard pounded on the steel door and demanded that they stop singing. And even then, as the liquor added spaciousness to the cell and an unexpected cogency to the *Standartenführer's* ravings, Schindler was listening for remote screams from upstairs or for the button-clicking Morse of some hopeless prisoner in the next cell. Only once did the true nature of the place dilute the effectiveness of the vodka. Next to his cot, partially obscured by the pallet, Philip discovered a minute statement in red pencil. He spent some idle moments deciphering it – not doing so well, his Polish much slower than Oskar's.

'"*My God,*"' he translated, '"*how they beat me!*" Well, it's a wonderful world, my friend Oskar. Isn't it?'

In the morning Schindler woke clearheaded. Hangovers had never plagued him, and he wondered why other people made such a fuss about them. But Philip was white-faced and depressed. During the morning he was taken away and came back to collect his belongings. He was to face a court-martial that afternoon, but had been given a new assignment at a training school in Stutthof, so he presumed they didn't intend to shoot him for desertion. He picked up his greatcoat from his cot and went off to explain his Polish dalliance. Alone, Oskar spent the day reading a Karl May book Ingrid had sent and, in the afternoon, speaking to his lawyer, a *Sudetendeutscher* who'd opened a practice in civil law in Cracow two years before. Oskar was comforted by the interview. The cause of the arrest was certainly as stated; they weren't using his transracial caresses as a pretext to hold him while they investigated his affairs. 'But it will probably come to the SS Court and you'll be asked why you aren't in the Army.'

'The reason is obvious,' said Oskar. 'I'm an essential war producer. You can get General Schindler to say so.'

Oskar was a slow reader and savoured the Karl May book – the hunter and the Indian sage in the American wilderness – a relationship of decency. He did not rush the reading, in any case. It could be a week before he came to court. The lawyer expected that there would be a speech by the president of the court about conduct unbecoming a member of the German race and then there would be a substantial fine. So be it. He'd leave court a more cautious man.

On the fifth morning, he had already drunk the half-litre of black *ersatz* coffee they'd given him for breakfast when an NCO and two guards came for him. Past the mute doors he was taken upstairs to one of the front offices. He found there a man he'd met at cocktail parties, *Obersturmbannführer* Rolf Czurda, head of the Cracow SD. Czurda looked like a businessman in his good suit.

'Oskar, Oskar,' said Czurda like an old friend reproving. 'We give you those Jewish girls at five marks a day. You should kiss *us*, not them.'

Oskar explained that it had been his birthday. He'd been impetuous. He'd been drinking.

Czurda shook his head. 'I never knew you were such a big-timer, Oskar,' he said. 'Calls from as far away as Breslau, from our friends in the *Abwehr*. Of course it would be ridiculous to keep you from your work just because you felt up some Jewess.'

'You're very understanding, *Herr Obersturmbannführer*,' said Oskar, feeling the request for some sort of gratuity building up in Czurda. 'If ever I'm in a position to return your liberal gesture . . .'

'As a matter of fact,' said Czurda, 'I have an old aunt whose flat has been bombed out.'

Yet another old aunt. Schindler made a compassionate click with his tongue and said that a representative of chief Czurda would be welcome any time in Lipowa Street to make a selection from the range of products turned out there. But it did not do to let men like Czurda think of his release as an absolute favour – and of the kitchenware as the least that the luckily released prisoner could offer. When Czurda said he could go, Oskar objected.

'I can't very well just call my car, *Herr Obersturmbannführer*. After all, my fuel resources are limited.'

Czurda asked if Herr Schindler expected the SD to take him home.

Oskar shrugged. He *did* live on the far side of the city, he said. It was a long way to walk.

Czurda laughed. 'Oskar, I'll have one of my own drivers take you back.'

But when the limousine was ready, engine running, at the bottom of the main steps, and Schindler, glancing at the blank windows above him, wanted a sign from that other republic, the realm of torture, of unconditional imprisonment – the hell beyond bars of those who had no pots and pans to barter – Rolf Czurda detained him by the elbow.

'Jokes aside, Oskar, my dear fellow. You'd be a fool if you got a real taste for some little Jewish skirt. They don't *have* a future, Oskar. That's not just old-fashioned Jew-hate talking, I assure you. It's policy.'

13

Even that summer, people inside the walls were clinging to the idea of the ghetto as a small but permanent realm. The idea had been easy enough to credit during 1941. There had been a post office; there had even been ghetto postage stamps. There had been a ghetto newspaper, even though it contained little else than edicts from the Wawel and Pomorska Street. A restaurant had been permitted in Lwówska Street: Foerster's Restaurant, where the Rosner brothers, back from the perils of the countryside and the changeable passions of the peasants, played the violin and the accordion. It had seemed for a brief time that schooling would proceed here in formal classrooms, that orchestras would gather and regularly perform, that Jewish life would be communicated like a benign organism along the streets, from artisan to artisan, from scholar to scholar. It had not yet been demonstrated finally by the SS bureaucrats of Pomorska Street that the idea of that sort of ghetto was to be considered not simply a whimsy but an insult to the rational direction of history.

So when *Untersturmführer* Brandt had *Judenrat* president Artur Rosenzweig around to Pomorska for a beating with the handle of a riding crop, he was trying to correct the man's incurable vision of the ghetto as a region of permanent residence. The ghetto was a depot, a siding, a walled bus station. Anything that would have encouraged the opposite view had, by 1942, been abolished.

So it was different here from the ghettos old people remembered even affectionately. Music was no profession here. There *were* no professions. Henry Rosner went to work in the *Luftwaffe* mess at the air base. There he met a young German chef/manager named Richard, a laughing boy hiding, as a chef can, from the history of the twentieth century among the elements of cuisine and bar management. He and Henry Rosner got on so well that Richard would send the violinist across town to pick up the *Luftwaffe* Catering Corps pay – you couldn't trust a German, said Richard; the last one had run off to Hungary with the payroll.

Richard, like any barman worthy of his station, heard things and attracted the affection of officials. On the first day of June, he came to the ghetto with his girlfriend, a *Volksdeutsche* girl wearing a sweeping cape – which, on account of the June showers, didn't seem too excessive a garment. Through his profession, Richard knew a number of policemen, including *Wachtmeister* Oswald Bosko, and had no trouble being admitted to the ghetto, even though it was officially out-of-bounds to him. Once inside the gate, Richard crossed Plac Zgody and found Henry Rosner's address. Henry was surprised to see them. He had left Richard at the mess only a few hours before, yet here he was with his girl, both dressed as if for a formal visit. It reinforced for Henry the strangeness of the season. For the past two days, ghetto people had been lining up at the old Polish Savings Bank building in Józefińska Street for the new identity cards. To your yellow *Kennkarte* with its sepia passport photograph and its large blue J, the German clerks now attached – if you were lucky – a blue sticker. People could be seen to leave the bank waving their cards with the *Blauschein* attached as if it proved their right to breathe, their permanent validity. Workers at the *Luftwaffe* mess, the *Wehrmacht* garage, at the Madritsch works, at Oskar Schindler's Emalia, at the Progress factory all had no trouble getting the *Blauschein*. But those who were refused it felt that their citizenship even of the ghetto was under question.

Richard said that young Olek Rosner should come and stay with his girlfriend at her apartment. You could tell that he'd heard something in the mess. He can't just walk out the gate, said Henry. It's fixed with Bosko, said Richard.

Henry and Manci were hesitant and consulted with each other as the girl in the cape promised to fatten Olek up on chocolate.

An *Aktion?* Henry Rosner asked in a murmur. Is there going to be an *Aktion?*

Richard answered with a question. You've got your *Blauschein?* he asked. Of course, said Henry. And Manci? Manci too. But Olek hasn't, said Richard. In the drizzling dusk, Olek Rosner, only child, newly six years old, walked out of the ghetto under the cape of Richard the chef's girlfriend. Had some policeman bothered to lift the cape, both Richard and the girl could have been shot for their friendly subterfuge. Olek too would vanish. In the childless corner of their room, the Rosners hoped they'd been wise.

Poldek Pfefferberg, runner for Oskar Schindler, had earlier in the year been ordered to begin tutoring the children of Symche Spira, exalted glazier, chief of the OD.

It was a contemptuous summons, as if Spira were saying, 'Yes, we know you're not fit for *man's* work, but at least you can pass on to my kids some of the benefits of your education.'

Pfefferberg amused Schindler with stories of the tutorial sessions at Symche's house. The police chief was one of the few Jews to have an entire floor to himself. There, amid two-dimensional paintings of nineteenth-century rabbis, Symche paced, listening to the instruction Pfefferberg gave, seeming to want to see knowledge, like petunias, sprout from his children's ears. A man of destiny with his hand hooked inside his jacket, he believed that this Napoleonic mannerism was a gesture universal to men of influence.

Symche's wife was a shadowy woman, a little bemused by her husband's unexpected power, perhaps a little excluded by old friends. The children, a boy of about twelve and a girl of fourteen, were biddable but no great scholars.

In any case, when Pfefferberg went to the Polish Savings Bank he expected to be given the *Blauschein* without any trouble. He was sure his labour with the Spira children would be counted as essential work. His yellow card identified him as a HIGH SCHOOL

PROFESSOR, and in a rational world as yet only partly turned upside down, it was an honourable label.

The clerks refused to give him the sticker. He argued with them and wondered if he should appeal to Oskar or to Herr Szepessi, the Austrian bureaucrat who ran the German Labour Office down the street. Oskar had been asking him for a year to come to Emalia, but Pfefferberg had always thought it would be too constricting of his illegal activities to have full-time work.

As he emerged from the bank building, details of the German Security Police, the Polish Blue Police, and the political detail of the OD were at work on the pavements, inspecting everyone's card and arresting those who did not have the sticker. A line of rejects, hangdog men and women, already stood in the middle of Józefińska Street. Pfefferberg affected his Polish military bearing and explained that of course, he had a number of trades. But the *Schupo* he spoke to shook his head, saying, 'Don't argue with me; no *Blauschein;* you join that line. Understand, Jew?'

Pfefferberg went and joined the line. Mila, the delicate, pretty wife he'd married eighteen months before, worked for Madritsch and already had her *Blauschein*. So there was that.

When the line had grown to more than a hundred, it was marched around the corner, past the hospital, and into the yard of the old Optima confectionery plant. There hundreds were already waiting. The early comers had taken the shady areas of what used to be the stable, where the Optima horses used to be harnessed between the shafts of drays laden with crèmes and liqueur chocolates. It was not a rowdy group. There were professional men, bankers like the Holzers, pharmacists and dentists. They stood in clusters, talking quietly. The young pharmacist Bachner stood speaking to an old couple named Wohl. There were many old people in here. The old and poor who depended on the *Judenrat* ration. This summer the *Judenrat* itself, the distributor of food and even of space, had been less equitable than it had been last.

Nurses from the ghetto hospital moved among these detainees

with buckets of water, which was said to be good for stress and disorientation. It was, in any case, just about the only medicine, other than some black-market cyanide, that the hospital had to give. The old, the poor families from the *shtetls*, took the water in restive silence.

Throughout the day, police of three varieties would enter the yard with lists, and lines of people would be formed to be met at the gate of the yard by SS details and moved out to the Prokocim Railway Station. In some people the urge rose to evade this next movement by keeping to the far corners of the yard. But it was Pfefferberg's style to hang around the gate, looking for some official to whom he could make a claim. Perhaps Spira would be there, dressed up like a movie actor and willing – with a little heavy-handed irony – to release him. In fact there stood by the gatekeeper's hut a sad-faced boy in an OD hat studying a list, holding the corner of the page in delicate fingers. Pfefferberg not only had served briefly with the boy in the OD, but in the first year of his teaching career at Kosciuszko High School in Podgórze had taught his sister.

The boy looked up. Panie Pfefferberg, he murmured with a respect from those vanished days. As if the yard were full of practiced criminals, he asked what Panie Pfefferberg was doing here.

It's nonsense, said Pfefferberg, but I haven't got a *Blauschein* yet.

The boy shook his head. Follow me, he said. He walked Pfefferberg to a senior uniformed *Schupo* at the gate and saluted. He did not look heroic in his funny OD cap and with his skinny, vulnerable neck. Later, Pfefferberg supposed that that had given him greater credibility.

'This is Herr Pfefferberg from the *Judenrat*,' he lied with a deft combination of respect and authority. 'He has been visiting some relatives.' The *Schupo* seemed bored by the mass of police work proceeding in the yard. Negligently he waved Pfefferberg out the gate. Pfefferberg had no time to thank the boy or to reflect on the mystery of why a child with a skinny neck will lie for you even unto death just because you taught his sister how to use the Roman rings.

Pfefferberg rushed straight to the Labour Office and broke into the waiting line. Behind the desk were Frauleins Skoda and Knosalla, two hearty Sudeten German girls. *'Liebchen, Liebchen,'* he told Skoda, 'they want to take me away because I don't have the sticker. Look at me, I ask you.' (He was built like a bull, and had played hockey for his country and belonged to the Polish ski team.) 'Am I not exactly the sort of fellow you'd like to keep around here?'

In spite of the crowds who'd given her no rest all day, Skoda raised her eyebrows and failed to suppress a smile. She took his *Kennkarte*. 'I can't help you, Herr Pfefferberg,' she told him. 'They didn't give it to you, so I can't. A pity . . . .'

'But you *can* give it to me, *Liebchen*,' he insisted in a loud, seductive, soap-opera voice. 'I have trades, *Liebchen*, I have trades.'

Skoda said that only Herr Szepessi could help him, and it was impossible to get Pfefferberg in to see Szepessi. It would take days. 'But you *will* get me in, *Liebchen*,' Pfefferberg insisted. And she did. That is where her reputation as a decent girl came from, because she abstracted from the massive drift of policy and could, even on a crowded day, respond to the individual face. A warty old man might not have done so well with her, however.

Herr Szepessi, who also had a humane reputation even though he serviced the monstrous machine, looked quickly at Pfefferberg's permit, murmuring, 'But we don't need gym teachers.'

Pfefferberg had always refused Oskar's offers of employment because he saw himself as an operator, an individualist. He didn't want to work long shifts for small pay over in dreary Zablocie. But he could see now that the era of individuality was vanishing. People needed, as a staple of life, a trade. 'I'm a metal polisher,' he told Szepessi. He had worked for short periods with a Podgórze uncle of his who ran a small metal factory in Rekawka.

Herr Szepessi eyed Pfefferberg from behind spectacles. 'Now,' he said, '*that's* a profession.' He took a pen, thoroughly crossing out HIGH SCHOOL PROFESSOR, cancelling the Jagiellonian education of which Pfefferberg was so proud, and over the top he wrote METAL POLISHER. He reached for a rubber stamp and a pot of paste and took from his desk a blue sticker. '*Now,*' he said, handing the document back to Pfefferberg – 'now should you meet a *Schupo*, you can assure him that you're a useful member of society.'

Later in the year they would send poor Szepessi to Auschwitz for being so persuadable.

14

From diverse sources – from the policeman Toffel as well as drunken Bosch of *Ostfaser*, the SS textile operation, Oskar Schindler heard rumors that 'procedures in the ghetto' (whatever that meant) were growing more intense. The SS were moving into Cracow some tough *Sonderkommando* units from Lublin, where they had already done sterling work in matters of racial purification. Toffel had suggested that unless Oskar wanted a break in production, he ought to set up some camp beds for his night shift until after the first Sabbath in June.

So Oskar set up dormitories in the offices and upstairs in the munitions section. Some of the night shift were happy to bed down there. Others had wives, children, parents waiting back in the ghetto. Besides, they had the *Blauschein*, the holy blue sticker, on their *Kennkartes*.

On June 3, Abraham Bankier, Oskar's office manager, didn't turn up at Lipowa Street. Schindler was still at home, drinking coffee in Straszewskiego Street, when he got a call from one of his secretaries. She'd seen Bankier marched out of the ghetto, not even stopping at Optima, straight to the Prokocim depot. There'd been other Emalia workers in the group too. There'd been Reich, Leser . . . as many as a dozen.

Oskar called for his car to be brought to him from the garage. He drove over the river and down Lwówska toward Prokocim. There he showed his pass to the guards at the gate. The depot yard itself was full of strings of cattle cars, the station crowded with the ghetto's dispensable citizens standing in orderly lines, convinced still – and perhaps they were right – of the value of passive and orderly response. It was the first time Oskar had seen this juxtaposition of humans and cattle cars, and it was a greater shock than hearing of it; it made him pause on the edge of the platform. Then he saw a jeweller he knew. Seen Bankier? he asked. 'He's already in one of the cars, Herr Schindler,' said the jeweller. 'Where are they taking you?' Oskar asked the man. 'We're going to a labour camp, they say. Near Lublin. Probably no worse than . . .' The man waved a hand toward distant Cracow.

Schindler took a pack of cigarettes from his pocket, found some 10-złoty bills and handed the pack and the notes to the jeweller, who thanked him. They had made them leave home without anything this time. They said they'd be forwarding the baggage.

Late the previous year, Schindler had seen in the SS *Bulletin of Budget and Construction* an invitation for bids for the construction of some crematoria in a camp southeast of Lublin. Bełżec. Schindler considered the jeweller. Sixty-three or -four. A little thin; had probably had pneumonia last winter. Worn pin-striped suit, too warm for the day. And in the clear, knowing eyes a capacity to bear finite suffering. Even in the summer of 1942 it was impossible to guess at the connections between such a man as this and those ovens of extraordinary cubic capacity. Did they intend to start epidemics among the prisoners? Was that to be the method?

Beginning from the engine, Schindler moved along the line of more than twenty cattle cars, calling Bankier's name to the faces peering down at him from the open grillwork high above the slats of the cars. It was fortunate for Abraham that Oskar did not ask himself why it was Bankier's name he called, that he did not pause and consider that Bankier's had only equal value to all the other names loaded aboard the *Ostbahn* rolling stock. An existentialist might have been defeated by the numbers at Prokocim, stunned by the equal appeal of all the names and voices. But Schindler was a philosophic innocent. He knew the people he knew. He knew the name of Bankier. '*Bankier! Bankier!*' he continued to call.

He was intercepted by a young SS *Oberscharführer*, an expert railroad shipper from Lublin. He asked for Schindler's pass. Oskar could see in the man's left hand an enormous list – pages of names.

My workers, said Schindler. Essential industrial workers. My office manager. It's idiocy. I have Armaments Inspectorate contracts, and here you are taking the workers I need to fulfill them.

You can't have them back, said the young man. They're on the list.... The SS NCO knew from experience that the list conferred an equal destination on all its members.

Oskar dropped his voice to that hard murmur, the growl of a reasonable man, well connected, who wasn't going to bring up all his heavy guns yet. Did the *Herr Oberscharführer* know how long it would take to train experts to replace those on the list? At my works, Deutsche Email Fabrik, I have a munitions section under the special protection of General Schindler, my namesake. Not only would the *Oberscharführer*'s comrades on the Russian Front be affected by the disruption of production, but the office of the Armaments Inspectorate would demand explanations as well.

The young man shook his head – just a harassed transit official. 'I've heard that kind of story before, sir,' he said. But he was worried. Oskar could tell it and kept leaning over him and speaking softly with an edge of menace. 'It's not my place to argue with the list,' said Oskar. 'Where is your superior officer?'

The young man nodded toward an SS officer, a man in his thirties wearing a frown above his spectacles. 'May I have your name, *Herr Untersturmführer?*' Oskar asked him, already pulling a notebook from his suit pocket.

The officer also made a statement about the holiness of the list. For this man it was the secure, rational, and sole basis for all this milling of Jews and movement of rail cars. But Schindler got crisper now. He'd heard about the list, he said. What he had asked was what the *Untersturmführer*'s name was. He intended to appeal directly to *Oberführer* Schemer and to General Schindler of the Armaments Inspectorate.

'Schindler?' asked the officer. For the first time he took a careful look at Oskar. The man was dressed like a tycoon, wore the right badge, had generals in the family. 'I believe I can guarantee you,

Herr Untersturmführer,' said Schindler in his benign grumble, 'that you'll be in southern Russia within the week.'

The NCO going ahead, Herr Schindler and the officer marched side by side between the ranks of prisoners and the loaded cattle cars. The locomotive was already steaming and the engineer leaning from his cabin, looking down the length of the train, waiting to be dispatched. The officer called to *Ostbahn* officials they passed on the platform to hold up. At last they reached one of the rear cars. There were a dozen workers in there with Bankier; they had all boarded together as if expecting a joint deliverance. The door was unlocked and they jumped down – Bankier and Frankel from the office; Reich, Leser, and the others from the factory. They were restrained, not wanting to permit anyone to detect their pleasure at being saved the journey. Those left inside began chattering merrily, as if they were fortunate to be travelling with so much extra room, while with emphasis in his pen strokes, the officer removed the Emalia workers one at a time from the list and required Oskar to initial the pages.

As Schindler thanked the officer and turned to follow his workers away, the man detained him by the elbow of his suit coat. 'Sir,' he said, 'it makes no difference to us, you understand. We don't care whether it's this dozen or that.'

The officer, who had been frowning when Oskar first saw him, now seemed calm, as if he had discovered the theorem behind the situation. You think your thirteen little tinsmiths are important? We'll replace them with another thirteen little tinsmiths and all your sentimentality for these will be defeated. 'It's the inconvenience to the list, that's all,' the officer explained.

Plump little Bankier admitted that the group of them had neglected to pick up *Blauscheins* from the old Polish Savings Bank. Schindler, suddenly testy, said to attend to it. But what his curtness covered was dismay at those crowds at Prokocim who, for want of a blue sticker, stood waiting for the new and decisive symbol of their status, the cattle car, to be hauled by heavy engine across their range of vision. Now, the cattle cars told them, we are all beasts together.

15

From the faces of his own workers, Oskar could read something of the ghetto's torment. For a person had no time to catch his breath there, no room to dig in, assert one's habits or set up family rituals. Many took refuge and a sort of comfort in suspicion of everyone – of the people in the same room as much as of the OD man in the street. But then, even the sanest were not sure whom to trust. 'Each tenant,' a young artist named Josef Bau wrote of a ghetto house, 'has his own world of secrets and mysteries.' Children suddenly stopped talking at a creaking in the stairwell. Adults woke from dreams of exile and dispossession to find themselves exiled and dispossessed in a crowded room in Podgórze – the events of their dreams, the very taste of fear in dreams, finding continuity in the fears of the day. Fierce rumors beset them in their room, on the street, on the factory floor. Spira had another list and it was either twice or three times as long as the last. All children would go to Tarnow to be shot, to Stutthof to be drowned, to Breslau to be indoctrinated, deracinated, operated upon. Do you have an elderly parent? They are taking everyone over fifty to the Wieliczka salt mines. To work? No. To seal them up in disused chambers.

All this hearsay, much of which reached Oskar, was based on a human instinct to prevent the evil by voicing it – to forestall the Fates by showing them that you could be as imaginative as they. But that June, all the worst of the dreams and whispers took concrete form, and the most unimaginable rumor became a fact.

South of the ghetto, beyond Rekawka Street, rose a hilly parkland. There was an intimacy, like that of mediaeval siege paintings, about the way you could look down over the ghetto's southern wall. As you rode along the brow of the hills, the ghetto's map was revealed, and you could see, as you passed them, what was happening in the streets below.

Schindler had noticed this advantage while riding here with Ingrid in the spring. Now, shocked by the sights of the Prokocim depot, he decided to go riding again. The morning after the rescue of Bankier, he rented horses from the stables in Park Bednarskiego. They were impeccably turned out, he and Ingrid, in long hacking jackets, riding breeches, and dazzling boots. Two *Sudeten* blonds high above the disturbed ant heap of the ghetto.

They rode up through the woods and had a short gallop over open meadows. From their saddles they could now see Wegierska Street, crowds of people around the hospital corner and, closer, a squad of SS working with dogs, entering houses, families pouring forth into the street, pulling on coats in spite of the heat, anticipating a long absence. Ingrid and Oskar reined in their horses in the shade of trees and considered this sight, beginning to notice refinements of the scene. OD men armed with truncheons worked with the SS. Some of these Jewish police seemed enthusiastic, for in a few minutes' view from the hill Oskar saw three reluctant women beaten across the shoulders. At first there was a naive anger in him. The SS were using Jews to flog Jews. It would become clear during the day, however, that some of the OD bludgeoned people to save them from worse things. And there was a new rule for the OD anyhow: if you failed to deliver a family into the street, your own family was forfeit.

Schindler noticed too that in Wegierska Street two lines were continually forming. One was stable, but the other, as it lengthened, was regularly marched away in segments around the corner into Józefińska and out of sight. It was not hard to interpret this assembling and movement, since Schindler and Ingrid, fringed by pine trees and elevated above the ghetto, were a distance of only two or three short blocks from the *Aktion*.

As families were routed out of the apartments, they were separated forcibly into two lines without regard to family considerations.

Adolescent daughters with the proper papers went to the static line, from which they called out to their middle-aged mothers in the other. A night-shift worker, still sullen from disturbed sleep, was pointed to one line, his wife and child to the other. In the middle of the street, the young man argued with an OD policeman. The man was saying, Screw the *Blauschein*! I want to go with Eva and the kid.

An armed SS man intervened. Beside the nondescript mass of *Ghettomenschen*, such a being, in his freshly pressed summer uniform, looked superbly fed and fresh. And from the hill you could see the oil on the automatic pistol in his hand. The SS man hit the Jew on the ear and was talking to him, loudly and harshly. Schindler, though he could not hear, was sure it was a speech he'd encountered before, at Prokocim Station. It doesn't make any difference to me. If you want to go with your frigging Jewish whore, go! The man was led from one line to another. Schindler saw him edge along it to embrace his wife, and under cover of this act of conjugal loyalty, another woman crept back indoors and was not seen by the SS *Sonderkommando*.

Oskar and Ingrid turned their horses, crossed a deserted avenue, and after a few metres, rode out onto a limestone platform facing directly down Krakusa. In its closer reaches, this street was not as hectic as Wegierska. A line of women and children, not so long, was being led away toward Piwna Street. A guard walked in front, another strolled behind. There was an imbalance in the line: far more children than the few women in it could themselves have borne. At the rear, dawdling, was a toddler, boy or girl, dressed in a small scarlet coat and cap. The reason it compelled Schindler's interest was that it made a statement, the way the argumentative shift worker in Wegierska had. The statement had to do, of course, with a passion for red.

Schindler consulted Ingrid. It was definitely a little girl, said Ingrid. Girls got obsessed by a colour, especially a colour like that.

As they watched, the *Waffen* SS man at the rear of the column would occasionally put out his hand and correct the drift of this scarlet node. He did not do it harshly – he could have been an elder brother. Had he been asked by his officers to do something to allay the sentimental concern of watching civilians, he could not have done better. So the moral anxiety of the two riders in Bednarskiego Park was, for a second, irrationally allayed. But it was brief comfort. For behind the departing column of women and children, to which the scarlet toddler placed a meandering period, SS teams with dogs worked north along either side of the street.

They rampaged through the foetid apartments; as a symptom of their rush, a suitcase flew from a second-story window and split open on the sidewalk. And, running before the dogs, the men and women and children who had hidden in attics or closets, inside drawerless dressers, the evaders of the first wave of search, jolted out onto the pavement, yelling and gasping in terror of the Doberman pinschers. Everything seemed speeded-up, difficult for the viewers on the hill to track. Those who had emerged were shot where they stood on the sidewalk, flying out over the gutters at the impact of the bullets, gushing blood into the drains. A mother and a boy, perhaps eight, perhaps a scrawny ten, had retreated under a windowsill on the western side of Krakusa Street. Schindler felt an intolerable fear for them, a terror in his own blood which loosened his thighs from the saddle and threatened to unhorse him. He looked at Ingrid and saw her hands knotted on the reins. He could hear her exclaiming and begging beside him.

His eyes slewed up Krakusa to the scarlet child. They were doing it within half a block of *her*; they hadn't waited for her column to turn out of sight into Józefińska. Schindler could not have explained at first how that compounded the murders on the sidewalk. Yet somehow it proved, in a way no one could ignore, their serious intent. While the scarlet child stopped in her column and turned to watch, they shot the woman in the neck, and one of them, when the boy slid down the wall whimpering, jammed a boot down on his head as if to hold it still and put the barrel against the back of the neck – the recommended SS stance – and fired.

Oskar looked again for the small red girl. She had stopped and turned and seen the boot descend. A gap had already widened between her and the next to last in the column. Again the SS guard corrected her drift fraternally, nudged her back into line. Herr Schindler could not see why he did not bludgeon her with his rifle butt, since at the other end of Krakusa Street, mercy had been cancelled.

At last Schindler slipped from his horse, tripped, and found himself on his knees hugging the trunk of a pine tree. The urge to throw up his excellent breakfast was, he sensed, to be suppressed, for he suspected it meant that all his cunning body was doing was making room to digest the horrors of Krakusa Street.

Their lack of shame, as men who had been born of women and had to write letters home (What did they put in them?), wasn't the worst aspect of what he'd seen. He *knew* they had no shame, since the guard at the base of the column had not felt any need to stop the red child from seeing things. But worst of all, if there was no shame, it meant there was official sanction. No one could find refuge anymore behind the idea of German culture, nor behind those pronouncements uttered by leaders to exempt anonymous men from stepping beyond their gardens, from looking out their office windows at the realities on the sidewalk. Oskar had seen in Krakusa Street a statement of his government's policy which could not be written off as a temporary aberration. The SS men were, Oskar believed, fulfilling there the orders of the leader, for otherwise their colleague at the rear of the column would not have let a child watch.

Later in the day, after he had absorbed a ration of brandy, Oskar understood the proposition in its clearest terms. They permitted witnesses, such witnesses as the red toddler, because they believed the witnesses all would perish too.

In the corner of Plac Zgody (Peace Square) stood an *Apotheke* run by Tadeus Pankiewicz. It was a pharmacy in the old style. Porcelain amphoras with the Latin names of ancient remedies marked on them, and a few hundred delicate and highly varnished drawers, hid the complexity of the pharmacopoeia from the citizens of Podgórze. Magister Pankiewicz lived above the shop by permission of the authorities and at the request of the doctors in the ghetto clinics. He was the only Pole permitted to remain within the ghetto walls. He was a quiet man in his early forties and had intellectual interests. The Polish impressionist Abraham Neumann, the composer Mordche Gebirtig, philosophical Leon Steinberg, and the scientist and philosopher Dr. Rappaport were all regular visitors at Pankiewicz'. The house was also a link, a mail drop for information and messages running between the Jewish Combat Organisation (ZOB) and the partisans of the Polish People's Army. Young Dolek Liebeskind and Shimon and Gusta Dranger, organisers of the Cracow ZOB, would sometimes call there, but discreetly. It was important not to implicate Tadeus Pankiewicz by their projects, which — unlike the cooperative policies of the *Judenrat* — involved furious and unequivocal resistance.

The square in front of Pankiewicz' pharmacy became in those first days of June a marshalling yard. 'It beggared belief,' Pankiewicz would always thereafter say of Peace Square. In the parkland in the middle, people were graded again and told to leave their baggage — No, no, it will be sent on to you! Against the blank wall at the western end of the square, those who resisted or were found carrying the secret option of Aryan papers in their pockets were shot without any explanation or excuses to the people in the middle. The astounding thunder of the rifles fractured conversation and hope. Yet in spite of the screams and wailing of those related to the victims, some people — shocked or focusing desperately on life — seemed almost unaware of the heap of corpses. Once the trucks rolled up, and details of Jewish men loaded the dead into the back, those left in the square would begin at once to talk of their futures again. And Pankiewicz would hear what he had been hearing all day from SS NCOs. 'I assure you, madam, you Jews are going to work. Do you think we can afford to squander you?' Frantic desire to believe would show blatantly on the faces of those women. And the SS rank and file, fresh from the executions against the wall, strolled among the crowd and advised people on how to label their luggage.

From Bednarskiego, Oskar Schindler had not been able to see into Plac Zgody. But Pankiewicz in the square, like Schindler on the hill, had never witnessed such dispassionate horror. Like Oskar, he was plagued by nausea, and his ears were full of an unreal sibilance, as if he had been struck on the head. He was so confused by the mass of noise and savagery, he did not know that among the dead in the square were his friends Gebirtig, composer of that famed song 'Burn City, Burn,' and gentle Neumann the artist. Doctors began to stumble into the pharmacy, panting, having run the two blocks from the hospital. They wanted bandages – they had dragged the wounded in from the streets. A doctor came in and asked for emetics. For in the crowd a dozen people were gagging or comatose from swallowing cyanide. An engineer Pankiewicz knew had slipped it into his mouth when his wife wasn't looking.

Young Dr. Idek Schindel, working at the ghetto hospital on the corner of Wegierska, heard from a woman who came in hysterical that they were taking the children. She'd seen the children lined up in Krakusa Street, Genia among them. Schindel had left Genia that morning with neighbors – he was her guardian in the ghetto; her parents were still hiding in the countryside, intending to slip back into the ghetto, which had been, until today, less perilous. This morning Genia, always her own woman, had wandered away from the woman who was minding her back to the house where she lived with her uncle. There she had been arrested. It was in this way that Oskar Schindler, from the park, had been drawn by her motherless presence in the column in Krakusa Street.

Taking off his surgical coat, Dr. Schindel rushed to the square and saw her almost at once, sitting on the grass, affecting composure within the wall of guards. Dr. Schindel knew how faked the performance was, having had to get up often enough to soothe her night terrors.

He moved around the periphery of the square and she saw him. *Don't call out*, he wanted to say; *I'll work it out*. He didn't want a scene because it could end badly for both of them. But he didn't need to be concerned, for he could see her eyes grow mute and unknowing. He stopped, transfixed by her pitiably admirable cunning. She knew well enough at the age of three years not to take the short-term comfort of calling out to uncles. She knew that there was no salvation in engaging the interest of the SS in Uncle Idek.

He was composing a speech he intended to make to the large *Oberscharführer* who stood by the execution wall. It was better not to approach the authorities too humbly or through anyone of lesser rank. Looking back again to the child, he saw the suspicion of a flutter of her eyes, and then, with a dazzling speculator's coolness, she stepped between the two guards nearest to her and out of the cordon. She moved with an aching slowness which, of course, galvanised her uncle's vision, so that afterward he would often see behind his closed eyes the image of her among the forest of gleaming SS knee boots. In Plac Zgody, no one saw her. She maintained her part-stumbling, part-ceremonial bluffer's pace all the way to Pankiewicz' corner and around it, keeping to the blind side of the street. Dr. Schindel repressed the urge he had to applaud. Though the performance deserved an audience, it would by its nature be destroyed by one.

He felt he could not move directly behind her without disclosing her feat. Against all his usual impulses, he believed that the instinct which had taken her infallibly out of Plac Zgody would provide her with a hiding place. He returned to the hospital by the alternative route to give her time.

Genia returned to the front bedroom in Krakusa Street that she shared with her uncle. The street was deserted now, or, if a few were by cunning or false walls still there, they did not declare themselves. She entered the house and hid under the bed. From the corner of the street, Idek, returning to the house, saw the SS, in a last sweep, come knocking. But Genia did not answer. She would not answer him when he arrived himself. It was just that he knew where to look, in the gap between curtain and window sash, and saw, shining in the drabness of the room, her red shoe beneath the hem of the bedspread.

By this time, of course, Schindler had returned his horse to the stable. He was not on the hill to see the small but significant triumph of red Genia's return to the place where the SS had first found her. He was already in his office at DEF, shut away for a time, finding the news too heavy to share with the day shift. Much later, in terms uncharacteristic of jovial Herr Schindler, Cracow's favourite party guest, Zablocie's big spender, in terms, that is, which showed – behind the playboy facade – an implacable judge, Oskar would lay special weight on this day. 'Beyond this day,' he would claim, 'no thinking person could fail to see what would happen. I was now resolved to do everything in my power to defeat the system.'

16

The SS kept at work in the Ghetto until Saturday evening. They operated with that efficiency which Oskar had observed in the executions in Krakusa Street. Their thrusts were hard to predict, and people who had escaped on Friday were caught on Saturday. Genia survived the week, however, through her precocious gift for maintaining silence and for being imperceptible in scarlet.

Over in Zablocie, Schindler did not dare believe that this red child had survived the *Aktion* process. He knew from talking to Toffel and other acquaintances from police headquarters in Pomorska Street that 7,000 people had been cleared from the ghetto. A Gestapo official from the Jewish Affairs Office was delighted to confirm the clearance. Up in Pomorska Street, among the paper pushers, the June *Aktion* was voted a triumph.

Oskar had now become more exact about this sort of information. He knew, for example, that the *Aktion* had been under the overall management of one Wilhelm Kunde but had been led by SS *Obersturmführer* Otto von Mallotke. Oskar kept no dossier, but he was preparing for another era when he would make a full report to either Canaris or the world. It would be made earlier than he expected. For the moment, he inquired after matters which he had in the past treated as temporary lunacies. He got his hard news from police contacts, but also from clear-headed Jews like Stern. Intelligence from other parts of Poland was piped into the ghetto, in part through Pankiewicz' pharmacy, by the partisans of the People's Army. Dolek Liebeskind, leader of the *Akiva Halutz* Resistance Group, also brought in information from other ghettos as a result of his official travelling job with the Jewish Communal Self-Help, an organisation which the

Germans – with half an eye on the Red Cross – permitted to exist.

It was no use bringing such tidings to the *Judenrat*. The *Judenrat* Council did not consider it civilly advisable to tell the ghetto dwellers anything about the camps. People would merely be distressed; there would be disorder in the streets, and it would not go unpunished. It was always better to let people hear wild rumors, decide they were exaggerated, fall back on hope. This had been the attitude of most Jewish Councillors even under decent Artur Rosenzweig. But Rosenzweig was gone. The salesman David Gutter, helped by his Germanic name, would soon become president of the *Judenrat*. Food rations were now diverted not only by certain SS officials but by Gutter and the new Councillors, whose vicar in the streets was high-booted Symche Spira. The *Judenrat* therefore had no interest anymore in informing the ghetto people about their probable destinations, since they were confident that they themselves would not be made to travel.

The beginning of knowledge for the ghetto, and the clinching news for Oskar, was the return to Cracow – eight days after he'd been shipped off from Prokocim – of the young pharmacist Bachner. No one knew how he had got back inside the ghetto, or the mystery of why he returned to a place from which the SS would simply send him off on another journey. But it was, of course, the pull of the known that brought Bachner home.

All the way down Lwówska and into the streets behind Plac Zgody he carried his story. He had seen the final horror, he said. He was mad-eyed, and in his brief absence his hair had silvered. All the Cracow people who had been rounded up in early June had been taken nearly to Russia, he said, to the camp of Bełżec. When the trains arrived at the railway station, the people were driven out by Ukrainians with clubs. There was a frightful stench about the place, but an SS man had kindly told people that that was due to the use of disinfectant. The people were lined up in front of two large warehouses, one marked 'CLOAK ROOM' and the other 'VALUABLES.' The new arrivals were made to undress, and a small Jewish boy passed among the crowd handing out lengths of string with which to tie their shoes together. Spectacles and rings were removed. So, naked, the prisoners had their heads shaved in the hairdresser's, an SS NCO telling them that their hair was needed to make something special for U-boat crews. It would grow again, he said, maintaining the myth of their continued usefulness. At last the victims were driven down a barbed-wire passage to bunkers which had copper Stars of David on their roofs and were labelled 'BATHS AND INHALATION ROOMS.' SS men reassured them all the way, telling them to breathe deeply, that it was an excellent means of disinfection. Bachner saw a little girl drop a bracelet on the ground, and a boy of three picked it up and went into the bunker playing with it.

In the bunkers, said Bachner, they were all gassed. And afterward, squads were sent in to disentangle the pyramid of corpses and take the bodies away for burial. It had taken barely two days, he said, before they were all dead, except for him. While waiting in an enclosure for his turn, he'd somehow got to a latrine and lowered himself into the pit. He'd stayed there three days, the human waste up to his neck. His face, he said, had been a hive of flies. He'd slept standing, wedged in the hole for fear of drowning there. At last he'd crawled out at night.

Somehow he'd walked out of Bełżec, following the railway tracks. Everyone understood that he had got out precisely because he was beyond reason. Likewise, he'd been cleaned by someone's hand – a peasant woman's, perhaps – and put into fresh clothes for his journey back to the starting point.

Even then there were people in Cracow who thought Bachner's story a dangerous rumor. Postcards had come to relatives from prisoners in Auschwitz. So if it was true of Bełżec, it couldn't be true of Auschwitz. And was it credible? On the short emotional rations of the ghetto, one got by through sticking to the credible.

The chambers of Bełżec, Schindler found out from his sources, had been completed by March of that year under the supervision of a Hamburg engineering firm and of SS engineers from Oranienburg. From Bachner's testimony, it seemed that 3,000 killings a day were not beyond their capacity. Crematoria were under construction, lest old-fashioned means of disposal of corpses put a brake on the new killing method. The same company involved in Bełżec had installed identical facilities at Sobibor, also in the Lublin district. Bids had been accepted, and construction was well advanced, for a similar installation at Treblinka, near Warsaw. And chambers and ovens were both in operation at the Auschwitz main camp and at the vast Auschwitz II camp a few kilometres away at Birkenau. The resistance claimed that 10,000 murders on a given day were within the capacity of Auschwitz II. Then, for the Łódź area, there was the camp at Chelmno, also equipped according to the new technology.

To write these things now is to state the commonplaces of history. But to find them out in 1942, to have them break upon you from a June sky, was to suffer a fundamental shock, a derangement in that area of the brain in which stable ideas about humankind and its possibilities are kept. Throughout Europe that summer some millions of people, Oskar among them, and the ghetto dwellers of Cracow too, tortuously adjusted the economies of their souls to the idea of Bełżec or of like enclosures in the Polish forests.

That summer also Schindler wound up the bankrupt estate of Rekord and, under the provisions of the Polish Commercial Court, acquired by a species of *pro forma* auction ownership of the property. Though the German armies were over the Don and on their way to the Caucasus oil fields, Oskar discerned by the evidence of what had happened in Krakusa Street that they could not finally succeed. Therefore it was a good season to legitimise to the limit his possession of the factory in Lipowa Street. He still hoped, in a way that was almost childlike and to which history would pay no regard, that the fall of the evil king would not bear away that legitimacy – that in the new era he would go on being Hans Schindler's successful boy from Zwittau.

Jereth of the box factory went on pressing him about building a hut – a refuge – on his patch of wasteland. Oskar got the necessary approvals from the bureaucrats. A rest area for the night shift was his story. He had the lumber for it – it had been donated by Jereth himself.

When finished in the autumn, it seemed a slight and comfortless structure. The planking had that crate-wood greenness and looked as if it would shrink as it got darker, and let in the slanting snow. But during an *Aktion* in October it was a haven for Mr. and Mrs. Jereth, for the workers from the box factory and the radiator works, and for Oskar's night shift.

The Oskar Schindler who comes down from his office on the frosty mornings of an *Aktion* to speak to the SS man, to the Ukrainian auxiliary, to the Blue Police, and to OD details who would have marched across from Podgórze to escort his night shift home; the Oskar Schindler who, drinking coffee, calls *Wachtmeister* Bosko's office near the ghetto and tells some lie about why his night shift must stay in Lipowa Street this morning – *that* Oskar Schindler has endangered himself now beyond the limit of cautious business practice. The men of influence who have twice sprung him from prison cannot do it indefinitely even if he is generous to them on their birthdays. This year they are putting men of influence in Auschwitz. If they die there, their widows get a terse and unregretful telegram from the Commandant. 'YOUR HUSBAND HAS DIED IN KONZENTRATIONSLAGER AUSCHWITZ.'

Bosko himself was lanky, thinner than Oskar. Gruff-voiced, and like him a German Czech. His family, like Oskar's, was conservative and looked to the old Germanic values. He had, for a brief season, felt a pan-Germanic anticipation at the rise of Hitler, exactly the way Beethoven had felt a grand European fervor for Napoleon. In Vienna, where he had been studying theology, he'd joined the SS – partly as an alternative to conscription into the *Wehrmacht*, partly from an evanescent ardour. He regretted that ardour now and was, more fully than Oskar knew, expiating it. All that Oskar understood about him at the time was that he was always pleased to undermine an *Aktion*. His responsibility was the perimeter of the ghetto, and from his office beyond the walls he looked inward at the *Aktion* with a precise horror, for he, like Oskar, considered himself a potential witness.

Oskar did not know that in the October *Aktion*, Bosko had

smuggled some dozens of children out of the ghetto in cardboard boxes. Oskar did not know either that the *Wachtmeister* provided, ten at a time, general passes for the underground. The Jewish Combat Organisation (ZOB) was strong in Cracow. It was made up mainly of youth-club members, especially of members of Akiva – a club named after the legendary Rabbi Akiva ben Joseph, scholar of the Mishna. The ZOB was led by a married couple, Shimon and Gusta Dranger – her diary would become a classic of the Resistance – and by Dolek Liebeskind. Its members needed to pass freely into and out of the ghetto, for purposes of recruitment and to carry currency, forged documents, and copies of the underground newspaper. They had contacts with the left-wing Polish People's Army, which was based in the forests around Cracow, and which also needed the documents Bosko provided. Bosko's contacts with ZOB and the People's Army were therefore sufficient to hang him; but still he secretly mocked and despised himself and had contempt for partial rescues. For Bosko wanted to save everyone, and would soon try to, and would perish because of it.

Danka Dresner, cousin of red Genia, was fourteen years old and had by then outgrown the sure infantile instincts which had led her small relative safely out of the cordon in Plac Zgody. Though she had work as a cleaning woman at the *Luftwaffe* base, the truth was that by autumn any woman under fifteen or more than forty could be taken away to the camps anyhow.

Therefore, on the morning an SS *Sonderkommando* and squads of Security Police rolled into Lwówska Street, Mrs. Dresner took Danka with her down to Dabrowski, to the house of a neighbor who had a false wall. The neighbor was a woman in her late thirties, a servant at the Gestapo mess near the Wawel, who could therefore expect some preferential treatment. But she had elderly parents who were automatic risks. So she had bricked up a 60-centimetre cavity for her parents, a costly project, since bricks had to be smuggled into the ghetto in barrows under heaps of legal goods – rags, firewood, disinfectant. God knew what her bricked-up secret space had cost her – maybe 5,000 zł., maybe 10,000.

She'd mentioned it a number of times to Mrs. Dresner. If there was an *Aktion*, Mrs. Dresner could bring Danka and come herself. Therefore, on the morning Danka and Mrs. Dresner heard from around the corner of Dabrowski the startling noise, the bark of Dalmatians and Dobermans, the megaphoned roaring of *Oberscharführers*, they hurried to their friend's place.

When the Dresners had gone up the stairs and found the right room, they could see that the clamour had had an effect on their friend. 'It sounds bad,' said the woman. 'I have my parents in there already. I can fit the girl in. But not you.'

Danka stared, captivated, at the end wall, at its stained wallpaper. In there, sandwiched in brick, rats perhaps worrying at their feet, their senses stretched by darkness, were this woman's elderly mother and father.

Mrs. Dresner could tell that the woman wasn't rational. The girl, but not you, she kept saying. It was as if she thought that should the SS penetrate the wall they would be more forgiving on account of Danka's lesser poundage. Mrs. Dresner explained that she was scarcely obese, that the *Aktion* seemed to be concentrating on this side of Lwówska Street, and that she had nowhere else to go. And that she could fit. Danka was a reliable girl, said Mrs. Dresner, but she would feel safer with her mother in there. You could see by measuring the wall with your eyes that four people could fit abreast in the cavity. But shots from two blocks distant swept away the last of the woman's reason. 'I can fit the girl!' she screamed. 'I want you to go!'

Mrs. Dresner turned to Danka and told her to go into the wall. Later Danka would not know why she had obeyed her mother and gone so mutely into hiding. The woman took her to the attic, removed a rug from the floor, then lifted a raft of floorboards. Then Danka descended into the cavity. It wasn't black in there; the parents were burning a stub of candle. Danka found herself beside the woman – someone else's mother but, beyond the unwashed smell, with the same warm, protective musk of motherhood. The woman smiled at her briefly. The husband stood on the far side of his wife, keeping his eyes closed, not to be distracted from signals from outside.

After a time the friend's mother motioned to her that she could sit if she wanted. So Danka crouched sideways and found a comfortable posture on the floor of the cavity. No rats troubled her. She heard no sound – not a word from her mother and the friend beyond the wall. Above everything else she felt unexpectedly safe. And with the sensation of safety came displeasure at herself for obeying her mother's order so woodenly, and then fear for her mother, who was out there in the world of *Aktions*.

Mrs. Dresner did not leave the house at once. The SS were in Dabrowski Street now. She thought she might as well stay on. If she was taken, it was no loss to her friend. It might, in fact, be a positive help. If they took a woman from this room, it would probably increase their satisfaction with their task, exempt them from a sharper inspection of the state of the wallpaper.

But the woman had convinced herself no one would survive the search if Mrs. Dresner stayed in the room; and, Mrs. Dresner could see, no one would if the woman remained in that state. Therefore she stood up, calmly despairing of herself, and left. They would find her on the steps or in the hall. Why not on the street? she wondered. It was so much an unwritten rule that ghetto natives must stay on quivering in their rooms until discovered that anyone found moving on the stairways was somehow guilty of defiance of the system.

A figure in a cap prevented her from going out. He appeared on the front step, squinting down the dark corridor to the cold blue light of the courtyard beyond. Staring at her, he recognised her, as she did him. It was an acquaintance of her elder son's; but you could not be sure that that counted for anything; you could not know what pressures they'd put on the OD boys. He stepped into the hall and approached her. 'Pani Dresner,' he said. He pointed at the stairwell. 'They'll be gone in ten minutes. You stay under the stairs. Go on. Get under the stairs.'

As numbly as her daughter had obeyed her, she now obeyed

the OD youth. She crouched down under the stairs, but knew it was no good. The autumn light from the courtyard revealed her. If they wanted to look at the courtyard, or at the apartment door at the rear of the hallway, she would be seen. Since upright or cowering made no difference, she stood upright. From near the front door, the OD man urged her to stay there. Then he went. She heard yells, orders, and appeals, and it all seemed to be as close as next door.

At last, he was back with others. She heard the boots at the front door. She heard him say in German that he'd searched the ground floor and no one was at home. There were occupied rooms upstairs, though. It was such a prosaic conversation he had with the SS men that it didn't seem to her to do justice to the risk he was taking. He was staking his existence against the likelihood that having worked down Lwówska and so far down Dabrowski they might by now be incompetent enough not to search the ground floor themselves and therefore not to find Mrs. Dresner, whom he dimly knew, beneath the stairs.

In the end they took his word. She heard them on the stairs, opening and slamming doors on the first landing, their boots clattering on the floor in the room of the cavity. She heard her friend's raised, shrewish voice . . . *of course I have a work permit, I work over at the Gestapo mess, I know all the gentlemen*. She heard them come down from the second floor with someone; with more than one; a couple, a family. *Substitutes for me*, she would later think. A middle-aged male voice with an edge of bronchitis to it said, 'But surely, gentlemen, we can take some clothing.' And in a tone as indifferent as that of a railway porter asked for time-table information, the SS man telling him in Polish, 'There's no need for it. At these places they provide everything.'

The sound receded. Mrs. Dresner waited. There was no second sweep. The second sweep would be tomorrow or the day after. They would return again and again now, culling the ghetto. What in June had been seen as a culminating horror had become by October a daily process. And as grateful as she was to the OD boy, it was clear as she went upstairs to get Danka that when murder is as scheduled, habitual, industrial as it was here in Cracow you could scarcely, with tentative heroism, redirect the overriding energy of the system. The more Orthodox of the ghetto had a slogan – 'An hour of life is still life.' The OD boy had given her that hour. She knew there was no one who could give her more.

Upstairs, the woman was a little shamefaced. 'The girl can come whenever she wishes,' she said. That is, I didn't exclude you out of cowardice, but as a matter of policy. And the policy stands. You can't be accepted, but the girl can.

Mrs. Dresner did not argue – she had a sense that the woman's stance was part of the same equation that had saved her in the downstairs hall. She thanked the woman. Danka might need to accept her hospitality again.

From now on, since she looked young for her forty-two years and still had her health, Mrs. Dresner would attempt to survive on that basis – the economic one, the putative value of her strength to the Armaments Inspectorate or to some other wing of the war effort. She wasn't confident of the idea. These days anyone with half a grasp on truth could tell that the SS believed the death of the socially unappeasable Jew outbalanced any value he might have as an item of labour. And the question is, in such an era, Who saves Juda Dresner, factory purchasing officer? Who saves Janek Dresner, auto mechanic at the *Wehrmacht* garage? Who saves Danka Dresner, *Luftwaffe* cleaning woman, on the morning the SS finally choose to ignore their economic value?

While the OD man was arranging Mrs. Dresner's survival in the hallway of the house in Dabrowski, the young Zionists of the *Halutz* Youth and the ZOB were preparing a more visible act of resistance. They had acquired uniforms of the *Waffen* SS and, with them, the entitlement to visit the SS-reserved Cyganeria Restaurant in św Ducha Plac, across the square from the Słowacki Theatre. In the Cyganeria they left a bomb which blew the tables through the roof, tore seven SS men to fragments, and injured some forty more.

When Oskar heard about it, he knew he could have been there, buttering up some official.

It was the deliberate intent of Shimon and Gusta Dranger and their colleagues to run against the ancient pacifism of the ghetto, to convert it to universal rebellion. They bombed the SS-only Bagatella Cinema in Karmelicka Street. In the dark, Leni Riefenstahl flickered the promise of German womanhood to the wandering soldier frayed from performing the nation's works in the barbarous ghetto or on the increasingly risky streets of Polish Cracow, and the next second a vast yellow spear of flame extinguished the sight.

The ZOB would in a few months sink patrol boats on the Vistula, fire-bomb sundry military garages throughout the city, arrange *Passierscheins* for people who were not supposed to have them, smuggle passport photographs out to centres where they could be used in the forging of Aryan papers, derail the elegant Army-only train that ran between Cracow and Bochnia, and get their underground newspaper into circulation. They would also arrange for two of OD Chief Spira's lieutenants, Spitz and Forster, who had drawn up lists for the imprisonment of thousands, to walk into a Gestapo ambush. It was a variation of an old undergraduate trick. One of the underground, posing as an informer, made an appointment to meet the two policemen in a village near Cracow. At the same time, a separate supposed informer told the Gestapo that two leaders of the Jewish partisan movement could be found at a particular rendezvous point. Spitz and Forster were both mown down while running from the Gestapo.

Still, the style of resistance for the ghetto dwellers remained that of Artur Rosenzweig, who, when asked in June to make a list of thousands for deportation, had placed his own name, his wife's, his daughter's at the top.

Over in Zablocie, in the backyard of Emalia, Mr. Jereth and Oskar Schindler were pursuing their own species of resistance by planning a second barracks.

17

An Austrian dentist named Sedlacek had now arrived in Cracow and was making wary enquiries about Schindler. He had come by train from Budapest and carried a list of possible Cracow contacts and, in a false-bottomed suitcase, a quantity of Occupation złoty, which, since Governor General Frank had abolished the major denominations of Polish money, took up an unconscionable space.

Though he pretended to be travelling on business, he was a courier for a Zionist rescue organisation in Budapest.

Even in the autumn of 1942, the Zionists of Palestine, let alone the population of the world, knew nothing but rumors of what was happening in Europe. They had set up a bureau in Istanbul to gather hard information. From an apartment in the Beyoglu section of the city, three agents sent out postcards addressed to every Zionist body in German Europe. The postcards read: 'Please let me know how you are. *Eretz* is longing for you.' *Eretz* meant the 'land' and, to any Zionist, Israel. Each of the postcards was signed by one of the three, a girl named Sarka Mandelblatt, who had a convenient Turkish citizenship.

The postcards had gone into the void. No one answered. It meant that the addressees were in prison, or in the forest, or at labour in some camp, or in a ghetto, or dead. All the Zionists of Istanbul had was the ominous negative evidence of silence.

In the late autumn of 1942, they at last received one reply, a postcard with a view of the Belvaros of Budapest. The message on it read: 'Encouraged by your interest in my situation. *Rahamim maher* [urgent help] is much needed. Please keep in touch.'

This reply had been composed by a Budapest jeweller named Samu Springmann, who'd first received and then puzzled out the message on Sarka Mandelblatt's postcard. Samu was a slight man, jockey size, in the prime of his thirties. Since the age of thirteen, despite an inalienable probity, he had been oiling officials, doing favours for the diplomatic corps, bribing the heavy-handed Hungarian Secret Police. Now the Istanbul people let him know that they wanted to use him to pipe rescue money into the German empire and to transmit through them to the world some definite intelligence on what was happening to European Jewry.

In the German-allied Hungary of General Horthy, Samu Springmann and his Zionist colleagues were as bereft of solid news from beyond the Polish border as the people in Istanbul. But he began to recruit couriers who, for a percentage of the bag or else out of conviction, would be willing to penetrate the German territories. One of his couriers was a diamond dealer, Erich Popescu, an agent of the Hungarian Secret Police. Another was an underworld carpet smuggler, Bandi Grosz, who had also assisted the secret police, but who began to work for Springmann to expiate all the grief he had caused his late mother. A third was Rudi Schulz, an Austrian safecracker, an agent for the Gestapo Management Bureau in Stuttgart. Springmann had a gift for playing with double agents such as Popescu, Grosz, and Schulz, by touching their sentimentality, their greed, and, if any, their principles.

Some of his couriers *were* idealists, working from firm premises. Sedlacek, who asked after Herr Schindler in Cracow near the end of 1942, belonged to that species. He had a successful dental practice in Vienna and, in his mid-forties, did not need to lug false-bottomed suitcases into Poland. But here he was, with a list in his pocket, the list having come from Istanbul. And the second name on the list, Oskar's!

It meant that someone – Itzhak Stern, the businessman Ginter, Dr. Alexander Biberstein – had forwarded Schindler's name to the Zionists in Palestine. Without knowing it, Herr Schindler had been nominated for the post of righteous person.

Dr. Sedlacek had a friend in the Cracow garrison, a fellow Viennese, a patient he'd got to know in his practice. It was Major Franz Von Korab of the *Wehrmacht*. On his first evening in Cracow, the dentist met Major Von Korab at the Hotel Cracovia for a drink. Sedlacek had had a miserable day; had gone to the grey Vistula and looked across at Podgórze, the cold fortress of barbed wire and lofty gravestoned walls, a cloud of a special dimness above it this mean winter's day, a sharper rain falling there beyond the fake eastern gate where even the policemen looked accursed. When it was time to go and meet Von Korab, he went gratefully.

In the suburbs of Vienna it had always been rumored that Von Korab had a Jewish grandmother. Patients would idly say so – in the Reich, genealogical gossip was as acceptable small talk as was the weather. People would seriously speculate over drinks whether it was true that Reinhard Heydrich's grandmother had married a Jew named Suss. Once, against all good sense but for the sake of friendship, Von Korab had confessed to Sedlacek that the rumor was true in his case. This confession had been a gesture of trust, which it would now be safe to return. Sedlacek therefore asked the major about some of the people on the Istanbul list. To Schindler's name, Von Korab responded with an indulgent laugh. He knew Herr Schindler, had dined with him. He was physically impressive, said the major, and made money hand over fist. He was much brighter than he pretended to be. I can call him right now and make an appointment, said Von Korab.

At ten the next morning they entered the Emalia office. Schindler accepted Sedlacek politely but watched Major Von Korab, measuring *his* trust of the dentist. After a time Oskar warmed to the stranger, and the major excused himself and would not stay for morning coffee. 'Very well,' said Sedlacek, when Von Korab was gone, 'I'll tell you exactly where I come from.'

He did not mention the money he had brought, nor the likelihood that in the future trusted contacts in Poland would be handed small fortunes in Jewish Joint Distribution Committee cash. What the dentist wanted to know, without any financial colouring, was what Herr Schindler knew and thought about the war against Jewry in Poland.

Once Sedlacek had the question out, Schindler hesitated. In that second, Sedlacek expected a refusal. Schindler's expanding workshop employed 550 Jews at the SS rental rate. The Armaments Inspectorate guaranteed a man like Schindler a continuity of rich contracts; the SS promised him, for no more than 7.50 Reichsmarks a day per person, a continuity of slaves. It should not be a surprise if he sat back in his padded leather chair and claimed ignorance.

'There is one problem, Herr Sedlacek,' he growled. 'It's this. What they are doing to people in this country is *beyond* belief.'

'You mean,' said Dr. Sedlacek, 'that you're concerned my principals won't believe you?'

Schindler said, 'Since I scarcely believe it myself.' He rose, went to the liquor cabinet, poured two snifters of cognac and brought one for Dr. Sedlacek. Returning to his own side of the desk with the other, he took a swallow, frowned at an invoice, picked it up, went to the door on the balls of his feet and swung it open as if to trap an eavesdropper. For a while he stood there framed. Then Sedlacek heard him talking calmly to his Polish secretary about the invoice. In a few minutes, closing the door, he returned to Sedlacek, took a seat behind the desk, and after another deep swallow, began to talk.

Even among Sedlacek's own small cell, his Viennese anti-Nazi club, it was not imagined that the pursuit of the Jews had grown quite so systematic. Not only was the story Schindler told him startling simply in moral terms: one was asked to believe that in the midst of a desperate battle, the National Socialists would devote thousands of men, the resources of precious railroads, an enormous cubic footage of cargo space, expensive techniques of engineering, a fatal margin of their research-and-development scientists, a substantial bureaucracy, whole arsenals of automatic weapons, whole magazines of ammunition, all to an extermination which had no military or economic meaning but merely a psychological one. Dr. Sedlacek had expected mere horror stories –

hunger, economic strictures, violent pogroms in this city or that, violations of ownership — all the historically accustomed things.

Oskar's summary of events in Poland convinced Sedlacek precisely because of the sort of man Oskar was. He had done well from the Occupation; he sat at the heart of his own hive, a brandy snifter in his hand. There were both an impressive surface calm and a fundamental anger in him. He was like a man who had, to his regret, found it impossible to disbelieve the worst. He showed no tendency to be extravagant in the facts he relayed.

If I can arrange your visa, said Sedlacek, would you come to Budapest and pass on what you just told me to my principals and the others?

Schindler seemed momentarily surprised. You can write a report, he said. And surely you've heard this sort of thing from other sources. But Sedlacek told him no; there had been individual stories, details of this incident and that. No comprehensive picture. Come to Budapest, said Sedlacek. Mind you, it might be uncomfortable travelling.

Do you mean, asked Schindler, that I have to cross the border on foot?

Not as bad as that, said the dentist. You might have to travel in a freight train.

I'll come, said Oskar Schindler.

Dr. Sedlacek asked him about the other names on the Istanbul list. At the top of the list, for instance, stood a Cracow dentist. Dentists were always easy to visit, said Sedlacek, since everyone on earth has at least one *bona fide* cavity. No, said Herr Schindler. Don't visit this man. He's been compromised by the SS.

Before he left Cracow to return to Mr. Springmann in Budapest, Dr. Sedlacek arranged another meeting with Schindler. In Oskar's office at DEF, he handed over nearly all the currency Springmann had given him to bring to Poland. There was always some risk, in view of Schindler's hedonistic taste, that he would spend it on black-market jewellery. But neither Springmann nor Istanbul required any assurances. They could never hope to play the auditor.

It must be stated that Oskar behaved impeccably and gave the cash to his contacts in the Jewish community to spend according to their judgment.

Mordecai Wulkan, who like Mrs. Dresner would in time come to know Herr Oskar Schindler, was a jeweller by trade. Now, late in the year, he was visited at home by one of Spira's political OD. This wasn't trouble, the OD man said. Certainly Wulkan had a record. A year before, he had been picked up by the OD for selling currency on the black market. When he had refused to work as an agent for the Currency Control Bureau, he had been beaten up by the SS, and Mrs. Wulkan had had to visit *Wachtmeister* Beck in the ghetto police office and pay a bribe for his release.

This June he'd been seized for transport to Bełżec, but an OD man he'd known had arrived to pick him up and led him straight out of the Optima yard. For there were Zionists in the OD, however small their chances of ever beholding Jerusalem might be.

The OD man who visited him this time was no Zionist. The SS, he told Wulkan, urgently needed four jewellers. Symche Spira had been given three hours to find them. In this way Herzog, Friedner, Grüner, and Wulkan, four jewellers, were assembled at the OD station and marched out of the ghetto to the old Technical Academy, now a warehouse for the SS Economic and Administrative Main Office.

It was obvious to Wulkan as he entered the Academy that a great security operated here. At every door stood a guard. In the front hall, an SS officer told the four jewellers that should they speak to anyone about their work here, they could expect to be sent to a labour camp. They were to bring with them, he said, every day, their diamond-grading kits, their equipment for assessing the karat value of gold.

They were led down into the basement. Around the walls stood racks laden with suitcases and towering layers of briefcases, each with a name studiously and futilely printed on it by its past owner. Beneath the high windows stood a line of wooden crates. As the four jewellers squatted in the centre of the floor, two SS men took down a suitcase, laboured across the cellar with it, and emptied it in front of Herzog. They returned to the rack for another, which they emptied in front of Grüner. Then they brought a cascade of gold for Friedner, then for Wulkan. It was old gold – rings, brooches, bracelets, watches, lorgnettes, cigarette holders. The jewellers were to grade the gold, separate the gold plate from the solid. Diamonds and pearls were to be valued. They were to classify everything, according to value and karat weight, in separate heaps.

At first they picked up individual pieces tentatively, but then worked faster as old professional habits asserted themselves. As the gold and jewellery went into their piles, the SS men loaded the stuff into its appropriate crate. Every time a crate was filled, it was labelled in black paint – SS REICHSFÜHRER BERLIN. The SS *Reichsführer* was Himmler himself, in whose name the confiscated jewellery of Europe was deposited in the *Reichsbank*. There were quantities of children's rings, and one had to keep a cool rational control of one's knowledge of their provenance. Only once did the jewellers falter: when the SS men opened a suitcase and out of it tumbled gold teeth still smeared with blood. There in a pile at Wulkan's knees, the mouths of a thousand dead were represented, each one calling for him to join them by standing and flinging his grading stone across the room and declaring the tainted origin of all this precious stuff. Then, after the hiatus, Herzog and Grüner, Wulkan and Friedner commenced to grade again, aware now, of course, of the radiant value of whatever gold they themselves carried in their mouths, fearful that the SS would come prospecting for it.

It took six weeks for them to work through the treasures of the Technical Academy. After they had finished there, they were taken to a disused garage which had been converted to a silver warehouse. The lubrication pits were filled to spilling over with solid silver – rings, pendants, Passover platters, *yad* pointers, breastplates, crowns, candelabra. They separated the solid silver from the silver plate; they weighed it all. The SS officer in charge complained that some of these objects were awkward to pack, and Mordecai Wulkan suggested that perhaps they might consider melting them down. It seemed to Wulkan, though he was not pious, that it would be somehow better, a minor triumph, if the Reich inherited silver from which the Judaic form had been removed. But for some reason the SS officer refused. Perhaps the objects were intended for some didactic museum inside the Reich. Or perhaps the SS liked the artistry of synagogue silverware.

When this appraisal work ran out, Wulkan was again at a loss for employment. He needed to leave the ghetto regularly to find enough food for his family, especially for his bronchitic daughter. For a time he worked at a metal factory in Kazimierz, getting to know an SS moderate, *Oberscharführer* Gola. Gola found him work as a maintenance man at the SA barracks near Wawel. As Wulkan entered the mess with his wrenches, he saw above the door the inscription, FÜR JUDEN UND HUNDE EINTRITT VERBOTEN: *Entrance forbidden to Jews and dogs*. This sign, together with the hundred thousand teeth he had appraised at the Technical Academy, convinced him that deliverance could not in the end be expected from the offhand favour of *Oberscharführer* Gola. Gola drank here without noticing the sign; and neither would he notice the absence of the Wulkan family on the day they were taken to Belzec or some place of equal efficiency. Therefore Wulkan, like Mrs. Dresner and some fifteen thousand other dwellers in the ghetto, knew that what was needed was a special and startling deliverance. They did not believe for a moment that it would be provided.

18

Dr. Sedlacek had promised an uncomfortable journey, and so it was. Oskar travelled in a good overcoat with a suitcase and a bag full of various comforts which he badly needed by the end of the trip. Though he had the appropriate travel documents, he did not want to have to use them. It was considered better if he did not have to present them at the border. He could always then deny that he had been to Hungary that December.

He rode in a freight van filled with bundles of the Party newspaper, *Völkischer Beobachter*, for sale in Hungary. Closeted with the redolence of printer's ink and among the heavy Gothic print of Germany's official newspaper, he was rocked south over the winter-sharp mountains of Slovakia, across the Hungarian border, and down to the valley of the Danube.

A reservation had been made for him at the Pannonia, near the University, and on the afternoon of his arrival, little Samu Springmann and an associate of his, Dr. Rezso Kastner, came to see him. The two men who rose to Schindler's floor in the elevator had heard fragments of news from refugees. But refugees could give you little but threads. The fact that they had avoided the threat meant that they knew little of its geography, its intimate functioning, the numbers it ran to. Kastner and Springmann were full of anticipation, since – if Sedlacek could be believed – the *Sudeten* German upstairs could give them the whole cloth, the first full-bodied report on the Polish havoc.

In the room the introductions were brief, for Springmann and Kastner had come to listen and they could tell that Schindler was anxious to talk. There was no effort, in this city obsessed with coffee, to formalise the event by calling Room Service for coffee and cakes. Kastner and Springmann, after shaking the enormous German by the hand, sat down. But Schindler paced. It seemed that far from Cracow and the realities of *Aktion* and ghetto, his knowledge disturbed him more than it had when he'd briefly informed Sedlacek. He rampaged across the carpet. They would have heard his steps in the room below – their chandelier would have shaken when he stamped his foot, miming the action of the SS man in the execution squad in Krakusa, the one who'd pinned his victim's head down with a boot in full sight of the red child at the tail of the departing column.

He began with personal images of the cruel parishes of Cracow, what he had beheld in the streets or heard from either side of the wall, from Jews and from the SS. In that connection, he said, he was carrying letters from members of the ghetto, from the physician Chaim Hilfstein, from Dr. Leon Salpeter, from Itzhak Stern. Dr. Hilfstein's letter, said Schindler, was a report on hunger. 'Once the body fat's gone,' said Oskar, 'it starts to work on the brain.'

The ghettos were being wound down, Oskar told them. It was true equally of Warsaw as of Łódź and of Cracow. The population of the Warsaw ghetto had been reduced by four-fifths, Łódź by two-thirds, Cracow by half. Where were the people who had been transferred? Some were in work camps; but the gentlemen here this afternoon had to accept that at least three-fifths of them had disappeared into camps that used the new scientific methods. Such camps were not exceptional. They had an official SS name – *Vernichtungslager:* Extermination Camp.

In the past few weeks, said Oskar, some 2,000 Cracow ghetto dwellers had been rounded up and sent not to the chambers of Bełżec, but to labour camps near the city. One was at Wieliczka, one at Prokocim, both of these being railway stations on the *Ostbahn* line which ran toward the Russian front. From Wieliczka and Prokocim, these prisoners were being marched every day to a site at the village of Płaszów, on the edge of the city, where the foundations for a vast labour camp were being laid. Their life in such a labour camp, said Schindler, would be no holiday – the barracks of

Wieliczka and Prokocim were under the command of an SS NCO named Horst Pilarzik who had earned a reputation last June when he had helped clear from the ghetto some 7,000 people, of whom only one, a chemist, had returned. The proposed camp at Płaszów would be under a man of the same calibre. What was in favour of the labour camps was that they lacked the technical apparatus for methodical slaughter. There was a different rationale behind them. They had economic reasons for existing – prisoners from Wieliczka and Prokocim were marched out every day to work on various projects, just as they were from the ghetto. Wieliczka, Prokocim, and the proposed camp at Płaszów were under the control of the chiefs of police for Cracow, Julian Scherner and Rolf Czurda, whereas the *Vernichtungslagers* were run by the central management of the SS Administrative and Economic Main Office at Oranienburg near Berlin. The *Vernichtungslagers* also used people as labour for a time, but their ultimate industry was death and its by-products – the recycling of the clothes, of remaining jewellery or spectacles, of toys, and even of the skin and hair of the dead.

In the midst of explaining the distinction between extermination camps and those for forced labour, Schindler suddenly stepped toward the door, wrenched it open, and looked up and down the empty hallway. 'I know the reputation of this city for eavesdropping,' he explained. Little Mr. Springmann rose and came to his elbow. 'The Pannonia isn't so bad,' he told Oskar in a low voice. 'It's the Victoria that's the Gestapo hotbed.'

Schindler surveyed the hallway once more, closed the door, and returned across the room. He stood by the windows and continued his grim report. The forced-labour camps would be run by men appointed for their severity and efficiency in clearing the ghettos. There would be sporadic murders and beatings, and there would certainly be corruption involving food and therefore short rations for the prisoners. But that was preferable to the assured death of the *Vernichtungslagers*. People in the labour camps could get access to extra comforts, and individuals could be taken out and smuggled to Hungary.

These SS men are as corruptible as any other police force, then? the gentleman of the Budapest rescue committee asked Oskar. 'In my experience,' growled Oskar, 'there isn't one of them who isn't.'

When Oskar finished, there was, of course, silence. Kastner and Springmann were not readily astounded. All their lives they'd lived under the intimidation of the Secret Police. Their present activities were both vaguely suspected by the Hungarian police – rendered safe only by Samu's contacts and bribes – and at the same time disdained by respectable Jewry. Samuel Stern, for example, president of the Jewish Council, member of the Hungarian Senate, would dismiss this afternoon's report by Oskar Schindler as pernicious fantasy, an insult to German culture, a reflection on the decency of the intentions of the Hungarian Government. These two were used to hearing the worst.

So it was not that Springmann and Kastner were unmanned by Schindler's testimony as much as that their minds were painfully expanding. Their resources seemed minute now that they knew what they were set against – not just any average and predictable Philistine giant, but Behemoth itself. Perhaps already they were reaching for the idea that as well as individual bargaining – some extra food for *this* camp, rescue for *this* intellectual, a bribe to temper the professional ardour of *this* SS man – some vaster rescue scheme would have to be arranged at breathtaking expense.

Schindler threw himself into a chair. Samu Springmann looked across at the exhausted industrialist. He had made an enormous impression on them, said Springmann. They would, of course, send a report to Istanbul on all Oskar had told them. It would be used to stir the Palestinian Zionists and the Joint Distribution Committee to greater action. At the same time it would be transmitted to the governments of Churchill and Roosevelt. Springmann said that he thought Oskar was right to worry about people's belief in what he'd say; he was right to say it was all incredible. 'Therefore,' said Samu Springmann, 'I urge you to go to Istanbul yourself and speak to the people there.'

After a little hesitation – whether to do with the demands of the enamelware business or with the dangers of crossing so many borders – Schindler agreed. Toward the end of the year, said Springmann. 'In the meantime you will see Dr. Sedlacek in Cracow regularly.'

They stood up, and Oskar could see that they were changed men. They thanked him and left, becoming simply, on the way downstairs, two pensive Budapest professional men who'd heard disturbing news of mismanagement in the branch offices.

That night Dr. Sedlacek called at Oskar's hotel and took him out into the brisk streets to dinner at the Hotel Gellert. From their table they could see the Danube, its illuminated barges, the city glowing on the far side of the water. It was like a prewar city, and Schindler began to feel like a tourist again. After his afternoon's temperance, he drank the dense Hungarian burgundy called Bull's Blood with a slow, assiduous thirst, and created a rank of empty bottles at their table.

Halfway through their meal they were joined by an Austrian journalist, Dr. Schmidt, who'd brought with him his mistress, an exquisite, golden Hungarian girl. Schindler admired the girl's jewellery and told her that he was a great fancier of gems himself. But over apricot brandy, he became less friendly. He sat with a mild frown, listening to Schmidt talk of real estate prices and automobile dealings and horse races. The girl listened raptly to Schmidt, since she wore the results of his business coups around her neck and at her wrists. But Oskar's unexpected disapproval was clear. Dr. Sedlacek was secretly amused: perhaps Oskar was seeing a partial reflection of his own new wealth, his own tendencies toward trading on the fringes.

When the dinner was over, Schmidt and his girl left for some nightclub, and Sedlacek made sure he took Schindler to a different one. They sat drinking unwise further quantities of *barack* and watching the floor show.

'That Schmidt,' said Schindler, wanting to clear up the question so that he could enjoy the small hours. 'Do you use him?'

'Yes.'

'I don't think you ought to use men like that,' said Oskar. 'He's a thief.'

Dr. Sedlacek turned his face, and its half-smile, away.

'How can you be sure he delivers any of the money you give him?' Oskar asked.

'We let him keep a percentage,' said Dr. Sedlacek.

Oskar thought about it for a full half-minute. Then he murmured, 'I don't want a damned percentage. I don't want to be offered one.'

'Very well,' said Sedlacek.

'Let's watch the girls,' said Oskar.

19

Even as Oskar Schindler returned by freight car from Budapest, where he'd predicted that the ghetto would soon be closed, an SS *Untersturmführer* named Amon Goeth was on his way from Lublin to bring about that liquidation, and to take command of the resultant Forced Labour Camp *(Zwangsarbeitslager)* at Płaszów. Goeth was some eight months younger than Schindler, but shared more with him than the mere year of birth. Like Oskar he had been raised a Catholic and had ceased observing the rites of the Church as late as 1938, when his first marriage had broken up. Like Oskar too, he had graduated from high school in the *Realgymnasium* – Engineering, Physics, Maths. He was therefore a practical man, no thinker, but considered himself a philosopher.

A Viennese, he had joined the National Socialist Party early, in 1930. When the nervous Austrian Republic banned the party in 1933, he was already a member of its security force, the SS. Driven underground, he had emerged onto the streets of Vienna after the *Anschluss* of 1938 in the uniform of an SS noncommissioned officer. In 1940 he had been raised to the rank of SS *Oberscharführer* and in 1941 achieved the honour of commissioned rank, immensely harder to come by in the SS than in *Wehrmacht* units. After training in infantry tactics, he was put in charge of *Sonderkommandos* during *Aktionen* in the populous ghetto of Lublin and, by his performance there, earned the right to liquidate Cracow.

Untersturmführer Amon Goeth then, speeding on the *Wehrmacht* special between Lublin and Cracow, there to take command of well-tried *Sonderkommandos*, shared with Oskar not only his year of birth, his religion, his weakness for liquor, but a massive physique as well. Goeth's face was open and pleasant, rather longer than Schindler's. His hands, though large and muscular, were long-fingered. He was sentimental about his children, the children of his second marriage whom, because of his foreign service, he had not seen often in the past three years. As a substitute, he was sometimes attentive to the children of brother officers. He could be a sentimental lover too, but though he resembled Oskar in terms of general sexual voraciousness, his tastes were less conventional, running sometimes to his brother SS men, frequently to the beating of women. Both his former wives could have testified that once the first blaze of infatuation had died, he could become physically abusive. He considered himself a sensitive man, and thought that his family's trade proved it. His father and grandfather were Viennese printers and binders of books on military and economic history, and he liked to list himself on official papers as a *Literat:* a man of letters. And though, at this moment, he would have told you that he looked forward to his taking of control of the liquidation operation – that this was the major chance of his career and carried with it the promise of promotion – his service in Special Actions seemed to him to have altered the flow of his nervous energies. He had been plagued with insomnia for two years now and, if he had his way, stayed up till three or four and slept late in the mornings. He had become a reckless drinker and believed he held his liquor with an ease he had not known in his youth. Again like Oskar, he never suffered the hangovers he deserved. He thanked his hardworking kidneys for this benefit.

His orders, entrusting him with the extinction of the ghetto and the kingship of the Płaszów camp, were dated February 12, 1943. He hoped that after consulting with his senior NCOs, with Wilhelm Kunde, commander of the SS guard detail for the ghetto, and with Willi Haase, Schemer's deputy, it would be possible to begin the clearing of the ghetto within a month of the date on his commission.

Commandant Goeth was met at the Cracow Central Station

by Kunde himself and by the tall young SS man Horst Pilarzik, who was temporarily in charge of the work camps at Prokocim and Wieliczka. They piled into the back of a Mercedes and were driven off for a reconnaissance of the ghetto and the site of the new camp. It was a bitter day, and snow began to fall as they crossed the Vistula. *Untersturmführer* Goeth was pleased for a pull on a flask of schnapps Pilarzik carried with him. They passed through the fake-Oriental portals and down the trolley lines of Lwówska Street, which cut the ghetto into two icy portions. The dapper Kunde, who had been a customs agent in civilian life and was adept at reporting to superiors, gave a deft sketch of the ghetto. The portion on their left was Ghetto B, said Kunde. Its inhabitants, about 2,000 of them, had escaped earlier *Aktionen* or had been previously employed in industry. But new identification cards had been issued since then, with appropriate initials – either W for Army employees, Z for employees of the civil authorities, or R for workers in essential industries. The inhabitants of Ghetto B lacked these new cards and were to be shipped away for *Sonderbehandlung* (Special Treatment). In clearing the ghetto, it might be preferable to start on that side first, though that sort of tactical decision was entirely up to the Herr Commandant.

The greater portion of the ghetto stood to the right and contained some 10,000 people still. They would of course be the initial labour force for the factories of the Płaszów camp. It was expected that the German entrepreneurs and supervisors – Bosch, Madritsch, Beckmann, the *Sudetenlander* Oskar Schindler – would want to move all or part of their operations out of town into the camp. As well as that there was a cable-making plant no more than half a mile from the proposed camp, and labourers would be marched there and back each day.

Would the Herr Commandant, asked Kunde, care to continue down the road a few kilometres and have a look at the campsite itself?

Oh, yes, said Amon, I think that would be advisable.

They turned off the highway where the cable-factory yard, snow lying on the giant spools, marked the beginning of Jerozolimska Street. Amon Goeth had a glimpse of a few groups of hunched and bescarved women dragging segments of huts – a wall panel, an eaves section – across the highway and up Jerozolimska from the direction of the railway station at Cracow-Płaszów. They were women from the Prokocim camp, Pilarzik explained. When Płaszów was ready, Prokocim would of course be disbanded and these labouring women would come under the management of the Herr Commandant.

Goeth estimated the distance the women had to carry the frames to be some three-quarters of a kilometre. 'All uphill,' said Kunde, putting his head on one shoulder, then on the other, as if to say, So it's a satisfactory form of discipline, but it slows up construction.

The camp would need a railway spur, said *Untersturmführer* Goeth. He would make an approach to *Ostbahn*.

They passed on the right a synagogue and its mortuary buildings, and a half-tumbled wall showed gravestones like teeth in the cruelly exposed mouth of winter. Part of the campsite had been until this month a Jewish cemetery. 'Quite extensive,' said Wilhelm Kunde. The Herr Commandant uttered a witticism which would come to his lips often during his residency at Płaszów. 'They won't have to go far to get buried.'

There was a house to the right which would be suitable as a temporary residence for the Commandant, and then a large new building to serve as an administration centre. The synagogue mortuary, already partly dynamited, would become the camp stable. Kunde pointed out that the two limestone quarries within the camp area could be seen from here. One stood in the bottom of the little valley, the other up on the hill behind the synagogue. The Herr Commandant might be able to notice the tracks being laid for trolleys which would be used in hauling stones. Once the heavy weather let up, the construction of the track would continue.

They drove to the southeast end of the proposed camp, and a

trail, just passable in the snow, took them along the skyline. The trail ended at what had once been an Austrian military earthwork, a circular mound surrounding a deep and broad indentation. To an artilleryman it would have appeared an important redoubt from which cannon could be sighted to enfilade the road from Russia. To *Untersturmführer* Goeth it was a place suited for disciplinary punishment.

From up here, the camp area could be seen whole. It was a rural stretch, graced with the Jewish cemetery, and folded between two hills. It was in this weather two pages of a largely blank book opened and held at an angle, sideways, to the observer on the fort hill. A grey, stone country dwelling was stuck at the entrance to the valley, and past it, along the far slope and among the few finished barracks, moved teams of women, black as bunches of musical notations, in the strange darkling luminescence of a snowy evening. Emerging from the icy alleys beyond Jerozolimska, they toiled up the white slope under the urgings of Ukrainian guards and dropped the sections of frames where the SS engineers, wearing homburgs and civilian clothes, instructed them.

Their rate of work was a limitation, *Untersturmführer* Goeth remarked. The ghetto people could not, of course, be moved here until the barracks were up and the watchtowers and fences completed. He had no complaints about the pace at which the prisoners on the far hill were working, he told them, confidingly. He was in fact secretly impressed that so late on a biting day, the SS men and Ukrainians on the far slope were not letting the thought of supper and warm barracks slow the pace of operations.

Horst Pilarzik assured him that it was all closer to completion than it looked: the land had been terraced, the foundations dug despite the cold, and a great quantity of prefabricated sections carried up from the railway station. The *Herr Untersturmführer* would be able to consult with the entrepreneurs tomorrow – a meeting had been arranged for 10 A.M. But modern methods combined with a copious supply of labour meant that these places could be put up almost overnight, weather permitting.

Pilarzik seemed to believe that Goeth was in genuine danger of demoralisation. In fact Amon was exhilarated. From what he could see here, he could discern the final shape of the place. Nor was he worried about fences. The fences would be a mental comfort to the prisoners rather than an essential precaution. For after the established methodology of SS liquidation had been applied to the Podgórze ghetto, people would be grateful for the barracks of Płaszów. Even those with Aryan papers would come crawling in here, seeking an obscure berth high up in the green, hoarfrosted rooftrees. For most of them, the wire was needed only as a prop, so that they might reassure themselves that they were prisoners against their will.

The meeting with the local factory owners and *Treuhänders* took place in Julian Scherner's office in central Cracow early the following day. Amon Goeth arrived smiling fraternally and, in his freshly tailored *Waffen* SS uniform, designed precisely for his enormous frame, seemed to dominate the room. He was sure he could charm the independents, Bosch and Madritsch and Schindler, into transferring their Jewish labour behind camp wire. Besides that, an investigation of the skills available among the ghetto dwellers helped him to see that Płaszów could become quite a business. There were jewellers, upholsterers, tailors who could be used for special enterprises under the Commandant's direction, filling orders for the SS, the *Wehrmacht*, the wealthy German officialdom. There would be the clothing workshops of Madritsch, the enamel factory of Schindler, a proposed metal plant, a brush factory, a warehouse for recycling used, damaged, or stained *Wehrmacht* uniforms from the Russian Front, a further warehouse for recycling Jewish clothing from the ghettos and dispatching it for the use of bombed-out families at home. He knew from his experiences of the SS jewellery and fur warehouses of Lublin, having seen his superiors at work there and taken his proper cut, that from most of these prison enterprises he could expect a personal percentage. He had reached that happy point in his career at which duty and financial opportunity coincided. The convivial SS police chief, Julian Scherner, over dinner last night, had talked to Amon about what a great opportunity Płaszów would be for a young officer – for them both.

Scherner opened the meeting with the factory people. He spoke solemnly about the 'concentration of labour,' as if it were a great economic principle new-hatched by the SS bureaucracy. You'll have your labour on site, said Scherner. All factory maintenance will be undertaken at no cost to you, and there will be no rent. All the gentlemen were invited to inspect the workshop sites inside Płaszów that afternoon.

The new Commandant was introduced. He said how pleased he was to be associated with these businessmen whose valuable contributions to the war effort were already widely known.

Amon pointed out on a map of the camp area the section set aside for the factories. It was next to the men's camp; the women – he told them with an easy and quite charming smile – would have to walk a little farther, one or two hundred metres downhill, to reach the workshops. He assured the gentlemen that his main task was to oversee the smooth functioning of the camp and that he had no wish to interfere with their factory policies or to alter the managerial autonomy they enjoyed here in Cracow. His orders, as *Oberführer* Schemer could verify, forbade in so many words that sort of intrusion. But the *Oberführer* had been correct in pointing out the mutual advantages of moving an industry inside the camp perimeter. The factory owners did not have to pay for the premises, and he, the Commandant, did not have to provide a guard to march the prisoners to town and back. They could understand how the length of the journey and the hostility of the Poles to a column of Jews would erode the worth of the workers.

Throughout this speech, Commandant Goeth glanced frequently at Madritsch and Schindler, the two he particularly wished to win over. He knew he could already depend on Bosch's local knowledge and advice. But Herr Schindler, for example, had a munitions section, small and merely in the developmental stage as yet. It would, however, if transferred, give Płaszów a great respectability with the Armaments Inspectorate.

Herr Madritsch listened with a considered frown, and Herr Schindler watched the speaker with an acquiescent half-smile. Commandant Goeth could tell instinctively, even before he'd finished speaking, that Madritsch would be reasonable and move in, that Schindler would refuse. It was hard to judge by these separate decisions which one of the two felt more paternal toward his Jews – Madritsch, who wanted to be inside Płaszów with them, or Schindler, who wanted to have his with him in Emalia.

Oskar Schindler, wearing that same face of avid tolerance, went with the party to inspect the campsite. Płaszów had the form of a camp now – an improvement in the weather had permitted the assembly of barracks; a thawing of the ground permitted the digging of latrines and postholes. A Polish construction company had installed the miles of perimeter fence. Thick-legged watchtowers were going up along the skyline toward Cracow, and also at the mouth of the valley down toward Wieliczka Street, away at the far end of the camp, and up here on this eastern hill where the official party, in the shadow of the Austrian hill fort, watched the fast work of this new creation. Off to the right, Oskar noticed, women were hustling up muddy tracks in the direction of the railway, heavy sections of barracks tilted between them. Below, from the lowest point of the valley and all the way up the far side, the terraced barracks ran, assembled by male prisoners who raised and slotted and hammered with an energy which at this distance resembled willingness.

On the choicest, most level ground beneath the official party, a number of long wooden structures were available for industrial occupation. Cement floors could be poured should heavy machinery need to be installed. The transfer of all plant machinery would be handled by the SS. The road that serviced the area was admittedly little more than a country track, but the engineering firm of Klug had been approached to build a central street for the camp, and the *Ostbahn* had promised to provide a spur to the camp gate itself, to the quarry down there on the right. Limestone from the quarries and some of what Goeth called 'Polish-defaced' gravestones from over in the cemetery would be broken up to provide other interior roads. The gentlemen should not worry about roads, said Goeth, for he intended to maintain a permanently strong quarrying and road-building team.

A small railroad had been laid for the rock trolleys. It ran from the quarry up past the Administration Building and the large stone barracks that were being built for the SS and Ukrainian garrison. Trolleys of limestone, each weighing six tons, were hauled by teams of women, thirty-five or forty of them to a team, dragging on cables set either side of the rock truck, to compensate for the unevenness in the rail line. Those who tripped or stumbled were trampled or else rolled out of the way, for the teams had their own organic momentum and no individual could abdicate from it. Watching this insidious Egyptian-looking industry, Oskar felt the same surge of nausea, the same prickling of the blood he had experienced on the hill above Krakusa Street. Goeth had assumed the businessmen were a safe audience, that they were all spiritual kinfolk of his. He was not embarrassed by that savage hauling down there. The question arose, as it had in Krakusa Street: What *could* embarrass the SS? What could embarrass Amon?

The energy of the barracks builders had, even to an informed observer like Oskar, the specious appearance of men working hard to put up shelter for their women. But though Oskar had not yet heard the rumor of it, Amon had performed a summary execution in front of those men this morning, so that now they knew what the full terms of their labour were. After the early-morning meeting with the engineers, Amon had been strolling down Jerozolimska and had come to the SS barracks where the work was under the supervision of an excellent NCO, soon to be promoted to officer rank, named Albert Hujar. Hujar had marched up and made his report. A section of the foundations of the barracks had collapsed, said Hujar, his face flushed. At the same time, Amon had noticed a girl walking around the half-finished building, speaking to teams of men, pointing, directing. Who was that? he asked Hujar. She was a prisoner named Diana Reiter, said Hujar, an architectural engineer who had been assigned to the construction of the barracks. She was claiming that the foundations hadn't been correctly excavated, and she wanted all the stone and cement dug up and the work on that section of the building to begin again from scratch.

Goeth had been able to tell from the colour of Hujar's face that he had had a tough argument with the woman. Hujar had, in fact, been reduced to screaming at her, 'You're building barracks, not the frigging Hotel Europa!'

Now Amon half-smiled at Hujar. We're not going to have arguments with these people, he said, as if it were a promise. Bring me the girl.

Amon could tell, from the way she walked toward him, the bogus elegance with which her middle-class parents had raised her, the European manners they had imbued her with, sending her – when the honest Poles wouldn't take her in their universities – off to Vienna or Milan to give her a profession and a heightened protective colouration. She walked toward him as if his rank and hers would bind them in the battle against oafish NCOs and the inferior craft of whichever SS engineer had supervised the digging of the foundations. She did not know that he hated her the worst – the type who thought, even against the evidence of his SS uniform, of these rising structures, that their Jewishness was not visible.

'You've had occasion to quarrel with *Oberscharführer* Hujar,' Goeth told her as a fact. She nodded firmly. The Herr Commandant would understand, the nod suggested, even though that idiot Hujar couldn't. The entire foundations at that end must be redug, she told him energetically. Of course, Amon knew 'they' were like that, they liked to string out tasks and so ensure that the labour force was safe for the duration of the project. If everything is not redug, she told him, there will be at least subsidence at the southern end of the barracks. There could be collapse.

She went on arguing the case, and Amon nodded and presumed she must be lying. It was a first principle that you never listened to a Jewish specialist. Jewish specialists were in the mould of Marx, whose theories were aimed at the integrity of government, and of Freud, who had assaulted the integrity of the Aryan mind. Amon felt that this girl's argument threatened his personal integrity.

He called Hujar. The NCO returned uneasily. He thought he was going to be told to take the girl's advice. The girl did too. Shoot her, Amon told Hujar. There was, of course, a pause while Hujar digested the order. Shoot her, Amon repeated.

Hujar took the girl's elbow to lead her away to some place of private execution.

Here! said Amon. Shoot her here! On my authority, said Amon.

Hujar knew how it was done. He gripped her by the elbow, pushed her a little to his front, took the Mauser from his holster, and shot her in the back of the neck.

The sound appalled everyone on the work site, except – it seemed – the executioners and the dying Miss Diana Reiter herself. She knelt and looked up once. *It will take more than that*, she was saying. The knowingness in her eyes frightened Amon, justified him, elevated him. He had no idea and would not have believed that these reactions had clinical labels. He believed, in fact, that he was being awarded the inevitable exaltation that follows an act of political, racial, and moral justice. Even so, a man paid for that, for by evening the fullness of this hour would be followed by such emptiness that he would need, to avoid being blown away like a husk, to augment his size and permanence by food, liquor, contact with a woman.

Apart from these considerations, the shooting of this Diana Reiter, the cancelling of her Western European diploma, had this practical value: that no erector of huts or roads in Płaszów would consider himself essential to the task – that if Miss Diana Reiter could not save herself with all her professional skill, the only chance of the others was prompt and anonymous labour. Therefore the women lugging frames up from the Cracow-Płaszów railway station, the quarry teams, the men assembling the huts all worked with an energy appropriate to what they'd learned from Miss Reiter's assassination.

As for Hujar and his colleagues, they knew now that instantaneous execution was to be the permitted style of Płaszów.

20

Two days after the visit of the factory heads to Płaszów, Schindler turned up at Commandant Goeth's temporary office in the city, bringing with him the compliments of a bottle of brandy. The news of Diana Reiter's assassination had by this time reached the front office of Emalia and was the sort of item that confirmed Oskar in his intention to keep his factory outside Płaszów.

The two big men sat opposite each other and there was a mutual knowingness in them too, just as there had been in the brief relationship between Amon and Miss Reiter. What they knew was that each of them was in Cracow to make a fortune; that therefore Oskar would pay for favours. At that level Oskar and the Commandant understood each other well. Oskar had the characteristic salesman's gift of treating men he abhorred as if they were spiritual brothers, and it would deceive the Herr Commandant so completely that Amon would always believe Oskar a friend.

But from the evidence of Stern and others it is obvious that, from the time of their earlier contacts, Oskar abominated Goeth as a man who went to the work of murder as calmly as a clerk goes to his office. Oskar could speak to Amon the administrator, Amon the speculator, but knew at the same time that nine-tenths of the Commandant's being lay beyond the normal rational processes of humans. The business and social connections between Oskar and Amon worked well enough to tempt the supposition that Oskar was somehow and despite himself fascinated by the evil of the man. In fact, no one who knew Oskar at this time or later saw a sign of any such enthrallment. Oskar despised Goeth in the simplest and most passionate terms. His contempt would grow without limit, and his career would dramatically demonstrate it. Just the same, the reflection can hardly be avoided that Amon was Oskar's dark brother, was the berserk and fanatic executioner Oskar might, by some unhappy reversal of his appetites, have become.

With a bottle of brandy between them, Oskar explained to Amon why it was impossible for him to move into Płaszów. His plant was too substantial to be shifted. He believed his friend Madritsch intended to move his Jewish workers in, but Madritsch's machinery was more easily transferred – it was basically a series of sewing machines. There were different problems involved in moving heavy metal presses, each of which, as a sophisticated machine will, had developed special quirks. His skilled workers had become accustomed to these quirks. But on a new factory floor the machines would display an entirely new set of eccentricities. There'd be delays; the settling-in period would take longer than it would for his esteemed friend Julius Madritsch. The *Untersturmführer* would understand that with important war contracts to fulfill, DEF could not spare such a lapse of time. Herr Beckmann, who had the same sort of problem, was firing all his Jews over at the Corona works. He didn't want the fuss of the Jews marching out from Płaszów to the factory in the morning and back in the evenings. Unfortunately, he, Schindler, had hundreds more *skilled* Jewish workers than Beckmann did. If he got rid of them, Poles would have to be trained in their place and there would again be a production delay, an even greater one than if he accepted Goeth's attractive offer and moved into Płaszów.

Amon secretly thought that Oskar might be worried that a move into Płaszów would impinge on any sweetly running little deals he had going in Cracow. The Commandant therefore hurried to reassure Herr Schindler that there'd be no interference in the management of the enamel factory.

'It's purely the industrial problems that worry me,' said Schindler piously. He didn't want to inconvenience the Commandant, but he would be grateful, and he was sure the Armaments Inspectorate would also be grateful, if DEF were permitted to stay in its present location.

Among men like Goeth and Oskar, the word 'gratitude' did not have an abstract meaning. Gratitude was a payoff. Gratitude was liquor and diamonds. I understand your problems, Herr Schindler, said Amon. I shall be happy, once the ghetto is liquidated, to provide a guard to escort your workers from Płaszów to Zablocie.

Itzhak Stern, coming to Zablocie one afternoon on business for the Progress factory, found Oskar depressed and sensed in him a dangerous feeling of impotence. After Klonowska had brought in the coffee, which the *Herr Direktor* drank as always with a shot of cognac, Oskar told Stern that he'd been to Płaszów again: ostensibly to look at the facilities; in fact to gauge when it would be ready for the *Ghettomenschen*. 'I took a count,' said Oskar. He'd counted the terraced barracks on the far hill and found that if Amon intended to cram 200 women into each, as was likely, there was now room for some 6,000 women up there in the top compound. The men's sector down the hill did not have so many finished buildings, but at the rate things were done in Płaszów it could be finished in days.

Everyone on the factory floor knows what's going to happen, said Oskar. And it's no use keeping the night shift on the premises here, because after this one, there'll be no ghetto to go back to. All I can tell them, said Oskar, taking a second slug of cognac, is that they shouldn't try to hide unless they're sure of the hiding place. He'd heard that the pattern was to tear the ghetto apart after it had been cleared. Every wall cavity would be probed, every attic carpet taken up, every niche revealed, every cellar plumbed. All I can tell them, said Oskar, is not to resist.

So it happened oddly that Stern, one of the targets of the coming *Aktion*, sat comforting *Herr Direktor* Schindler, a mere witness. Oskar's attention to his Jewish labourers was being diffused, tempted away by the wider tragedy of the ghetto's coming end. Płaszów was a labour institution, said Stern. Like all institutions, it could be outlived. It wasn't like Bełżec, where they made death in the same manner in which Henry Ford made cars. It was degrading to have to line up for Płaszów on orders, but it wasn't the end of things. When Stern had finished arguing, Oskar put both thumbs under the bevelled top of his desk and seemed for a few seconds to want to tear it off. You know, Stern, he said, that that's damn well not good enough!

It is, said Stern. It's the only course. And he went on arguing, quoting and hairsplitting, and was himself frightened. For Oskar seemed to be in crisis. If Oskar lost hope, Stern knew, all the Jewish workers of Emalia would be fired, for Oskar would wish to be purified of the entire dirty business.

There'll be time to do something more positive, said Stern. But not yet.

Abandoning the attempt to tear the lid from his desk, Oskar sat back in his chair and resumed his depression. 'You know that Amon Goeth,' he said. 'He's got charm. He could come in here now and charm you. But he's a lunatic.'

On the ghetto's last morning – a *Shabbat*, as it happened, March 13 – Amon Goeth arrived in Plac Zgody, Peace Square, at an hour which officially preceded dawn. Low clouds obscured any sharp distinctions between night and day. He saw that the men of the *Sonderkommando* had already arrived and stood about on the frozen earth of the small park in the middle, smoking and laughing quietly, keeping their presence a secret from the ghetto dwellers in the streets beyond Herr Pankiewicz' pharmacy. The roads down which they'd move were clear, as in a model of a town. The remaining snow lay heaped and tarnished in gutters and against walls. It is safe to guess that sentimental Goeth felt paternal as he looked out at the orderly scene and saw the young men, comradely before action, in the middle of the square.

Amon took a pull of cognac while he waited there for the middle-aged *Sturmbannführer* Willi Haase, who would have strategic, though not tactical, control of today's *Aktion*. Today Ghetto

A, from Plac Zgody westward, the major section of the ghetto, the one where all the working (healthy, hoping, opinionated) Jews dwelt, would be emptied. Ghetto B, a small compound a few blocks square at the eastern end of the ghetto, contained the old, the last of the unemployable. They would be uprooted overnight, or tomorrow. They were slated for Commandant Rudolf Höss's greatly expanded extermination camp at Auschwitz. Ghetto B was straightforward, honest work. Ghetto A was the challenge.

Everyone wanted to be here today, for today was history. There had been for more than seven centuries a Jewish Cracow, and by this evening – or at least by tomorrow – those seven centuries would have become a rumor, and Cracow would be *judenrein* (clean of Jews). And every petty SS official wanted to be able to say that he had seen it happen. Even Unkelbach, the *Treuhänder* of the Progress cutlery factory, having some sort of reserve SS rank, would put on his NCO's uniform today and move through the ghetto with one of the squads. Therefore the distinguished Willi Haase, being of field rank and involved in the planning, had every right to be counted in.

Amon would be suffering his customary minor headache and be feeling a little drained from the feverish insomnia in which he'd spent the small hours. Now he was here, though, he felt a certain professional exhilaration. It was a great gift which the National Socialist Party had given to the men of the SS, that they could go into battle without physical risk, that they could achieve honour without the contingencies that plagued the whole business of being shot at. Psychological impunity had been harder to achieve. Every SS officer had friends who had committed suicide. SS training documents, written to combat these futile casualties, pointed out the simplemindedness of believing that because the Jew bore no visible weapons he was bereft of social, economic, or political arms. He was, in fact, armed to the teeth. Steel yourself, said the documents, for the Jewish child is a cultural time bomb, the Jewish woman a biology of treasons, the Jewish male a more incontrovertible enemy than any Russian could hope to be.

Amon Goeth was steeled. He knew he could not be touched, and the very thought of that gave him the same delicious excitement a long-distance runner might have before an event he feels sure about. Amon despised in a genial sort of way those officers who fastidiously left the act itself to their men and NCOs. He sensed that in some way that might be more dangerous than lending a hand yourself. He would show the way, as he had with Diana Reiter. He knew the euphoria that would build during the day, the gratification that would grow, along with a taste for liquor, as noon came and the pace picked up. Even under the low squalor of those clouds, he knew that this was one of the best days, that when he was old and the race extinct, the young would ask with wonder about days like this.

Less than a kilometre away, a doctor of the ghetto's convalescent hospital, Dr. H, sat among his last patients, in darkness, grateful that they were isolated like this on the hospital's top floor, high above the street, alone with their pain and fever.

For at street level everyone knew what had happened at the epidemic hospital near Plac Zgody. An SS detachment under *Oberscharführer* Albert Hujar had entered the hospital to close it down and had found Dr. Rosalia Blau standing among the beds of her scarlet fever and tuberculosis patients, who, she said, should not be moved. The whooping cough children she had sent home earlier. But the scarlet fever sufferers were too dangerous to move, both for their own sakes and for the community's, and the tuberculosis cases were simply too sick to walk out.

Since scarlet fever is an adolescent disease, many of Dr. Blau's patients were girls between the age of twelve and sixteen. Faced with Albert Hujar, Dr. Blau pointed, as warranty for her professional judgment, to these wide-eyed, feverish girls.

Hujar himself, acting on the mandate he'd received the week before from Amon Goeth, shot Dr. Blau in the head. The infectious patients, some trying to rise in their beds, some detached in their own delirium, were executed in a rage of automatic fire. When Hujar's squad had finished, a detail of ghetto men was sent up the stairs to deal with the dead, to pile the bloodied linen, and to wash down the walls.

The convalescent hospital was situated in what had been before the war a Polish police station. Throughout the life of the ghetto, its three floors had been cluttered with the sick. Its director was a respected physician named Dr. B. By the bleak morning of March 13, Doctors B and H had reduced its population to four, all of them immovable. One was a young workman with galloping consumption; the second, a talented musician with terminal kidney disease. It seemed important to Dr. H that they somehow be spared the final panic of a mad volley of fire. Even more so the blind man afflicted by a stroke, and the old gentleman whose earlier surgery for an intestinal tumor had left him weakened and burdened with a colostomy.

The medical staff here, Dr. H included, were of the highest calibre. From this ill-equipped ghetto hospital would derive the first Polish accounts of Weil's erythroblastic disease, a condition of the bone marrow, and of the Wolff-Parkinson-White syndrome. This morning, though, Dr. H was concerned with the question of cyanide.

With an eye to the option of suicide, H had acquired a supply of cyanic acid solution. He knew that other doctors had too. This past year depression had been endemic to the ghetto. It had infected Dr. H. He was young; he was formidably healthy. Yet history itself seemed to have gone malignant. To know he had access to cyanide had been a comfort for Dr. H on his worst days. By this late stage of the ghetto's history, it was the one pharmaceutical left to him and to the other doctors in quantity. There had rarely been any sulpha. Emetics, ether, and even aspirin were used up. Cyanide was the single sophisticated drug remaining.

This morning before five, Dr. H had been awakened in his room in Wit Stwosz Street by the noise of trucks pulling up beyond the wall. Looking down from his window, he saw the *Sonderkommandos* assembling by the river and knew that they had come to take some decisive action in the ghetto. He rushed to the hospital and found

Dr. B and the nursing staff already working there on the same premise, arranging for every patient who could move to be taken downstairs and brought home by relatives or friends. When all except the four had gone, Dr. B told the nurses to leave, and all of them obeyed except for one senior nurse. Now she and Doctors B and H remained with the last four patients in the nearly deserted hospital.

Doctors B and H did not speak much as they waited. They each had access to the cyanide, and soon H would be aware that Dr. B's mind was also sadly preoccupied with it. There was suicide, yes. But there was euthanasia as well. The concept terrified H. He had a sensitive face and a marked delicacy about the eyes. He suffered painfully from a set of ethics as intimate to him as the organs of his own body. He knew that a physician with common sense and a syringe and little else to guide him could add up like a shopping list the values of either course – to inject the cyanide, or to abandon the patients to the *Sonderkommando*. But H knew that these things were never a matter of calculating sums, that ethics was higher and more tortuous than algebra.

Sometimes Dr. B would go to the window, look out to see if the *Aktion* had begun in the streets, and turn back to H with a level, professional calm in his eyes. Dr. B, H could tell, was also running through the options, flicking the faces of the problem like the faces of riffled cards, then starting again. Suicide. Euthanasia. Hydrocyanic acid. One appealing concept: Stand and be found among the beds like Rosalia Blau. Another: Use the cyanide on oneself as well as on the sick. The second idea appealed to H, seeming not as passive as the first. As well as that, waking depressed these past three nights, he'd felt something like a physical desire for the fast poison, as if it were merely the drug or stiff drink that every victim needed to soften the final hour.

To a serious man like Dr. H, this allure was a compelling reason *not* to take the stuff. For him the precedents for suicide had been set in his scholarly childhood, when his father had read to him in Josephus the account of the Dead Sea Zealots' mass suicide on the eve of capture by the Romans. The principle was, death should not be entered like some snug harbour. It should be an unambiguous refusal to surrender. Principle is principle, of course, and terror on a grey morning is another thing. But H was a man of principle.

And he had a wife. He and his wife had another escape route, and he knew it. It led through the sewers near the corner of Piwna and Krakusa Streets. The sewers and a risky escape to the forest of Ojców. He feared that more than the easy oblivion of cyanide. If Blue Police or Germans stopped him, however, and dragged his trousers down, he would pass the test, thanks to Dr. Lachs. Lachs was a distinguished plastic surgeon who had taught a number of young Cracow Jews how to lengthen their foreskins bloodlessly by sleeping with a weight – a bottle containing a gradually increasing volume of water – attached to themselves. It was, said Lachs, a device that had been used by Jews in periods of Roman persecution, and the intensity of SS action in Cracow had caused Lachs to revive its use in the past eighteen months. Lachs had taught his young colleague Dr. H the method, and the fact that it had worked with some success allowed H even less ground for suicide.

At dawn the nurse, a calm woman about forty years old, came to Dr. H and made a morning report. The young man was resting well, but the blind man with the stroke-affected speech was in a state of anxiety. The musician and the anal-fistula case had both had a painful night. It was all very quiet in the convalescent hospital now, however; the patients snuffled in the last of their sleep or the intimacy of their pain; and Dr. H went out onto the freezing balcony above the courtyard to smoke a cigarette and once more examine the question.

Last year Dr. H had been at the old epidemic hospital in Rekawka when the SS decided to close that section of the ghetto and relocate the hospital. They had lined the staff up against the wall and dragged the patients downstairs. H had seen old Mrs. Reisman's leg caught between the balusters, and an SS man hauling her by the other leg did not stop and extricate her but pulled until the trapped limb snapped with an audible crack. That was how patients were moved in the ghetto. But last year no one had thought of mercy-killing. Everyone had still hoped at that stage that things might improve.

Now, even if he and Dr. B made their decision, H didn't know if he had the rigour to feed the cyanide to the ill, or to watch someone else do it and maintain a professional dispassion. It was absurdly like the argument, in one's youth, about whether you should approach a girl you were infatuated with. And when you'd decided, it still counted for nothing. The act still had to be faced.

Out there on the balcony he heard the first noise. It began early and came from the eastern end of the ghetto. The *Raus, raus!* of megaphones, the customary lie about baggage which some people still chose to believe. In the deserted streets, and among the tenements in which no one moved, you could hear all the way from the cobblestones of Plac Zgody and up by the river in Nadwiślanska Street an indefinite terror-sick murmur which made H himself tremble.

Then he heard the first volley, loud enough to wake the patients. And a sudden stridency after the firing, a bull megaphone raging at some plangent feminine voice; and then the wailing snapped off by a further burst of fire, and a different wailing succeeding, the bereaved being hurried along by the SS bullhorns, by anxious OD men, and by neighbors, unreasonable grief fading into the far corner of the ghetto where there was a gate. He knew that it all might well have cut through even the precomatose state of the musician with the failed kidneys.

When he returned to the ward, he could see that they were watching him – even the musician. He could sense rather than see the way their bodies stiffened in their beds, and the old man with the colostomy cried out with the muscular exertion. 'Doctor, doctor!' someone said. 'Please!' answered Dr. H, by which he meant, *I'm here and they're a long way off yet.* He looked at Dr. B, who narrowed his eyes as the noise of evictions broke out again three blocks away. Dr. B nodded at him, walked to the small locked pharmaceutical chest at the end of the ward, and came back with the bottle of hydrocyanic acid. After a pause, H moved to his colleague's side. He could have stood and left it to Dr. B. He guessed that the man had the strength to do it alone, without the approval of colleagues. But it would be shameful, H thought, not to cast his own vote, not to take some of the burden. Dr. H, though younger than Dr. B, had been associated with the Jagiellonian University, was a specialist, a thinker. He wanted to give Dr. B the backing of all that.

'Well,' said Dr. B, displaying the bottle briefly to H. The word was nearly obscured by a woman's screaming and ranting official orders from the far end of Józefińska Street. Dr. B called the nurse. 'Give each patient forty drops in water.' 'Forty drops,' she repeated. She knew what the medication was. 'That's right,' said Dr. B. Dr. H also looked at her. Yes, he wanted to say. I'm strong now; I could give it myself. But if I did, it would alarm them. Every patient knows that nurses bring the medicine around.

As the nurse prepared the mixture, H wandered down the ward and laid his hand on the old man's. 'I have something to help you, Roman,' he told him. Dr. H sensed with amazement the old man's history through the touch of skin. For a second, like a surge of flame, the young man Roman was there, growing up in Franz Josef's Galicia, a lady-killer in the sweet little nougat of a city, the *petit* Wien, the jewel of the Vistula, Cracow. Wearing Franz Josef's uniform and going to the mountains for spring manoeuvres. Chocolate-soldiering in Rynek Glowny with the girls of Kazimierz, in a city of lace and patisseries. Climbing the Kosciuszko Mound and stealing a kiss among the shrubbery. How could the world have come so far in one manhood? asked the young man in old Roman. From Franz Josef to the NCO who had had a sanction to put Rosalia Blau and the scarlet fever girls to death?

'Please, Roman,' said the doctor, meaning that the old man should unclench his body. He believed the *Sonderkommando* was coming within the hour. Dr. H felt, but resisted, a temptation to let him in on the secret. Dr. B had been liberal with the dosage.

A few seconds of breathlessness and a minor amazement would be no new or intolerable sensation to old Roman.

When the nurse came with four medicine glasses, none of them even asked her what she was bringing them. Dr. H would never know if any of them understood. He turned away and looked at his watch. He feared that when they drank it, some noise would begin, something worse than the normal hospital gasps and gaggings. He heard the nurse murmuring, 'Here's something for you.' He heard an intake of breath. He didn't know if it was patient or nurse. *The woman is the hero of this*, he thought.

When he looked again, the nurse was waking the kidney patient, the sleepy musician, and offering him the glass. From the far end of the ward, Dr. B looked on in a clean white coat. Dr. H moved to old Roman and took his pulse. There was none. In a bed at the far end of the ward, the musician forced the almond-smelling mixture down.

It was all as gentle as H had hoped. He looked at them – their mouths agape, but not obscenely so, their eyes glazed and immune, their heads back, their chins pointed at the ceiling – with the envy any ghetto dweller would feel for escapees.

21

Poldek Pfefferberg shared a room on the second floor of a nineteenth-century house at the end of Józefińska Street. Its windows looked down over the ghetto wall at the Vistula, where Polish barges passed upstream and down in ignorance of the ghetto's last day and SS patrol boats puttered as casually as pleasure craft. Here Pfefferberg waited with his wife, Mila, for the *Sonderkommando* to arrive and order them out into the street. Mila was a small, nervous girl of twenty-two, a refugee from Łódź whom Poldek had married in the first days of the ghetto. She came from generations of physicians, her father having been a surgeon who had died young in 1937, her mother a dermatologist who, during an *Aktion* in the ghetto of Tarnow last year, had suffered the same death as Rosalia Blau of the epidemic hospital, being cut down by automatic fire while standing among her patients.

Mila had lived a sweet childhood, even in Jew-baiting Łódź, and had begun her own medical education in Vienna the year before the war. She had met Poldek when Łódź people were shipped down to Cracow in 1939. Mila had found herself billeted in the same apartment as the lively Poldek Pfefferberg.

Now he was already, like Mila, the last of his family. His mother, who had once redecorated Schindler's Straszewskiego Street apartment, had been shipped with his father to the ghetto of Tarnow. From there, it would be discovered in the end, they were taken to Bełżec and murdered. His sister and brother-in-law, on Aryan papers, had vanished in the Pawiak prison in Warsaw. He and Mila had only each other. There was a temperamental gulf between them: Poldek was a neighborhood boy, a leader, an organiser; the type who, when authority appeared and asked what in God's name was happening, would step forward and speak up. Mila was quieter, rendered more so by the unspeakable destiny that had swallowed her family. In a peaceable era, the mix between them would have been excellent. She was not only clever but wise; she was a quiet centre. She had a gift for irony, and Poldek Pfefferberg often needed her to restrain his torrents of oratory. Today, however, on this impossible day, they were in conflict.

Though Mila was willing, should the chance come, to leave the ghetto, even to entertain a mental image of herself and Poldek as partisans in the forest, she feared the sewers. Poldek had used them more than once as a means of leaving the ghetto, even though the police were sometimes to be found at one end or the other. His friend and former lecturer, Dr. H, had also mentioned the sewers recently as an escape route which might not be guarded on the day the *Sonderkommando* moved in. The thing would be to wait for the early winter dusk. The door of the doctor's house was mere metres from a manhole cover. Once down in there, you took the left-hand tunnel, which brought you beneath the streets of non-ghetto Podgórze to an outlet on the embankment of the Vistula near the Zatorska Street canal. Yesterday Dr. H had given him the definite news. The doctor and his wife would attempt the sewer exit, and the Pfefferbergs were welcome to join them. Poldek could not at that stage commit Mila and himself. Mila had a fear, a reasonable one, that the SS might flood the sewers with gas or might resolve the matter anyhow by arriving early at the Pfefferbergs' room at the far end of Józefińska Street.

It was a slow, tense day up in the attic room, waiting to find out which way to jump. Neighbors must also have been waiting. Perhaps some of them, not wanting to deal with the delay, had marched up the road already with their packages and hopeful suitcases, for in a way it was a mix of sounds fit to draw you down the stairs – violent noise dimly heard from blocks away, and here a silence in which you could hear the ancient, indifferent timbers of the house ticking away the last and worst hours of your tenancy. At murky noon Poldek and Mila chewed on their brown bread, the 300g each they had in stock. The recurrent noises of the *Aktion* swept up to the corner of Wegierska, a long block away, and then, toward midafternoon, receded again. There was near-silence then. Someone tried uselessly to flush the recalcitrant toilet on the first-floor landing. It was nearly possible at that hour to believe that they had been overlooked.

The last dun afternoon of their life in No. 2 Józefińska refused, in spite of its darkness, to end. The light, in fact, was poor enough, thought Poldek, for them to try for the sewer earlier than dusk. He wanted, now that it was quiet, to go and consult with Dr. H.

Please, said Mila. But he soothed her. He would keep off the streets, moving through the network of holes that connected one building with another. He piled up the reassurances. The streets at this end seemed to be clear of patrols. He would evade the occasional OD or wandering SS man at the intersections, and be back within five minutes. Darling, darling, he told her, I *have* to check with Dr. H.

He went down the back stairs and into the yard through the hole in the stable wall, not emerging into the open street until he'd reached the Labour Office. There he risked crossing the broad carriageway, entering the warrens of the triangular block of houses opposite, meeting occasional groups of confused men conveying rumors and discussing options in kitchens, sheds, yards, and corridors. He came out into Krakusa Street just across from the doctor's place. He crossed unnoticed by a patrol working down near the southern limit of the ghetto, three blocks away, in the area where Schindler had witnessed his first demonstration of the extremities of Reich racial policy.

Dr. H's building was empty, but in the yard Poldek met a dazed middle-aged man who told him that the *Sonderkommando* had already visited the place and that the doctor and his wife had first hidden, then gone for the sewers. Perhaps it's the right thing to do, said the man. They'll be back, the SS. Poldek nodded; he knew now the tactics of the *Aktion*, having already survived so many.

He went back the way he'd come and again was able to cross the road. But he found No. 2 empty, Mila vanished with their baggage, all doors opened, all rooms vacant. He wondered if in fact they were not all hidden down at the hospital – Dr. H and his wife; Mila. Perhaps the Hs had called for her out of respect for her anxiety and her long medical lineage.

Poldek hurried out through the stable again, and by alternative passageways reached the hospital courtyard. Like disregarded flags of surrender, bloodied bedding hung from the balconies of both the upper floors. On the cobblestones was a pile of victims. They lay, some of them, with their heads split open, their limbs twisted. They were not, of course, the terminal patients of Doctors B and H. They were people who had been detained here during the day and then executed. Some of them must have been imprisoned upstairs, shot, then tumbled into the yard.

Always thereafter, when questioned about the corpses in the ghetto hospital yard, Poldek would say 60 to 70, though he had no time to count that tangled pyramid. Cracow being a provincial town and Poldek having been raised as a very sociable child in Podgórze and then in the Centrum, visiting with his mother the affluent and distinguished people of the city, he recognised in that heap familiar faces: old clients of his mother's; people who had asked him about school at the Kosciuszko High School, got precocious answers in reply, and fed him cake and candy for his looks and charm. Now they were shamefully exposed and jumbled in that blood-red courtyard.

Somehow it did not occur to Pfefferberg to look for the bodies of his wife and the Hs. He sensed why he had been placed there. He believed unshakably in better years to come, years of just tribunals. He had that sense of being a witness which Schindler had experienced on the hill beyond Rekawka.

He was distracted by the sight of a crowd of people in Wegierska Street beyond the courtyard. They moved toward the Rekawka gate with the dull but not desperate languor of factory workers on a Monday morning, or even of supporters of a defeated football team. Among this wave of people he noticed neighbors from Józefińska Street. He walked out of the yard, carrying like a weapon up his sleeve his memory of it all. What had happened to Mila? Did any of them know? She'd already left, they said. The *Sonderkommando's* been through. She'd already be out the gate, on her way to the place. To Płaszów.

He and Mila, of course, had had a contingency plan for an impasse like this. If one of them ended up in Płaszów, it would be better for the other to attempt to stay out. He knew that Mila had her gift for unobtrusiveness, a good gift for prisoners; but also she could be racked by extraordinary hunger. He'd be her supplier from the outside. He was sure these things could be managed. It was no easy decision, though – the bemused crowds, barely guarded by the SS, now making for the south gate and the barbed-wire factories of Płaszów were an indication of where most people, probably quite correctly, considered that long-term safety lay.

The light, though late now, was sharp, as if snow were coming on. Poldek was able to cross the road and enter the empty apartments beyond the pavement. He wondered whether they were in fact empty or full of ghetto dwellers concealed cunningly or naively – those who believed that wherever the SS took you, it led in the end to the extermination chambers.

Poldek was looking for a first-class hiding place. He came by back passages to the lumberyard on Józefińska. Lumber was a scarce commodity. There were no great structures of cut timber to hide behind. The place that looked best was behind the iron gates at the yard entrance. Their size and blackness seemed a promise of the coming night. Later he would not be able to believe that he'd chosen them with such enthusiasm.

He hunched in behind the one that was pushed back against the wall of the abandoned office. Through the crack left between the gate and the gatepost, he could see up Józefińska in the direction he'd come from. Behind that freezing iron leaf he watched the slice of cold evening, a luminous grey, and pulled his coat across his chest. A man and his wife hurried past, rushing for the gate, dodging among the dropped bundles, the suitcases labelled with futile large letters. KLEINFELD, they proclaimed in the evening light. LEHRER, BAUME, WEINBERG, SMOLAR, STRUS, ROSENTHAL, BIRMAN, ZEITLIN. Names against which no receipts would be issued. 'Heaps of goods laden with memories,' the young artist Josef Bau had written of such scenes. 'Where are my treasures?'

From beyond this battleground of fallen luggage he could hear the aggressive baying of dogs. Then into Józefińska Street, striding on the far pavement, came three SS men, one of them dragged along by a canine flurry which proved to be two large police dogs. The dogs hauled their handler into No. 41 Józefińska, but the other two men waited on the pavement. Poldek had paid most of his attention to the dogs. They looked like a cross between Dalmatians and German shepherds. Pfefferberg still saw Cracow as a genial city, and dogs like that looked foreign, as if they'd been brought in from some other and harsher ghetto. For even in this last hour, among the litter of packages, behind an iron gate, he was grateful for the city and presumed that the ultimate frightfulness was always performed in some other, less gracious place. This last assumption was wiped away in the next half-minute. The worst thing, that is, occurred in Cracow. Through the crack of the gate, he saw the event which revealed that if there was a pole of evil it was not situated in Tarnow, Czestochowa, Lwów or Warsaw, as you thought. It was at the north side of Józefińska Street a hundred and twenty paces away. From 41 came a screaming woman and a child. One dog had the woman by the cloth of her dress, the flesh of her hip. The SS man who was the servant of the dogs took the child and flung it against the wall. The sound of it made Pfefferberg close his eyes, and he heard the shot which put an end to the woman's howling protest.

Just as Pfefferberg would think of the pile of bodies in the hospital yard as 60 or 70, he would always testify that the child was two or three years of age.

Perhaps before she was even dead, certainly before he himself even knew he had moved, as if the decision had came from some mettlesome gland behind his forehead, Pfefferberg gave up the freezing iron gate, since it would not protect him from the dogs, and found himself in the open yard. He adopted at once the military bearing he'd learned in the Polish Army. He emerged from the lumberyard like a man on a ceremonial assignment, and bent and began lifting the bundles of luggage out of the carriageway and heaping them against the walls of the yard. He could hear the three SS men approaching; the dogs' snarling breath was palpable, and the whole evening was stretched to breaking by the tension in their leashes. When he believed they were some ten paces off, he straightened and permitted himself, playing the biddable Jew of some European background, to notice them. He saw that their boots and riding breeches were splashed with blood, but they were not abashed to appear before other humans dressed that way. The officer in the middle was tallest. He did not look like a murderer; there was a sensitivity to the large face and a subtle line to the mouth.

Pfefferberg in his shabby suit clicked his cardboard heels in the Polish style and saluted this tall one in the middle. He had no knowledge of SS ranks and did not know what to call the man. 'Herr,' he said. 'Herr Commandant!'

It was a term his brain, under threat of its extinction, had thrown forth with electric energy. It proved to be the precise word, for the tall man was Amon Goeth in the full vitality of his afternoon, elated at the day's progress and as capable of instant and instinctive exercises of power as Poldek Pfefferberg was of instant and instinctive subterfuge.

'Herr Commandant, I respectfully report to you that I received an order to put all the bundles together to one side of the road so that there will be no obstruction of the thoroughfare.'

The dogs were craning toward him through their collars. They expected, on the basis of their black training and the rhythm of today's *Aktion*, to be let fly at Pfefferberg's wrist and groin. Their snarls were not simply feral, but full of a frightful confidence in the outcome, and the question was whether the SS man on the Herr Commandant's left had enough strength to restrain them. Pfefferberg didn't expect much. He would not be surprised to be buried by dogs and after a time to be delivered from their ravages by a bullet. If the woman hadn't got away with pleading her motherhood, he stood little chance with stories of bundles, of clearing a street in which human traffic had in any case been abolished.

But the Commandant was more amused by Pfefferberg than he had been by the mother. Here was a *Ghettomensch* playing soldier in front of three SS officers and making his report, servile if true, and almost endearing if not. His manner was, above all, a break in style for a victim. Of all today's doomed, not one other had tried heel-clicking. The Herr Commandant could therefore exercise the kingly right to show irrational and unexpected amusement. His head went back; his long upper lip retracted. It was a broad, honest laugh, and his colleagues smiled and shook their heads at its extent.

In his excellent baritone, *Untersturmführer* Goeth said, 'We're looking after everything. The last group is leaving the ghetto. *Verschwinde!*' That is, Disappear, little Polish clicking soldier!

Pfefferberg began to run, not looking back, and it would not have surprised him if he had been felled from behind. Running, he got to the corner of Wegierska and turned it, past the hospital yard where some hours ago he had been a witness. The dark came down as he neared the gate, and the ghetto's last familiar alleys faded. In Podgórze Square, the last official huddle of prisoners stood in a loose cordon of SS men and Ukrainians.

'I must be the last one out alive,' he told people in that crowd.

Or if not he it was Wulkan the jeweller and his wife and son. Wulkan had been working these past months in the Progress factory and, knowing what was to happen, had approached *Treuhänder* Unkelbach with a large diamond concealed for two years in the lining of a coat. 'Herr Unkelbach,' he told the supervisor, 'I'll go wherever I'm sent, but my wife isn't up to all that noise and violence.' Wulkan and his wife and son would wait at the OD police station under the protection of a Jewish policeman they knew, and then perhaps during the day Herr Unkelbach would come and convey them bloodlessly to Płaszów.

Since this morning they had sat in a cubicle in the police station, but it had been as frightful a wait as if they'd stayed in their kitchen, the boy alternately terrified and bored, and his wife continuing to hiss her reproaches. Where *is* he? Is he going to come at *all*? These people, these people! Early in the afternoon, Unkelbach did in fact appear, came into the *Ordnungsdienst* to use the lavatory and have coffee. Wulkan, emerging from the office in which he'd been waiting, saw a *Treuhänder* Unkelbach he had never known before: a man in the uniform of an SS NCO, smoking and exchanging animated conversation with another SS man; using one hand to take hungry mouthfuls of coffee, to bite off mouthfuls of smoke, to savage a lump of brown bread while his pistol, still held in the left hand, lay like a resting animal on the police-station counter and dark spatters of blood ran across the breast of his uniform. The eyes he turned to meet Wulkan's did not see the jeweller. Wulkan knew at once that Unkelbach was not backing out of the deal, he simply did not remember it. The man was drunk, and not on liquor. If Wulkan had called to him, the answer would have been a stare of ecstatic incomprehension. Followed, very likely, by something worse.

Wulkan gave it up and returned to his wife. She kept saying, 'Why don't you talk to him? I'll talk to him if he's still there.' But then she saw the shadow in Wulkan's eyes and sneaked a look around the edge of the door. Unkelbach was getting ready to leave. She saw the unaccustomed uniform, the blood of small traders and their wives splashed across its front. She uttered a whimper and returned to her seat.

Like her husband, she now fell into a well-founded despair, and the waiting became somehow easier. The OD man they knew restored them to the usual pulse of hope and anxiety. He told them that all the OD, apart from Spira's praetorians, had to be out of the ghetto by 6 P.M. and on the Wieliczka Road to Płaszów. He would see if there was a way of getting the Wulkans into one of the vehicles.

After dark had fallen in the wake of Pfefferberg's passage up Wegierska, after the last party of prisoners had assembled at the gate into Podgórze Square, while Dr. H and his wife were moving eastward in the company and under the cover of a group of rowdy Polish drunks, and while the squads of the *Sonderkommando* were resting and taking a smoke before the last search of the tenements, two horse-drawn wagons came to the door of the police station. The Wulkan family were hidden by the OD men under cartons of paperwork and bundles of clothing. Symche Spira and his associates were not in sight, were on the job somewhere in the streets, drinking coffee with NCOs, celebrating their permanence within the system.

But before the wagons had turned out of the ghetto gate, the Wulkans, flattened to the boards, heard the nearly continuous sound of rifle and small-arms fire from the streets behind them. It meant that Amon Goeth and Willi Haase, Albert Hujar, Horst Pilarzik, and some hundreds of others were bursting into the attic niches, the false ceilings, the crates in cellars, and finding those who all day had maintained a hopeful silence.

More than 4,000 such people were discovered overnight and executed in the streets. In the next two days their bodies were taken to Płaszów on open-platform trucks and buried in two mass graves in the woods beyond the new camp.

22

We do not know in What Condition of soul Oskar Schindler spent March 13, the ghetto's last and worst day. But by the time his workers returned to him under guard from Płaszów, he was back in the mood for collecting data to pass on to Dr. Sedlacek on the dentist's next visit. He found out from the prisoners that *Zwangsarbeitslager* Płaszów – as it was known in SS bureaucratese – was to be no rational kingdom. Goeth had already pursued his passion against engineers by letting the guards beat Zygmunt Grünberg into a coma and bring him so late to the clinic up near the women's camp that his death was assured. From the prisoners who ate their hearty noonday soup at DEF, Oskar heard also that Płaszów was being used not only as a work camp but as a place of execution as well. Though all the camp could hear the executions, some of the prisoners had been witnesses.

The prisoner M,† for example, who had had a prewar decorating business in Cracow. In the first days of the camp he was in demand to decorate the houses of the SS, the few small country villas that flanked the lane on the north side of the camp. Like any especially valued artisan he had more freedom of movement, and one afternoon that spring he had been walking from the villa of *Untersturmführer* Leo John up the track toward the hill called Chujowa Górka, on whose crest stood the Austrian fort. Before he was ready to turn back down the slope to the factory yard, he had to pause to let an Army truck grind past him uphill. M had noticed that beneath its canopy were women under the care of white-coveralled Ukrainian guards. He had hidden between stacks of

†Now living in Vienna, the man does not want his real name used.

lumber and got an incomplete view of the women, disembarked and marched inside the fort, refusing to undress. The man yelling the orders in there was the SS man Edmund Sdrojewski. Ukrainian NCOs marched among the women hitting them with whip handles. M presumed they were Jewish, probably women caught with Aryan papers, brought here from Montelupich prison. Some cried out at the blows, but others were silent, as if to refuse the Ukrainians that much satisfaction. One of them began to intone the *Shema Yisroel*, and the others took it up. The verses rose vigorously above the mound, as if it had just occurred to the girls – who till yesterday had played straight Aryans – that now the pressure was off, they were freer than anyone to celebrate their tribal difference in the faces of Sdrojewski and the Ukrainians. Then, huddling for modesty and the bite of the spring air, they were all shot. At night the Ukrainians took them away in wheelbarrows and buried them in the woods on the far side of Chujowa Górka.

People in the camp below had also heard that first execution on the hill now profanely nicknamed 'Prick Hill.' Some told themselves that it was partisans being shot up there, intractable Marxists or crazy nationalists. It was another country up there. If you obeyed the ordinances within the wire, you need never visit it. But the more clearheaded of Schindler's workers, marched up Wieliczka Street past the cable factory and over to Zablocie to work at DEF – *they* knew why prisoners from Montelupich were being shot at the Austrian hill fort, why the SS did not seem alarmed if the truckloads were seen arriving or the noise was heard throughout Płaszów. The reason was that the SS did not look on the prison population as ultimate witnesses. If there had been concern about a time in court, a mass of future testimony, they would have taken the women deeper into the woods. The conclusion to be drawn, Oskar decided, was not that Chujowa Górka was a separate world from Płaszów, but that all of them, those brought to the mound fort by truck and those behind the wire down the hill, were under sentence.

*

The first morning Commandant Goeth stepped out his front door and murdered a prisoner at random, there was a tendency to see *this* also, like the first execution on Chujowa Górka, as a unique event, discrete from what would become the customary life of the camp. In fact, of course, the killings on the hill would soon prove to be habitual, and so would Amon's morning routine.

Wearing a shirt and riding breeches and boots on which his orderly had put a high shine, he would emerge on the steps of his temporary villa. (They were renovating a better place for him down at the other end of the camp perimeter.) As the season wore on he would appear without his shirt, for he loved the sun. But for the moment he stood in the clothes in which he had eaten breakfast, a pair of binoculars in one hand and a sniper's rifle in the other. He would scan the camp area, the work at the quarry, the prisoners pushing or hauling the quarry trucks on the rails which passed by his door. Those glancing up could see the smoke from the cigarette which he held clamped between his lips, the way a man smokes without hands when he is too busy to put down the tools of his trade. Within the first few days of the camp's life he appeared thus at his front door and shot a prisoner who did not seem to be pushing hard enough at a cart loaded with limestone. No one knew Amon's precise reason for settling on that prisoner – Amon certainly did not have to document his motives. With one blast from the doorstep, the man was plucked from the group of pushing and pulling captives and hurled sideways in the road. The others stopped pushing, of course, their muscles frozen in expectation of a general slaughter. But Amon waved them on, frowning, as if to say that he was pleased for the moment with the standard of work he was getting from them.

Apart from such excesses with prisoners, Amon was also breaking one of the promises he'd made to the entrepreneurs. Oskar got a telephone call from Madritsch – Madritsch wanted them both to complain. Amon had said he would not interfere in the business of the factories. At least, he was not interfering from within. But he held up shifts by detaining the prison population for hours on the *Appellplatz* (parade ground) at roll call. Madritsch mentioned a case in which a potato had been found in a given hut, and therefore every prisoner from that barracks had to be publicly flogged in front of the thousands of inmates. It is no fast matter to have a few hundred people drag their pants and underwear down, their shirts or dresses up, and treat each of them to twenty-five lashes. It was Goeth's rule that the flogged prisoner call out the numbers for the guidance of the Ukrainian orderlies who did the flogging. If the victim lost track of the count, it was to begin again. Commandant Goeth's roll calls on the *Appellplatz* were full of just such time-consuming trickery.

Therefore shifts would arrive hours late at the Madritsch clothing factory inside the Płaszów camp, and an hour later still at Oskar's place in Lipowa Street. They would arrive shocked, too, unable to concentrate, muttering stories of what Amon or John or Scheidt or some other officer had done that morning. Oskar complained to an engineer he knew at the Armaments Inspectorate. It's no use complaining to the police chiefs, said the engineer. They're not involved in the same war we are. What I ought to do, said Oskar, is keep the people on the premises. Make my own camp.

The idea amused the engineer. Where would you put them, old man? he asked. You don't have much room.

If I can acquire the space, said Oskar, would you write a supporting letter?

When the engineer agreed, Oskar called an elderly couple named Bielski who lived in Stradom Street. He wondered if they would consider an offer for the land abutting his factory. He drove across the river to see them. They were delighted by his manner. Because he had always been bored by the rituals of haggling, he began by offering them a boom-time price. They gave him tea and, in a state of high excitement, called their lawyer to draw up the papers while Oskar was still on the premises. From their apartment, Oskar drove out, as a courtesy, and told Amon that he intended to make a subcamp of Płaszów in his own factory yard. Amon was quite taken with the idea. 'If the SS generals approve,' he said, 'you can expect my cooperation. As long as you don't want my musicians or my maid.'

The next day a full-scale appointment was arranged with *Oberführer* Schemer at Pomorska Street. Somehow both Amon and General Schemer knew that Oskar could be made to foot the whole bill for a new camp. They could detect that when Oskar pushed the industrial argument – 'I want my workers on the premises so that their labour can be more fully exploited' – he was at the same time pushing some other intimate craze of his in which expense was no question. They thought of him as a good enough fellow who'd been stricken with a form of Jew-love as with a virus. It was a corollary to SS theory that the Jewish genius so pervaded the world, could achieve such magical effects, that Herr Oskar Schindler was to be pitied as much as was a prince turned into a frog. But he would have to pay for his disease.

The requirements of *Obergruppenführer* Friedrich-Wilhelm Krüger, police chief of the Government General and superior of Schemer and Czurda, were based on the regulations set down by the Concentration Camp Section of General Oswald Pohl's SS Main Administrative and Economic Office, even though as yet Płaszów was run independently of Pohl's bureau. The basic stipulations for an SS Forced Labour Subcamp involved the erection of fences nine feet tall, of watchtowers at given intervals according to the length of the camp perimeter, of latrines, barracks, a clinic, a dental office, a bathhouse and delousing complex, a barbershop, a food store, a laundry, a barracks office, a guard block of somewhat better construction than the barracks themselves, and all the accessories. What had occurred to Amon, Schemer, and Czurda was that Oskar, as was only proper, would meet the expenses either out of economic motives or because of the cabalistic enchantment he lay under.

And even though they would make Oskar pay, his proposal suited them. There was still a ghetto in Tarnow, forty-five miles east, and when it was abolished the population would need to be absorbed into Płaszów. Likewise the thousands of Jews now arriving at Płaszów from the *shtetls* of southern Poland. A subcamp in Lipowa Street would ease that pressure.

Amon also understood, though he would never say it aloud to the police chiefs, that there would be no need to supply a Lipowa Street camp too precisely with the minimum food requirements as laid down in General Pohl's directive. Amon – who could hurl thunderbolts from his doorstep without meeting protest, who believed in any case in the official idea that a certain attrition should take place in Płaszów – was already selling a percentage of the prison rations on the open market in Cracow through an agent of his, a Jew named Wilek Chilowicz, who had contacts with factory managements, merchants, and even restaurants in Cracow.

Dr. Alexander Biberstein, now a Płaszów prisoner himself, found that the daily ration varied between 700 and 1,100 calories. At breakfast a prisoner received a half-litre of black *ersatz* coffee, tasting of acorns, and a lump of rye bread weighing 175g, an eighth of one of the round loaves collected by barracks mess orderlies each morning at the bakery. Hunger being such a disruptive force, each mess orderly cut up the loaf with his back to the others and called, 'Who wants this piece? Who wants this one?' At midday a soup was distributed – carrots, beets, sago substitute. Some days it had a fuller body than on others. Better food came in with the work parties who returned each evening. A small chicken could be carried under a coat, a French roll down a trouser leg. Yet Amon tried to prevent this by having the guards search returning details at dusk in front of the Administration Building. He did not want the work of natural wastage to be frustrated, nor the ideological wind to be taken out of his food dealings through Chilowicz. Since, therefore, he did not indulge his own prisoners, he felt that if Oskar chose to take a thousand Jews, he could indulge them at his own expense, without too regular a supply of bread and beets from the storerooms of Płaszów.

That spring, it was not only the police chiefs of the Cracow region whom Oskar had to talk to. He went into his backyard, persuading the neighbors. Beyond the two shabby huts constructed of Jereth's pineboard, he came to the radiator factory run by Kurt Hoderman. It employed a horde of Poles and about 100 Płaszów inmates. In the other direction was Jereth's box factory, supervised by the German engineer Kuhnpast. Since the Płaszów people were such a small part of their staff, they didn't take to the idea with any passion, but they weren't against it. For Oskar was offering to house their Jews 50 metres from work instead of 5 kilometres.

Next Oskar moved out into the neighborhood to talk to engineer Schmilewski at the *Wehrmacht* garrison office a few streets away. He employed a squad of Płaszów prisoners. Schmilewski had no objections. His name, with Kuhnpast's and Hoderman's, was appended to the application Schindler sent off to Pomorska Street.

SS surveyors visited Emalia and conferred with surveyor Steinhauser, an old friend of Oskar's from the Armaments Inspectorate. They stood and frowned at the site, as surveyors will, and asked questions about drainage. Oskar had them all into his office upstairs for a morning coffee and a cognac, and then everyone parted amiably. Within a few days the application to establish a Forced Labour Subcamp in the factory backyard was accepted.

That year DEF would enjoy a profit of 15.8 million Reichsmarks. It might be thought that the 300,000 RM. Oskar now spent on building materials for the Emalia camp was a large but not fatal overhead. The truth was though that he was only beginning to pay.

Oskar sent a plea to the *Bauleitung*, or Construction Office, of Płaszów for the help of a young engineer named Adam Garde. Garde was still working on the barracks of Amon's camp and, after leaving instructions for the barracks builders, would be marched under individual guard from Płaszów to Lipowa Street to supervise the setting up of Oskar's compound. When Garde first turned up in Zablocie, he found two rudimentary huts already occupied by close to 400 prisoners. There was a fence patrolled by an SS squad, but the inmates told Garde that Oskar did not let the SS into the encampment or onto the factory floor, except, of course, when senior inspectors came to look over the place. Oskar, they said, kept the small SS garrison of the Emalia factory well liquored and happy with their lot. Garde could see that the Emalia prisoners themselves were content between the shrinking fragile boards of their two huts, the men's and the women's. Already they called themselves *Schindlerjuden*, using the term in a mood of cautious self-congratulation, the way a man recovering from a heart attack might describe himself as a lucky beggar.

They'd already dug some primitive latrines, which engineer Garde, much as he approved the impulse behind the work, could smell from the factory entrance. They washed at a pump in the DEF yard.

Oskar asked him to come up to the office and look at the plans. Six barracks for up to 1,200 people. The cookhouse at this end, the SS barracks – Oskar was temporarily accommodating the SS in a part of the factory – beyond the wire at the far end. I want a really first-rate shower block and laundry, Oskar told him. I have the welders who can put it together under your direction. Typhus, he growled, half-smiling at Garde. None of us wants typhus. The lice are already biting in Płaszów. We need to be able to boil clothes.

Adam Garde was delighted to go to Lipowa Street each day. Two engineers had already been punished at Płaszów for their diplomas, but at DEF experts were still experts. One morning, as his guard was marching him up Wieliczka Street toward Zablocie, a black limousine materialised, braking hard at their heels. From it emerged *Untersturmführer* Goeth. He had that restless look about him.

One prisoner, one guard, he observed. What does it mean? The Ukrainian begged to inform the Herr Commandant that he had orders to escort this prisoner each morning to Herr Oskar

Schindler's Emalia. They both hoped, Garde and the Ukrainian, that the mention of Oskar's name would give them immunity. One guard, one prisoner? asked the Commandant again, but he was appeased and got back into his limousine without resolving the matter in any radical way. Later in the day he approached Wilek Chilowicz, who besides being his agent was also chief of the Jewish camp police – or 'firemen,' as they were called. Symche Spira, recently the Napoleon of the ghetto, still lived there and spent each day supervising the searching out and the digging up of the diamonds, gold, and cash hidden away and unrecorded by people who were now ashes on the pine needles of Bełżec. In Płaszów, however, Spira had no power, the centre of prison power being Chilowicz. No one knew where Chilowicz' authority came from. Perhaps Willi Kunde had mentioned his name to Amon; perhaps Amon had recognised and liked his style. But all at once, here he was chief of firemen in Płaszów, hander-out of the caps and armbands of authority in that debased kingdom and, like Symche, limited enough in imagination to equate his power with that of tsars.

Goeth approached Chilowicz and said that he had better send Adam Garde to Schindler full-time and get it over with. We have engineers to burn, said Goeth with distaste. He meant that engineering had been a soft option for Jews who weren't allowed into the medical faculties of the Polish universities. First, though, said Amon, before he goes to Emalia, he has to finish the work on my conservatory.

This news came to Adam Garde in his barracks, at his place in the four-tiered bunks of Hut 21. He would be delivered to Zablocie at the end of a trial. He would be building at Goeth's back door, where, as Reiter and Grünberg might have told him, the rules were unpredictable.

In the midst of his work for the Commandant, a large beam was lifted to its place in the rooftree of Amon's conservatory. As he worked, Adam Garde could hear the Commandant's two dogs, named Rolf and Ralf, names from a newspaper cartoon – except that Amon had permitted them in the past week to rip the breast from a female prisoner suspected of idling. Amon himself, with his half-completed technical education, would return again and again to take a professional stance and watch the roof beams lifted by pulley. He came to ask questions when the centre beam was being slotted into place. It was an immense length of heavy pine, and across it Goeth called his question. Adam Garde could not catch the meaning and put his hand to his ear. Again Goeth asked it, and worse than not hearing it, Garde could not understand it. 'I don't understand, Herr Commandant,' he admitted. Amon grabbed the rising beam with both long-fingered hands, dragged back the end of it, and swung it toward the engineer. Garde saw the massive timber spinning toward his head and understood that it was a mortal instrument. He lifted his right hand and the beam took it, shattering the knuckles and the metacarpals and hurling him to the ground. When Garde could see again through the fog of pain and nausea, Amon had turned and walked away. Perhaps he would come again tomorrow for a *satisfactory* answer . . . .

Lest he be seen as deformed and unfit, engineer Garde avoided favouring his shattered hand on the way to the *Krankenstube* (infirmary). Carried normally, it weighed at his side, a bladder of torment. He let Dr. Hilfstein talk him into accepting a plaster cast. So he continued to supervise the construction of the conservatory and each day marched to the Emalia works, hoping that the long sleeve of his coat helped conceal the cast. When he was unsure about this, he cut his hand free of the thing. Let the hand mend crookedly. He wanted to ensure his transfer to Schindler's subcamp by presenting an unmaimed appearance.

Within a week, carrying a shirt and some books in a bundle, he was marched to Lipowa Street for good.

23

Among prisoners who knew, there was already competition to get into Emalia. Prisoner Dolek Horowitz, a purchasing officer inside the Płaszów camp, knew that he would not be allowed to go to Schindler's place himself. But he had a wife and two children.

Richard, the younger of the children, woke up early these spring mornings as the earth gave off its last winter humour in mist, got down from his mother's bunk in the women's quarters, and ran down the hillside to the men's camp, his mind on the coarse morning bread. He had to be with his father for morning roll call on the *Appellplatz*. His path took him past Chilowicz' Jewish Police post and, even on foggy mornings, within sight of two watchtowers. But he was safe because he was known. He was a Horowitz child. His father was considered invaluable by Herr Bosch, who in turn was a drinking companion of the Commandant's. Richard's unselfconscious freedom of movement derived from his father's expertise; he moved charmed under the eyes in the towers, finding his father's barracks and climbing to his cot and waking him with questions. Why is there mist in the mornings and not in the afternoons? Will there be trucks? Will it take long on the *Appellplatz* today? Will there be floggings?

Through Richard's morning questions, Dolek Horowitz had it borne in on him that Płaszów was unfit even for privileged children. Perhaps he could contact Schindler – Schindler came out here now and then and walked around the Administration Building and the workshops, under the guise of doing business, to leave small gifts and exchange news with old friends like Stern and Roman Ginter and Poldek Pfefferberg. When Dolek did not seem to be able to make contact this way, it struck him that perhaps

Schindler could be approached through Bosch. Dolek believed they met a lot. Not out here so much, but perhaps in offices in town and at parties. You could tell they were not friends, but were bound together by dealings, by mutual favours.

It was not only, and perhaps not mainly, Richard whom Dolek wanted to get into Schindler's compound. Richard could diffuse his terror in clouds of questions. It was his ten-year-old daughter, Niusia, who no longer asked questions; who was just another thin child past the age of frankness; who – from a window in the brushworks shop where she sewed the bristles into the wooden backs – saw the daily truckloads arriving at the Austrian hill fort and carried her terror insupportably, the way adults will, unable to climb onto a parental chest and transfer the fear. To soothe her hunger in Płaszów, Niusia had taken to smoking onion leaves in newspaper wrappings. The solid rumors about Emalia were that such precocious methods weren't necessary there.

So Dolek appealed to Bosch during one of his tours of the clothing warehouse. He presumed on Bosch's earlier kindnesses, he said, to beg him to talk to Herr Schindler. He repeated his pleadings and repeated the children's names again, so that Bosch, whose memory was eroded by schnapps, might still remember. Herr Schindler is probably my best friend, said Bosch. He'd do anything for me.

Dolek expected little from the talk. His wife, Regina, had no experience of making shells or enamelware. Bosch himself never mentioned the request again. Yet within the week they marched out on the next Emalia list, cleared by Commandant Goeth in return for a little envelope of jewellery. Niusia looked like a thin, reserved adult in the women's barracks at Emalia, and Richard moved as he had in Płaszów, everyone knowing him in the munitions section and the enamel shops, the guards accepting his familiarity. Regina kept expecting Oskar to come up to her in the enamel factory and say, 'So you're Dolek Horowitz' wife?' Then the only question would be how to frame her thanks. But he never did. She was delighted to find that she was not very visible at

Lipowa Street, and neither was her daughter. They understood that Oskar knew who they were, since he often chatted with Richard by name. They knew, too, by the altered nature of Richard's questions, the extent of what they had been given.

The Emalia camp had no resident commandant to tyrannise the inmates. There were no permanent guards. The garrison was changed every two days, two truckloads of SS and Ukrainians coming up to Zablocie from Płaszów to take over the security of the subcamp. The Płaszów soldiers liked their occasional duty at Emalia. The *Herr Direktor*'s kitchens, more primitive even than Płaszów's, turned out better meals. Since the *Herr Direktor* started raging and making phone calls to *Oberführer* Schemer if any guard, instead of just patrolling the perimeter, entered the camp, the garrison kept to their side of the fence. Duty in Zablocie was pleasurably dull.

Except for inspection by senior SS men, the prisoners who worked at DEF rarely got a close view of their guards. One barbed-wire passageway took the inmates to their work in the enamel plant; another ran to the door of the munitions section. Those Emalia Jews who worked at the box factory, the radiator plant, the garrison office were marched to work and back by Ukrainians – different Ukrainians every second day. No guard had the time to develop a fatal grudge against a prisoner.

Therefore, though the SS may have set the limits to the life people led in Emalia, Oskar set its tone. The tone was one of fragile permanence. There were no dogs. There were no beatings. The soup and the bread were better and more plentiful than in Płaszów – about 2,000 calories a day, according to a doctor who worked in Emalia as a factory hand. The shifts were long, often twelve hours, for Oskar was still a businessman with war contracts to fill and a conventional desire for profit. It must be said, though, that no shift was arduous and that many of his prisoners seem to have believed at the time that their labour was making a contribution in measurable terms to their survival. According to accounts Oskar presented after the war to the Joint Distribution Committee, he spent 1,800,000 złoty ($360,000) on food for the Emalia camp. Cosmetic entries could be found, written off to similar expenditure, in the books of Farben and Krupp – though nowhere near as high a percentage of the profit as in Oskar's accounts. The truth is, though, that no one collapsed and died of overwork, beatings, or hunger in Emalia. Whereas at I. G. Farben's Buna plant alone, 25,000 prisoners out of a work force of 35,000 would perish at their labour.

Long afterward, Emalia people would call the Schindler camp a paradise. Since they were by then widely scattered, it cannot have been a description they decided on after the fact. The term must have had some currency while they were in Emalia. It was, of course, only a relative paradise, a heaven by contrast with Płaszów. What it inspired in its people was a sense of almost surreal deliverance, something preposterous which they didn't want to look at too closely for fear it would evaporate. New DEF hands knew of Oskar only by report. They did not want to put themselves in the *Herr Direktor*'s path or risk speaking to him. They needed time for recovery and for adjustment to Schindler's unorthodox prison system.

A girl named Lusia, for example. Her husband had recently been separated out from the mass of prisoners on the *Appellplatz* at Płaszów and shipped off with others to Mauthausen. With what would turn out to be mere realism, she grieved like a widow. Grieving, she'd been marched to Emalia. She worked at carrying dipped enamelware to the furnaces. You were permitted to heat up water on the warm surfaces of machinery, and the floor was warm. For her, hot water was Emalia's first beneficence.

She saw Oskar at first only as a large shape moving down an aisle of metal presses or traversing a catwalk. It was somehow not a threatening shape. She sensed that if she were noticed, the nature of the place – the lack of beatings, the food, the absence of guards in the camp – might somehow reverse itself. She wanted only unobtrusively to work her shift and return down the barbed-wire tunnel to her hut in the compound.

After a while she found herself giving an answering nod to Oskar and even telling him that, yes, thank you, *Herr Direktor*, she was quite well. Once he gave her some cigarettes, better than gold both as a comfort and as a means of trading with the Polish workers. Since she knew friends vanished, she feared his friendship; she wanted him to continue to be a presence, a magical parent. A paradise run by a friend was too fragile. To manage an enduring heaven, you needed someone both more authoritative and more mysterious than that.

Many of the Emalia prisoners felt the same.

There was a girl named Regina Perlman living, at the time Oskar's factory subcamp came into existence, in the city of Cracow on forged South American papers. Her dark complexion made the papers credible, and under them she worked as an Aryan in the office of a factory in Podgórze. She would have been safer from blackmailers if she'd gone to Warsaw, Łódź, or Gdansk. But her parents were in Płaszów, and she carried forged papers for their sakes too, so that she could supply them with food, comforts, medicine. She knew from the days in the ghetto that it was an adage in the Jewish mythology of Cracow that Herr Schindler could be expected to take extreme pains. She also knew the reports from Płaszów, from the quarry, the Commandant's balcony. She would have to break cover to do it, but she believed it essential that she get her parents into Schindler's backyard camp.

The first time she visited DEF she wore a safely anonymous faded floral dress and no stockings. The Polish gateman went through the business of calling Herr Schindler's office upstairs, and through the glass she could see him disapproving of her. It's nobody – some grubby girl from one of the other factories. She had the normal fear of people on Aryan papers that a hostile Pole would somehow spot her Jewishness. This one looked hostile.

It's of no great importance, she told him when he returned shaking his head. She wanted to put him off her track. But the Pole did not even bother to lie to her. 'He won't see you,' he said. The hood of a BMW glowered in the factory yard, she could see, and it could belong only to Herr Schindler. He was in, but not to visitors who couldn't afford stockings. She went away trembling at her escape. She'd been saved from making to Herr Schindler a confession which, even in her sleep, she feared making to anyone.

She waited a week before she could get more time off from the factory in Podgórze. She devoted an entire half-day to her approach. She bathed and got black-market stockings. From one of her few friends – a girl on Aryan papers could not risk having many – she borrowed a blouse. She had an excellent jacket of her own and bought a lacquered straw hat with a veil. She made up her face, achieving a dark radiance appropriate to a woman living beyond threat. In the mirror she looked like her prewar self, an elegant Cracovienne of exotic racial derivation – Hungarian businessman father, perhaps, and a mother from Rio.

This time, as she had intended, the Pole in the gatehouse did not even recognise her. He let her inside while he rang Miss Klonowska, the *Herr Direktor*'s secretary, and then was put on to speak to Schindler himself. *Herr Direktor*, said the Pole, there is a lady here to see you on important business. Herr Schindler seemed to want details. A very well-dressed young lady, said the Pole, and then, bowing while holding the telephone, a very beautiful young lady, he said. As if he had a hunger to see her, or perhaps as if she might be some forgotten girl who'd embarrass him in the outer office, Schindler met her on the steps. He smiled when he saw he did not know her. He was very pleased to meet her, this Fraulein Rodriguez. She could see that he had a respect for pretty women, that it was at the same time childlike and yet sophisticated. With flourishes like those of a matinee idol, he indicated she should follow him upstairs. She wanted to talk to him in confidence? Of course she should. He led her past Klonowska. Klonowska took it calmly. The girl could mean anything – black-market or currency business. She could even be a chic partisan. Love might be the least of motivations. In any case, a worldly girl like Klonowska didn't expect to own Oskar, or to be owned in return.

Inside the office, Schindler placed a chair for her and walked behind his desk beneath the ritual portrait of the *Führer*. Would she like a cigarette? Perhaps a Pernod or a cognac? No, she said, but he must, of course, feel free to take a drink. He poured himself one from his cocktail cabinet. What's this very important business? he asked, not quite with that crisp grace he'd shown on the stairs. For her manner had changed now the door to the outer office was closed. He could tell she'd come to do hard business. She leaned forward. For a second it seemed ridiculous for her, a girl whose father had paid 50,000 zł. for Aryan papers, to say it without a pause, to give it all away to a half-ironic, half-worried *Sudetendeutscher* with a snifter of cognac in his hand. Yet in some ways it was the easiest thing she'd ever done.

I have to tell you, Herr Schindler, I'm not a Polish Aryan. My real name is Perlman. My parents are in Płaszów. They say, and I believe it, that coming to Emalia is the same as being given a *Lebenskarte* – a card of life. I have nothing I can give you; I borrowed clothes to get inside your factory. Will you bring them here for me?

Schindler put down his drink and stood up. You want to make a secret arrangement? I don't make secret arrangements. What you suggest, Fraulein, is illegal. I have a factory here in Zablocie and the only question I ask is whether or not a person has certain skills. If you care to leave your Aryan name and address, it might be possible to write to you at some stage and inform you that I need your parents for their work skills. But not now, and not on any other ground.

But they can't come as skilled workers, said Fraulein Perlman. My father's an importer, not a metalworker.

We have an office staff, said Schindler. But mainly we need skills on the factory floor.

She was defeated. Half-blind with tears, she wrote her false name and real address – he could do with it whatever he wanted.

But on the street she understood and began to revive. Maybe Schindler thought she might be an agent, that she might have been there for entrapment. Just the same, he'd been cold. There hadn't even been an ambiguous, nonindictable gesture of kindness in the manner in which he'd thrown her out of his office.

Within a month Mr. and Mrs. Perlman came to Emalia from Płaszów. Not on their own, as Regina Perlman had imagined it would happen should Herr Oskar Schindler decide to be merciful, but as part of a new detail of 30 workers. Sometimes she would go around to Lipowa Street and bribe her way onto the factory floor to see them. Her father worked dipping the enamel, shovelling coal, clearing the floor of scrap. 'But he talks again,' said Mrs. Perlman to her daughter. For in Płaszów he'd gone silent.

In fact, despite the draughty huts, the plumbing, here at Emalia there was a certain mood, a fragile confidence, a presumption of permanence such as she, living on risky papers in sullen Cracow, could not hope to feel until the day the madness stopped.

Miss Perlman-Rodriguez did not complicate Herr Schindler's life by storming his office in gratitude or writing effusive letters. Yet she always left the yellow gate of DEF with an unquenchable envy for those who stayed inside.

Then there was a campaign to get Rabbi Menasha Levartov, masquerading as a metalworker in Płaszów, into Emalia. Levartov was a scholarly city rabbi, young and black-bearded. He was more liberal than the rabbis from the *shtetls* of Poland, the ones who believed the Sabbath was more important even than life and who, throughout 1942 and 1943, were shot by the hundreds every Friday evening for refusing work in the forced-labour cantonments of Poland. He was one of those men who, even in the years of peace, would have advised his congregation that while God may well be honoured by the inflexibility of the pious, he might also be honoured by the flexibility of the sensible.

Levartov had always been admired by Itzhak Stern, who worked in the Construction Office of Amon Goeth's Administration

Building. In the old days, Stern and Levartov would, if given the leisure, have sat together for hours over a glass of *herbata*, letting it grow cold while they talked about the influence of Zoroaster on Judaism, or the other way round, or the concept of the natural world in Taoism. Stern, when it came to comparative religion, got greater pleasure out of talking to Levartov than he could ever have received from bluff Oskar Schindler, who nonetheless had a fatal weakness for discoursing on the same subject.

During one of Oskar's visits to Płaszów, Stern told him that somehow Menasha Levartov had to be got into Emalia, or else Goeth would surely kill him. For Levartov had a sort of visibility – it was a matter of presence. Goeth was drawn to people of presence; they were, like idlers, another class with high target priority. Stern told Oskar how Goeth had attempted to murder Levartov.

Amon Goeth's camp now held more than 30,000 people. On the near side of the *Appellplatz*, near the Jewish mortuary chapel which had now become a stable, stood a Polish compound which could hold some 1,200 prisoners. *Obergruppenführer* Krüger was so pleased by his inspection of the new, booming camp that he now promoted the Commandant two SS grades to the rank of *Hauptsturmführer*.

As well as the crowd of Poles, Jews from the East and from Czechoslovakia would be held in Płaszów while space was made for them farther west in Auschwitz-Birkenau or Gröss-Rosen. Sometimes the population rose above 35,000 and the *Appellplatz* teemed at roll call. Amon therefore often had to cull his early comers to make way for new prisoners. And Oskar knew that the Commandant's quick method was to enter one of the camp offices or workshops, form up two lines, and march one of them away. The line marched away would be taken either to the Austrian hill fort, for execution by firing squads, or else to the cattle cars at the Cracow-Płaszów Station or, when it was laid down in the autumn of 1943, to the railway siding by the fortified SS barracks.

On just such a culling exercise, Stern told Oskar, Amon had entered the metalworks in the factory enclosure some days past. The supervisors had stood at attention like soldiers and made their eager reports, knowing that they could die for an unwise choice of words. 'I need twenty-five metalworkers,' Amon told the supervisors when the reports were finished. 'Twenty-five and no more. Point out to me the ones who are skilled.'

One of the supervisors pointed to Levartov and the rabbi joined the line, though he could see that Amon took a special note of his selection. Of course, one never knew which line would be moved out or where it would be moved to, but it was in most cases a safer bet to be on the line of the skilled.

So the selection continued. Levartov had noticed that the metal shops were strangely empty that morning, since a number of those who worked or filled in time by the door had got forewarning of Goeth's approach and had slipped over to the Madritsch garment factory to hide among the bolts of linen or appear to be mending sewing machines. The forty or so slow or inadvertent who had stayed on in the metalworks were now in two lines between the benches and the lathes. Everyone was fearful, but those in the smaller line were the more uneasy.

Then a boy of indeterminate age, perhaps as young as sixteen or as old as nineteen, had called from the midst of the shorter line, 'But, Herr Commandant, I'm a metal specialist too.'

'Yes, *Liebchen*?' murmured Amon, drawing his service revolver, stepping to the child and shooting him in the head. The enormous blast in this place of metal threw the boy against the wall. He was dead, the appalled Levartov believed, before he fell to the workshop floor.

The even shorter line was now marched out to the railroad depot, the boy's corpse was taken over the hill in a barrow, the floor was washed, the lathes returned to operation. But Levartov, making gate hinges slowly at his bench, was aware of the recognition that had flashed for an instant in Amon's eye – the look that had said, *There's one*. It seemed to the rabbi that the boy had, by crying out, only temporarily distracted Amon from Levartov himself, the more obvious target.

A few days had passed, Stern told Schindler, before Amon returned to the metalworks and found it crowded, and went around making his own selections for the hill or the transports. Then he'd halted by Levartov's bench, as Levartov had known he would. Levartov could smell Amon's after-shave lotion. He could see the starched cuff of Amon's shirt. Amon was a splendid dresser.

'What are you making?' asked the Commandant.

'Herr Commandant,' said Levartov, 'I am making hinges.' The rabbi pointed, in fact, to the small heap of hinges on the floor.

'Make me one now,' Amon ordered. He took a watch from his pocket and began timing. Levartov earnestly cut a hinge, his fingers urging the metal, pressuring the lathe; convinced labouring fingers, delighted to be skilled. Keeping tremulous count in his head, he turned out a hinge in what he believed was fifty-eight seconds, and let it fall at his feet.

'Another,' murmured Amon. After his speed trial, the rabbi was now more assured and worked confidently. In perhaps another minute the second hinge slid to his feet.

Amon considered the heap. 'You've been working here since six this morning,' said Amon, not raising his eyes from the floor. 'And you can work at a rate you've just shown me – and yet, such a tiny little pile of hinges?'

Levartov knew, of course, that he had crafted his own death. Amon walked him down the aisle, no one bothering or brave enough to look up from his bench. To see what? A death walk. Death walks were commonplace in Płaszów.

Outside, in the midday air of spring, Amon stood Menasha Levartov against the workshop wall, adjusting him by the shoulder, and took out the pistol with which he'd slaughtered the child two days before.

Levartov blinked and watched the other prisoners hurry by, wheeling and toting the raw materials of the Płaszów camp, eager to be out of range, the Cracovians among them thinking, *My*

God, it's Levartov's turn. Privately, he murmured the *Shema Yisroel* and heard the mechanisms of the pistol. But the small internal stirrings of metal ended not in a roar but in a click like that of a cigarette lighter which won't give a flame. And like a dissatisfied smoker, with just such a trivial level of annoyance, Amon Goeth extracted and replaced the magazine of bullets from the butt of the pistol, again took his aim, and fired. As the rabbi's head swayed to the normal human suspicion that the impact of the bullet could be absorbed as could a punch, all that emerged from Goeth's pistol was another click.

Goeth began cursing prosaically. '*Donnerwetter! Zum Teufel!*' It seemed to Levartov that at any second Amon would begin to run down faulty modern workmanship, as if they were two tradesmen trying to bring off some simple effect – the threading of a pipe, a drill hole in the wall. Amon put the faulty pistol away in its black holster and withdrew from a jacket pocket a pearl-handled revolver, of a type Rabbi Levartov had only read of in the Westerns of his boyhood. *Clearly,* he thought, *there are going to be no remissions due to technical failure. He'll keep on. I'll die by cowboy revolver, and even if all the firing pins are filed down,* Hauptsturmführer *Goeth will fall back on more primitive weapons.*

As Stern relayed it to Schindler, when Goeth aimed again and fired, Menasha Levartov had already begun to look about in case there was some object in the neighborhood that could be used, together with these two astounding failures of Goeth's service pistol, as a lever. By the corner of the wall stood a pile of coal, an unpromising item in itself. 'Herr Commandant,' Levartov began to say, but he could already hear the small murderous hammers and springs of the barroom pistol acting on each other. And again the click of a defective cigarette lighter. Amon, raging, seemed to be attempting to tear the barrel of the thing from its socket.

Now Rabbi Levartov adopted the stance he had seen the supervisors in the metalworks assume. 'Herr Commandant, I would beg to report that my heap of hinges was so unsatisfactory for the reason that the machines were being recalibrated this morning. And therefore instead of hinge-work I was put on to shovelling that coal.'

It seemed to Levartov that he had violated the rules of the game they had been playing together, the game that was to be closed by Levartov's reasonable death just as surely as Snakes and Ladders ends with the throwing of a six. It was as if the rabbi had hidden the dice and now there could be no conclusion. Amon hit him on the face with a free left hand, and Levartov tasted blood in his mouth, lying on the tongue like a guarantee.

Hauptsturmführer Goeth then simply abandoned Levartov against the wall. The contest, however, as both Levartov and Stern could tell, had merely been suspended.

Stern whispered this narrative to Oskar in the Building Office of Płaszów. Stern, stooping, eyes raised, hands joined, was as generous with detail as ever. 'It's no problem,' Oskar murmured. He liked to tease Stern. 'Why the long story? There's always room at Emalia for someone who can turn out a hinge in less than a minute.'

When Levartov and his wife came to the Emalia factory subcamp in the summer of '43, he had to suffer what at first he believed to be Schindler's little religious witticisms. On Friday afternoons, in the munitions hall of DEF where Levartov operated a lathe, Schindler would say, 'You shouldn't be here, Rabbi. You should be preparing for *Shabbat*.' But when Oskar slipped him a bottle of wine for use in the ceremonies, Levartov knew that the *Herr Direktor* was not joking. Before dusk on Fridays, the rabbi would be dismissed from his workbench and would go to his barracks behind the wire in the backyard of DEF. There, under the strings of sourly drying laundry, he would recite *Kiddush* over a cup of wine among the roof-high tiers of bunks. Under, of course, the shadow of an SS watchtower.

24

The Oskar Schindler who dismounted from his horse these days in the factory yard of Emalia was still the prototypical tycoon. He looked sleekly handsome in the style of the film stars George Sanders and Curt Jürgens, to both of whom people would always compare him. His hacking jacket and jodhpurs were tailored; his riding boots had a high shine. He looked like a man to whom it was profit all the way.

Yet he would return from his rural rides and go upstairs to face the sort of bills novel even to the history of an eccentric enterprise like DEF.

Bread shipments from the bakery at Płaszów to the factory camp in Lipowa Street, Zablocie, were a few hundred loaves delivered twice a week and an occasional token half-truckload of turnips. These few high-backed and lightly laden trucks were no doubt written large and multiplied in Commandant Goeth's books, and such trusties as Chilowicz sold off on behalf of the *Herr Hauptsturmführer* the difference between the mean supplies that arrived at Lipowa Street and the plenteous and phantom convoys that Goeth put down on paper. If Oskar had depended on Amon for prison food, his 900 internees would each have been fed perhaps three-quarters of a kilo of bread a week and soup every third day. On missions of his own and through his manager, Oskar was spending 50,000 zł. a month on black-market food for his camp kitchen. Some weeks he had to find more than three thousand round loaves. He went to town and spoke to the German supervisors in the big bakeries, and had in his briefcase Reichsmarks and two or three bottles.

Oskar did not seem to realise that throughout Poland that

summer of 1943, he was one of the champion illicit feeders of prisoners; that the malign pall of hunger which should by SS policy hang over the great death factories and over every one of the little, barbed-wired forced-labour slums was lacking in Lipowa Street in a way that was dangerously visible.

That summer a host of incidents occurred which augmented the Schindler mythology, the almost religious supposition among many prisoners of Płaszów and the entire population of Emalia that Oskar was a provider of outrageous salvation.

Early in the career of every subcamp, senior officers from the parent camp, or *Lager*, paid a visit to ensure that the energy of the slave labourers was stimulated in the most radical and exemplary manner. It is not certain exactly which members of Płaszów's senior staff visited Emalia, but some prisoners and Oskar himself would always say that Goeth was one of them. And if not Goeth it was Leo John, or Scheidt. Or else Josef Neuschel, Goeth's protégé. It is no injustice to mention any of their names in connection with 'stimulating energy in a radical and exemplary manner.' Whoever they were, they had already in the history of Płaszów taken or condoned fierce action. And now, visiting Emalia, they spotted in the yard a prisoner named Lamus pushing a barrow too slowly across the factory yard. Oskar himself later declared that it was Goeth who was there that day and saw Lamus' slow trundling and turned to a young NCO named Grün – Grün being another Goeth protégé, his bodyguard, a former wrestler. It was certainly Grün who was ordered to execute Lamus.

So Grün made the arrest, and the inspectors continued on into other parts of the factory camp. It was someone from the metal hall who rushed up to the *Herr Direktor*'s office and alerted Schindler. Oskar came roaring down the stairs even faster than on the day Miss Regina Perlman had visited, and reached the yard just as Grün was positioning Lamus against the wall.

Oskar called out, You can't do that here. I won't get work out of my people if you start shooting. I've got high-priority war contracts, et cetera. It was the standard Schindler argument and carried the suggestion that there were senior officers known to Oskar to whom Grün's name would be given if he impeded production in Emalia.

Grün was cunning. He knew the other inspectors had passed on to the workshops, where the whumping of metal presses and the roaring of lathes would cover any noise he chose, or failed, to make. Lamus was such a small concern to men like Goeth and John that no investigation would be made afterward. 'What's in it for me?' the SS man asked Oskar. 'Would vodka do?' said Oskar.

To Grün it was a substantial prize. For working all day behind the machine guns during *Aktions*, the massed and daily executions in the East – for shooting hundreds – you were given half a litre of vodka. The boys lined up to be on the squad so that they could take that prize of liquor back to their messes in the evening. And here the *Herr Direktor* offered him three times that for one act of omission.

'I don't see the bottle,' he said. Herr Schindler was already nudging Lamus away from the wall and pushing him out of range. 'Disappear!' Grün yelled at the wheelbarrow man. 'You may collect the bottle,' said Oskar, 'from my office at the end of the inspection.'

Oskar took part in a similar transaction when the Gestapo raided the apartment of a forger and discovered, among other false documents completed or near-completed, a set of Aryan papers for a family called the Wohlfeilers – mother, father, three adolescent children, all of them workers at Schindler's camp. Two Gestapo men therefore came to Lipowa Street to collect the family for an interrogation which would lead, through Montelupich prison, to Chujowa Górka. Three hours after entering Oskar's office both men left, reeling on the stairs, beaming with the temporary bonhomie of cognac and, for all anyone knew, of a payoff. The confiscated papers now lay on Oskar's desk, and he picked them up and put them in the fire.

Next, the brothers Danziger, who cracked a metal press one Friday. Honest, bemused men, semiskilled, looking up with staring *shtetl* eyes from the machine they had just loudly shattered. The *Herr Direktor* was away on business, and someone – a factory spy, Oskar would always say – denounced the Danzigers to the administration in Płaszów. The brothers were taken from Emalia and their hanging advertised at the next morning's roll call in Płaszów. *Tonight* (it was announced), *the people of Płaszów will witness the execution of two saboteurs.* What of course qualified the Danzigers above all for execution was their Orthodox aura.

Oskar returned from his business trip to Sosnowiec at three o'clock on Saturday afternoon, three hours before the promised execution. News of the sentence was waiting on his desk. He drove out through the suburbs to Płaszów at once, taking cognac with him and some fine *kielbasa* sausage. He parked by the Administration Building and found Goeth in his office. He was pleased not to have to rouse the Commandant from an afternoon nap. No one knows the extent of the deal that was struck in Goeth's office that afternoon, in that office akin to Torquemada's, where Goeth had had ringbolts attached to the wall from which to hang people for discipline or instruction. It is hard to believe, however, that Amon was satisfied simply with cognac and sausage. In any case, his concern for the integrity of the Reich's metal presses was soothed by the interview, and at six o'clock, the hour of their execution, the Danziger brothers returned in the back seat of Oskar's plush limousine to the sweet squalor of Emalia.

All these triumphs were, of course, partial. It is an aspect of Caesars, Oskar knew, to remit as irrationally as they condemn. Emil Krautwirt, by day an engineer in the radiator factory beyond the Emalia barracks, was an inmate of Oskar's SS subcamp. He was young, having got his diploma in the late Thirties. Krautwirt, like the others in Emalia, called the place Schindler's camp, but by taking Krautwirt away to Płaszów for an exemplary hanging, the SS demonstrated whose camp it really was, at least for some aspects of its existence.

For the fraction of Płaszów people who would live on into the peace, the hanging of engineer Krautwirt was the first story, other than their own intimate stories of pain and humiliation, which they would relate. The SS were ever economical with their scaffolds, and at Płaszów the gallows resembled a long, low set of goalposts, lacking the majesty of the gibbets of history, of the Revolutionary guillotine, the Elizabethan scaffold, the tall solemnity of jailhouse gallows in the sheriff's backyard. Seen in peacetime, the gallows of Płaszów and Auschwitz would intimidate not by their solemnity but by their ordinariness. But as mothers of children would discover in Płaszów, it was still possible, even with such a banal structure, for five-year-olds to see too much of an execution from within the mass of prisoners on the *Appellplatz*. With Krautwirt, a sixteen-year-old boy named Haubenstock was also to be hanged. Krautwirt had been condemned for some letters he had written to seditious persons in the city of Cracow. But with Haubenstock, it was that he had been heard singing 'Volga, Volga,' 'Kalinka Maya,' and other banned Russian songs with the intention, according to his death sentence, of winning the Ukrainian guards over to Bolshevism.

The rules for the rite of execution inside Płaszów involved silence. Unlike the festive hangings of earlier times, the drop was performed in utter stillness. The prisoners stood in phalanxes, and were patrolled by men and women who knew the extent of their power: by Hujar and John; by Scheidt and Grün; by the NCOs Landsdorfer, Amthor, and Grimm, Ritschek and Schreiber; and by the SS women supervisors recently assigned to Płaszów, both of them accomplished with the truncheon – Alice Orlowski and Luise Danz. Under such supervision, the pleadings of the condemned were heard in silence.

Engineer Krautwirt himself seemed at first stunned and had nothing to say, but the boy was vocal. In an uneven voice he reasoned with the *Hauptsturmführer*, who stood beside the scaffold. 'I am not a Communist, Herr Commandant. I hate Communism. They were just songs. Ordinary songs.' The hangman, a Jewish butcher of Cracow, pardoned for some earlier crime on condition that he undertake this work, stood Haubenstock on a stool and placed the noose around his neck. He could tell Amon wanted the boy hanged first, didn't want the debate to drag on. When the butcher kicked the support out from beneath Haubenstock, the rope broke, and the boy, purple and gagging, noose around his neck, crawled on his hands and knees to Goeth, continuing his pleadings, ramming his head against the Commandant's ankles and hugging his legs. It was the most extreme submission; it conferred on Goeth again the kingship he'd been exercising these fevered months past. Amon, in an *Appellplatz* of gaping mouths uttering no sound but a low hiss, a susurrus like a wind in sand dunes, took his pistol from his holster, kicked the boy away, and shot him through the head.

When poor engineer Krautwirt saw the horror of the boy's execution, he took a razor blade that he'd concealed in his pocket and slashed his wrists. Those prisoners at the front could tell that Krautwirt had injured himself fatally in both arms. But Goeth ordered the hangman to proceed in any case, and splashed with the gore from Krautwirt's injuries, two Ukrainians lifted him to the scaffold, where, gushing from both wrists, he strangled in front of the Jews of southern Poland.

It was natural to believe with one part of the mind that each such barbarous exhibition might be the last, that there might be a reversal of methods and attitudes even in Amon, or if not in him, then in those unseen officials who in some high office with French windows and waxed floors, overlooking a square where old women sold flowers, must formulate half of what happened in Płaszów and condone the rest.

On the second visit of Dr. Sedlacek from Budapest to Cracow, Oskar and the dentist devised a scheme which might to a more introverted man than Schindler have seemed naive. Oskar suggested to Sedlacek that perhaps one of the reasons Amon Goeth behaved so savagely was the bad liquor he drank, the gallons of local so-called cognac which weakened even further Amon's faulty sense of ultimate consequences. With a portion of the Reichsmarks Dr.

Sedlacek had just brought to Emalia and handed to Oskar, a crate of first-rate cognac should be bought – not such an easy or inexpensive item in post-Stalingrad Poland. Oskar should deliver it to Amon, and in the progress of conversation suggest to Goeth that one way or another the war would end at some time, and that there would be investigations into the actions of individuals. That perhaps even Amon's friends would remember the times he'd been too zealous.

It was Oskar's nature to believe that you could drink with the devil and adjust the balance of evil over a snifter of cognac. It was not that he found more radical methods frightening. It was that they did not occur to him. He'd always been a man of transactions.

Wachtmeister Oswald Bosko, who had earlier had control of the ghetto perimeter, was, in contrast, a man of ideas. It had become impossible for him to work within the SS scheme, passing a bribe here, a forged paper there, placing a dozen children under the patronage of his rank while a hundred more were marched out the ghetto gate. Bosko had absconded from his police station in Podgórze and vanished into the partisan forests of Niepolomice. In the People's Army he would try to expiate the callow enthusiasm he'd felt for Nazism in the summer of 1938. Dressed as a Polish farmer, he'd be recognised in the end in a village west of Cracow and shot for treason. Bosko would therefore become a martyr.

Bosko had gone to the forest because he had no other option. He lacked the financial resources with which Oskar greased the system. But it accorded with the natures of both men that one be found with nothing but a cast-off rank and uniform, that the other would make certain he had cash and trade goods. It is not to praise Bosko or denigrate Schindler that one says that if ever Oskar suffered martyrdom, it would be by accident, because some business he was transacting had turned sour on him. But there were people who still drew breath – the Wohlfeilers, the Danziger brothers, Lamus – because Oskar worked that way. Because Oskar worked that way, the unlikely camp of Emalia stood in Lipowa

Street, and there, on most days, a thousand were safe from seizure, and the SS stayed outside the wire. No one was beaten there, and the soup was thick enough to sustain life. In proportion to their natures, the moral disgust of both Party members, Bosko and Schindler, was equal, even if Bosko manifested his by leaving his empty uniform on a coat hanger in Podgórze, while Oskar put on his big Party pin and went to deliver high-class liquor to mad Amon Goeth in Płaszów.

It was late afternoon, and Oskar and Goeth sat in the salon of Goeth's white villa. Goeth's girlfriend Majola looked in, a small-boned woman, a secretary at the Wagner factory in town. She did not spend her days amid the excesses of Płaszów. She had sensitive manners, and this delicacy helped a rumor to emerge that Majola had threatened not to sleep with Goeth if he continued arbitrarily gunning people down. But no one knew whether that was the truth or just one of those therapeutic interpretations which arise in the minds of prisoners desperate to make the earth habitable.

Majola did not stay long with Amon and Oskar that afternoon. She could tell there would be a drinking session. Helen Hirsch, the pale girl in black who was Amon's maid, brought them the necessary accompaniments – cakes, canapés, sausage. She reeled with exhaustion. Last night Amon had beaten her for preparing food for Majola without his permission; this morning he had made her run up and down the villa's three flights of stairs fifty times on the double because of a flyspeck on one of the paintings in the corridor. She had heard certain rumors about Herr Schindler but had not met him until now. This afternoon she took no comfort from the sight of these two big men, seated either side of the low table, fraternal and in apparent concord. There was nothing here to interest her, for the certainty of her own death was a first premise. She thought only about the survival of her young sister, who worked in the camp's general kitchen. She kept a sum of money hidden in the hope that it would effect her sister's survival. There was no sum, she believed, no deal, that could influence her own prospects.

So they drank through the camp's twilight and into the dark. Long after the prisoner Tosia Lieberman's nightly rendition of Brahms's 'Lullaby' had calmed the women's camp and insinuated itself between the timbers of the men's, the two big men sat on. Their prodigious livers glowed hot as furnaces. And at the right hour, Oskar leaned across the table and, acting out of an amity which, even with this much cognac aboard, did not go beyond the surface of the skin . . . Oskar, leaning toward Amon and cunning as a demon, began to tempt him toward restraint.

Amon took it well. It seemed to Oskar that he was attracted by the thought of moderation – a temptation worthy of an emperor. Amon could imagine a sick slave on the trolleys, a returning prisoner from the cable factory, staggering – in that put-upon way one found so hard to tolerate – under a load of clothing or lumber picked up at the prison gate. And the fantasy ran with a strange warmth in Amon's belly that he would forgive that laggard, that pathetic actor. As Caligula might have been tempted to see himself as Caligula the Good, so the image of Amon the Good exercised the Commandant's imagination for a time. He would, in fact, always have a weakness for it. Tonight, his blood running golden with cognac and nearly all the camp asleep beyond his steps, Amon was more definitely seduced by mercy than by the fear of reprisal. But in the morning he would remember Oskar's warning and combine it with the day's news that Russian threats were developing on the Front at Kiev. Stalingrad had been an inconceivable distance from Płaszów. But the distance to Kiev was imaginable.

For some days after Oskar's bout with Amon, news came to Emalia that the dual temptation was having its result with the Commandant. Dr. Sedlacek, going back to Budapest, would report to Samu Springmann that Amon had given up, for the time being at least, arbitrarily murdering people. And gentle Samu, among the diverse cares he had in the list of places from Dachau and Drancy in the west to Sobibor and Bełżec in the east, hoped for a time that the hole at Płaszów had been plugged.

But the allure of clemency vanished quickly. If there was a brief respite, those who were to survive and give testimony of their days in Płaszów would not be aware of it. The summary assassinations would seem continual to them. If Amon did not appear on his balcony this morning or the next, it did not mean he would not appear the morning after that. It took much more than Goeth's temporary absence to give even the most deluded prisoner some hope of a fundamental change in the Commandant's nature. And then, in any case, there he would be, on the steps in the Austrian-style cap he wore to murders, looking through his binoculars for a culprit.

Dr. Sedlacek would return to Budapest not only with overly hopeful news of a reform in Amon but with more reliable data on the camp at Płaszów. One afternoon a guard from Emalia turned up at Płaszów to summon Stern to Zablocie. Once Stern arrived at the front gate, he was led upstairs into Oskar's new apartment. There Oskar introduced him to two men in good suits. One was Sedlacek; the other a Jew – equipped with a Swiss passport – who introduced himself as Babar. 'My dear friend,' Oskar told Stern, 'I want you to write as full a report on the situation in Płaszów as you can manage in an afternoon.' Stern had never seen Sedlacek or Babar before this and thought that Oskar was being indiscreet. He bent over his hands, murmuring that before he undertook a task like that he would like a word in private with the *Herr Direktor*.

Oskar used to say that Itzhak Stern could never make a straight statement or request unless it arrived smuggled under a baggage of talk of the Babylonian Talmud and purification rites. But now he was more direct. 'Tell me, please, Herr Schindler,' he asked, 'don't you believe this is a dreadful risk?'

Oskar exploded. Before he got control of himself, the strangers would have heard him in the other room. 'Do you think I'd ask you, if there was a risk?' Then he calmed and said, 'There's always risk, as you know better than I. But not with these two men. These two are safe.'

In the end, Stern spent all afternoon on his report. He was a scholar and accustomed to writing in exact prose. The rescue organisation in Budapest, the Zionists in Istanbul would receive from Stern a report they could rely on. Multiply Stern's summary by the 1,700 large and small forced-labour camps of Poland, and then you had a tapestry to stun the world!

Sedlacek and Oskar wanted more than that of Stern. On the morning after the Amon-Oskar binge, Oskar dragged his heroic liver back out to Płaszów before office-opening time. In between the suggestions of tolerance Oskar had tried to drop into Amon's ear the night before, he'd also got a written permit to take two 'brother industrialists' on a tour of this model industrial community. Oskar brought the two into the grey Administration Building that morning and demanded the services of *Häftling* (prisoner) Itzhak Stern for a tour of the camp. Sedlacek's friend Babar had some sort of miniature camera, but he carried it openly in his hand. It was almost possible to believe that if an SS man had challenged him, he would have welcomed the chance to stand and boast for five minutes about this little gadget he'd got on a recent business trip to Brussels or Stockholm.

As Oskar and the visitors from Budapest emerged from the Administration Building, Oskar took the thin, clerkly Stern by the shoulder. His friends would be happy to see the workshops and the living quarters, said Oskar. But if there was anything Stern thought they were missing out on, he was just to bend down and tie his shoestring.

On Goeth's great road paved with fractured gravestones, they moved past the SS barracks. Here, almost at once, prisoner Stern's shoestring needed tying. Sedlacek's associate snapped the teams hauling truckloads of rock up from the quarry, while Stern murmured, 'Forgive me, gentlemen.' Yet he took his time with the tying so that they could look down and read the monumental fragments. Here were the gravestones of Bluma Gemeinerowa (1859-1927); of Matylde Liebeskind, deceased at the age of 90 in 1912; of Helena Wachsberg, who died in childbirth in 1911; of

Rozia Groder, a thirteen-year-old who had passed on in 1931; of Sofia Rosner and Adolf Gottlieb, who had died in the reign of Franz Josef. Stern wanted them to see that the names of the honourable dead had been made into paving stones.

Moving on, they passed the *Puffhaus*, the SS and Ukrainian brothel staffed by Polish girls, before reaching the quarry, the excavations running back into the limestone cliff. Stern's shoelaces required reef knots here; he wanted this recorded. They destroyed men at this rock face, working them on the hammers and wedges. None of the scarred men of the quarry parties showed any curiosity about their visitors this morning. Ivan, Amon Goeth's Ukrainian driver, was on duty here, and the supervisor was a bullet-headed German criminal named Erik. Erik had already demonstrated a capacity for murdering families, having killed his own mother, father, sister. He might by now have been hanged or at least been put in a dungeon if the SS had not realised that there were worse criminals still than patricides and that Erik should be employed as a stick to beat them with. As Stern had mentioned in his report, a Cracow physician named Edward Goldblatt had been sent here from the clinic by SS Dr. Blancke and his Jewish protégé, Dr. Leon Gross. Erik loved to see a man of culture and speciality enter the quarry and report soft-handed for work, and the beatings began in Goldblatt's case with the first display of uncertainty in handling the hammer and spikes. Over a period of days, Erik and sundry SS and Ukrainian enlisted men beat Goldblatt. The doctor was forced to work with a ballooning face, now half again its normal size, with one eye sealed up. No one knew what error of quarry technique set Erik to give Dr. Goldblatt his final beating. Long after the doctor lost consciousness, Erik permitted him to be carried to the *Krankenstube*, where Dr. Leon Gross refused to admit him. With this medical sanction Erik and an SS enlisted man continued to kick the dying Goldblatt as he lay, rejected for treatment, on the threshold of the hospital.

Stern bent and tied his shoelace at the quarry because, like Oskar and some others in the Płaszów complex, he believed in a future of judges who might ask, Where – in a word – did this act occur?

Oskar was able to give his colleagues an overview of the camp, taking them up to Chujowa Górka and the Austrian mound, where the bloodied wheelbarrows used to transport the dead to the woods stood unabashedly at the mouth of the fort. Already thousands were buried down there in mass graves in or on the verges of those eastern pinewoods. When the Russians came from the east, that wood with its population of victims would fall to them before living and half-dying Płaszów.

As for Płaszów as an industrial wonder, it was bound to disappoint any serious observer. Amon, Bosch, Leo John, Josef Neuschel all thought it a model city on the ground that it was making them rich. It would have shocked them to find that one of the reasons their sweet billet in Płaszów continued was not any delight on the part of the Armaments Inspectorate with the economic miracles they were performing.

In fact the only economic miracles within Płaszów were the personal fortunes made by Amon and his clique. It was a surprise to any calm outsider that war contracts came to the workshops of Płaszów at all, considering that their plant was so poor and old-fashioned. But shrewd Zionist prisoners inside Płaszów put pressure on convinced outsiders, people like Oskar and Madritsch, who could in turn put pressure on the Armaments Inspectorate. On the ground that the hunger and sporadic murders of Płaszów were still to be preferred to the assured annihilations of Auschwitz and Bełżec, Oskar was willing to sit down with the purchasing officers and engineers of General Schindler's Arms Inspectorate. These gentlemen would make faces and say, 'Come on, Oskar! Are you serious?' But in the end they would find contracts for Amon Goeth's camp, orders for shovels manufactured from the collected scrap iron of Oskar's Lipowa Street factory, orders for funnels turned out of offcuts of tin from a jam factory in Podgórze. The chances of full delivery of the shovels and their handles ever being made to the *Wehrmacht* were small. Many of Oskar's friends among the officers of the Armaments Inspectorate understood what they were doing, that prolonging the life of the slave-labour camp of Płaszów was the same thing as prolonging the life of a number of the slaves. With some of them it stuck in the craw, because they knew what a crook Goeth was, and their serious and old-fashioned patriotism was affronted by Amon's sybaritic life out there in the countryside.

The divine irony of Forced Labour Camp Płaszów – that some of the slaves were conspiring for their own purposes to maintain Amon's kingdom – can be seen in the case of Roman Ginter. Ginter, former entrepreneur and now one of the supervisors in the metalworks from which Rabbi Levartov had already been rescued, was summoned to Goeth's office one morning and, as he closed the door, took the first of a number of blows. While he beat Ginter, Amon raged incoherently. Then he dragged him out-of-doors and down the steps to a stretch of wall by the front entrance. May I ask something? said Ginter against the wall, spitting out two teeth, offhandedly, lest Amon think him an actor, a self-pitier. You bastard, roared Goeth, you haven't delivered the handcuffs I ordered! My desk calendar tells me that, you pig's-ass. But Herr Commandant, said Ginter, I beg to report that the order for handcuffs was filled yesterday. I asked *Herr Oberscharführer* Neuschel what I should do with them and he told me to deliver them to your office, which I did.

Amon dragged bleeding Ginter back to the office and called the SS man Neuschel. Why, yes, said young Neuschel. Look in your second-top drawer on the left, Herr Commandant. Goeth looked and found the manacles. I almost killed him, he complained to his young and not-so-gifted Viennese protégé.

This same Roman Ginter, complaisantly spitting up his teeth against the foundation of Amon's grey Administration Building – this Jewish cipher whose accidental murder would have caused Amon to blame Neuschel – this Ginter is the man who under special pass goes to Herr Schindler's DEF to talk to Oskar about workshop supplies for Płaszów, about large scrap metal without which the whole metal-shop crew would be railroaded off to Auschwitz. Therefore, while the pistol-waving Amon Goeth believes he maintains Płaszów by his special administrative genius, it is as much the bloody-mouthed prisoners who keep it running.

25

To some people it now seemed that Oskar was spending like a compulsive gambler. Even from the little they knew of him, his prisoners could sense that he would ruin himself for them if that was the price. Later – not now, for now they accepted his mercies in the same spirit in which a child accepts Christmas presents from its parents – they would say, Thank God he was more faithful to us than to his wife. And like the prisoners, sundry officials could also ferret Oskar's passion out.

One such official, a Dr. Sopp, physician to the SS prisons in Cracow and to the SS Court‡ in Pomorska, let Herr Schindler know through a Polish messenger that he was willing to do a brand of business. In Montelupich prison was a woman named Frau Helene Schindler. Dr. Sopp knew she was no relative of Oskar's, but her husband had invested some money in Emalia. She had questionable Aryan papers. Dr. Sopp did not need to say that for Mrs. Schindler this portended a truck ride to Chujowa Górka. But if Oskar would put up certain amounts, said Sopp, the doctor was willing to issue a medical certificate saying that, in view of her condition, Mrs. Schindler should be permitted to take the cure indefinitely at Marienbad, down in Bohemia.

Oskar went to Sopp's office, where he found out that the doctor wanted 50,000 zł. for the certificate. It was no use arguing. After three years of practice, a man like Sopp could tell to within a few złoty the price to put on favours. During the afternoon, Oskar raised the money. Sopp knew he could, knew that Oskar was the

‡The SS had its own judiciary section.

sort of man who had black-market money stashed, money with no recorded history.

Before making the payment, Oskar set some conditions. He would need to go to Montelupich with Dr. Sopp to collect the woman from her cell. He would himself deliver her to mutual friends in the city. Sopp did not object. Under a bare light bulb in freezing Montelupich, Mrs. Schindler was handed her costly documents.

A more careful man, a man with an accountant's mind, might reasonably have repaid himself for his trouble from the money Sedlacek brought from Budapest. All together, Oskar would be handed nearly 150,000 Reichsmarks carried to Cracow in false-bottomed suitcases and in the lining of clothes. But Oskar, partly because his sense of money (whether owed or owing) was so inexact, partly because of his sense of honour, passed on to his Jewish contacts all the money he ever received from Sedlacek, except for the sum spent on Amon's cognac.

It was not always a straightforward business. When in the summer of '43 Sedlacek arrived in Cracow with 50,000 RM., the Zionists inside Płaszów to whom Oskar offered the cash feared it might be a setup.

Oskar first approached Henry Mandel, a welder in the Płaszów metal shop and a member of *Hitach Dut*, a Zionist youth and labour movement. Mandel did not want to touch the money. Look, said Schindler, I've got a letter in Hebrew to go with it, a letter from Palestine. But of course, if it was a setup, if Oskar had been compromised and was being used, he *would* have a letter from Palestine. And when you hadn't enough bread for breakfast, it was quite a sum to be offered: 50,000 RM. – 100,000 złoty. To be offered that for your discretionary use. It just wasn't credible.

Schindler then tried to pass the money, which was sitting there, inside the boundary of Płaszów in the trunk of his car, to another member of *Hitach Dut*, a woman named Alta Rubner. She had some contacts, through prisoners who went to work in the cable factory, through some of the Poles in the Polish prison, with the underground in Sosnowiec. Perhaps, she said to Mandel, it would be best to refer the whole business to the underground, and let them decide on the provenance of the money Herr Oskar Schindler was offering.

Oskar kept trying to persuade her, raising his voice at her under cover of Madritsch's chattering sewing machines. 'I guarantee with all my heart that this isn't a trap!' *With all my heart*. Exactly the sentiment one would expect from an *agent provocateur*!

Yet after Oskar had gone away and Mandel had spoken to Stern, who declared the letter authentic, and then conferred again with the girl, a decision was made to take the money. They knew now, however, that Oskar wouldn't be back with it. Mandel went to Marcel Goldberg at the Administration Office. Goldberg had also been a member of *Hitach Dut*, but after becoming the clerk in charge of lists – of labour lists and transport lists, of the lists of living and dead – he had begun taking bribes. Mandel could put pressure on him, though. One of the lists Goldberg could draw up – or at least, add to and subtract from – was the list of those who went to Emalia to collect scrap metal for use in the workshops of Płaszów. For old times' sake, and without having to disclose his reason for wanting to visit Emalia, Mandel was put on *this* list.

But arriving in Zablocie and sneaking away from the scrap-metal detail to get to Oskar, he'd been blocked in the front office by Bankier. Herr Schindler was too busy, said Bankier.

A week later Mandel was back. Again Bankier wouldn't let him in to speak to Oskar. The third time, Bankier was more specific. You want that Zionist money? You didn't want it before. And now you want it. Well, you can't have it. That's the way life goes, Mr. Mandel!

Mandel nodded and left. He presumed wrongly that Bankier had already lifted at least a segment of the cash. In fact, however, Bankier was being careful. The money did finish in the hands of Zionist prisoners in Płaszów, for Alta Rubner's receipt for the funds was delivered to Springmann by Sedlacek. It seems that the amount was used in part to help Jews who came from other cities than Cracow and therefore had no local sources of support.

Whether the funds that came to Oskar and were passed on by him were spent mainly on food, as Stern would have preferred, or largely on underground resistance – the purchase of passes or weapons – is a question Oskar never investigated. None of this money, however, went to buy Mrs. Schindler out of Montelupich prison or to save the lives of such people as the Danziger brothers. Nor was the Sedlacek money used to replace the 30,000-kilogram bribes of enamelware Oskar would pay out to major and minor SS officials during 1943 to prevent them from recommending the closure of the Emalia camp.

None of it was spent on the 16,000-zł. set of gynaecological instruments Oskar had to buy on the black market when one of the Emalia girls got pregnant – pregnancy being, of course, an immediate ticket to Auschwitz. Nor did any of it go to purchase the broken-down Mercedes from *Untersturmführer* John. John offered Oskar the Mercedes for sale at the same time as Oskar presented a request for 30 Płaszów people to be transferred to Emalia. The car, bought by Oskar one day for 12,000 zł., was requisitioned the next by Leo John's friend and brother officer, *Untersturmführer* Scheidt, to be used in the construction of fieldworks on the camp perimeter. Perhaps they'll carry soil in the trunk, Oskar raged to Ingrid at the supper table. In a later informal account of the incident, he commented that he was glad to be of assistance to both gentlemen.

26

Raimund Titsch was making payments of a different order. Titsch was a quiet, clerkly Austrian Catholic with a limp some said came from the first war and others from a childhood accident. He was ten years or more older than either Amon or Oskar. Inside the Płaszów camp, he managed Julius Madritsch's uniform factory, a business of 3,000 seamstresses and mechanics.

One way he paid was through his chess matches with Amon Goeth. The Administration Building was connected with the Madritsch works by telephone, and Amon would often call Titsch up to his office for a game. The first time Raimund had played Amon, the game had ended in half an hour and not in the *Hauptsturmführer's* favour. Titsch, with the restrained and not so very triumphal 'Mate!' dying on his lips, had been amazed at the tantrum Amon had thrown. The Commandant had grabbed for his coat and gun belt, buttoning and buckling them on, ramming his cap on his head. Raimund Titsch, appalled, believed that Amon was about to go down to the trolley line looking for a prisoner to chastise for his – for Raimund Titsch's – minor victory at chess. Since that first afternoon, Titsch had taken a new direction. Now he could take as long as three hours to lose to the Commandant. When workers in the Administration Building saw Titsch limping up Jerozolimska to do this chess duty, they knew the afternoon would be saner for it. A modest sense of security spread from them down to the workshops and even to the miserable trolley pushers.

But Raimund Titsch did not only play preventive chess. Independently of Dr. Sedlacek and of the man with the pocket camera whom Oskar had brought to Płaszów, Titsch had begun photographing. Sometimes from his office window, sometimes from the corners of workshops, he photographed the stripe-uniformed prisoners in the trolley line, the distribution of bread and soup, the digging of drains and foundations. Some of these photographs of Titsch's are probably of the illegal supply of bread to the Madritsch workshop. Certainly round brown loaves were bought by Raimund himself, with Julius Madritsch's consent and money, and delivered to Płaszów by truck beneath bales of rags and bolts of cloth. Titsch photographed round rye being hurried from hand to hand into Madritsch's storeroom, on the side away from the towers and screened from the main access road by the bulk of the camp stationery plant.

He photographed the SS and the Ukrainians marching, at play, at work. He photographed a work party under the supervision of engineer Karp, who was soon to be set on by the killer dogs, his thigh ripped open, his genitals torn off. In a long shot of Płaszów, he intimated the size of the camp, its desolation. It seems that on Amon's sun deck he even took close-ups of the Commandant at rest in a deck chair, a hefty Amon approaching now the 120 kg at which newly arrived SS Dr. Blancke would say to him, 'Enough, Amon; you have to take some weight off.' Titsch photographed Rolf and Ralf loping and sunning, and Majola holding one of the dogs by the collar and pretending to enjoy it. He also took Amon in full majesty on his big white horse.

As the reels were shot, Titsch did not have them developed. As an archive, they were safer and more portable in roll form. He hid them in a steel box in his Cracow apartment. There also he kept some of the remaining goods of the Madritsch Jews. Throughout Płaszów you found people who had a final treasure; something to offer – at the moment of greatest danger – to the man with the list, the man who opened and closed the doors on the cattle cars. Titsch understood that only the desperate deposited goods with him. That prison minority who had a stock of rings and watches and jewellery hidden somewhere in Płaszów didn't need him. *They* traded regularly for favours and comforts. But into the same hiding as Titsch's photographs went the final resources of a dozen families – Auntie Yanka's brooch, Uncle Mordche's watch.

In fact, when the Płaszów regimen passed, when Schemer and Czurda had fled, and when the impeccable files of the SS Main Economic and Administrative Office had been baled up in trucks and moved away as evidence, Titsch had no need to develop the photographs, and every reason not to. In the files of ODESSA, the postwar secret society of former SS men, he would be listed as a traitor. For the fact that he'd supplied the Madritsch people with some 30,000 loaves of bread, as well as many chickens and some kilos of butter, and that for his humanity he had been honoured by the Israeli Government, had received some publicity in the press. Some people made threats and hissed at him as he passed in the streets of Vienna. 'Jew-kisser.' So the Płaszów reels would lie for twenty years in the soil of a small park in the suburbs of Vienna where Titsch had buried them, and might well have stayed there forever, the emulsion drying on the dark and secret images of Amon's love Majola, his killing dogs, his nameless slave labourers. It might therefore have been seen as a sort of triumph for the population of Płaszów when, in November 1963, a Schindler survivor (Leopold Pfefferberg) secretly bought the box and its contents for $500 from Raimund Titsch, who was then suffering from terminal heart disease. Even then, Raimund didn't want the rolls developed until after his death. The nameless shadow of ODESSA frightened him more than had the names of Amon Goeth, of Scherner, of Auschwitz, in the days of Płaszów.

After his burial, the reels were developed. Nearly all the pictures came out.

Not one of that small body of Płaszów inmates who would survive Amon and the camp itself would ever have anything accusatory to say of Raimund Titsch. But he was never the sort of man concerning whom mythologies arose. Oskar was. From late 1943, there is a story about Schindler which runs among the survivors with the electric excitement of a myth. For the thing about a myth is not whether it is true or not, nor whether it *should* be true, but that it is somehow truer than truth itself. Through listening to such stories, one can see that to the Płaszów people, while Titsch may have been the good hermit, Oskar had become a minor god of deliverance, double-faced – in the Greek manner – as any small god; endowed with all the human vices; many-handed; subtly powerful; capable of bringing gratuitous but secure salvation.

One story concerns the time when the SS police chiefs were under pressure to close Płaszów, as its reputation as an efficient industrial complex was not high with the Armaments Inspectorate. Helen Hirsch, Goeth's maid, often encountered officers, dinner guests, who wandered into the hallway or kitchen of the villa to escape Amon for a while and to shake their heads. An SS officer named Tibritsch, turning up in the kitchen, had said to Helen, 'Doesn't he know there are men giving their lives?' He meant on the Eastern Front, of course, not out there in the dark of Płaszów. Officers with less imperial lives than Amon were becoming outraged by what they saw at the villa or, perhaps more dangerously, envious.

As the legend has it, it was on a Sunday evening that General Julius Schindler himself visited Płaszów to decide whether its existence was of any real value to the war effort. It was an odd hour for a grand bureaucrat to be visiting a plant, but perhaps the Armaments Inspectorate, in view of the perilous winter now falling on the Eastern Front, were working desperate hours. The inspection had been preceded by dinner at Emalia, at which wine and cognac flowed, for Oskar is associated like Bacchus with the Dionysian line of gods.

Because of the dinner, the inspection party rolling out to Płaszów in their Mercedeses were in a mood of less than professional detachment. In making this claim, the story ignores the fact that Schindler and his officers were all production experts and engineers with nearly four years of detachment behind them. But Oscar would be the last to be awed by that fact.

The inspection started at the Madritsch clothing factory. This was Płaszów's showplace. During 1943, it had produced *Wehrmacht* uniforms at a monthly rate of better than twenty thousand. But the question was whether Herr Madritsch would do better to forget Płaszów, to spend his capital on expanding his more efficient and better-supplied Polish factories in Podgórze and Tarnow. The ramshackle conditions of Płaszów were no encouragement to Madritsch or any other investor to install the sort of machinery a sophisticated factory would need.

The official party had just begun its inspection when all the lights in all the workshops went out, the power circuit broken by friends of Itzhak Stern's in the Płaszów generator shed. To the handicaps of drink and indigestion which Oskar had imposed on the gentlemen of the Armaments Inspectorate were now added the limitations of bad light. The inspection went ahead by flashlight, in fact, and the machinery on the benches remained inoperative and therefore less of a provocation to the inspectors' professional feelings.

As General Schindler squinted along the beam of a flashlight at the presses and lathes in the metalworks, 30,000 Płaszówians, restless in tiered bunks, waited on his word. Even on the overladen lines of the *Ostbahn*, they knew, the higher technology of Auschwitz was but a few hours' journey west. They understood that they could not expect from General Schindler compassion as such. *Production* was his specialty. For him, *Production* was meant to be an overriding value.

Because of Schindler's dinner and the power failure, says the myth, the people of Płaszów were saved. It is a generous fable, because in fact only a tenth of Płaszów people would be alive at the end. But Stern and others would later celebrate the story, and most of its details are probably true. For Oskar always had recourse to liquor when puzzled as to how to treat officials, and he would have liked the trickery of plunging them into darkness. 'You have to remember,' said a boy whom Oskar would later save, 'that Oskar had a German side but a Czech side too. He was the good soldier Schweik. He loved to foul up the system.'

It is ungracious to the myth to ask what the exacting Amon Goeth thought when the lights went out. Maybe, even on the level of literal event, he was drunk or dining elsewhere. The question is whether Płaszów survived because General Schindler was deceived by dim light and alcohol-dimmed vision, or whether it continued because it was such an excellent holding centre for those weeks when the great terminus at Auschwitz-Birkenau was overcrowded. But the story says more of people's expectations of Oskar than it does of the frightful compound of Płaszów or the final end of most of its inmates.

And while the SS and the Armaments Inspectorate considered the future of Płaszów, Josef Bau – a young artist from Cracow, whom Oskar would in the end come to know well – was falling into conspicuous and unconditional love with a girl named Rebecca Tannenbaum. Bau worked in the Construction Office as a draughtsman. He was a solemn boy with an artist's sense of destiny. He had, so to speak, *escaped* into Płaszów, because he had never held the correct ghetto papers. Since he had had no trade of use to the ghetto factories, he had been hidden by his mother and by friends. During the liquidation in March 1943, he'd escaped out of the walls and attached himself to the tail of a labour detail going to Płaszów. For in Płaszów there was a new industry which had had no place in the ghetto. Construction. In the same sombre two-winged building in which Amon had his office, Josef Bau worked on blueprints. He was a protégé of Itzhak Stern's, and Stern had mentioned him to Oskar as an accomplished draughtsman and as a boy who had, potentially at least, skills as a forger.

He was lucky not to come into too much contact with Amon, because he displayed the air of genuine sensibility which had, before today, caused Amon to reach for his revolver. Bau's office was on the far side of the building from Amon's. Some prisoners worked on the ground floor, with offices near the Commandant's. There were the purchasing officers; the clerks; Mietek Pemper, the stenographer. They faced not only a daily risk of an unexpected bullet but, more certainly than that, assaults on their sense of outrage. Mundek Korn, for example, who had been a buyer for a string of Rothschild subsidiaries before the war and who now bought the fabrics, sea grass, lumber, and iron for the prison workshops, had to work not only in the Administration Building but in the same wing where Amon had his office. One morning Korn looked up from his desk and saw through the window, across Jerozolimska Street and by the SS barracks, a boy of twenty or so years, a Cracovian of his acquaintance, urinating against the base of one of the stacks of lumber there. At the same time he saw white-shirted arms and two ham fists appear through the bathroom window at the end of the wing. The right hand held a revolver. There were two quick shots, at least one of which entered the boy's head and drove him forward against the pile of cut wood. When Korn looked once more at the bathroom window, one white-shirted arm and free hand were engaged in closing the window.

On Korn's desk that morning were requisition forms signed with Amon's open-vowelled but not deranged scrawl. His gaze ranged from the signature to the unbuttoned corpse at the box of lumber. Not only did he wonder if he had seen what he had seen. He sensed the seductive concept inherent in Amon's methods. That is, the temptation to agree that if murder was no more than a visit to the bathroom, a mere pulse in the monotony of form signing, then perhaps all death should now be accepted – with whatever despair – as routine.

It does not seem that Josef Bau was exposed to such radical persuasion. He missed too the purge of the administrative staff on the ground floor right and centre. It had begun when Josef Neuschel, Goeth's protégé, complained to the Commandant that a girl in the office had acquired a rind of bacon. Amon had come raging down the corridor from his office. 'You're all getting fat!' he had screamed. He had divided the office staff into two lines then. It had been, to Korn, like a scene from the Podgórze High School: the girls in the other line so familiar to him, daughters of families he'd grown up with, Podgórze families. It could have been that a teacher was sorting them out into those who would visit the Kosciuszko Monument and those for the museum at the Wawel. In fact, the girls in the other line were taken straight from their desks to Chujowa Górka and, for the decadence of that bacon rind, gunned down by one of Pilarzik's squads.

Though Josef Bau was not involved in such office turmoil, no one could have said that he was leading a sheltered life in Płaszów. But it had been less perilous than the experience of the girl of his choice. Rebecca Tannenbaum was an orphan, though in the clannish life of Jewish Cracow, she had not been bereft of kindly aunts and uncles. She was nineteen, sweet-faced, and neatly built. She could speak German well and made pleasant and generous conversation. Recently she'd begun to work in Stern's office behind the Administration Building, away from the most immediate environs of the Commandant's berserk interference. But her job in the Construction Office was only half her labour. She was a manicurist. She treated Amon weekly; she tended the hands of *Untersturmführer* Leo John, those of Dr. Blancke and of his lover, the harsh Alice Orlowski. Taking Amon's hands, she had found them long and well made, with tapering fingers – not a fat man's hands at all; certainly not those of a savage.

When a prisoner had first come to her and told her that the Herr Commandant wanted to see her, she had begun to run away, fleeing among the desks and down the back stairs. The prisoner had followed and cried after her, 'For God's sake, don't! He'll punish *me* if I don't bring you back.'

So she had followed the man down to Goeth's villa. But before going into the salon, she first visited the stinking cellar – this was in Goeth's first residence, and the cellar had been dug down into the boundaries of an ancient Jewish graveyard. Down amid the grave soil, Rebecca's friend Helen Hirsch had been nursing bruises. You have a problem, Helen admitted. But just do the job and see. That's all you can do. Some people he likes a professional manner from, some people he doesn't. And I'll give you cake and sausage when you come. But don't just take food; ask me first. Some people take food without asking, and I don't know what I have to cover up for.

Amon did accept Rebecca's professional manner, presenting his fingers and chatting in German. It could have been the Hotel Cracovia again, and Amon a crisp-shirted, overweight young German tycoon come to Cracow to sell textiles or steel or chemicals. There were, however, two aspects to these meetings that detracted from their air of timeless geniality. The Commandant always kept his service revolver at his right elbow, and frequently one or the other of the dogs drowsed in the salon. She had seen them, on the *Appellplatz*, tear the flesh of engineer Karp. Yet sometimes, as the dogs snuffled in sleep and she and Amon compared notes on prewar visits to the spa at Carlsbad, the roll call of horrors seemed remote and beyond belief. One day she felt confident enough to ask him why the revolver was always at his elbow. His answer chilled the back of her neck as she bent over his hand. 'That's in case you ever nick me,' he told her.

If she ever needed proof that a chat about spas was all the same to Amon as an act of madness, she had it the day she entered the hallway and saw him dragging her friend Helen Hirsch out of the salon by the hair – Helen striving to keep her balance and her auburn hair coming out by the roots, and Amon, if he lost his grip one second, regaining it the next in his giant, well-tended hands. And further proof came on the evening she entered the salon and one of those dogs – Rolf or Ralf – materialised, leaped at her, and, holding her by the shoulders, opened its jaw on her breast. She looked across the room and saw Amon lolling on the sofa and smiling. 'Stop shaking, you stupid girl,' he told her, 'or I won't be able to save you from the hound.'

During the time she tended the Commandant's hands, he would shoot his shoeshine boy for faulty work; hang his fifteen-year-old orderly, Poldek Deresiewicz, from the ringbolts in his office because a flea had been found on one of the dogs; and execute his servant Lisiek for lending a *dróżka* and horse to Bosch without first checking. Yet twice a week, the pretty orphan entered the salon and philosophically took the beast by the hand.

She met Josef Bau one grey morning when he stood outside the *Bauleitung* holding up a blueprint frame toward the low autumn cloud. His thin body seemed overburdened by the weight. She asked if she could help him. 'No,' he said. 'I'm just waiting for the sunshine.' 'Why?' she asked. He explained how his transparency drawings for a new building were clamped in the frame beside sensitised blueprint paper. If the sun, he said, were only to shine harder, a mysterious chemical union would transfer the drawing from the transparency to the blueprint. Then he said, 'Why don't you be my magical sunshine?'

Pretty girls weren't used to delicacy from boys in Płaszów. Sexuality there took its harsh impetus from the volleys heard on Chujowa Górka, the executions on the *Appellplatz*. Imagine a day, for instance, when a chicken is found among the work party returning from the cable factory on Wieliczka. Amon is ranting on the *Appellplatz*, for the chicken was discovered lying in a bag in front of the camp gate during a spot check. Whose bag was it? Amon wants to know. Whose chicken? Since no one on the *Appellplatz* will admit anything, Amon takes a rifle from an SS man and shoots the prisoner at the head of the line. The bullet, passing through the body, also fells the man behind. No one speaks, though. 'How you love one another!' roars Amon, and prepares to execute the next man in line. A boy of fourteen steps out of the line. He is shuddering and weeping. He can say who brought the chicken in, he tells the Herr Commandant. 'Who, then?' The boy points to one of the two dead men. 'That one!' the boy screams. Amon astonishes the entire *Appellplatz* by believing the boy, and puts his head back and laughs with the sort of classroom incredulity teachers like to exhibit. *These people . . . can't they understand now why they're all forfeit?*

After an evening like that, in the hours of free movement between 7 and 9 P.M. most prisoners felt that there was no time for leisurely courtship. The lice plaguing your groin and armpits made a mockery of formality. Young males mounted girls without ceremony. In the women's camp they sang a song which asked the virgin why she'd bound herself up with string and for whom she thought she was saving herself.

The atmosphere was not as desperate at Emalia. In the enamel workshop, niches had been designed among the machinery on the factory floor to permit lovers to meet at greater length. There was only a theoretical segregation in the cramped barracks. The absence of daily fear, the fuller ration of daily bread made for a little less frenzy. Besides, Oskar still maintained that he would not let the SS garrison go inside the prison without his permission.

One prisoner recalls wiring installed in Oskar's office in case any SS official did demand entry to the barracks. While the SS man was on his way downstairs, Oskar could punch a button connected to a bell inside the camp. It warned men and women, first, to stub out the illicit cigarettes supplied daily by Oskar. ('Go to my apartment,' he would tell someone on the factory floor almost daily, 'and fill this cigarette case.' He would wink significantly.) The bell also warned men and women to get back to their appointed bunks.

To Rebecca, it was something close to a shock, a remembrance of a vanished culture, to meet in Płaszów a boy who courted as if he'd met her in a patisserie in the Rynek.

Another morning when she came downstairs from Stern's office, Josef showed her his work desk. He was drawing plans for yet more barracks. What's your barrack number, and who's your barrack *Alteste*? She let him know with the correct reluctance. She had seen Helen Hirsch dragged down the hallway by the hair and would die if she accidentally jabbed the cuticle of Amon's thumb. Yet this boy had restored her to coyness, to girlhood. I'll come and speak to your mother, he promised. I don't have a mother, said Rebecca. Then I'll speak to the *Alteste*.

That was how the courting began – with the permission of elders and as if there *were* world enough and time. Because he was such a fantastical and ceremonious boy, they did not kiss. It was, in fact, under Amon's roof that they first managed a proper embrace. It was after a manicure session. Rebecca had got hot water and soap from Helen and crept up to the top floor, vacant because of renovations pending, to wash her blouse and her change of underwear. Her washtub was her mess can. It would be needed tomorrow to hold her soup.

She was working away on that small bucket of suds when Josef appeared. Why are you here? she asked him. I'm measuring for my drawings, for the renovations, he told her. And why are you here yourself? You can see, she told him. And please don't talk too loudly.

He danced around the room, flashing the tape measure up walls and along mouldings. Do it carefully, she told him, anxious because she was aware of Amon's exacting standards.

While I'm here, he told her, I might as well measure you. He ran the tape along her arms and down her back from the nape of her neck to the small of her spine. She did not resist the way his thumb touched her, marking her dimensions. But when they had embraced each other thoroughly for a while, she ordered him out. This was no place for a languorous afternoon.

There were other desperate romances in Płaszów, even among the SS, but they proceeded less sunnily than this very proper romance between Josef Bau and the manicurist. *Oberscharführer* Albert Hujar, for example, who had shot Dr. Rosalia Blau in the ghetto and Diana Reiter after the foundations of the barracks collapsed, had fallen in love with a Jewish prisoner. Madritsch's daughter had been captivated by a Jewish boy from the Tarnow ghetto – he had, of course, worked in Madritsch's Tarnow plant until the expert ghetto-liquidator Amon had been brought in at the end of the summer to close down Tarnow as he had Cracow. Now he was in the Madritsch workshop inside Płaszów; the girl could visit him there. But nothing could come of it. The prisoners themselves had niches and shelters where lovers and spouses could meet. But everything – the law of the Reich and the strange code of the prisoners – resisted the affair between Fraulein Madritsch and her young man. Similarly, honest Raimund Titsch had fallen in love with one of his machinists. That too was a gentle, secretive, and largely abortive love. As for *Oberscharführer* Hujar, he was ordered by Amon himself to stop being a fool. So Albert took the girl for a walk in the woods and with fondest regrets shot her through the nape of the neck.

It seemed, in fact, that death hung over the passions of the SS. Henry Rosner, the violinist, and his brother Leopold, the accordionist, spreading Viennese melodies around Goeth's dinner table, were aware of it. One night a tall, slim, grey officer in the *Waffen* SS had visited Amon for dinner and, drinking a lot, had kept asking the Rosners for the Hungarian song 'Gloomy Sunday.' The song is an emotional outpouring in which a young man is about to commit suicide for love. It had exactly the sort of excessive feeling which, Henry had noticed, appealed to SS men at their leisure. It had, in fact, enjoyed notoriety in the Thirties – governments in Hungary, Poland, and Czechoslovakia had considered banning it because its popularity had brought on a rash of thwarted-love suicides. Young men about to blow their heads off would sometimes quote its lyrics in their suicide notes. It had long been a song proscribed by the Reich Propaganda Office. Now this tall, elegant guest, old enough to have teen-age sons and daughters, themselves caught up in the excesses of puppy love, kept walking up to the Rosner boys and saying, 'Play "Gloomy Sunday."' And though Dr. Goebbels would not have permitted it, no one in the wilds of southern Poland was going to argue with an SS field officer with unhappy memories of an affair.

After the guest had demanded the song four or five times, an unearthly conviction took hold of Henry Rosner. In its tribal origins, music was always magic. And no one in Europe had a better sense of the potency of the violin than a Cracovian Jew like Henry, who came from the sort of family in which music is not so much learned as inherited, in the same way as the status of *cohen*, or hereditary priest. It came to Henry now that, as he would say later – 'God, if I have the power, maybe this son-of-a-bitch will kill himself.'

The proscribed music of 'Gloomy Sunday' had gained legitimacy in Amon's dining room through being repeated, and now Henry declared war with it, Leopold playing with him and reassured by the stares of almost grateful melancholy the handsome officer directed at them.

Henry sweated, believing that he was so visibly fiddling up the SS man's death that at any moment Amon would notice and come and take him out behind the villa for execution. As for Henry's performance, it is not relevant to ask was it good or bad. It was possessed. And only one man, the officer, noticed and assented and, across the hubbub of drunken Bosch and Schemer, Czurda and Amon, continued to look up from his chair directly into Henry's eyes, as if he were going to jump up at any second and say, 'Of course, gentlemen. The violinist is absolutely right. There's no sense in enduring a grief like this.'

The Rosners went on repeating the song beyond the limit at which Amon would normally have shouted, 'Enough!' At last the guest stood up and went out onto the balcony. Henry knew at once that everything he could do to the man had been done. He and his brother slid into some Von Suppé and Lehar, covering their tracks with full-bodied operetta. The guest remained alone on the balcony and after half an hour interrupted a good party by shooting himself through the head.

Such was sex in Płaszów. Lice, crabs, and urgency inside the wire; murder and lunacy on its fringes. And in its midst Josef Bau and Rebecca Tannenbaum pursued their ritual dance of courtship.

In the midst of the snows that year, Płaszów underwent a change of status adverse to all lovers inside the wire. In the early days of January 1944, it was designated a *Konzentrationslager* (Concentration Camp) under the central authority of General Oswald Pohl's SS Main Economic and Administrative Office in Oranienburg, on the outskirts of Berlin. Subcamps of Płaszów – such as Oskar Schindler's

Emalia – now also came under Oranienburg's control. Police chiefs Schemer and Czurda lost their direct authority. The labour fees of all those prisoners employed by Oskar and Madritsch no longer went to Pomorska Street, but to the office of General Richard Glücks, head of Pohl's Section D (Concentration Camps). Oskar, if he wanted favours now, had not only to drive out to Płaszów and sweeten Amon, not only to have Julian Schemer to dinner, but also to reach certain officials in the grand bureaucratic complex of Oranienburg.

Oskar made an early opportunity to travel to Berlin and meet the people who would be dealing with his files. Oranienburg had begun as a concentration camp. Now it had become a sprawl of administrative barracks. From the offices of Section D, every aspect of prison life and death was regulated. Its chief, Richard Glücks, had responsibility as well, in consultation with Pohl, for establishing the balance between labourers and candidates for the chambers, for the equation in which X represented slave labour and Y represented the more immediately condemned.

Glücks had laid down procedures for every event, and from his department came memos drafted in the anaesthetic jargon of the planner, the paper shuffler, the detached specialist.

SS Main Office of Economics and Administration
Section Chief D (Concentration Camps)
D1-AZ:14fl-Ot-S-
GEH TGB NO 453-44

To the Commandants of Concentration Camps
Da, Sah, Bu, Mau, Slo, Neu, Au I-III,
Gr-Ro, Natz, Stu, Rav, Herz, A-L-Bels,
Gruppenl. D.Riga, Gruppenl. D.Cracow (Płaszów).

Applications from Camp Commandants for punishment by flogging in cases of sabotage by prisoners in the war production industries are increasing.

I request that in future in all *proved* cases of sabotage (a report from the management must be enclosed), an application for execution by hanging should be made. The execution should take place before the assembled members of the work detachment concerned. The reason for the execution is to be made known so as to act as a deterrent.

(Signed)
SS *Obersturmführer*

In this eerie chancellory, some files discussed the length a prisoner's hair should be before it was considered of economic use for 'the manufacture of hair-yarn socks for U-boat crews and hair-felt footwear for the Reichs railway,' while others debated whether the form registering 'death cases' should be filed by eight departments or merely covered by letter and appended to the personnel records as soon as the index card had been brought up to date. And here Herr Oskar Schindler of Cracow came to talk about his little industrial compound in Zablocie. They appointed someone of middle status to handle him, a personnel officer of field rank.

Oskar wasn't distressed. There were larger employers of Jewish prison labour than he. There were the megaliths, Krupp, of course, and I. G. Farben. There was the Cable Works at Płaszów. Walter C. Toebbens, the Warsaw industrialist whom Himmler had tried to force into the *Wehrmacht*, was a heavier employer of labour than Herr Schindler. Then there were the steelworks at Stalowa Wola, the aircraft factories at Budzyn and Zakopane, the Steyr-Daimler-Puch works at Radom.

The personnel officer had the plans of Emalia on his desk. I hope, he said curtly, you don't want to increase the size of your camp. It would be impossible to do it without courting a typhus epidemic.

Oskar waved that suggestion aside. He was interested in the permanence of his labour force, he said. He had had a talk on that matter, he told the officer, with a friend of his, Colonel Erich Lange. The name, Oskar could tell, meant something to the SS man. Oskar produced a letter from the Colonel, and the personnel officer sat back reading it. The office was silent – all you could hear from other rooms was pen-scratch and the whisper of papers and quiet, earnest talk, as if none here knew that they lay at the core of a network of screams.

Colonel Lange was a man of influence, Chief of Staff of the Armaments Inspectorate at Army Headquarters, Berlin. Oskar had met him at a party at General Schindler's office in Cracow. They had liked each other almost at once. It happened a lot at parties that two people could sense in each other a certain resistance to the regime and might retire to a corner to test each other out and perhaps establish friendship. Erich Lange had been appalled by the factory camps of Poland – by the I. G. Farben works at Buna, for example, where foremen adopted the SS 'work tempo' and made prisoners unload cement on the run; where the corpses of the starved, the broken were hurled into ditches built for cables and covered, together with the cables, with cement. 'You are not here to live but to perish in concrete,' a plant manager had told newcomers, and Lange had heard the speech and felt damned.

His letter to Oranienburg had been preceded by some phone calls, and calls and letter both promoted the same proposition: Herr Schindler, with his mess kits and his 45mm antitank shells, is considered by this Inspectorate to be a major contributor to the struggle for our national survival. He has built up a staff of skilled specialists, and nothing should be done to disrupt the work they perform under the *Herr Direktor* Schindler's supervision.

The personnel officer was impressed and said he would speak frankly to Herr Schindler. There were no plans to alter the status or interfere with the population of the camp in Zablocie. However, the *Herr Direktor* had to understand that the situation of Jews, even skilled armaments workers, was always risky. Take the case of our own SS enterprises. Ostindustrie, the SS company, employs prisoners in a peat works, a brush factory and iron foundry in Lublin, equipment factories in Radom, a fur works in Trawniki. But other branches of the SS shoot the work force continually, and now Osti is for all practical purposes out of business. Likewise, at the killing centres, the staff never retains a sufficient percentage of prisoners for factory work. This has been a matter of frequent correspondence, but they're intransigent, those people in the field. 'Of course,' said the personnel officer, tapping the letter, 'I'll do what I can for you.'

'I understand the problem,' said Oskar, looking up at the SS man with that radiant smile. 'If there is any way I can express my gratitude . . . .'

In the end, Oskar left Oranienburg with at least some guarantees about the continuity of his backyard camp in Cracow.

The manner in which the new status of Płaszów impinged on lovers was that a proper penal separation of the sexes – such as was provided for in a series of SS Main Office of Economics and Administration memos – was created. The fences between the men's prison and the women's, the perimeter fence, the fence around the industrial sector were all electrified. The voltage, the spacing of wires, the number of electrified strands and insulators were all provided for by Main Office directives. Amon and his officers were not slow to notice the disciplinary possibilities involved. Now you could stand people for twenty-four hours at a time between the electrified outer fence and the inner, neutral, original fence. If they staggered with weariness, they knew that inches behind their backs ran the hundreds of volts. Mundek Korn, for example, found himself, on returning to camp with a work party from which one prisoner was missing, standing in that narrow gulf for a day and a night.

But perhaps worse than the risk of falling against the wire was the way the current ran, from the end of evening roll call to reveille in the morning, like a moat between man and woman. Time for contact was now reduced to the short phase of milling on the *Appellplatz*, before the orders for falling into line were shouted. Each couple devised a tune, whistling it among the crowds, straining to pick up the answering refrain amid a forest of sibilance. Rebecca

Tannenbaum also settled on a code tune. The requirements of General Pohl's Main SS Office had forced the prisoners of Płaszów to adopt the mating stratagems of birds. And by these means, the formal romance of Rebecca and Josef went forward.

Then Josef somehow got a dead woman's dress from the clothing warehouse. Often, after roll call in the men's lines, he would go to the latrines, put on the long gown, and place an Orthodox bonnet on his hair. Then he would come out and join the women's lines. His short hair would not have amazed any SS guard, since most of the women had been shorn because of lice. So, with 13,000 women prisoners, he would pass into the women's compound and spend the night sitting up in Hut 57 keeping Rebecca company.

In Rebecca's barracks, the older women took Josef at his word. If Josef required a traditional courtship, they would fall into their traditional roles as chaperones. Josef was therefore a gift to them too, a licence to play their prewar ceremonious selves. From their four-tiered bunks they looked down on the two children until everyone fell asleep. If any one of them thought, *Let's not be too fussy in times like these about what the children get up to in the dead of night*, it was never said. In fact, two of the older women would crowd onto one narrow ledge so that Josef could have a bunk of his own. The discomfort, the smell of the other body, the risk of the migration of lice from your friend to yourself – none of that was as important, as crucial to self-respect as that the courtship should be fulfilled according to the norms.

At the end of winter, Josef, wearing the armband of the Construction Office, went out into the strangely immaculate snow in the strip between the inner fence and the electrified barrier and, steel measure in hand, under the eyes of the domed watchtowers, pretended to be sizing up no-man's-land for some architectural reason.

At the base of the concrete stanchions studded with porcelain insulators grew the first tiny flowers of that year. Flashing his steel ruler, he picked them and shoved them into his jacket. He brought the flowers across the camp, up Jerozolimska Street. He was passing Amon's villa, his chest stuffed with blossoms, when Amon himself appeared from the front door and advanced, towering, down the steps. Josef Bau stopped. It was most dangerous to stop, to appear to be in arrested motion in front of Amon. But having stopped, he seemed frozen there. He feared that the heart he'd so energetically and honestly signed over to the orphan Rebecca would likely now become just another of Amon's targets.

But when Amon walked past him, not noticing him, not objecting to his standing there with an idle ruler in his hands, Josef Bau concluded that it meant some kind of guarantee. No one escaped Amon unless it was a sort of destiny. All dolled up in his shooting uniform, Amon had entered the camp unexpectedly one day through the back gate and had found the Warrenhaupt girl lolling in a limousine at the garage, staring at herself in the rearview mirror. The car windows she'd been assigned to clean were still smudged. He had killed her for that. And there was that mother and daughter Amon had noticed through a kitchen window. They had been peeling potatoes too slowly. So he'd leaned in on the sill and shot both of them. Yet here at his steps was something he hated, a stock-still Jewish lover and draughtsman, steel ruler dangling in his hands. And Amon had walked by. Bau felt the urge to confirm this outrageous good luck by some emphatic act. Marriage was, of course, the most emphatic act of all.

He got back to the Administration Building, climbed the stairs to Stern's office and, finding Rebecca, asked her to marry him. Urgency, Rebecca was pleased and concerned to notice, had entered the business now.

That evening, in the dead woman's dress, he visited his mother again and the council of chaperones in Hut 57. They awaited only the arrival of a rabbi. But if rabbis came, they remained only a few days on their way to Auschwitz – not long enough for people requiring the rites of *kiddushin* and *nissuin* to locate them and ask them, before they stepped into the furnace, for a final exercise of their priesthood.

Josef married Rebecca on a Sunday night of fierce cold in February. There was no rabbi. Mrs. Bau, Josef's mother, officiated. They were Reformed Jews, so that they could do without a *ketubbah* written in Aramaic. In the workshop of Wulkan the jeweller someone had made up two rings out of a silver spoon Mrs. Bau had had hidden in the rafters. On the barracks floor, Rebecca circled Josef seven times and Josef crushed glass – a spent light bulb from the Construction Office – beneath his heel.

The couple had been given the top bunk of the tier. For the sake of privacy, it had been hung with blankets. In darkness Josef and Rebecca climbed to it, and all around them the earthy jokes were running. At weddings in Poland there was always a period of truce when profane love was given its chance to speak. If the wedding guests didn't wish to voice the traditional double entendres themselves, they could bring in a professional wedding jester. Women who might in the Twenties and Thirties have sat up at weddings making disapproving faces at the risqué hired jester and the belly-laughing men, only now and then permitting themselves, as mature women, to be overcome with amusement, stepped tonight into the place of all the absent and dead wedding jesters of southern Poland.

Josef and Rebecca had not been together more than ten minutes on the upper bunk when the barracks lights came on. Looking through the blankets, Josef saw *Untersturmführer* Scheidt patrolling the canyons of bunks. The same old fearful sense of destiny overcame Josef. They'd found he was missing from his barracks, of course, and sent one of the worst of the officers to look for him in his mother's hut. Amon had been blinded to him that day outside the villa only so that Scheidt, who was quick on the trigger, could come and kill him on his wedding night!

He knew too that all the women were compromised – his mother, his bride, the witnesses, the ones who'd uttered the most exquisitely embarrassing jokes. He began murmuring apologies, pleas to be forgiven. Rebecca told him to be quiet. She took down the screen of blankets. At this time of night, she reasoned, Scheidt wasn't going to climb to a top bunk unless provoked. The women on the lower bunks were passing their small straw-filled pillows to her. Josef might well have orchestrated the courtship, but he was now the child to be concealed. Rebecca pushed him hard up into the corner of the bunk and covered him with pillows. She watched Scheidt pass below her, leave the barracks by its back door. The lights went out. Among a last spatter of dark, earthy jokes, the Baus were restored to their privacy.

Within minutes, the sirens began to sound. Everyone sat up in the darkness. The noise meant to Bau that yes, they *were* determined to stamp out this ritual marriage. They *had* found his empty bunk over in the men's quarters and were now seriously hunting him.

In the dark aisle, the women were milling. They knew it too. From the top bunk he could hear them saying it. His old-fashioned love would kill them all. The barracks *Alteste*, who'd been so decent about the whole thing, would be shot first once the lights came on and they found a bridegroom there in token female rags.

Josef Bau grabbed his clothes. He kissed his wife perfunctorily, slid to the floor, and ran from the hut. In the darkness outside, the wail of the sirens pierced him. He ran in dirty snow, with his jacket and old dress bundled up under his armpits. When the lights came on, he would be seen by the towers. But he had the berserk idea that he could beat the lights over the fence, that he could even climb it between the alternations of its current. Once back in the men's camp, he could make up some story about diarrhea, about having gone to the latrines and collapsed on the floor, being brought back to consciousness by the noise of sirens.

But even if electrocuted, he understood as he sprinted, he could not then confess what woman he was visiting. Racing for the fatal wire, he did not understand that there would have to be a classroomlike scene on the *Appellplatz* and that Rebecca would be made, one way or another, to step forward.

In the fence between the men's and women's camps in Płaszów ran nine electrified strands. Josef Bau launched himself high, so that his feet would find purchase on the third of the strands and his hands, at the stretch, might reach the second from the top. He imagined himself then as racing over the strands with a ratlike quickness. In fact he landed in the mesh of wire and simply hung there. He thought the coldness of the metal in his hands was the first message of the current. But there was no current. There were no lights. Josef Bau, stretched on the fence, did not speculate on the reason there wasn't any voltage. He got to the top and vaulted into the men's camp. *You're a married man*, he told himself. He slid into the latrines by the washhouses. 'A frightful diarrhea, *Herr Oberscharführer.*' He stood gasping in the stench. Amon's blindness on the day of the flowers . . . the consummation, waited for with an untoward patience, twice interrupted . . . Scheidt and the sirens . . . a problem with the lights and the wire – staggering and gagging, he wondered if he could support the ambiguity of his life. Like others, he wanted a more definite rescue.

He wandered out to be one of the last to join the lines in front of his hut. He was trembling, but sure the *Alteste* would cover up for him. 'Yes, *Herr Untersturmführer*, I gave *Häftling* Bau permission to visit the latrines.'

They weren't looking for him at all. They were looking for three young Zionists who'd escaped in a truckload of product from the upholstery works, where they made *Wehrmacht* mattresses out of sea grass.

27

On April 28, 1944, Oskar – by looking sideways at himself in a mirror – was able to tell that his waist had thickened for his thirty-sixth birthday. But at least today, when he embraced the girls, no one bothered to denounce him. Any informer among the German technicians must have been demoralised, since the SS had let Oskar out of Pomorska and Montelupich, both of them centres supposed impregnable to influence.

To mark the day, Emilie sent the usual greetings from Czechoslovakia, and Ingrid and Klonowska gave him gifts. His domestic arrangements had scarcely changed in the four and a half years he had spent in Cracow. Ingrid was still a consort, Klonowska a girlfriend, Emilie an understandably absent wife. Whatever grievances and bewilderment each suffered goes unrecorded, but it would become obvious in this, his thirty-seventh, year that some coolness had entered his relations with Ingrid; that Klonowska, always a loyal friend, was content with a merely sporadic liaison; and that Emilie still considered their marriage indissoluble. For the moment, they gave their presents and kept their counsel.

Others took a hand in the celebration. Amon permitted Henry Rosner to bring his violin to Lipowa Street in the evening under the guard of the best baritone in the Ukrainian garrison. Amon was, at this stage, very pleased with his association with Schindler. In return for his continuing support for the Emalia camp, Amon had one day recently requested and got the permanent use of Oskar's Mercedes – not the jalopy Oskar had bought from John for a day, but the most elegant car in the Emalia garage.

The recital took place in Oskar's office. No one attended except

Oskar. It was as if he were tired of company. When the Ukrainian went to the lavatory, Oskar revealed his depression to Henry. He was upset about the war news. His birthday had come in a hiatus. The Russian armies had halted behind the Pripet Marshes in Belorussia and in front of Lwów. Oskar's fears puzzled Henry. *Doesn't he understand*, he wondered, *that if the Russians aren't held off, it's the end of his operation here?*

'I've often asked Amon to let you come here permanently,' Oskar told Rosner. 'You and your wife and child. He won't hear of it. He appreciates you too much. But eventually . . .'

Henry was grateful. But he felt he had to point out that his family might be as safe as any in Płaszów. His sister-in-law, for example, had been discovered by Goeth smoking at work, and he had ordered her execution. But one of the NCOs had begged to put before the Herr Commandant's notice the fact that this woman was Mrs. Rosner, wife of Rosner the accordionist. 'Oh,' Amon had said, pardoning her. 'Well, remember, girl, I won't have smoking on the job.'

Henry told Oskar that night that it had been this attitude of Amon's – that the Rosners were immune because of their musical talent – which had persuaded him and Manci to bring their eight-year-old son, Olek, into the camp. He had been hiding with friends in Cracow, but that was becoming a less and less secure business every day. Once inside, Olek could blend into that small crowd of children, many unregistered in the prison records, whose presence in Płaszów was connived at by prisoners and tolerated by some of the junior camp officials. Getting Olek into the place, however, had been the risky part. Poldek Pfefferberg, who'd had to drive a truck to town to pick up toolboxes, had smuggled the boy in. The Ukrainians had nearly discovered him at the gate, while he was still an outsider and living in contravention of every racial statute of the Reich Government General. His feet had burst out of the end of the box that lay between Pfefferberg's ankles. 'Mr. Pfefferberg, Mr. Pfefferberg,' Poldek had heard while the Ukrainians searched the back of the truck. 'My feet are sticking out.'

Henry could laugh at that now, though warily, since there were still rivers to be crossed. But Schindler reacted dramatically, with a gesture that seemed to grow from the slightly alcoholic melancholy which had beset him on this evening of his birthday. He lifted his office chair by its back and raised it to the portrait of the *Führer*. It seemed for a second that he was about to lash into the icon. But he spun again on his heel, lowered the chair deliberately until its four legs hung equidistant from the floor, and rammed them into the carpet, shaking the wall.

Then he said, 'They're burning bodies out there, aren't they?'

Henry grimaced as if the stench were in the room. 'They've started,' he admitted.

Now that Płaszów was – in the language of the bureaucrats – a Concentration Camp, its inmates found that it was safer to encounter Amon. The chiefs in Oranienburg did not permit summary execution. The days when slow potato-peelers could be expunged on the spot were gone. They could now be destroyed only by due process. There had to be a hearing, a record sent in triplicate to Oranienburg. The sentence had to be confirmed not only by General Glücks's office but also by General Pohl's Department W (Economic Enterprises). For if a commandant killed essential workers, Department W could find itself hit with claims for compensation. Allach-Munich, Ltd., for example, porcelain manufacturers using slave labour from Dachau, had recently filed a claim for 31,800 RM. because 'as a result of the typhoid epidemic which broke out in January 1943, we had no prison labour at our disposal from January 26, 1943, until March 3, 1943. In our opinion we are entitled to compensation under Clause 2 of the Businesses Compensation Settlement Fund . . .'

Department W was all the more liable for compensation if the loss of skilled labour arose from the zeal of a trigger-happy SS officer.

So, to avoid the paperwork and the departmental complications, Amon held his hand on most days. The people who appeared within his range in the spring and early summer of '44 somehow understood it was safer, though they knew nothing of Department W and Generals Pohl and Glücks. It was to them a remission as mysterious as Amon's madness itself.

Yet, as Oskar had mentioned to Henry Rosner, they were now burning bodies at Płaszów. In preparation for the Russian offensive, the SS was abolishing its institutions in the East. Treblinka, Sobibor, and Bełżec had been evacuated the previous autumn. The *Waffen* SS who had run them had been ordered to dynamite the chambers and the crematoria, to leave no recognisable trace, and had then been posted to Italy to fight partisans. The immense complex at Auschwitz, in its safe ground in Upper Silesia, would complete the great task in the East, and once that was concluded, the crematoria would be ploughed under the earth. For without the evidence of the crematoria, the dead could offer no witness, were a whisper behind the wind, an inconsequential dust on the aspen leaves.

Płaszów was not as simple a case, for its dead lay everywhere around it. In the enthusiasm of the spring of 1943, bodies – notably the bodies of those killed in the ghetto's last two days – were thrown randomly into mass graves in the woods. Now Department D charged Amon with finding them all.

Estimates of the numbers of bodies vary widely. Polish publications, based on the work of the Main Commission for the Investigation of Nazi Crimes in Poland and on other sources, claim that 150,000 prisoners, many of them in transit to other places, went through Płaszów and its five subcamps. Of these, the Poles believe that 80,000 died there, mainly in mass executions inside Chujowa Górka or else in epidemics.

These figures baffle the surviving Płaszów inmates who remember the fearsome work of burning the dead. They say the number they exhumed was somewhere between 8,000 and 10,000 – a multitude frightful in itself and which they have no desire to exaggerate. The distance between the two estimates looks narrower when it is remembered that executions of Poles, Gypsies, and Jews would continue at Chujowa Górka and at other points around Płaszów throughout most of that year, and that the SS themselves took up the practice of burning bodies immediately after mass killings in the Austrian hill fort. Besides, Amon would not succeed in his intention of removing all bodies from the woods. Some thousands more would be found in postwar exhumations, and today, as the suburbs of Cracow close Płaszów in, bones are still discovered during the digging of foundations.

Oskar saw the line of pyres on the ridge above the workshops during a visit just before his birthday. When he came back a week later, the activity had increased. The bodies were dug up by male prisoners who worked masked and gagging. On blankets and barrows and litters the dead were brought to the burning site and laid on log frames. So the pyre was built, layer by layer, and when it reached the height of a man's shoulder, was doused in fuel and lit. Pfefferberg was horrified to see the temporary life the flames gave to the dead, the way the corpses sat forward, throwing the burning logs away, their limbs reaching, their mouths opening for a last cry. A young SS man from the delousing station ran among the pyres waving a pistol and roaring frenetic orders.

The dust of the dead fell in hair and on the clothing hung in the back gardens of junior officers' villas. Oskar was bemused to see the way the personnel took the smoke as if the grit in the air were some sort of honest and inevitable industrial fallout. And through the fogs, Amon went riding with Majola, both of them calm in the saddle. Leo John took his twelve-year-old son off to catch tadpoles in the marshy ground in the wood. The flames and the stench did not distract them from their daily lives.

Oskar, leaning back in the driver's seat of his BMW, the windows up and a handkerchief clamped over his mouth and nose, thought how they must be burning the Spiras with all the rest. He'd been astounded when they'd executed all the ghetto policemen and their families last Christmas, as soon as Symche Spira had finished directing the dismantling of the ghetto. They had brought them all, and their wives and children, up here on a grey afternoon and shot them as the cold sun vanished. They'd shot the most faithful (Spira and Zellinger) as well as the most grudging. Spira and bashful Mrs. Spira and the ungifted Spira children whom Pfefferberg had patiently tutored – they'd all stood naked within a circle of rifles, shivering against each other's flanks, Spira's Napoleonic OD uniform now just a heap of clothing for recycling, flung down at the fort entrance. And Spira still assuring everyone that it could not happen.

That execution had shocked Oskar because it showed that there was no obedience or obeisance a Jew could make to guarantee survival. And now they were burning the Spiras as anonymously, as ungratefully, as they had executed them.

Even the Gutters! It had happened after a dinner at Amon's the year before. Oskar had gone home early, but later heard what had happened after he left. John and Neuschel had started in on Bosch. They thought he was squeamish. He'd made a fuss about being a veteran of the trenches. But they had not seen him perform any executions. They kept it going for hours – the joke of the evening. In the end, Bosch had ordered David Gutter and his son roused in their barracks and Mrs. Gutter and the Gutter girl fetched from theirs. Again, it was a matter of faithful servants. David Gutter had been the last president of the *Judenrat* and had cooperated in everything – had never gone to Pomorska Street and tried to start any argument over the scope of the SS *Aktions* or the size of transports sent to Bełżec. Gutter had signed everything and thought every demand reasonable. Besides that, Bosch had used Gutter as an agent inside and outside Płaszów, sending him up to Cracow with truckloads of newly upholstered furniture or pocketfuls of jewellery to sell on the black market. And Gutter had done it because he was a scoundrel anyhow, but mainly because he believed it would make his wife and children immune.

At two o'clock that polar morning, a Jewish policeman, Zauder, a friend of Pfefferberg's and of Stern's, later to be shot by Pilarzik during one of that officer's drunken rampages, but on duty at the women's gate that night, heard it – Bosch ordering the Gutters into position in a depression in the ground near the women's camp. The children pleading, but David and Mrs. Gutter taking it calmly, knowing there was no argument. And now as Oskar watched, all of that evidence – the Gutters, the Spiras, the rebels, the priests, the children, the pretty girls found on Aryan papers – all of it was returning to that mad hill to be obliterated in case the Russians came to Płaszów and made too much of it.

Care, said Oranienburg in a letter to Amon, is to be taken with the future disposal of all bodies, and for that purpose they were sending a representative of a Hamburg engineering firm to survey the site for crematoria. In the meantime, the dead were to be kept, awaiting retrieval, at well-marked burial sites.

When, on that second visit, Oskar saw the extent of the fires on Chujowa Górka, his first impulse was to stay in the car, that sane German mechanism, and drive home. Instead he went calling on friends of his in the workshop, and then visited Stern's office. He thought that with all that grit falling on the windows, it wasn't out of the question that people inside Płaszów would consider suicide. Yet he was the one who seemed depressed. He didn't ask any of his usual questions, such as 'All right, Herr Stern, if God made man in His image, which race is most like Him? Is a Pole more like Him than a Czech?' There was none of that whimsy today. Instead he growled, 'What does everyone think?' Stern told him that the prisoners were like prisoners. They did their work and hoped for survival.

'I'm going to get you out,' Oskar grunted all at once. He put a balled fist on the desk. 'I'm going to get you *all* out.'

'All?' asked Stern. He couldn't help himself. Such massive Biblical rescues didn't suit the era.

'You, anyhow,' said Oskar. '*You*.'

28

In Amon's office in the Administration Building there were two typists. One was a young German woman, a Frau Kochmann; the other, a studious young prisoner, Mietek Pemper. Pemper would one day become secretary to Oskar, but in the summer of '44 he worked with Amon, and like anyone else in that situation was not too sanguine about his chances.

He first came into close contact with Amon as accidentally as had Helen Hirsch, the maid. Pemper was summoned to Amon's office after someone had recommended him to the Commandant. The young prisoner was a student of accounting, a touch typist, and could take dictation in both Polish and German shorthand. His powers of memory were said to be a byword. So, a prisoner of his skills, Pemper found himself in Płaszów's main office with Amon, and would also sometimes take dictation from Amon at the villa.

The irony was that Pemper's photographic memory would in the end, more than the memory of any other prisoner, bring about the hanging of Amon in Cracow. But Pemper did not believe such an era would come. In 1944, if he'd had to guess who'd be the most likely victim of his near-perfect recall, he would have had to say Mietek Pemper himself.

Pemper was meant to be the backup typist. For confidential documents, Amon was to use Frau Kochmann, a woman not nearly as competent as Mietek and slow at dictation. Sometimes Amon would break the rule and let young Pemper take confidential dictation. And Mietek, even while he sat across Amon's desk with the pad on his knee, could not stop contradictory suspicions from distracting him. The first was that all these inside reports and memoranda, whose details he was retaining, would make him a prime witness on the remote day when he and Amon stood before a tribunal. The other suspicion was that Amon would, in the end, have to erase him as one later would a classified tape.

Nonetheless, Mietek prepared each morning not only his own sets of typing paper, carbons, and duplicates, but a dozen for the German girl. After the girl had done her typing, Pemper would pretend to destroy the carbons, but in fact would keep and read them. He kept no written records, but he had had this reputation for memory since school days. He knew that if that tribunal ever met, if he and Amon sat in the body of the court, he would astound the Commandant with the precise dating of his evidence.

Pemper saw some astonishing classified documents. He read, for example, memoranda on the flogging of women. Camp commanders were to be reminded that it should be done to maximum effect. It was demeaning to involve SS personnel, and therefore Czech women were to be flogged by Slovak women, Slovaks by Czechs. Russians and Poles were to be bracketed for the same purposes. Commandants were to use their imagination in exploiting other national and cultural differences.

Another bulletin reminded them that they did not hold in their own persons the right to impose the death sentence. Commandants could seek authorisation by telegram or letter to the Reich Security Main Office. Amon had done this in the spring with two Jews who'd escaped from the subcamp at Wieliczka and whom he proposed to hang. A telegram of permission had returned from Berlin, signed, Pemper noticed, by Dr. Ernst Kaltenbrunner, Chief of the Reich Security Main Office.

Now, in April, Pemper read a memorandum from Gerhard Maurer, the Labour Allocation Chief of General Glücks's Section D. Maurer wanted Amon to tell him how many Hungarians could be held temporarily at Płaszów. They were meant ultimately to go to the German Armament Works, DAW, which was a subsidiary of Krupp making artillery-shell fuses in the enormous complex at Auschwitz. Given that Hungary had only recently been taken over as a German Protectorate, these Hungarian Jews and dissidents were in a better state of health than those who had had years of ghettoisation and prison life. They were therefore a windfall for the factories of Auschwitz. Unfortunately, accommodation at DAW was not yet ready for them, and if the commandant of Płaszów would take up to 7,000, pending the proper arrangements, Section D would be extremely grateful.

Goeth's answer, either seen or typed by Pemper, was that Płaszów was up to capacity and that there was no building space left inside the electric fences. However, Amon could accept up to 10,000 transit prisoners if (a) he were permitted to liquidate the unproductive element inside the camp; and (b) he were at the same time to impose double bunking. Maurer wrote in reply that double bunking could not be permitted in summer for fear of typhus, and that ideally, according to the regulations, there should be a minimum 3 cubic metres of air per person. But he was willing to authorise Goeth to undertake the first option. Section D would advise Auschwitz-Birkenau – or at least, the extermination wing of that great enterprise – to expect a shipment of reject prisoners from Płaszów. At the same time, *Ostbahn* transport would be arranged with cattle cars, of course, run up the spur from the main line to the very gate of Płaszów.

Amon therefore had to conduct a sorting-out process inside his camp.

With the blessing of Maurer and Section D, he would in a day abolish as many lives as Oskar Schindler was, by wit and reckless spending, harbouring in Emalia. Amon named his selection session *Die Gesundheitaktion*, the Health Action.

He managed it as one would manage a country fair. When it began, on the morning of Sunday, May 7, the *Appellplatz* was hung with banners: 'FOR EVERY PRISONER, APPROPRIATE WORK!' Loudspeakers played ballads and Strauss and love songs. Beneath them was set a table where Dr. Blancke, the SS physician, sat with Dr. Leon Gross and a number of clerks. Blancke's concept of 'health' was as eccentric as that of any doctor in the SS. He had rid the prison clinic of the chronically ill by injecting benzine into their bloodstreams. These injections could not by anyone's definition be called mercy killings. The patient was seized by convulsions which ended in a choking death after a quarter of an hour. Marek Biberstein, once president of the *Judenrat* and now, after his two-year imprisonment in Montelupich Street, a citizen of Płaszów, had suffered heart failure and been brought to the *Krankenstube*. Before Blancke could get to him with a benzine syringe, Dr. Idek Schindel, uncle of that Genia whose distant figure had galvanised Schindler two years before, had come to Biberstein's bedside with a number of colleagues. One had injected a more merciful dose of cyanide.

Today, flanked by the filing cabinets of the entire prison population, Blancke would deal with the prisoners a barracks at a time, and when he finished with one battery of cards it would be taken away and replaced by the next.

As they reached the *Appellplatz*, prisoners were told to strip. They were lined up naked and run back and forth in front of the doctors. Blancke and Leon Gross, the collaborating Jewish physician, would make notations on the card, point at this prisoner, call on that one to verify his name. Back the prisoners would run, the physicians looking for signs of disease or muscular weakness. It was an odd and humiliating exercise. Men with dislocated backs (Pfefferberg, for example, whose back Hujar had thrown out with the blow of a whip handle); women with chronic diarrhea, red cabbage rubbed into their cheeks to give them colour – all of them running for their lives and understanding that it was so. Young Mrs. Kinstlinger, who'd sprinted for Poland at the Berlin Olympics, knew that all that had been just a game. *This* was the true contest. With your stomach turning and your breath thin, you ran – beneath the throb of the lying music – for your golden life.

No prisoner found out the results until the following Sunday when, under the same banners and band music, the mass of inmates was again assembled. As names were read out and the rejects of the *Gesundheitaktion* were marched to the eastern end of the square, there were cries of outrage and bewilderment. Amon had expected a riot and had sought the help of the *Wehrmacht* garrison of Cracow, who were on standby in case of a prisoner uprising. Nearly 300 children had been discovered during the inspection the previous Sunday, and as they were now dragged away, the protests and wailings of parents were so loud that most of the garrison, together with Security Police detachments called in from Cracow, had to be thrown into the cordon separating the two groups. This confrontation lasted for hours, the guards forcing back surges of demented parents and telling the usual lies to those who had relatives among the rejects. Nothing had been announced, but everyone knew that those down there had failed the test and had no future. Blurred by waltzes and comic songs from the loudspeakers, a pitiable babel of messages was shouted from one group to the other. Henry Rosner, himself in torment, his son, Olek, in fact hidden somewhere in the camp, had the bizarre experience of facing a young SS man who, with tears in his eyes, denounced what was happening and made a pledge to volunteer for the Eastern Front. But officers shouted that unless people showed a little discipline, they would order their men to open fire. Perhaps Amon hoped that a justifiable outbreak of shooting would further reduce the overcrowding.

At the end of the process, 1,400 adults and 268 children stood, hedged in by weapons, at the eastern rim of the *Appellplatz*, ready for fast shipment to Auschwitz. Pemper would see and memorise the figures, which Amon would consider disappointing. Though it was not the number for which Amon had hoped, it would create immediate room for a large temporary intake of Hungarians.

In Dr. Blancke's card-file system, the children of Płaszów had not been as precisely registered as the adults. Many of them chose to spend both these Sundays in hiding, both they and their parents knowing instinctively that their age and the absence of their names and other details from the camp's documentation would make them obvious targets of the selection process.

Olek Rosner hid in the ceiling of a hut on the second Sunday. There were two other children with him all day above the rafters, and all day they kept the discipline of silence, all day held their bladders among the lice and the little packages of prisoners' belongings and the rooftop rats. For the children knew as well as any adult that the SS and the Ukrainians were wary of the spaces above the ceiling. They believed them typhus-ridden, and had been informed by Dr. Blancke that it took but a fragment of louse faeces in a crack in your skin to bring on epidemic typhus. Some of Płaszów's children had been housed for months near the men's prison in the hut marked ACHTUNG TYPHUS.

This Sunday, for Olek Rosner, Amon's health *Aktion* was far more perilous than typhus-bearing lice. Other children, some of the 268 separated out of the mass that day, had in fact begun the *Aktion* in hiding. Each Płaszów child, with that same toughness of mind, had chosen a favourite hiding place. Some favoured depressions beneath huts, some the laundry, some a shed behind the garage. Many of these hideouts had been discovered either this Sunday or last, and no longer offered refuge.

A further group had been brought without suspicion to the *Appellplatz*. There were parents who knew this or that NCO. It was as Himmler had once complained, for even SS *Oberscharführers* who did not flinch in the act of execution had their favourites, as if the place were a school playground. If there was a question about the children, some parents thought, you could appeal to an SS man who knew you.

The previous Sunday a thirteen-year-old orphan thought he'd be safe because he had, at other roll calls, passed for a young man. But naked, he wasn't able to argue away the childlikeness of his body. He had been told to dress and been marked down for the children's group. Now, as parents at the other end of the *Appellplatz* cried out for their rounded-up children and while the loudspeakers brayed forth a sentimental song called '*Mammi, kauf mir ein Pferdchen*' (Mummy, buy me a pony), the boy simply passed from one group to another, moved with that infallible instinct which had once characterised the movement of the red-capped child in Plac Zgody. And as with Redcap, no one had seen him. He stood, a plausible adult among the others, as the hateful music roared and his heart sought to beat its way through his rib cage. Then, faking the cramps of diarrhea, he asked a guard to let him go to the latrine.

The long latrines lay beyond the men's camp, and arriving there the boy stepped over the plank on which men sat while defecating. An arm either side of the pit, he lowered himself, trying to find knee- and toeholds in either wall. The stench blinded him, and flies invaded his mouth and ears and nostrils. As he entered the larger foulness and touched the bottom of the pit, he seemed to hear what he believed to be a hallucinatory murmur of voices behind the rage of flies. *Were they behind you?* said one voice. And another said, *Dammit, this is* our *place!*

There were ten children in there with him.

Amon's report made use of the compound word *Sonderbehandlung* – Special Treatment. It was a term that would become famous in later years, but this was the first time that Pemper had come across it. Of course, it had a sedative, even medical ring, but Mietek could tell by now that medicine was not involved.

A telegram Amon dictated that morning to be transmitted to Auschwitz gave more than a hint of its meaning. Amon explained that to make escape more difficult he had insisted that those selected for Special Treatment should drop any remnants of civilian clothing they still possessed at the rail siding and should put on striped prison clothes there. Since a great shortage of such garments prevailed, the stripes in which the Płaszów candidates for Special Treatment turned up at Auschwitz should be sent back at once to Concentration Camp Płaszów for reuse.

And all the children left in Płaszów, of whom the greatest number were those who shared the latrine with the tall orphan, hid out or impersonated adults until later searches discovered them and took them to the *Ostbahn* for the slow day's journey 60 kilometres to Auschwitz. The cattle cars were used that way all through high summer, taking troops and supplies east to the stalemated lines near Lwów and, on the return trip, wasting time at sidings while SS doctors watched ceaseless lines of the naked run before them.

29

Oskar, sitting in Amon's office, the windows flung open to a breathless summer's day, had the impression from the start that this meeting was a fake. Perhaps Madritsch and Bosch felt the same, for their gaze kept drifting away from Amon toward the limestone trolleys outside the window, toward any passing truck or wagon. Only *Untersturmführer* Leo John, who took notes, felt the need to sit up straight and keep his top button done up.

Amon had described it as a security conference. Though the Front had now been stabilised, he said, the advance of the Russian centre to the suburbs of Warsaw had encouraged partisan activity all over the Government General. Jews who heard of it were encouraged to attempt escapes. They did not know, of course, Amon pointed out, that they were better off behind the wire than exposed to those Jew-killers among the Polish partisans. In any case, everyone had to beware of partisan attack from outside and, worst of all, of collusion between the partisans and the prisoners.

Oskar tried to imagine the partisans invading Płaszów, letting all the Poles and Jews pour out, making of them an instant army. It was a daydream, and who could believe it? But there was Amon, straining to convince them all that *he* believed it. It had a purpose, this little act. Oskar was sure of that.

Bosch said, 'If the partisans are coming out to your place, Amon, I hope it's not a night when I've been invited.'

'Amen, amen,' murmured Schindler.

After the meeting, whatever it meant, Oskar took Amon to his car, parked outside the Administration Building. He opened the trunk. Inside lay a richly tooled saddle worked with designs characteristic of the Zakopane region in the mountains south of

Cracow. It was necessary for Oskar to keep priming Amon with such gifts even now that payment for the forced labour of DEF no longer went anywhere near *Hauptsturmführer* Goeth but, instead, was sent directly to the Cracow area representative of General Pohl's Oranienburg headquarters.

Oskar offered to drive both Amon and his saddle down to the Commandant's villa.

On such a blistering day, some of the trolley-pushers were showing a little less than the required zeal. But the saddle had mollified Amon, and in any case, it was no longer permitted for him to jump from a car and shoot people down in their tracks. The car rolled past the garrison barracks and came to the siding where a string of cattle cars stood. Oskar could tell, by the haze hanging above the cars and blending with and wavering in the heat rebounding from the roofs, that they were full. Even above the sound of the engine, you could hear the mourning from inside, the pleas for water.

Oskar braked his car and listened. This was permitted him, in view of the splendid multizłoty saddle in the trunk. Amon smiled indulgently at his sentimental friend. They're partly Płaszów people, said Amon, and people from the work camp at Szebnie. And Poles and Jews from Montelupich. They're going to Mauthausen, Amon said whimsically. They're complaining now? They don't know what complaint is . . . .

The roofs of the cars were bronzed with heat. You have no objection, said Oskar, if I call out your fire brigade?

Amon gave a What-will-you-think-of-next? sort of laugh. He implied that he wouldn't let anyone else summon the firemen, but he'd tolerate Oskar because Oskar was such a character and the whole business would make a good dinner-party anecdote.

But as Oskar sent Ukrainian guards to ring the bell for the Jewish firemen, Amon was bemused. He knew that Oskar knew what Mauthausen meant. If you hosed the cars for people, you were making them promises about a future. And would not such promises constitute, in anyone's code, a true cruelty? So disbelief mingled with tolerant amusement in Amon as the hoses were run out and jets of water fell hissing on the scalding cartops. Neuschel also came down from the office to shake his head and smile as the people inside the cars moaned and roared with gratitude. Grün, Amon's bodyguard, stood chatting with *Untersturmführer* John and clapped his side and hooted as the water rained down. Even at full extension the hoses reached only halfway down the line of cars. Next, Oskar was asking Amon for the loan of a truck or wagon and of a few Ukrainians to drive into Zablocie and fetch the fire hoses from DEF. They were 200-metre hoses, Oskar said. Amon, for some reason, found that sidesplitting. 'Of course I'll authorise a truck,' said Amon. Amon was willing to do anything for the sake of the comedy of life.

Oskar gave the Ukrainians a note for Bankier and Garde. While they were gone, Amon was so willing to enter the spirit of the event that he permitted the doors of the cars to be opened and buckets of water to be passed in and the dead, with their pink, swollen faces, to be lifted out. And still, all around the railway siding stood amused SS officers and NCOs. 'What does he think he's saving them from?'

When the large hoses from DEF arrived and all the cars had been drenched, the joke took on new dimensions. Oskar, in his note to Bankier, had instructed that the manager also go into Oskar's own apartment and fill a hamper with liquor and cigarettes, some good cheeses and sausages, and so on. Oskar now handed the hamper to the NCO at the rear of the train. It was an open transaction, and the man seemed a little embarrassed at the largesse, shoving it quickly into the rear van in case one of the officers of KL Płaszów reported him. Yet Oskar seemed to be in such curious favour with the Commandant that the NCO listened to him respectfully. 'When you stop near stations,' said Oskar, 'will you open the car doors?'

Years later, two survivors of the transport, Doctors Rubinstein and Feldstein, would let Oskar know that the NCO had frequently ordered the doors opened and the water buckets regularly filled on the tedious journey to Mauthausen. For most of the transport, of course, that was no more than a comfort before dying.

As Oskar moves along the string of cars, accompanied by the laughter of the SS, bringing a mercy which is in large part futile, it can be seen that he's not so much reckless anymore but possessed. Even Amon can tell that his friend has shifted into a new gear. All this frenzy about getting the hoses as far as the farthest car, then bribing an SS man in full view of the SS personnel – it would take just a shift in degree or so in the laughter of Scheidt or John or Hujar to bring about a mass denunciation of Oskar, a piece of information the Gestapo could not ignore. And then Oskar *would* go into Montelupich and, in view of previous racial charges against him, probably on to Auschwitz. So Amon was horrified by the way Oskar insisted on treating those dead as if they were poor relations travelling third class but bound for a genuine destination.

Some time after two, a locomotive hauled the whole miserable string of cattle cars away toward the main line, and all the hoses could again be wound up. Schindler delivered Amon and his saddle to the Goeth villa. Amon could see that Oskar was still preoccupied and, for the first time in their association, gave his friend some advice about living. You have to relax, said Amon. You can't go running after every trainload that leaves this place.

Adam Garde, engineer and prisoner of Emalia, also saw symptoms of this shift in Oskar. On the night of July 20, an SS man had come into Garde's barracks and roused him. The *Herr Direktor* had called the guardhouse and said it was necessary to see engineer Garde, professionally, in his office.

Garde found Oskar listening to the radio, his face flushed, a bottle and two glasses in front of him on the table. Behind the desk these days was a relief map of Europe. It had never been there in the days of German expansion, but Oskar seemed to take a sharp interest in the shrinkage of the German Fronts. Tonight he had the radio tuned to the *Deutschlandsender*, not – as was usually the case – to the BBC. Inspirational music was being played, as it often was as prelude to important announcements.

Oskar seemed to be listening avidly. When Garde came in, he stood up and hustled the young engineer to a seat. He poured cognac and passed it hurriedly across the desk. 'There's been an attempt on Hitler's life,' said Oskar. It had been announced earlier in the evening, and the story then was that Hitler had survived. They'd promised that he would soon be speaking to the German people. But it hadn't happened. Hours had passed and they hadn't been able to produce him. And they kept playing a lot of Beethoven, the way they had when Stalingrad fell.

Oskar and Garde sat together for hours. A seditious event, a Jew and a German listening together – all night if necessary – to discover if the *Führer* had died. Adam Garde, of course, suffered that same breathless surge of hope. He noticed that Oskar kept gesturing limply, as if the possibility that the Leader was dead had unstrung his muscles. He drank devoutly and urged Garde to drink up. If it was true, said Oskar, then Germans, ordinary Germans like himself, could begin to redeem themselves. Purely because someone close to Hitler had had the guts to remove him from the earth. It's the end of the SS, said Oskar. Himmler will be in jail by morning.

Oskar blew clouds of smoke. Oh, my God, he said, the relief to see the end of this system!

The 10 P.M. news brought only the earlier statement. There had been an attempt on the *Führer*'s life but it had failed and the *Führer* would be broadcasting in a few minutes. When, as the hour passed, Hitler did not speak, Oskar turned to a fantasy which would be popular with many Germans as the war drew to a close. 'Our troubles are over,' he said. 'The world's sane again. Germany can ally itself with the West against the Russians.'

Garde's hopes were more modest. At worst, he hoped for a ghetto which was a ghetto in the old Franz Josef sense.

And as they drank and the music played, it seemed more and more reasonable that Europe would yield them that night the death vital to its sanity. They were citizens of the continent again; they were not the prisoner and the *Herr Direktor*. The radio's promises to produce a message from the *Führer* recurred, and every time, Oskar laughed with increasing point.

Midnight came and they paid no attention anymore to the promises. Their very breath was lighter in this new post-*Führer* Cracow. By morning, they surmised, there would be dancing in every square, and it would go unpunished. The *Wehrmacht* would arrest Frank in the Wawel and encircle the SS complex in Pomorska Street.

A little before 1 A.M., Hitler was heard broadcasting from Rastenberg. Oskar had been so convinced that *that* voice was a voice he would never need to hear again that for a few seconds he did not recognise the sound, in spite of its familiarity, thinking it just another temporising Party spokesman. But Garde heard the speech from its first word, and knew whose voice it was.

'My German comrades!' it began. 'If I speak to you today, it is first in order that you should hear my voice and should know that I am unhurt and well, and, second, that you should know of a crime unparallelled in German history.'

The speech ended four minutes later with a reference to the conspirators. 'This time we shall settle accounts with them in the manner to which we National Socialists are accustomed.'

Adam Garde had never quite bought the fantasy Oskar had been pushing all evening. For Hitler was more than a man: he was a *system* with ramifications. Even if he died, it was no guarantee the system would alter its character. Besides, it was not in the nature of a phenomenon such as Hitler to perish in the space of a single evening.

But Oskar had been believing in the death with a feverish conviction for hours now, and when it turned out to be an illusion, it was young Garde who found himself cast as the comforter, while Oskar spoke with an almost operatic grief. 'All our vision of deliverance is futile,' he said. He poured another glass of cognac each, then pushed the bottle across the desk, opening his cigarette box. 'Take the cognac and some cigarettes and get some sleep,' he said. 'We'll have to wait a little longer for our freedom.'

In the confusion of the cognac, of the news and of its sudden reversal in the small hours, Garde did not think it strange that Oskar was talking about 'our freedom,' as if they had an equivalent need, were both prisoners who had to wait passively to be liberated. But back in his bunk Garde thought, It's amazing that *Herr Direktor* should have talked like that, like someone easily given to fantasies and fits of depression. Usually, he was so pragmatic.

Pomorska Street and the camps around Cracow crawled with rumors, that late summer, of some imminent rearrangement of prisoners. The rumors troubled Oskar in Zablocie, and at Płaszów, Amon got unofficial word that the camps would be disbanded.

In fact that meeting about security had to do not with saving Płaszów from partisans, but with the coming closure of the camp. Amon had called Madritsch and Oskar and Bosch out to Płaszów and held the meeting just to give himself protective colouration. It then became plausible for him to drive into Cracow and call on Wilhelm Koppe, the new SS police chief of the Government General. Amon sat on the far side of Koppe's desk wearing a fake frown, cracking his knuckles as if from the stress of a besieged Płaszów. He told Koppe the same story he'd given Oskar and the others – that partisan organisations had sprung up inside the camp, that Zionists within the wire had had communication with radicals of the Polish People's Army and the Jewish Combat Organisation. As the *Obergruppenführer* could appreciate, that sort of communication was difficult to stamp out – messages could come in in a smuggled loaf of bread. But at the first sign of active rebellion, he – Amon Goeth – as Commandant, would need to be able to take summary action. The question Amon wanted to ask was, if he fired first and did the paperwork for Oranienburg afterward, would the distinguished *Obergruppenführer* Koppe stand by him?

No problem, said Koppe. He didn't really approve of bureaucrats either. In years past, as police chief of the Wartheland, he'd commanded the fleet of extermination trucks which carried *Untermenschen* out into the countryside and which then, running the engines at full throttle, pumped the exhaust back into the locked interior. That too was an off-the-cuff operation, not permitting precise paperwork. Of course, you have to use your judgment, he told Amon. And if you do, I'll back you.

Oskar had sensed at the meeting that Amon was not really worried about partisans. Had he known then that Płaszów was to be liquidated, he would have understood the deeper meaning of Amon's performance. For Amon was worried about Wilek Chilowicz, his Jewish chief of camp police. Amon had often used Chilowicz as an agent on the black market. Chilowicz knew Cracow. He knew where he could sell the flour, rice, butter the Commandant held back from the camp supplies. He knew the dealers who would be interested in product from the custom jewellery shop staffed by interns like Wulkan. Amon was worried about the whole Chilowicz clique: Mrs. Marysia Chilowicz, who enjoyed conjugal privileges; Mietek Finkelstein, an associate; Chilowicz' sister Mrs. Ferber; and Mr. Ferber. If there had been an aristocracy inside Płaszów, it had been the Chilowiczes. They had had power over prisoners, but their knowledge was double-edged: they knew as much about Amon as they did about some miserable machinist in the Madritsch factory. If, when Płaszów closed, they were shipped to another camp, Amon knew they would try to barter their inside knowledge of his rackets as soon as they found themselves in the wrong line. Or more likely, as soon as they were hungry.

Of course, Chilowicz was uneasy too, and Amon could sense in him the doubt that he would be allowed to leave Płaszów. Amon decided to use Chilowicz' very concern as a lever. He called Sowinski, an SS auxiliary recruited from the High Tatras of Czechoslovakia, into his office for a conference. Sowinski was to approach Chilowicz and pretend to offer him an escape deal. Amon was sure that Chilowicz would be eager to negotiate.

Sowinski went and did it well. He told Chilowicz he could get the whole clan out of the camp in one of the large fuel-burning trucks. You could sit half a dozen people in the wood furnace if you were running on gas.

Chilowicz was interested in the proposition. Sowinski would of course need to deliver a note to friends on the outside, who would provide a vehicle. Sowinski would deliver the clan to the rendezvous point in the truck. Chilowicz was willing to pay in diamonds. But, said Chilowicz, as an earnest of their mutual trust, Sowinski must provide a weapon.

Sowinski reported the meeting to the Commandant, and Amon gave him a .38-calibre pistol with the pin filed down. This was passed to Chilowicz, who of course had neither need nor opportunity to test-fire it. Yet Amon would be able to swear to both Koppe and Oranienburg that he had found a weapon on the prisoner.

It was a Sunday in mid-August when Sowinski met the Chilowiczes in the building-material shed and hid them in the truck. Then he drove down Jerozolimska to the gate. There should be routine formalities there; then the truck could roll out into the countryside. In the empty furnace, in the pulses of the five escapees was the febrile, almost insupportable hope of leaving Amon behind.

At the gate, however, were Amon and Amthor and Hujar, and the Ukrainian Ivan Scharujew. A leisurely inspection was made. Lumbering with half-smiles across the bed of the truck, the gentlemen of the SS saved the wood furnace till last. They mimed surprise when they discovered the pitiable Chilowicz clan sardine-tight in the wood hole. As soon as Chilowicz had been dragged out, Amon 'found' the illegal gun tucked into his boot. Chilowicz' pockets were laden with diamonds, bribes paid him by the desperate inmates of the camp.

Prisoners at their day of rest heard that Chilowicz was under sentence down there at the gate. The news made for the same awe, the confusion of emotions that had operated the night the year before when Symche Spira and his OD had been executed. Nor could any prisoner decipher what it meant to his own chances.

The Chilowicz crowd were executed one at a time with pistols. Amon, very yellow now from liver disease, at the height of his obesity, wheezing like an elderly uncle, put the muzzle to Chilowicz' neck. Later the corpses were displayed in the *Appellplatz* with placards tied to their chests: 'THOSE WHO VIOLATE JUST LAWS CAN EXPECT A SIMILAR DEATH.'

That, of course, was not the moral the prisoners of Płaszów took from the sight.

Amon spent the afternoon drafting two long reports, one to Koppe, one to General Glücks's Section D, explaining how he had saved Płaszów from an insurgency in its first phase – the one in which a group of key conspirators escaped from the camp – by executing the plot's leaders. He did not finish revising either draft till 11 P.M. Frau Kochmann was too slow for such late work, and so the Commandant had Mietek Pemper roused from his barracks and brought to the villa. In the front parlor, Amon stated levelly that he believed the boy had been party to Chilowicz' escape attempt. Pemper was astounded and did not know how to answer. Looking around him for some sort of inspiration, he saw the seam of his pants leg, which had come unsewn. How could I pass on the outside in this sort of clothing? he asked.

The balance of frank desperation in his answer satisfied Amon. He told the boy to sit down and instructed him how the typing was to be set out and the pages numbered. Amon hit the papers with his spatulate fingertips. 'I want a first-class job done.' And Pemper thought, *That's the way of it – I can die now for being an escapee, or later in the year for having seen these justifications of Amon's.*

When Pemper was leaving the villa with the drafts in his hand, Goeth followed him out onto the patio and called a last order. 'When you type the list of insurgents,' Amon called companionably, 'I want you to leave room above my signature for another name to be inserted.'

Pemper nodded, discreet as any professional secretary. He stood just a half-second, trying for inspiration, some fast answer that would reverse Amon's order about the extra space. The space for his name. *Mietek Pemper*. In that hateful torrid silence of Sunday evening in Jerozolimska, nothing plausible came to him.

'Yes, Herr Commandant,' said Pemper.

As Pemper stumbled up the road to the Administration Building, he remembered a letter Amon had had him type earlier that summer. It had been addressed to Amon's father, the Viennese publisher, and was full of filial concern for an allergy which had troubled the old man that spring. Amon hoped that it had lifted by now. The reason Pemper remembered that letter out of all the others was that half an hour before he'd been called into Amon's office to take it down, the Commandant had dragged a girl filing clerk outside and executed her. The juxtaposition of the letter and the execution proved to Pemper that, for Amon, murder and allergies were events of equal weight. And if you told a tractable stenographer to leave a space for his name, it was a matter of course that he left it.

Pemper sat at the typewriter for more than an hour, but in the end left the space for himself. Not to do that would be even more suddenly fatal. There had been a rumor among Stern's friends that Schindler had some movement of people in mind, some rescue or other, but tonight rumors from Zablocie meant nothing anymore. Mietek typed; Mietek left in each report the space for his own death. And all his remembrance of the Commandant's criminal carbons which he'd so industriously memorised – all that was made futile by the space he left.

When both typescripts were word-perfect, he returned to the villa. Amon kept him waiting by the French windows while he himself sat in the parlor reading the documents. Pemper wondered if his own body would be displayed with some declamatory lettering: 'So Die All Jewish Bolshevists!'

At last Amon appeared at the windows. 'You may go to bed,' he said.

'Herr Commandant?'

'I said, you may go to bed.'

Pemper went. He walked less steadily now. After what he had seen, Amon could not let him live. But perhaps the Commandant believed there would be leisure to kill him later. In the meantime, life for a day was still life.

The space, as it proved, was for an elderly prisoner who, by unwise dealings with men like John and Hujar, had let it be known he had a cache of diamonds somewhere outside the camp. While Pemper sank into the sleep of the reprieved, Amon had the old man summoned to the villa, offered him his life for the diamonds' location, was shown the place, and, of course, executed the old man and added his name to the reports to Koppe and Oranienburg – to his humble claim of having snuffed out the spark of rebellion.

30

The orders, labelled OKH (Army High Command), already sat on Oskar's desk. Because of the war situation, the Director of Armaments told Oskar, KL Płaszów and therefore the Emalia camp were to be disbanded. Prisoners from Emalia would be sent to Płaszów, awaiting relocation. Oskar himself was to fold his Zablocie operation as quickly as possible, retaining on the premises only those technicians necessary for dismantling the plant. For further instructions, he should apply to the Evacuation Board, OKH, Berlin.

Oskar's initial reaction was a cool rage. He resented the tone, the sense of a distant official trying to absolve him from further concern. There was a man in Berlin who, not knowing of the black-market bread that bound Oskar and his prisoners together, thought it was reasonable for a factory owner to open the gate and let the people be taken. But the worst arrogance was that the letter did not define 'relocation.' Governor General Frank was more honest than that and had made a notorious speech a little earlier in the year. 'When we ultimately win the war, then as far as I'm concerned, Poles, Ukrainians, and all that rabble idling around here can be made into mincemeat, into anything you like.' Frank had the courage to put an accurate name to the process. In Berlin, they wrote 'relocation' and believed themselves excused.

Amon knew what 'relocation' meant and, during Oskar's next visit to Płaszów, freely told him so. All Płaszów men would be sent to Gröss-Rosen. The women would go to Auschwitz. Gröss-Rosen was a vast quarry camp in Lower Silesia. The German Earth & Stone Works, an SS enterprise with branches throughout Poland, Germany, and the conquered territories, consumed the prisoners of Gröss-Rosen. The processes at Auschwitz were, of course, more direct and modern.

When the news of the abolition of Emalia reached the factory floor and ran through the barracks, some Schindler people thought it was the end of all sanctuary. The Perlmans, whose daughter had come out of Aryan cover to plead for them, packed their blankets and talked philosophically to their bunk neighbors. Emalia has given us a year's rest, a year's soup, a year's sanity. Perhaps it might be enough. But they expected to die now. It was apparent from their voices.

Rabbi Levartov was resigned too. He was going back to unfinished business with Amon. Edith Liebgold, who'd been recruited by Bankier for the night shift in the first days of the ghetto, noticed that although Oskar spent hours talking solemnly with his Jewish supervisors, he did not come up to people and make dizzying promises. Perhaps he was as baffled and diminished by these orders from Berlin as the rest. So he wasn't quite the prophet he'd been the night she'd first come here more than three years ago.

Just the same, at the end of summer, as his prisoners packed their bundles and were marched back to Płaszów, there was a rumor among them that Oskar had spoken of buying them back. He had said it to Garde; he had said it to Bankier. You could almost hear him saying it – that level certainty, the paternal rumble of the throat. But as you went up Jerozolimska Street, past the Administration Building, staring in newcomer's disbelief at the hauling gangs from the quarry, the memory of Oskar's promises was very nearly just another burden.

The Horowitz family were back in Płaszów. Their father, Dolek, had last year manoeuvered them to Emalia, but here they were back. The six-year-old boy, Richard; the mother, Regina. Niusia, eleven now, was again sewing bristles onto brush paddles and watching, from the high windows, the trucks roll up to the Austrian hill fort, and the black cremation smoke rise over the hill. As Płaszów was when she had left it last year, so it continued. It was impossible for her to believe that it would ever end.

But her father believed that Oskar would make a list of people and extricate them. Oskar's list, in the mind of some, was already more than a mere tabulation. It was a *List*. It was a sweet chariot which might swing low.

Oskar raised the idea of taking Jews away from Cracow with him one night at Amon's villa. It was a still night at the end of summer. Amon seemed pleased to see him. Because of Amon's health – both Doctors Blancke and Gross warning him that if he didn't cut his eating and drinking he would die – there had not been so many visitors to the villa of late.

They sat together, drinking at Amon's new rate of moderation. Oskar sprang the news on him. He wanted to move his factory to Czechoslovakia. He wanted to take his skilled workers with him. He might need other skills from among the Płaszów workers too. He would seek the help of the Evacuation Board in finding an appropriate site, somewhere down in Moravia, and of the *Ostbahn* in making the shift southwest from Cracow. He let Amon know that he'd be very grateful for any support. The mention of gratitude always excited Amon. Yes, he said, if Oskar could get all the cooperation he needed from the boards involved, Amon would then allow a list of people to be drawn up.

When that was settled, Amon wanted a game of cards. He liked blackjack, a version of the French *vingt-et-un*. It was a hard game for junior officers to fake losing without being obvious. It did not permit of too much sycophancy. It was therefore true sport, and Amon preferred it. Besides, Oskar wasn't interested in losing this evening. He would be paying enough to Amon for that list.

The Commandant began by betting modestly, in 100-złoty bills, as if his doctors had advised moderation in this as well. He kept busting however, and when the beginning stake had been raised to 500 zł., Oskar got a 'natural,' an ace and a jack, which meant that Amon had to pay him double the stake.

Amon was disconsolate about that, but not too testy. He called for Helen Hirsch to bring coffee. She came in, a parody of a gentleman's servant, crisply dressed still in black but her right eye blinded by swelling. She was so small that Amon would need to stoop to beat her up. The girl knew Oskar now, but did not look at him. Nearly a year past, he had promised to get her out. Whenever he came to the villa he managed to slip down the corridor to the kitchen and ask her how she was. It meant something, but it had not touched the substance of her life. A few weeks back, for example, when the soup hadn't been the correct temperature – Amon was pernickety about soup, flyspecks in the corridor, fleas on dogs – the Commandant had called for Ivan and Petr and told them to take her to the birch tree in the garden and shoot her. He'd watched from the French windows as she walked in front of Petr's Mauser, pleading under her breath with the young Ukrainian. 'Petr, who's this you're going to shoot? It's Helen. Helen who gives you cakes. You couldn't shoot Helen, could you?' And Petr answering in the same manner, through clenched teeth, 'I know, Helen. I don't want to. But if I don't, he'll kill *me*.' She'd bent her head toward the spotted birch bark. Having often asked Amon why he wouldn't kill her, she wanted to die simply, to hurt him by her willing acceptance. But it wasn't possible. She was trembling so hard that he could have seen it. Her legs were shaking. And then she'd heard Amon call from the windows, 'Bring the bitch back. There's plenty of time to shoot her. In the meantime, it might still be possible to educate her.'

Insanely, in between his spates of savagery, there were brief phases in which he tried to play the benign master. He had said to her one morning, 'You're really a very well-trained servant. If after the war you need a reference, I shall be happy to give you one.' She knew it was just talk, a daydream. She turned her deaf ear, the one whose eardrum he had perforated with a blow. Sooner or later, she knew, she would die of his customary fury.

In a life like hers, a smile from visitors was only a momentary comfort. Tonight she placed the enormous silver pot of coffee beside the Herr Commandant – he still drank it by the bucket in cups laden with sugar – made her obeisance, and left.

Within an hour, when Amon was 3,700 zł. in debt to Oskar

and complaining sourly about his luck, Oskar suggested a variation on the betting. He would need a maid in Moravia, he said, when he moved to Czechoslovakia. There you couldn't get them as intelligent and well trained as Helen Hirsch. They were all country girls. Oskar suggested therefore that he and Amon play one hand, double or nothing. If Amon won, Oskar would pay him 7,400 zł. If he hit a 'natural,' it would be 14,800 zł. But if *I* win, said Oskar, then you give me Helen Hirsch for my list.

Amon wanted to think about that. Come on, said Oskar, she's going to Auschwitz anyhow. But there was an attachment there. Amon was so used to Helen that he couldn't easily wager her away. When he'd thought of an end for her, it had probably always been that he would finish her by his own hand, with personal passion. If he played cards for her and lost, he would be under pressure, as a Viennese sportsman, to give up the pleasure of intimate murder.

Much earlier in Płaszów's history, Schindler had asked that Helen be assigned to Emalia. But Amon had refused. It seemed only a year ago that Płaszów would exist for decades, and that the Commandant and his maid would grow old together, at least until some perceived fault in Helen brought about the abrupt end of the connection. This time a year ago, no one would have believed that the relationship would be resolved because the Russians were outside Lwów. As for Oskar's part in this proposal, he had made it lightly. He did not seem to see, in his offer to Amon, any parallel with God and Satan playing cards for human souls. He did not ask himself by what right he made a bid for the girl. If he lost, his chance of extracting her some other way was slim. But all chances were slim that year. Even his own.

Oskar got up and bustled around the room, looking for stationery with an official letterhead on it. He wrote out the marker for Amon to sign should he lose: '*I authorise that the name of prisoner Helen Hirsch be added to any list of skilled workers relocated with Herr Oskar Schindler's DEF Works.*'

Amon was dealer and gave Oskar an 8 and a 5. Oskar asked

to be dealt more. He received a 5 and an ace. It would have to do. Then Amon dealt to himself. A 4 came up, and then a king. God in heaven! said Amon. He was a gentleman cusser; he seemed to be too fastidious to use obscenities. I'm out. He laughed a little but was not really amused. My first cards, he explained, were a three and a five. With a four I should have been safe. Then I got this damned king.

In the end, he signed the marker. Oskar picked up all the chits he'd won that evening from Amon and returned them. Just look after the girl for me, he said, till it's time for us all to leave.

Out in her kitchen, Helen Hirsch did not know she'd been saved over cards.

Probably because Oskar reported his evening with Amon to Stern, rumors of Oskar's plan were heard in the Administration Building and even in the workshops. There *was* a Schindler list. It was worth everything to be on it.

31

At some point in any discussion of Schindler, the surviving friends of the *Herr Direktor* will blink and shake their heads and begin the almost mathematical business of finding the sum of his motives. For one of the commonest sentiments of Schindler Jews is still 'I don't know why he did it.' It can be said to begin with that Oskar was a gambler, was a sentimentalist who loved the transparency, the simplicity of doing good; that Oskar was by temperament an anarchist who loved to ridicule the system; and that beneath the hearty sensuality lay a capacity to be outraged by human savagery, to react to it and not to be overwhelmed. But none of this, jotted down, added up, explains the doggedness with which, in the autumn of 1944, he prepared a final haven for the graduates of Emalia.

And not only for them. In early September he drove to Podgórze and visited Madritsch, who at that point employed more than 3,000 prisoners in his uniform factory. This plant would now be disbanded. Madritsch would get his sewing machines back, and his workers would vanish. If we made a combined approach, said Oskar, we could get more than four thousand out. Mine and yours as well. We could relocate them in something like safety. Down in Moravia.

Madritsch would always and justly be revered by his surviving prisoners. The bread and chickens smuggled into his factory were paid for from his pocket and at continuous risk. He would have been considered a more stable man than Oskar. Not as flamboyant, and not as subject to obsession. He had not suffered arrest. But he had been much more humane than was safe and, without wit and energy, would have ended in Auschwitz.

Now Oskar presented to him a vision of a Madritsch-Schindler camp somewhere in the High Jeseniks; some smoky, safe little industrial hamlet.

Madritsch was attracted by the idea but did not rush to say yes. He could tell that though the war was lost, the SS system had become more instead of less implacable. He was correct in believing that, unhappily, the prisoners of Płaszów would – in coming months – be consumed in death camps to the west. For if Oskar was stubborn and possessed, so were the SS Main Office and their prize field operatives, the commandants of the Concentration Camps.

He did not say no, however. He needed time to think about it. Though he couldn't say it to Oskar, it is likely he was afraid of sharing factory premises with a rash, demonic fellow like Herr Schindler.

Without any clear word from Madritsch, Oskar took to the road. He went to Berlin and bought dinner for Colonel Erich Lange. I can go completely over to the manufacture of shells, Oskar told Lange. I can transfer my heavy machinery.

Lange was crucial. He could guarantee contracts; he could write the hearty recommendations Oskar needed for the Evacuation Board and the German officials in Moravia.

Later, Oskar would say of this shadowy staff officer that he had given consistent help. Lange was still in that state of exalted desperation and moral disgust characteristic of many who had worked inside the system but not always for it. We can do it, said Lange, but it will take some money. Not for me. For others.

Through Lange, Oskar talked with an officer of the Evacuation Board at OKH on Bendler Street. It was likely, said this officer, that the evacuation would be approved in principle. But there was a major obstacle. The Governor *cum* Gauleiter of Moravia, ruling from a castle at Liberec, had followed a policy of keeping Jewish labour camps *out* of his province. Neither the SS nor the Armaments Inspectorate had so far persuaded him to change his attitude. A good man to discuss this impasse with, said the officer, would be a middle-aged *Wehrmacht* engineer down in the Troppau office of the Armaments Inspectorate, a man named Sussmuth. Oskar could talk to Sussmuth too about what relocation sites were available in Moravia. Meanwhile, Herr Schindler could count on the support of the Main Evacuation Board. 'But you can understand that in view of the pressure they are under, and the inroads the war has made on their personal comforts, they are more likely to give a quick answer if you could be considerate to them in some way. We poor city fellows are short of ham, cigars, liquor, cloth, coffee . . . that sort of thing.'

The officer seemed to think that Oskar carried around with him half the peacetime produce of Poland. Instead, to get together a gift parcel for the gentlemen of the board, Oskar had to buy luxuries at the Berlin black-market rate. An old gentleman on the desk at the Hotel Adlon was able to acquire excellent schnapps for Herr Schindler for a discount price of about 80 RM. a bottle. And you couldn't send the gentlemen of the board less than a dozen. Coffee, however, was like gold, and Havanas were at an insane price. Oskar bought them in quantity and included them in the hamper. The gentlemen might need a head of steam if they were to bring the Governor of Moravia around.

In the midst of Oskar's negotiations, Amon Goeth was arrested.

Someone must have informed on him. Some jealous junior officer, or a concerned citizen who'd visited the villa and been shocked by Amon's sybaritic style. A senior SS investigator named Eckert began to look at Amon's financial dealings. The shots Amon had taken from the balcony were not germane to Eckert's investigation. But the embezzlements and the black-market dealings were, as were complaints from some of his SS inferiors that he had treated them severely.

Amon was on leave in Vienna, staying with his father, the publisher, when the SS arrested him. They also raided an apartment *Hauptsturmführer* Goeth kept in the city and discovered a cache of money, some 80,000 RM., which Amon could not explain to their satisfaction. They found as well, stacked to the ceiling, close to a million cigarettes. Amon's Viennese apartment, it seemed, was more warehouse than *pied à terre*.

It might be at first sight surprising that the SS – or rather, the officers of Bureau V of the Reich Security Main Office – should want to arrest such an effective servant as *Hauptsturmführer* Goeth. But they had already investigated irregularities in Buchenwald and tried to pin the Commandant, Koch. They had even attempted to find evidence for the arrest of the renowned Rudolf Höss, and had questioned a Viennese Jewess who, they suspected, was pregnant by this star of the camp system. So Amon, raging in his apartment while they ransacked it, had no cause to hope for much immunity.

They took him to Breslau and put him in an SS prison to await investigation and trial. They showed their innocence of the way affairs were run in Płaszów by going to the villa and questioning Helen Hirsch on suspicion of her being involved in Amon's swindles. Twice in coming months she would be taken to the cells beneath the SS barracks of Płaszów for interrogation. They fired questions at her about Amon's contacts on the black market – who his agents were, how he worked the jewellery shop at Płaszów, the custom-tailoring shop, the upholstery plant. No one hit her or threatened her. But it was their conviction that she was a member of a gang that tormented her. If Helen had ever thought of an unlikely and glorious salvation, she would not have dared dream that Amon would be arrested by his own people. But she felt her sanity going now in the interrogation room, when under their law they tried to shackle her to Amon.

Chilowicz might have been able to help you, she told them. But Chilowicz is dead.

They were policemen by trade, and after a time would decide she could give them nothing except a little information about the sumptuous cuisine at the villa Goeth. They could have asked her about her scars, but they knew they couldn't get Amon on grounds of sadism. Investigating sadism in the camp at Sachsenhausen, they'd been forced off the premises by armed guards. In Buchenwald they had found a material witness, an NCO, to testify against the Commandant, but the informer had been found dead in his cell. The head of that SS investigating team ordered that samples of a poison found in the NCO's stomach be administered to four Russian prisoners. He watched them die, and so had his proof against the Commandant and the camp doctor. Even though he got prosecutions for murder and sadistic practice, it was a strange justice. Above all, it made the camp personnel close ranks and dispose of living evidence. So the men of Bureau V did not question Helen about her injuries. They stuck to embezzlement, and in the end stopped troubling her.

They investigated Mietek Pemper too. He was wise enough not to tell them much about Amon, certainly not about his crimes against humans. He knew little but rumors of Amon's frauds. He played the neutral and well-mannered typist of nonclassified material. 'The Herr Commandant would never discuss such matters with me,' he pleaded continually. But beneath his performance, he must have suffered the same howling disbelief as Helen Hirsch. If there was one event most likely to guarantee *him* a chance of life, it was Amon's arrest. For there had been no more certain limit to his life than this: that when the Russians reached Tarnow, Amon would dictate his last letters and then assassinate the typist. What worried Mietek, therefore, was that they would release Amon too soon.

But they were not interested solely in the question of Amon's speculations. The SS judge who questioned Pemper had been told by *Oberscharführer* Lorenz Landsdorfer that *Hauptsturmführer* Goeth had let his Jewish stenographer type up the directives and plans to be followed by the Płaszów garrison in the case of an assault on the camp by partisans. Amon, in explaining to Pemper how the typing of these plans should be set out, had even shown him copies of similar plans for other concentration camps. The judge was so alarmed by this disclosure of secret documents to a Jewish prisoner that he ordered Pemper's arrest.

Pemper spent two miserable weeks in a cell beneath the SS barracks. He was not beaten, but was questioned regularly by a series of Bureau V investigators and by two SS judges. He thought he could read in their eyes the conclusion that the safest thing was to shoot him. One day during questioning about Płaszów's emergency plans, Pemper asked his interrogators, 'Why keep me here? A prison is a prison. I have a life sentence anyhow.' It was an argument calculated to bring a resolution, either release from the cells or else a bullet. After the session ended, Pemper spent some hours of anxiety until his cell door opened again. He was marched out and returned to his hut in the camp. It was not the last time, however, that he would be questioned on subjects relating to Commandant Goeth.

It seemed that following his arrest, Amon's juniors did not rush to give him references. They were careful. They waited. Bosch, who'd drunk so much of the Commandant's liquor, told *Untersturmführer* John that it was dangerous to try to bribe these determined investigators from Bureau V. As for Amon's seniors, Schemer was gone, assigned to hunting partisans, and would in the end be killed in an ambush in the forests of Niepolomice. Amon was in the hands of men from Oranienburg who'd never dined at the *Goethhaus* – or, if they had, had been either shocked or touched by envy.

After her release by the SS, Helen Hirsch, now working for the new Commandant, *Hauptsturmführer* Büscher, received a friendly note from Amon asking her to get together a parcel of clothes, some romances and detective novels, and some liquor to comfort him in his cell. It was, she thought, like a letter from a relative. *'Would you kindly gather for me the following,'* it said, and ended with *'Hoping to see you again soon.'*

Meanwhile Oskar had been down to the market city of Troppau to see engineer Sussmuth. He'd brought along liquor and diamonds, but they weren't needed in this case. Sussmuth told Oskar that he had already proposed that some small Jewish work camps be set up in the border towns of Moravia to turn out goods for the Armaments Inspectorate. Such camps would, of course, be under the central control of either Auschwitz or Gröss-Rosen, for the areas of influence of the big concentration camps crossed the Polish-Czechoslovak border. But there was more safety for prisoners in little work camps than could be found in the grand necropolis of Auschwitz itself. Sussmuth had got nowhere, of course. The Castle at Liberec had trampled on the proposal. He had never had a lever. Oskar – the support Oskar had from Colonel Lange and the gentlemen of the Evacuation Board – *that* could be the lever.

Sussmuth had in his office a list of sites suitable to receive plants evacuated from the war zone. Near Oskar's hometown of Zwittau, on the edge of a village called Brinnlitz, was a great textile plant owned by the Viennese brothers Hoffman. They'd been in butter and cheese in their home city, but had come to the *Sudetenland* behind the legions (just as Oskar had gone to Cracow) and become textile magnates. An entire annex of their plant lay idle, used as a storehouse for obsolete spinning machines. A site like that was served from the rail depot at Zwittau, where Schindler's brother-in-law was in charge of the freight yard. And a railway loop ran close to the gates. The brothers are profiteers, said Sussmuth, smiling. They have some local party backing – the County Council and the District Leader are in their pockets. But you have Colonel Lange behind you. I will write to Berlin at once, Sussmuth promised, and recommend the use of the Hoffman annex.

Oskar knew the Germanic village of Brinnlitz from his childhood. Its racial character was in its name, since the Czechs would have called it Brnenec, just as a Czech Zwittau would have become Zvitava. The Brinnlitz citizens would not fancy a thousand or more Jews in their neighborhood. The Zwittau people, from whom some of Hoffman's workers were recruited, would not like it either, this contamination, so late in the war, of their rustic-industrial backwater.

In any case, Oskar drove down to take a quick look at the site.

He did not approach Hoffman Brothers' front office, since that would give the tougher Hoffman brother, the one who chaired the company, too much warning. But he was able to wander into the annex without being challenged. It was an old-fashioned two-story industrial barracks built around a courtyard. The ground floor was high-ceilinged and full of old machines and crates of wool. The upper floor must have been intended as offices and for lighter equipment. Its floor would not stand the weight of the big pressing machines. Downstairs would do for the new workshops of DEF, as offices and, in one corner, the *Herr Direktor*'s apartment. Upstairs would be barracks for the prisoners.

He was delighted with the place. He drove back to Cracow yearning to get started, to spend the necessary money, to talk to Madritsch again. For Sussmuth could find a site for Madritsch too – perhaps even floor space in Brinnlitz.

When he got back, he found that an Allied bomber, shot down by a *Luftwaffe* fighter, had crashed on the two end barracks in the backyard prison. Its blackened fuselage sat crookedly across the wreckage of the flattened huts. Only a small squad of prisoners had been left behind in Emalia to wind up production and maintain the plant. They had seen it come down, flaming. There had been two men inside, and their bodies had burned. The *Luftwaffe* people who came to take them away had told Adam Garde that the bomber was a Stirling and that the men were Australian. One, who was holding the charred remnants of an English Bible, must have crashed with it in his hand. Two others had parachuted in the suburbs. One had been found, dead of wounds, still in his harness. The partisans had got to the other one first and were hiding him somewhere. What these Australians had been doing was dropping supplies to the partisans in the primeval forest east of Cracow.

If Oskar had wanted some sort of confirmation, this was it. That men should come all this way from unimaginable little towns in the Australian Outback to hasten the end in Cracow. He put a call through at once to the official in charge of rolling stock in the office of *Ostbahn* President Gerteis and invited him to dinner to talk about DEF's potential need of flatcars.

A week after Oskar spoke to Sussmuth, the gentlemen of the Berlin Armaments Board instructed the Governor of Moravia that Oskar's armaments company was to be allocated the annex of Hoffman's spinning mill in Brinnlitz. The Governor's bureaucrats could do nothing more, Sussmuth told Oskar by telephone, than slow the paperwork down. But Hoffman and other Party men in the Zwittau area were already conferring and passing resolutions against Oskar's intrusion into Moravia. The Party *Kreisleiter* in Zwittau wrote to Berlin complaining that Jewish prisoners from Poland would be a peril to the health of Moravian Germans. Spotted fever would very likely appear in the region for the first time in modern history, and Oskar's small armaments factory, of dubious value to the war effort, would also attract Allied bombers, with resultant damage to the important Hoffman mills. The population of Jewish criminals in the proposed Schindler camp would outweigh the small and decent population of Brinnlitz and be a cancer on the honest flank of Zwittau.

A protest of that kind didn't have a chance, since it went straight to the office of Erich Lange in Berlin. Appeals to Troppau were quashed by honest Sussmuth. Nonetheless, the posters went up on walls in Oskar's hometown: 'KEEP THE JEWISH CRIMINALS OUT.'

And Oskar was paying. He was paying the Evacuation Committee in Cracow to help speed up the permits for the transfer of his machinery. The Department of the Economy in Cracow had to be encouraged to provide the clearances of bank holdings. Currency wasn't favoured these days, so he paid in goods – in kilos of tea, in pairs of leather shoes, in carpets, in coffee, in canned fish. He spent his afternoons in the little streets off the market square of Cracow haggling at staggering prices for whatever the bureaucrats desired. Otherwise, he was sure, they would keep him waiting till his last Jew had gone to Auschwitz.

It was Sussmuth who told him that people from Zwittau were writing to the Armaments Inspectorate accusing Oskar of black-marketeering. If they're writing to me, said Sussmuth, you can bet the same letters are going to the police chief of Moravia, *Obersturmführer* Otto Rasch. You should introduce yourself to Rasch and show him what a charming fellow you are.

Oskar had known Rasch when he was SS police chief of Katowice. Rasch was, by happy chance, a friend of the chairman of Ferrum AG at Sosnowiec, from which Oskar had bought his steel. But in rushing down to Brno to head off informers, Oskar didn't rely on anything as flimsy as mutual friendships. He took a diamond cut in the *brilliant* style which, somehow, he introduced into the meeting. When it crossed the table and ended on Rasch's side of the desk, it secured Oskar's Brno front.

Oskar later estimated that he spent 100,000 RM. – nearly $40,000 – to grease the transfer to Brinnlitz. Few of his survivors would ever find the figure unlikely, though there were those who shook their heads and said, 'No, *more!* It would have to have been more than that.'

He had drawn up what he called a preparatory list and delivered it to the Administration Building. There were more than a thousand names on it – the names of all the prisoners of the backyard prison camp of Emalia, as well as new names. Helen Hirsch's name was freshly on the list, and Amon was not there to argue about it.

And the list would expand if Madritsch agreed to go to Moravia with Oskar. So Oskar kept working on Titsch, his ally at Julius Madritsch's ear. Those Madritsch prisoners who were closest to Titsch knew the list was under compilation, that they could have access to it. Titsch told them without any ambiguity: You must get on it. In all the reams of Płaszów paperwork, Oskar's dozen pages of names were the only pages with access to the future.

But Madritsch still could not decide whether he wanted an alliance with Oskar, whether he would add his 3,000 to the total.

There is again a haziness suitable to a legend about the precise chronology of Oskar's list. The haziness doesn't attach to the existence of the list – a copy can be seen today in the archives of the *Yad Vashem*. There is no uncertainty as we shall see about the names remembered by Oskar and Titsch at the last minute and attached to the end of the official paper. The names on the list are definite. But the circumstances encourage legends. The problem is that the list is remembered with an intensity which, by its very heat, blurs. The list is an absolute good. The list is life. All around its cramped margins lies the gulf.

Some of those whose names appeared on the list say that there was a party at Goeth's villa, a reunion of SS men and entrepreneurs to celebrate the times they'd had there. Some even believe that Goeth was there, but since the SS did not release on bail, that is impossible. Others believe that the party was held at Oskar's own apartment above his factory. Oskar had for more than two years given excellent parties there. One Emalia prisoner remembers the early hours of 1944 when he was on night watch duty and Oskar had wandered down from his apartment at one o'clock, escaping the noise upstairs and bringing with him two cakes, two hundred cigarettes, and a bottle for his friend the watchman.

At the Płaszów graduation party, wherever it took place, the guests included Dr. Blancke, Franz Bosch, and, by some reports, *Oberführer* Julian Schemer, on vacation from his partisan-hunting. Madritsch was there too, and Titsch. Titsch would later say that at it Madritsch informed Oskar for the first time that he would not be going to Moravia with him. 'I've done everything I can for the Jews,' Madritsch told him. It was a reasonable claim; he would not be persuaded although he said Titsch had been at him for days.

Madritsch was a just man. Later he would be honoured as such. He simply did not believe that Moravia would work. If he had, the indications are that he would have attempted it.

What else is known about the party is that an urgency operated there, because the Schindler list had to be handed in that evening.

This is an element in all the versions of the story survivors tell. The survivors could tell and expand upon it only if they had heard it in the first place from Oskar, a man with a taste for embellishing a story. But in the early 1960s, Titsch himself attested to the substantial truth of this one. Perhaps the new and temporary Commandant of Płaszów, a *Hauptsturmführer* Büscher, had said to Oskar, 'Enough fooling around, Oskar! We have to finalise the paperwork and the transportation.' Perhaps there was some other form of deadline imposed by the *Ostbahn*, by the availability of transport.

At the end of Oskar's list, therefore, Titsch now typed in, above the official signatures, the names of Madritsch prisoners. Almost seventy names were added, written in by Titsch from his own and Oskar's memories. Among them were those of the Feigenbaum family – the adolescent daughter who suffered from incurable bone cancer; the teen-age son Lutek with his shaky expertise in repairing sewing machines. Now they were all transformed, as Titsch scribbled, into skilled munitions workers. There was singing in the apartment, loud talk and laughter, a fog of cigarette smoke, and, in a corner, Oskar and Titsch quizzing each other over people's names, straining for a clue to the spelling of Polish patronyms.

In the end, Oskar had to put his hand on Titsch's wrist. We're over the limit, he said. They'll balk at the number we already have. Titsch continued to strain for names, and tomorrow morning would wake damning himself because one had come to him too late. But now he was at the limit, wrung out by this work. It was blasphemously close to creating people anew just by thinking of them. He did not begrudge doing it. It was what it said of the world – that was what made the heavy air of Schindler's apartment so hard for Titsch to breathe.

The list was vulnerable, however, through the personnel clerk, Marcel Goldberg. Büscher, the new Commandant, who was there merely to wind the camp down, himself could not have cared, within certain numerical limits, who went on the list. Therefore

Goldberg had the power to tinker with its edges. It was known to prisoners already that Goldberg would take bribes. The Dresners knew it. Juda Dresner – uncle of red Genia, husband of the Mrs. Dresner who'd once been refused a hiding place in a wall, and father of Janek and of young Danka – Juda Dresner knew it. 'He paid Goldberg,' the family would simply say to explain how they got on the Schindler list. They never knew what was given. Wulkan the jeweller presumably got himself, his wife, his son on the list in the same way.

Poldek Pfefferberg was told about the list by an SS NCO named Hans Schreiber. Schreiber, a young man in his mid-twenties, had as evil a name as any other SS man in Płaszów, but Pfefferberg had become something of a mild favourite of his in that way that was common to relationships – throughout the system – between individual prisoners and SS personnel. It had begun one day when Pfefferberg, as a group leader in his barracks, had had responsibility for window cleaning. Schreiber inspected the glass and found a smudge, and began browbeating Poldek in the style that was often a prelude to execution. Pfefferberg lost his temper and told Schreiber that both of them knew the windows were perfectly polished and if Schreiber wanted a reason to shoot him, he ought to do it without any more delay. The outburst had, in a contradictory way, amused Schreiber, who afterward occasionally used to stop Pfefferberg and ask him how he and his wife were, and sometimes even gave Poldek an apple for Mila. In the summer of 1944, Poldek had appealed to him desperately to extricate Mila from a trainload of women being sent from Płaszów to the evil camp at Stutthof on the Baltic. Mila was already in the lines boarding the cattle cars when Schreiber came waving a piece of paper and calling her name. Another time, a Sunday, he turned up drunk at Pfefferberg's barracks and, in front of Poldek and a few other prisoners, began to weep for what he called 'the dreadful things' he had done in Płaszów. He intended, he said, to expiate them on the Eastern Front. In the end, he would.

Now he told Poldek that Schindler had a list and that Poldek should do everything he could to get on it. Poldek went down to the Administration Building to beg Goldberg to add his name and Mila's to the list. Schindler had in the past year and a half often visited Poldek in the camp garage and had always promised rescue. Poldek had, however, become such an accomplished welder that the garage supervisors, who needed for their lives' sake to produce high-standard work, would never let him go. Now Goldberg sat with his hand on the list – he had already added his own name to it – and this old friend of Oskar's, once a frequent guest in the apartment in Straszewskiego, expected to have himself written down for sentiment's sake. 'Do you have any diamonds?' Goldberg asked Pfefferberg.

'Are you serious?' asked Poldek.

'For this list,' said Goldberg, a man of prodigious and accidental power, 'it takes diamonds.'

Now that the Viennese music lover *Hauptsturmführer* Goeth was in prison, the Rosner brothers, musicians to the court, were free to work their way onto the list. Dolek Horowitz also, who had earlier got his wife and children out to Emalia, now persuaded Goldberg to include him, his wife, his son, his young daughter. Horowitz had always worked in the central warehouse of Płaszów and had managed to put some small treasure away. Now it was paid to Marcel Goldberg.

Among those included in the list were the Bejski brothers, Uri and Moshe, officially described as machine fitter and draughtsman. Uri had a knowledge of weapons, and Moshe a gift for forging documents. The circumstances of the list are so clouded that it is not possible to say whether they were included for these talents or not.

Josef Bau, the ceremonious bridegroom, would at some stage be included, but without his knowing it. It suited Goldberg to keep everyone in the dark about the list. Given his nature, it is possible to assume that if Bau made any personal approach to Goldberg it could only have been on the basis that his mother, his wife, himself should all be included. He would not find out until too late that he alone would be listed for Brinnlitz.

As for Stern, the *Herr Direktor* had included him from the beginning. Stern was the only father confessor Oskar ever had, and Stern's suggestions had a great authority with him. Since October 1, no Jewish prisoner had been allowed out of Płaszów either to march to the cable factory or for any other purpose. At the same time, the trusties in the Polish prison had begun to put guards on the barracks to stop Jewish prisoners from trading with the Poles for bread. The price of illegal bread reached a level it would be hard to express in złoty. In the past you could have bought a loaf for your second coat, 250 gm. for a clean undershirt. Now – as with Goldberg – it took diamonds.

During the first week of October, Oskar and Bankier visited Płaszów for some reason and went as usual to see Stern in the Construction Office. Stern's desk was down the hallway from the vanished Amon's office. It was possible to speak more freely here than ever before. Stern told Schindler about the inflated price of rye bread. Oskar turned to Bankier. 'Make sure Weichert gets fifty thousand złoty,' murmured Oskar.

Dr. Michael Weichert was chairman of the former Jewish Communal Self-Help, now renamed Jewish Relief Office. He and his office were permitted to operate for cosmetic reasons and, in part, because of Weichert's powerful connections in the German Red Cross. Though many Polish Jews within the camps would treat him with understandable suspicion, and though this suspicion would bring him to trial after the war – he would be exonerated – Weichert was exactly the man to find 50,000 zł. worth of bread quickly and introduce it into Płaszów.

The conversation of Stern and Oskar moved on. The 50,000 złoty were a mere *obiter dicta* of their talk about the unsettled times and about how Amon might be enjoying his cell in Breslau. Later in the week black-market bread from town was smuggled into camp hidden beneath cargoes of cloth, coal, or scrap iron. Within a day, the price had fallen to its accustomed level.

It was a nice case of connivance between Oskar and Stern, and would be followed by other instances.

32

At least one of the Emalia people crossed off by Goldberg to make room for others – for relatives, Zionists, specialists, or payers – would blame Oskar for it.

In 1963, the Martin Buber Society would receive a pitiable letter from a New Yorker, a former Emalia prisoner. In Emalia, he said, Oskar had promised deliverance. In return, the people had made him wealthy with their labour. Yet some found themselves off the edge of the list. This man saw his own omission as a very personal betrayal and – with all the fury of someone who has been made to travel through the flames to pay for another man's lie – blamed Oskar for all that had happened afterward: for Gröss-Rosen, and for the frightful cliff at Mauthausen from which prisoners were thrown, and last of all for the death march with which the war would end.

Strangely, the letter, radiant with just anger, shows most graphically that life on the list was a feasible matter, while life off it was unutterable. But it seems unjust to condemn Oskar for Goldberg's fiddling with names. The camp authorities would, in the chaos of those last days, sign any list Goldberg gave them as long as it did not exceed too drastically the 1,100 prisoners Oskar had been granted. Oskar himself could not police Goldberg by the hour. His own day was spent speaking to bureaucrats, his evenings in buttering them up.

He had, for example, to receive shipment authorisations for his Hilo machines and metal presses from old friends in the office of General Schindler, some of whom delayed the paperwork, finding small problems which could confound the idea of Oskar's salvage of his 1,100.

One of these Inspectorate men had raised the problem that Oskar's armament machines had come to him by way of the procurement section of the Berlin Inspectorate, and under approval from its licensing section, specifically for use in Poland. Neither of these sections had been notified of the proposed move to Moravia. They would need to be. It could be a month before they gave their authorisation. Oskar did not have a month. Płaszów would be empty by the end of October; everyone would be in Gröss-Rosen or Auschwitz. In the end, the problem was cleared away by the accustomed gifts.

As well as such preoccupations, Oskar was concerned about the SS investigators who had arrested Amon. He half-expected to be arrested or – which was the same thing – heavily interrogated about his relationship with the former Commandant. He was wise to anticipate it, for one of the explanations Amon had offered for the 80,000 RM. the SS had found among his belongings was 'Oskar Schindler gave it to me so I'd go easy on the Jews.' Oskar therefore had to keep in contact with friends of his at Pomorska Street who might be able to tell him the direction Bureau V's investigation of Amon was taking.

Finally, since his camp at Brinnlitz would be under the ultimate supervision of KL Gröss-Rosen, he was already dealing with the Commandant of Gröss-Rosen, *Sturmbannführer* Hassebroeck. Under Hassebroeck's management, 100,000 would die in the Gröss-Rosen system, but when Oskar conferred with him on the telephone and drove across into Lower Silesia to meet him, he seemed the least of all Oskar's worries. Schindler was used by now to meeting charming killers and noticed that Hassebroeck even seemed grateful to him for extending the Gröss-Rosen empire into Moravia. For Hassebroeck *did* think in terms of empire. He controlled one hundred and three subcamps. (Brinnlitz would be one hundred and four and – with its more than 1,000 inmates and its sophisticated industry – a major addition.) Seventy-eight of Hassebroeck's camps were located in Poland, sixteen in Czechoslovakia, ten in the Reich. It was much bigger cheese than anything Amon had managed.

With so much sweetening, cajoling, and form-filling to occupy him in the week Płaszów was wound down, Oskar could not have found the time to monitor Goldberg, even if he had had the power. In any case, the account the prisoners give of the camp in its last day and night is one of milling and chaos, Goldberg – Lord of the Lists – at its centre, still holding out for offers.

Dr. Idek Schindel, for example, approached Goldberg to get himself and his two young brothers into Brinnlitz. Goldberg would not give an answer, and Schindel would not find out until the evening of October 15, when the male prisoners were marshalled for the cattle cars, that he and his brothers were not listed for the Schindler camp. They joined the line of Schindler people anyway. It is a scene from a cautionary engraving of Judgment Day – the ones without the right mark attempting to creep onto the line of the justified and being spotted by an angel of retribution, in this case *Oberscharführer* Muller, who came up to the doctor with his whip and slapped him, left cheek, right cheek, left and right again with the leather butt, while asking amusedly, 'Why would you want to get on that line?'

Schindel would be made to stay on with the small party involved in liquidating Płaszów and would then travel with a carload of sick women to Auschwitz. They would be placed in a hut in some corner of Birkenau and left to die. Yet most of them, overlooked by camp officials and exempt from the usual regimen of the place, would live. Schindel himself would be sent to Flossenburg and then – with his brothers – on a death march. He would survive by a layer of skin, but the youngest Schindel boy would be shot on the march on the next-to-last day of the war. That is an image of the way the Schindler list, without any malice on Oskar's side, with adequate malice on Goldberg's, still tantalises survivors, and tantalised them in those desperate October days.

Everyone has a story about the list. Henry Rosner lined up with the Schindler people, but an NCO spotted his violin and, knowing that Amon would require music should he be released from prison, sent Rosner back. Rosner then hid his violin under his coat, against his side, tucking the node of the sound post under his armpit. He lined up again and was let through to the Schindler cars. Rosner had been one of those to whom Oskar had made promises, and so had always been on the list. It was the same with the Jereths: old Mr. Jereth of the box factory and Mrs. Chaja Jereth, described in the list inexactly and hopefully as a *Metallarbeiterin* – a metalworker. The Perlmans were also on as old Emalia hands, and the Levartovs as well. In fact, in spite of Goldberg, Oskar got for the most part the people he had asked for, though there may have been some surprises among them. A man as worldly as Oskar could not have been amazed to find Goldberg himself among the inhabitants of Brinnlitz.

But there were more welcome additions than that. Poldek Pfefferberg, for example, accidentally overlooked and rejected by Goldberg for lack of diamonds, let it be known that he wanted to buy vodka – he could pay in clothing or bread. When he'd acquired the bottle, he got permission to take it down to the orderly building in Jerozolimska where Schreiber was on duty. He gave Schreiber the bottle and pleaded with him to force Goldberg to include Mila and himself. 'Schindler,' he said, 'would have written us down if he'd remembered.' Poldek had no doubt that he was negotiating for his life. 'Yes,' Schreiber agreed. 'The two of you must get on it.' It is a human puzzle why men like Schreiber didn't in such moments ask themselves, *If this man and his wife were worth saving, why weren't the rest?*

The Pfefferbergs would find themselves on the Schindler line when the time came. And so, to their surprise, would Helen Hirsch and the younger sister whose survival had always been Helen's own obsession.

The men of the Schindler list entrained at the Płaszów siding on a Sunday, October 15. It would be another full week before the women left. Though the 800 were kept separate during the loading of the train and were pushed into freight cars kept exclusively for Schindler personnel, they were coupled to cars containing 1,300 other prisoners all bound for Gröss-Rosen. It seems that some half-expected to have to pass through Gröss-Rosen on their way to Schindler's camp; but many others believed that the journey would be direct. They were prepared to endure a slow trip to Moravia – they accepted that they would be made to spend time sitting in the cars at junctions and on sidings. They might wait half a day at a time for traffic with higher priority to pass. The first snow had fallen in the last week, and it would be cold. Each prisoner had been issued only 300 gm. of bread to last the journey, and each car had been provided with a single water bucket. For their natural functions, the travellers would have to use a corner of the floor, or if packed too tightly, urinate and defecate where they stood. But in the end, despite all their griefs they would tumble out at a Schindler establishment. The 300 women of the list would enter the cars the following Sunday in the same sanguine state of mind.

Other prisoners noticed that Goldberg travelled as lightly as any of them. He must have had contacts outside Płaszów to hold his diamonds for him. Those who still hoped to influence him on behalf of an uncle, a brother, a sister allowed him enough space to sit in comfort. The others squatted, their knees pushed into their chins. Dolek Horowitz held six-year-old Richard in his arms. Henry Rosner made a nest of clothing on the floor for nine-year-old Olek.

It took three days. Sometimes, at sidings, their breath froze on the walls. Air was always scarce, but when you got a mouthful it was icy and foetid. The train halted at last on the dusk of a comfortless autumn day. The doors were unlocked, and passengers were expected to alight as quickly as businessmen with appointments to keep. SS guards ran among them shouting directions and blaming them for smelling. 'Take everything off!' the NCOs were roaring. 'Everything for disinfection!' They piled their clothing and marched naked into the camp. By six in the evening they stood in naked lines on the *Appellplatz* of this bitter destination. Snow stood in the surrounding woods; the surface of the parade ground was iced. It was not a Schindler camp. It was Gröss-Rosen. Those who had paid Goldberg glared at him, threatening murder, while SS men in overcoats walked along the lines, lashing the buttocks of those who openly shivered.

They kept the men on the *Appellplatz* all night, for there were no huts available. It was not until midmorning the next day that they would be put under cover. In speaking of that seventeen hours of exposure, of ineffable cold dragging down on the heart, survivors do not mention any deaths. Perhaps life under the SS, or even at Emalia, had tempered them for a night like this one. Though it was a milder evening than those earlier in the week, it was still murderous enough. Some of them, of course, were too distracted by the possibility of Brinnlitz to drift away with cold.

Later, Oskar would meet prisoners who had survived an even longer exposure to cold and frostbite. Certainly elderly Mr. Garde, the father of Adam Garde, lived through this night, as did little Olek Rosner and Richard Horowitz.

Toward eleven o'clock the next morning, they were taken to the showers. Poldek Pfefferberg, crowded in with the others, considered the nozzle above his head with suspicion, wondering if water or gas would rain down. It was water; but before it was turned on, Ukrainian barbers passed among them, shaving their heads, their pubic hair, their armpits. You stood straight, eyes front, while the Ukrainian worked at you with his unhoned razor. 'It's too dull,' one of the prisoners complained. 'No,' said the Ukrainian, and slashed the prisoner's leg to show that the blade still held a cutting edge.

After the showers, they were issued striped prison uniforms and crowded into barracks. The SS sat them in lines, like galley oarsmen, one man backed up between the legs of the man behind him, his own opened legs affording support to the man in front. By this method, 2,000 men were crammed into three huts. German *Kapos* armed with truncheons sat on chairs against the wall and watched. Men were wedged so tightly – every inch of the floor space covered – that to leave their rows for the latrines, even if the *Kapos* permitted it, meant walking on heads and shoulders and being cursed for it.

In the middle of one hut was a kitchen where turnip soup was being made and bread baked. Poldek Pfefferberg, coming back from a visit to the latrines, found the kitchen under the supervision of a Polish Army NCO he had known at the beginning of the war. The NCO gave Poldek some bread and permitted him to sleep by the kitchen fire. The others, however, spent their nights wedged in the human chain.

Each day they were stood at attention in the *Appellplatz* and remained there in silence for ten hours. In the evenings, however, after the issue of thin soup, they were allowed to walk around the hut, to talk to each other. The blast of a whistle at 9 P.M. was the signal for them to take up their curious positions for the night.

On the second day, an SS officer came to the *Appellplatz* looking for the clerk who had drawn up the Schindler list. It had not been sent off from Płaszów, it seemed. Shivering in his coarse prison uniform, Goldberg was led off to an office and asked to type out the list from memory. By the end of the day he had not finished the work and, back in the barracks, was surrounded by a spate of final pleas for inclusion. Here, in the bitter dusk, the list still enticed and tormented, even if all it had done so far for those on it was bring them to Gröss-Rosen. Pemper and others, moving in on Goldberg, began to pressure him to type Dr. Alexander Biberstein's name on the sheet in the morning. Biberstein was brother of the Marek Biberstein who had been that first, optimistic president of the Cracow *Judenrat*. Earlier in the week Goldberg had confused Biberstein, telling him that he *was* on the list. It was not till the trucks were loaded that the doctor found out he was not in the Schindler group. Even in such a place as Gröss-Rosen, Mietek Pemper was sure enough of a future to threaten Goldberg with postwar reprisals if Biberstein were not added.

Then, on the third day, the 800 men of Schindler's now revised list were separated out; taken to the delousing station for yet another wash; permitted to sit a few hours, speculating and chatting like villagers in front of their huts; and marched out once more to the siding. With a small ration of bread, they climbed up into cattle cars. None of the guards who loaded them admitted to knowing where they were going. They squatted on the floorboards in the prescribed manner. They kept fixed in their minds the map of Central Europe, and made continual judgments about the passage of the sun, gauging their direction by glimpses of light through small wire ventilators near the roofs of the cars. Olek Rosner was lifted to the ventilator in his car and said that he could see forests and mountains. The navigation experts claimed the train was travelling generally southeast. It all indicated a Czech destination, but no one wanted to say so.

This journey of a hundred miles took nearly two days; when the doors opened, it was early morning on the second day. They were at the Zwittau depot. They dismounted and were marched through a town not yet awake, a town frozen in the late Thirties. Even the graffiti on the walls – 'KEEP THE JEWS OUT OF BRINNLITZ' – looked strangely prewar to them. They had been living in a world where their very breath was begrudged. It seemed almost endearingly naive for the people of Zwittau to begrudge them a mere location.

Three or four miles out into the hills, following a rail siding, they came to the industrial hamlet of Brinnlitz, and saw ahead in thin morning light the solid bulk of the Hoffman annex transformed into *Arbeitslager* (Labour Camp) Brinnlitz, with watchtowers, a wire fence encircling it, a guard barracks inside the wire, and beyond that the gate to the factory and the prisoners' dormitories.

As they marched in through the outer gate, Oskar appeared from the factory courtyard, wearing a Tyrolean hat.

33

This camp, like Emalia, had been equipped at Oskar's expense. According to the bureaucratic theory, all factory camps were built at the owner's cost. It was thought that any industrialist got sufficient incentive from the cheap prison labour to justify a small expenditure on wire and lumber. In fact, Germany's darling industrialists, such as Krupp and Farben, built their camps with materials donated from SS enterprises and with a wealth of labour lent to them. Oskar was no darling and got nothing. He had been able to pry some wagonloads of SS cement out of Bosch at what Bosch would have considered a discount black-market price. From the same source he got two to three tons of gasoline and fuel oil for use in the production and delivery of his goods. He had brought some of the camp fencing wire from Emalia.

But around the bare premises of the Hoffman annex, he was required to provide high-tension fences, latrines, a guard barracks for 100 SS personnel, attached SS offices, a sickroom, and kitchens. Adding to the expense, *Sturmbannführer* Hassebroeck had already been down from Gröss-Rosen for an inspection and gone away with a supply of cognac and porcelainware, and what Oskar described as 'tea by the kilogram.' Hassebroeck had also taken away inspection fees and compulsory Winter Aid contributions levied by Section D, and no receipt had been given. 'His car had a considerable capacity for these things,' Oskar would later declare. He had no doubt in October 1944 that Hassebroeck was already doctoring the Brinnlitz books.

Inspectors sent directly by Oranienburg had also to be satisfied. As for the goods and equipment of DEF, much of it still in transit, it would require 250 freight cars before it had all arrived. It was astounding, said Oskar, how in a crumbling state, *Ostbahn* officials could, if properly encouraged, find such a number of rail cars.

And the unique aspect of all this, of Oskar himself, jaunty in his mountain hat, as he emerged from that frosty courtyard, is that unlike Krupp and Farben and all the other entrepreneurs who kept Jewish slaves, he had no serious industrial intention at all. He had no hopes of production; there were no sales graphs in his head. Though four years ago he had come to Cracow to get rich, he now had no manufacturing ambitions left.

It was a hectic industrial situation there in Brinnlitz. Many of the presses, drills, and lathes had not yet arrived, and new cement floors would have to be poured to take their weight. The annex was still full of Hoffman's old machinery. Even so, for these 800 supposed munitions workers who had just moved through the gate, Oskar was paying 7.50 RM. each day per skilled worker, 6 RM. per labourer. This would amount to nearly $14,000 U.S. each week for male labour; when the women arrived, the bill would top $18,000. Oskar was therefore committing a grand business folly, but celebrated it in a Tyrolean hat.

Some of Oskar's attachments had shifted too. Mrs. Emilie Schindler had come from Zwittau to live with him in his downstairs apartment. Brinnlitz, unlike Cracow, was too close to home to permit her to excuse their separation. For a Catholic like her, it was now a matter of either formalising the rift or living together again. There seemed to be at least a tolerance between them, a thorough mutual respect. At first sight she might have looked like a marital cipher, an abused wife who did not know how to get out. Some of the men wondered at first what she would think when she found the sort of factory Oskar kept, the sort of camp. They did not know yet that Emilie would make her own discrete contribution, that it would be based not on conjugal obedience but on her own ideas.

Ingrid had come with Oskar to Brinnlitz to work in the new plant, but she had taken lodgings outside the camp and was there only for office hours. There was a definite cooling in that relationship, and she would never live with Oskar again. But she would show no animosity, and throughout the coming months Oskar would frequently visit her in her apartment. The racy Klonowska, that chic Polish patriot, stayed behind in Cracow, but again there was no apparent bitterness. Oskar would have contact with her during visits to Cracow, and she would again help him when the SS caused trouble. The truth was that though his attachments to Klonowska and Ingrid were winding down in the most fortunate way, without any bitterness, it would have been a mistake to believe that he was turning conjugal.

He told the men, that day of their arrival, that the women could be confidently expected. He believed they would arrive after scarcely more delay than there had been with the men. The women's journey would, however, be different. After a short trip from Płaszów, their locomotive backed them, with some hundreds of other Płaszów women, through the arched gatehouse of Auschwitz-Birkenau. When the car doors opened, they found themselves in that immense concourse bisecting the camp, and practiced SS men and women, speaking calmly, began to grade them. The sorting of the people went on with a terrifying detachment. When a woman was slow in moving, she was hit with a truncheon, but the blow had no personal edge to it. It was all a matter of getting the numbers through. For the SS sections at the railside of Birkenau, it was all dutiful tedium. They had already heard every plea, every story. They knew every dodge anyone was ever likely to pull.

Under the floodlights, the women numbly asked each other what it meant. But even in their daze, their shoes already filling with the mud that was Birkenau's element, they were aware of SS women pointing to them, and telling uniformed doctors who showed any interest, '*Schindlergruppe!*' And the spruce young physicians would turn away and leave them alone for a time.

Feet sticking in the mud, they were marched to the delousing plant and stripped by order of tough young SS women with truncheons in their hands. Mila Pfefferberg was troubled by rumors of the type most prisoners of the Reich had by now heard – that some shower nozzles gave out a killing gas. These, she was delighted to find, gave mere icy water.

After their wash, some of them expected to be tattooed. They knew as much as that about Auschwitz. The SS tattooed your arm if they wanted to use you. If they intended to feed you into the machine, however, they did not bother. The same train that had brought the women of the list had brought also some 2,000 others who, not being *Schindlerfrauen*, were put through the normal selections. Rebecca Bau, excluded from the Schindler list, had passed and been given a number, and Josef Bau's robust mother had also won a tattoo in that preposterous Birkenau lottery. Another Płaszów girl, fifteen years old, had looked at the tattoo she'd been given and been delighted that it had two fives, a three, and two sevens – numbers enshrined in the *Tashlag*, or Jewish calendar. With a tattoo, you could leave Birkenau and go to one of the Auschwitz labour camps, where there was at least a chance.

But the Schindler women, left untattooed, were told to dress again and taken to a windowless hut in the women's camp. There, in the centre of the floor, stood a sheet-iron stove housed in bricks. It was the only comfort. There were no bunks. The *Schindlerfrauen* were to sleep two or three to a thin straw pallet. The clay floor was damp, and water would rise from it like a tide and drench the pallets, the ragged blankets. It was a death house at the heart of Birkenau. They lay there and dozed, frozen and uneasy in that enormous acreage of mud.

It confounded their imaginings of an intimate location, a village in Moravia. This was a great, if ephemeral, city. On a given day more than a quarter of a million Poles, Gypsies, and Jews kept brief residence here. There were thousands more over in Auschwitz I, the first but smaller camp where Commandant Rudolf Höss lived. And in the great industrial area named Auschwitz III, some tens of thousands worked while they could. The Schindler women had not been precisely informed of the statistics of Birkenau or of the Auschwitz duchy in itself. They could see, though, beyond birch trees at the western end of the enormous settlement, constant smoke rising from the four crematoria and the numerous pyres. They believed they were adrift now, and that the tide would take them down there. But not with all the capacity for making and believing rumors that characterises a life in prison would they have guessed how many people could be gassed there on a day when the system worked well. The number was – according to Höss – nine thousand.

The women were equally unaware that they had arrived in Auschwitz at a time when the progress of the war and certain secret negotiations between Himmler and the Swedish Count Folke Bernadotte were imposing a new direction on it. The secret of the extermination centres had not been kept, for the Russians had excavated the Lublin camp and found the furnaces containing human bones and more than five hundred drums of Zyklon B. News of this was published throughout the world, and Himmler, who wanted to be treated seriously as obvious postwar successor to the *Führer*, was willing to make promises to the Allies that the gassing of Jews would stop. He did not, however, issue an order on the matter until some time in October – the date is not certain. One copy went to General Pohl in Oranienburg; the other, to Kaltenbrunner, Chief of Reich Security. Both of them ignored the directive, and so did Adolf Eichmann. Jews from Płaszów, Theresienstadt, and Italy continued to be gassed up to the middle of November. The last selection for the gas chambers is believed, however, to have been made on October 30.

For the first eight days of their stay in Auschwitz, the Schindler women were in enormous danger of death by gassing. And even after that, as the last victims of the chambers continued to file throughout November toward the western end of Birkenau, and as the ovens and pyres worked on their backlog of corpses, they would not be aware of any change in the essential nature of the camp. All their anxieties would in any case be well founded, for most of those left after the gassing ceased would be shot – as happened to all the crematorium workers – or allowed to die of disease.

In any case, the Schindler women went through frequent mass medical inspections in both October and November. Some of them had been separated out in the first days and sent off to the huts reserved for the terminally ill. The doctors of Auschwitz – Josef Mengele, Fritz Klein, Doctors Konig and Thilo – not only worked on the Birkenau platform but roamed the camp, turning up at roll calls, invading the showers, asking with a smile, 'How old are you, Mother?' Mrs. Clara Sternberg found herself put aside in a hut for older women. Sixty-year-old Mrs. Lola Krumholz was also cut out of the *Schindlergruppe* and put into a barracks for the aged where she was meant to die at no expense to the administration. Mrs. Horowitz, believing that her fragile daughter of eleven years, Niusia, could not survive a 'bathhouse' inspection, hustled her into an empty sauna boiler. One of the SS girls who'd been appointed to the Schindler women – the pretty one, the blonde – saw her do it but did not give her away. She was a puncher, that one, short-tempered, and later she would ask Mrs. Horowitz for a bribe and get a brooch which Regina had somehow concealed till then. Regina handed it over philosophically. There was another, heavier, gentler one who made lesbian advances and may have required a more personal payoff.

Sometimes at roll call, one or more of the doctors would appear in front of the barracks. Seeing the medical gentlemen, women rubbed clay into their cheeks to induce a little bogus colour. At one such inspection, Regina found stones for her daughter, Niusia, to stand on, and silver-haired young Mengele came to her and asked her a soft-voiced question concerning her daughter's age and punched her for lying. Women felled like this at inspection were meant to be picked up by the guards while still semiconscious, dragged to the electrified fence at the edge of the women's camp, and thrown onto it. They had Regina halfway there when she revived and begged them not to fry her alive, to let her return to her line. They released her, and when she crept back into the ranks, there was her bird-boned, speechless daughter still, frozen to the pile of stone.

These inspections could occur at any hour. The Schindler women were called out one night to stand in the mud while their barracks was searched. Mrs. Dresner, who had once been saved by a vanished OD boy, came out with her tall teen-age daughter, Danka. They stood there in that eccentric mire of Auschwitz which, like the fabled mud of Flanders, would not freeze when everything else had frozen – the roads, the rooftops, the human traveller.

Both Danka and Mrs. Dresner had left Płaszów in the summer clothing that was all they had left. Danka wore a blouse, a light jacket, a maroon skirt. Since it had begun snowing earlier in the evening, Mrs. Dresner had suggested that Danka tear a strip off her blanket and wear it beneath the skirt. Now, in the course of the barracks inspection, the SS discovered the ripped blanket.

The officer who stood before the Schindler women called out the barracks *Alteste* – a Dutch woman whom, until yesterday, none of them had known – and said that she was to be shot, together with any other prisoner found with a blanket strip under her dress.

Mrs. Dresner began whispering to Danka. 'Take it off and I'll slip it back into the barracks.' It was a credible idea. The barracks stood at ground level and no step led up to them. A woman in the rear line might slip backward through the door. As Danka had obeyed her mother once before in the matter of the wall cavity in Dabrowski Street, Cracow, she obeyed her now, slipping from beneath her dress that strip of Europe's poorest blanket. In fact, while Mrs. Dresner was in the hut, the SS officer passed by and idly extracted a woman of Mrs. Dresner's age – it was probably Mrs. Sternberg – and had her taken away to some worse part of the camp, some place where there was no Moravian illusion.

Perhaps the other women in line did not let themselves understand what this simple act of weeding out meant. It was in fact a statement that no reserved group of so-called 'industrial prisoners' was safe in Auschwitz. No cry of *'Schindlerfrauen!'* would keep them immune for long. There had been other groups of 'industrial prisoners' who had vanished in Auschwitz. General Pohl's Section W had sent some trainloads of skilled Jewish workers from Berlin the year before. I. G. Farben had needed labour and was told by Section W to select its workers from these transports. In fact, Section W had suggested to Commandant Höss that the trains should be unloaded in the I. G. Farben works, not near the crematoria in Auschwitz-Birkenau. Of 1,750 prisoners, all male, in the first train, 1,000 were immediately gassed. Of 4,000 in the next four trainloads, 2,500 went at once to the 'bathhouses.' If the Auschwitz administration would not stay its hand for I. G. Farben and Department W, it was not going to be finicky about the women of some obscure German potmaker.

In barracks like those of the Schindler women, it was like living outdoors. The windows had no glass and served only to put an edge on the blasts of cold air out of Russia. Most of the girls had dysentery. Crippled with cramp, they limped in their clogs to the steel waste drum out in the mud. The woman who tended it did so for an extra bowl of soup. Mila Pfefferberg staggered out one evening, seized with dysentery, and the woman on duty – not a bad woman, a woman Mila had known as a girl – insisted that she could not use the drum but had to wait for the next girl out and then empty it with her help. Mila argued but could not shake the woman. Beneath the hungry stars this tending of the drum had become something like a profession, and there were rules. With the drum as pretext, the woman had come to believe that order, hygiene, sanity were possible.

The next girl out arrived at Mila's side, gasping and bent and desperate. But she too was young and, in peaceful days in Lodz, had known the woman on the can as a respectable married woman. So the two girls were obedient and lugged the thing 300 metres through the mud. The girl who shared the burden asked Mila, 'Where's Schindler now?'

Not everyone in the barracks asked that question, or asked it in that fierce, ironic way. There was an Emalia girl named Lusia, a widow of twenty-two, who kept saying, 'You'll see, it will all come out. We'll end up somewhere warm with Schindler's soup in us.' She did not know herself why she kept repeating such statements. In Emalia she had never been the type to make projections. She'd worked her shift, drunk her soup, and slept. She had never predicted grandiose events. Sufficient to her day had always been the survival thereof. Now she was ill and there was no reason for her to be prophetic. The cold and hunger were wasting her, and she too bore the vast obsessions of her hunger. Yet she amazed herself by repeating Oskar's promises.

Later in their stay in Auschwitz, when they had been moved to a hut closer to the crematoria and did not know if they were to go to the showers or the chambers, Lusia continued pushing the glad message. Even so, the tide of the camp having washed them to this geographic limit of the earth, this pole, this pit, despair wasn't quite the fashion for the *Schindlerfrauen*. You would still find women huddled in recipe talk and dreams of prewar kitchens.

In Brinnlitz when the men arrived, there was only the shell. There were no bunks yet; straw was strewn in the dormitories upstairs. But it was warm, with steam heat from the boilers. There were no cooks that first day. Bags of turnips lay around what would be the cookhouse, and men devoured them raw. Later, soup was brewed and bread baked, and the engineer Finder began the allocating of jobs. But from the start, unless there were SS men looking on, it was all slow. It is mysterious how a body of prisoners could sense that the *Herr Direktor* was no longer a party to any war effort. The pace of work grew very canny in Brinnlitz. Since Oskar was detached from the question of production, slow work became the prisoners' vengeance, their declaration.

It was a heady thing to withhold your labour. Everywhere else in Europe, the slaves worked to the limit of their 600 calories per day, hoping to impress some foreman and delay the transfer to the death camp. But here in Brinnlitz was the intoxicating freedom to use the shovel at half-pace and still survive.

None of this unconscious policy-making was evident in the first days. There were still too many prisoners anxious for their women. Dolek Horowitz had a wife and daughter in Auschwitz. The Rosner brothers had their wives. Pfefferberg knew the shock which something as vast, as appalling as Auschwitz would have on Mila. Jacob Sternberg and his teen-age son were concerned about Mrs. Clara Sternberg. Pfefferberg remembers the men clustering around Schindler on the factory floor and asking him again where the women were.

'I'm getting them out,' Schindler rumbled. He did not go into explanations. He did not publicly surmise that the SS in Auschwitz might need to be bribed. He did not say that he had sent the list of women to Colonel Erich Lange, or that he and Lange both intended to get them to Brinnlitz according to the list. Nothing of that. Simply 'I'm getting them out.'

The SS garrison who moved into Brinnlitz in those days gave Oskar some cause to hope. They were middle-aged reservists called up to allow younger SS men a place in the front line. There were not so many lunatics as at Płaszów, and Oskar would always keep them gentle with the specialties of his kitchen – plain food, but plenty. In a visit to their barracks, he made his usual speech about the unique skills of his prisoners, the importance of his manufacturing activities. Antitank shells, he said, and casings for a projectile still on the secret list. He asked that there be no intrusion by the garrison into the factory itself, for that would disturb the workers.

He could see it in their eyes. It suited them, this quiet town. They could imagine themselves lasting out the cataclysm here. They did not want to rampage round the workshops like a Goeth or a Hujar. They didn't want the *Herr Direktor* to complain about them.

Their commanding officer, however, had not yet arrived. He

was on his way from his previous post, the labour camp at Budzyn, which had, until the recent Russian advances, manufactured Heinkel bomber parts. He would be younger, sharper, more intrusive, Oskar knew. He might not readily take to being denied access to the camp.

Among all this pouring of cement floors, the knocking of holes in the roof so that the vast Hilos would fit, the softening of NCOs, amid the private uneasiness of settling into married life with Emilie again, Oskar was arrested a third time.

The Gestapo turned up at lunchtime. Oskar was not in his office, in fact had driven to Brno on some business earlier in the morning. A truck had just arrived at the camp from Cracow laden with some of the *Herr Direktor*'s portable wealth – cigarettes, cases of vodka, cognac, champagne. Some would later claim that this was Goeth's property, that Oskar had agreed to bring it into Moravia in return for Goeth's backing of his Brinnlitz plans. Since Goeth had now been a prisoner for a month and had no more authority, the luxuries on the truck could just as well be considered Oskar's.

The men doing the unloading thought so and became nervous at the sight of the Gestapo men in the courtyard. They had mechanics' privileges and so were permitted to drive the truck to a stream down the hill, where they threw the liquor into the water by the easeful. The two hundred thousand cigarettes on the truck were hidden more retrievably under the cover of the large transformer in the power plant.

It is significant that there were so many cigarettes and so much liquor in the truck: a sign that Oskar, always keen on trade goods, intended now to make his living on the black market.

They got the truck back to the garage as the siren for midday soup was blown. In past days the *Herr Direktor* had eaten with the prisoners, and the mechanics hoped that today he would do so again; they could then explain what had happened to such an expensive truckload.

He did in fact return from Brno soon after, but was stopped at the inner gate by one of the Gestapo men who stood there with his hand raised. The Gestapo man ordered him to leave his car at once.

'This is my factory,' a prisoner heard Oskar growl back. 'If you want to talk to me, you're welcome to jump in the car. Otherwise follow me to my office.'

He drove into the courtyard, the two Gestapo men walking quickly on either side of the vehicle.

In his office, they asked him about his connections with Goeth, with Goeth's loot. I do have a few suitcases here, he told them. They belong to Herr Goeth. He asked me to keep them for him until his release.

The Gestapo men asked to see them, and Oskar took them through to the apartment. He made formal and cold introductions between Frau Schindler and the men from Bureau V. Then he brought out the suitcases and opened them. They were full of Amon's civilian clothing, and old uniforms from the days when Amon had been a slim SS NCO. When they'd been through them and found nothing, they made the arrest.

Emilie grew aggressive now. They had no right, she said, to take her husband unless they could say what they were taking him for. The people in Berlin will not be happy about this, she said.

Oskar advised her to be silent. But you will have to call my friend Klonowska, he told her, and cancel my appointments.

Emilie knew what that meant. Klonowska would do her trick with the telephone again, calling Martin Plathe in Breslau, the General Schindler people, all the big guns. One of the Bureau V men took out handcuffs and put them on Oskar's wrists. They took him to their car, drove him to the station in Zwittau, and escorted him by train to Cracow.

The impression is that this arrest scared him more than the previous two. There are no stories of lovelorn SS colonels who shared a cell with him and drank his vodka. Oskar did later record some details, however. As the Bureau V men escorted him across the grand neoclassic loggia of the Cracow central station, a man named Huth approached them. He had been a civilian engineer in Płaszów. He had always been obsequious to Amon, but had a reputation for many secret kindnesses. It may have been an accidental meeting, but suggests that Huth may have been working with Klonowska. Huth insisted on shaking Oskar by his shackled hand. One of the Bureau V men objected. 'Do you really want to go around shaking hands with prisoners?' he asked Huth. The engineer at once made a speech, a testimonial to Oskar. This was the *Herr Direktor* Schindler, a man greatly respected throughout Cracow, an important industrialist. 'I can never think of him as a prisoner,' said Huth.

Whatever the significance of this meeting, Oskar was put into a car and taken across the familiar city to Pomorska Street again. They put him in a room like the one he had occupied during his first arrest, a room with a bed and a chair and a washbasin but with bars on the window. He was not easy there, even though his manner was one of bearlike tranquillity. In 1942, when they had arrested him the day after his thirty-fourth birthday, the rumor that there were torture chambers in the Pomorska cellars had been terrifying and indefinite. It wasn't indefinite anymore. He knew that Bureau V would torture him if they wanted Amon badly enough.

That evening Herr Huth came as a visitor, bringing with him a dinner tray and a bottle of wine. Huth had spoken to Klonowska. Oskar himself would never clarify whether or not Klonowska had prearranged that 'chance encounter.' Whichever it was, Huth told him now that Klonowska was rallying his old friends.

The next day he was interrogated by a panel of twelve SS investigators, one a judge of the SS Court. Oskar denied that he had given any money to ensure that the Commandant would, in the words of the transcript of Amon's evidence, 'go easy on the Jews.' I may have given him the money as a loan, Oskar admitted at one stage. Why would you give him a loan? they wanted to know. I run an essential war industry, said Oskar, playing the old tune. I have a body of skilled labour. If it is disturbed, there is loss to me, to the Armaments Inspectorate, to the war effort. If I found that in the mass of prisoners in Płaszów there was a skilled metalworker of a category I needed, then of course I asked the Herr Commandant for him. I wanted him fast, I wanted him without red tape. My interest was production, its value to me, to the Armaments Inspectorate. In consideration of the Herr Commandant's help in these matters, I may have given him a loan.

This defense involved some disloyalty to his old host, Amon. But Oskar would not have hesitated. His eyes gleaming with transparent frankness, his tone low, his emphasis discreet, Oskar – without saying it in so many words – let the investigators know that the money had been extorted. It didn't impress them. They locked him away again.

The interrogation went into a second, third, and fourth day. No one did him harm, but they were steely. At last he had to deny any friendship with Amon at all. It was no great task: he loathed the man profoundly anyhow. 'I'm not a fairy,' he growled at the gentlemen of Bureau V, falling back on rumors he'd heard about Goeth and his young orderlies.

Amon himself would never understand that Oskar despised him and was willing to help the case Bureau V had against him. Amon was always deluded about friendship. In sentimental moods, he believed that Mietek Pemper and Helen Hirsch were loving servants. The investigators probably would not have let him know that Oskar was in Pomorska and would have listened mutely to Amon urging them, 'Call in my old friend Schindler. He'll vouch for me.'

What helped Oskar most when he faced the investigators was that he had had few actual business connections with the man. Though he had sometimes given Amon advice or contacts, he had never had a share in any deal, never made a złoty out of Amon's sales of prison rations, of rings from the jewellery shop, of garments from the custom-tailoring plant or furniture from the upholstery section. It must also have helped him that his lies were disarming even to policemen, and that when he told the truth he was positively seductive. He never gave the impression that he was grateful for being believed. For example, when the gentlemen of Bureau V looked as if they might at least give standing room to the idea that the 80,000 RM. was a 'loan,' a sum extorted, Oskar asked them whether in the end the money might be returned to him, to *Herr Direktor* Schindler, the impeccable industrialist.

A third factor in Oskar's favour was that his credentials checked out. Colonel Erich Lange, when telephoned by Bureau V, stressed Schindler's importance to the conduct of the war. Sussmuth, called in Troppau, said that Oskar's plant was involved in the production of 'secret weapons.' It was not, as we will see, an untrue statement. But when said bluntly, it was misleading and carried a distorted weight. For the *Führer* had promised 'secret weapons.' The phrase itself was charismatic and extended its protection now to Oskar. Against a phrase like 'secret weapons,' any confetti of protest from the burghers of Zwittau did not count.

But even to Oskar it did not seem that the imprisonment was going well. About the fourth day, one of his interrogators visited him not to question him but to spit at him. The spittle streaked the left lapel of his suit. The man ranted at him, calling him a Jew-lover, a fucker of Jewesses. It was a departure from the strange legalism of the interrogations. But Oskar wasn't sure that it was not planned, that it did not represent the true impetus behind his imprisonment.

After a week, Oskar sent a message, by way of Huth and Klonowska, to *Oberführer* Schemer. Bureau V was putting such pressure on him, the message went, that he did not believe he could protect the former police chief much longer. Schemer left his counterinsurgency work (it was soon to kill him) and arrived in Oskar's cell within a day. It was a scandal what they were doing, said Schemer. What about Amon? Oskar asked, expecting Scherner to say that that was a scandal too. He deserves all he gets, said Schemer. It seemed that everyone was deserting Amon. Don't worry, said Schemer before leaving, we intend to get you out.

On the morning of the eighth day, they let Oskar out onto the street. Oskar did not delay his going – nor did he, this time, demand transport. Enough to be deposited on the cold sidewalk. He travelled across Cracow by streetcar and walked to his old factory in Zablocie. A few Polish caretakers were still there, and from the upstairs office he called Brinnlitz and told Emilie that he was free.

Moshe Bejski, a Brinnlitz draughtsman, remembers the confusion while Oskar was away – the rumors, all the questions about what it meant. But Stern and Maurice Finder, Adam Garde and others had consulted Emilie about food, about work arrangements, about the provision of bunks. They were the first to discover that Emilie was no mere passenger. She was not a happy woman, and her unhappiness was compounded by Bureau V's arrest of Oskar. It must have seemed cruel that the SS should intrude on this reunion before it had got properly started. But it was clear to Stern and the others that she was not there, keeping house in that little apartment on the ground floor, purely out of wifely duty. There was what you could call an ideological commitment too. A picture of Jesus with His heart exposed and in flames hung on a wall of the apartment. Stern had seen the same design in the houses of Polish Catholics. But there had been no ornament of that kind in either of Oskar's Cracow apartments. The Jesus of the exposed heart did not always reassure when you saw it in Polish kitchens. In Emilie's apartment, however, it hung like a promise, a personal one. Emilie's.

Early in November, her husband came back by train. He was unshaven and smelly from his imprisonment. He was amazed to find that the women were still in Auschwitz-Birkenau.

In planet Auschwitz, where the Schindler women moved as warily, as full of dread as any space travellers, Rudolf Höss ruled as founder, builder, presiding genius. Readers of William Styron's novel *Sophie's Choice* encountered him as the master of Sophie – a very different sort of master than Amon was to Helen Hirsch;

a more detached, mannerly, and sane man; yet still the unflagging priest of that cannibal province. Though in the 1920s he had murdered a Ruhr schoolteacher for informing on a German activist and had done time for the crime, he never murdered any Auschwitz prisoner by his own hand. He saw himself instead as a technician. As champion of Zyklon B, the hydrogen cyanide pellets which gave off fumes when exposed to air, he had engaged in a long personal and scientific conflict with his rival, *Kriminalkommissar* Christian Wirth, who had jurisdiction over the Bełżec camp and who was the head of the carbon monoxide school. There had been an awful day at Bełżec, which the SS chemical officer Kurt Gerstein had witnessed, when *Kommissar* Wirth's method took three hours to finish a party of Jewish males packed into the chambers. That Höss had backed the more efficient technology is partially attested to by the continuous growth of Auschwitz and the decline of Bełżec.

By 1943, when Rudolf Höss left Auschwitz to do a stint as Deputy Chief of Section D in Oranienburg, the place was already something more than a camp. It was even more than a wonder of organisation. It was a phenomenon. The moral universe had not so much decayed here. It had been inverted, like some black hole, under the pressure of all the earth's malice – a place where tribes and histories were sucked in and vaporised, and language flew inside out. The underground chambers were named 'disinfection cellars,' the aboveground chambers 'bathhouses,' and *Oberscharführer* Moll, whose task it was to order the insertion of the blue crystals into the roofs of the 'cellars,' the walls of the 'bathhouses,' customarily cried to his assistants, 'All right, let's give them something to chew on.'

Höss had returned to Auschwitz in May 1944 and presided over the entire camp at the time the Schindler women occupied a barracks in Birkenau, so close to the whimsical *Oberscharführer* Moll. According to the Schindler mythology, it was Höss himself with whom Oskar wrestled for his 300 women. Certainly Oskar had telephone conversations and other commerce with Höss. But he also had to deal with *Sturmbannführer* Fritz Hartjenstein, Commandant of Auschwitz II – that is, of Auschwitz-Birkenau – and with *Untersturmführer* Franz Hössler, the young man in charge, in that great city, of the suburb of women.

What is certain is that Oskar now sent a young woman with a suitcase full of liquor, ham, and diamonds to make a deal with these functionaries. Some say that Oskar then followed up the girl's visit in person, taking with him an associate, an influential officer in the S.A. (the *Sturmabteilung*, or Storm Troops), *Standartenführer* Peltze, who, according to what Oskar later told his friends, was a British agent. Others claim that Oskar stayed away from Auschwitz himself as a matter of strategy and went to Oranienburg instead, and to the Armaments Inspectorate in Berlin, to try to put pressure on Höss and his associates from that end.

The story as Stern would tell it years later in a public speech in Tel Aviv is as follows. After Oskar's release from prison, Stern approached Schindler and – 'under the pressure of some of my comrades' – begged Oskar to do something decisive about the women ensnared in Auschwitz. During this conference, one of Oskar's secretaries came in – Stern does not say which one. Schindler considered the girl and pointed to one of his fingers, which sported a large diamond ring. He asked the girl whether she would like this rather hefty piece of jewellery. According to Stern, the girl got very excited. Stern quotes Oskar as saying, 'Take the list of the women; pack a suitcase with the best food and liquor you can find in my kitchen. Then go to Auschwitz. You know the Commandant has a penchant for pretty women. If you bring it off, you'll get this diamond. And more still.'

It is a scene, a speech worthy of one of those events in the Old Testament when for the good of the tribe a woman is offered to the invader. It is also a Central European scene, with its gross, corruscating diamonds and its proposed transaction of the flesh.

According to Stern, the secretary went. When she did not return within two days, Schindler himself – in the company of the obscure Peltze – went to settle the matter.

According to Schindler mythology, Oskar *did* send a girlfriend of his to sleep with the Commandant – be that Höss, Hartjenstein, or Hössler – and leave diamonds on the pillow. While some, like Stern, say it was 'one of his secretaries,' others name an *Aufseher*, a pretty blond SS girl, ultimately a girlfriend of Oskar's and part of the Brinnlitz garrison. But this girl, it seems, was still in Auschwitz anyhow, together with the *Schindlerfrauen*.

According to Emilie Schindler herself, the emissary was a girl of twenty-two or twenty-three. She was a native of Zwittau, and her father was an old friend of the Schindler family. She had recently returned from occupied Russia, where she'd worked as a secretary in the German administration. She was a good friend of Emilie's, and volunteered for the task. It is unlikely that Oskar would demand a sexual sacrifice of a friend of the family. Even though he was a brigand in these matters, that side of the story is certainly myth. We do not know the extent of the girl's transactions with the officers of Auschwitz. We know only that she approached the dreadful kingdom and dealt courageously.

Oskar later said that in his own dealings with the rulers of necropolis Auschwitz, he was offered the old temptation. The women have been here some weeks now. They won't be worth much as labour anymore. Why don't you forget these three hundred? We'll cut another three hundred for you, out of the endless herd. In 1942, an SS NCO at Prokocim station had pushed the same idea at Oskar. Don't get stuck on these particular names, *Herr Direktor*.

Now as at Prokocim, Oskar pursued his usual line. There are irreplaceable skilled munitions workers. I have trained them myself over a period of years. They represent skills I cannot quickly replace. The names I know, that is, are the names I know.

A moment, said his tempter. I see listed here a nine-year-old, daughter of one Phila Rath. I see an eleven-year-old, daughter of one Regina Horowitz. Are you telling me that a nine-year-old and an eleven-year-old are skilled munitions workers?

They polish the forty-five-millimetre shells, said Oskar. They were selected for their long fingers, which can reach the interior of the shell in a way that is beyond most adults.

Such conversation in support of the girl who was a friend of the family took place, conducted by Oskar either in person or by telephone. Oskar would relay news of the negotiations to the inner circle of male prisoners, and from them the details were passed on to the men on the workshop floor. Oskar's claim that he needed children so that the innards of antitank shells could be buffed was outrageous nonsense. But he had already used it more than once. An orphan named Anita Lampel had been called to the *Appellplatz* in Płaszów one night in 1943 to find Oskar arguing with a middle-aged woman, the *Alteste* of the women's camp. The *Alteste* was saying more or less what Höss/Hössler would say later in Auschwitz. 'You can't tell me you need a fourteen-year-old for Emalia. You cannot tell me that Commandant Goeth has allowed you to put a fourteen-year-old on your roster for Emalia.' (The *Alteste* was worried, of course, that if the list of prisoners for Emalia had been doctored, she would be made to pay for it.) That night in 1943, Anita Lampel had listened flabbergasted as Oskar, a man who had never even seen her hands, claimed that he had chosen her for the industrial value of her long fingers and that the Herr Commandant had given his approval.

Anita Lampel was herself in Auschwitz now, but had grown tall and no longer needed the long-fingered ploy. So it was transferred to the benefit of the daughters of Mrs. Horowitz and Mrs. Rath.

Schindler's contact had been correct in saying that the women had lost nearly all their industrial value. At inspections, young women like Mila Pfefferberg, Helen Hirsch, and her sister could not prevent the cramps of dysentery from bowing and aging them. Mrs. Dresner had lost all appetite, even for the *ersatz* soup. Danka could not force the mean warmth of it down her mother's throat. It meant that she would soon become a *Mussulman*. The term was camp slang, based on people's memory of newsreels of famine in Muslim countries, for a prisoner who had crossed the borderline that separated the ravenous living from the good-as-dead.

Clara Sternberg, in her early forties, was isolated from the main Schindler group into what could be described as a *Mussulman* hut. Here, each morning, the dying women were lined up in front of the door and a selection was made. Sometimes it was Mengele leaning toward you. Of the 500 women in this new group of Clara Sternberg's, 100 might be detailed off on a given morning. On another, 50. You rouged yourself with Auschwitz clay; you kept a straight back if that could be managed. You choked where you stood rather than cough.

It was after such an inspection that Clara found herself with no further reserves left for the waiting, the daily risk. She had a husband and a teen-age son in Brinnlitz, but now they seemed more remote than the canals of the planet Mars. She could not imagine Brinnlitz, or them in it. She staggered through the women's camp looking for the electric wires. When she had first arrived, they'd seemed to be everywhere. Now that they were needed, she could not find them. Each turn took her into another quagmire street, and frustrated her with a view of identically miserable huts. When she saw an acquaintance from Płaszów, a Cracow woman like herself, Clara propped in front of her. 'Where's the electric fence?' Clara asked the woman. To her distraught mind, it was a reasonable question to ask, and Clara had no doubt that the friend, if she had any sisterly feeling, would point the exact way to the wires. The answer the woman gave Clara was just as crazed, but it was one that had a fixed point of view, a balance, a perversely sane core.

'Don't kill yourself on the fence, Clara,' the woman urged her. 'If you do that, you'll never know what happened to you.'

It has always been the most powerful of answers to give to the intending suicide. Kill yourself and you'll never find out how the plot ends. Clara did not have any vivid interest in the plot. But somehow the answer was adequate. She turned around. When she got back to her barracks, she felt more troubled than when she'd set out to look for the fence. But her Cracow friend had – by her reply – somehow cut her off from suicide as an option.

Something awful had happened at Brinnlitz. Oskar, the Moravian traveller, was away. He was trading in kitchenware and diamonds, liquor and cigars, all over the province. Some of it was crucial business. Biberstein speaks of the drugs and medical instruments that came into the *Krankenstube* at Brinnlitz. None of it was standard issue. Oskar must have traded for medicines at the depots of the *Wehrmacht*, or perhaps in the pharmacy of one of the big hospitals in Brno.

Whatever the cause of his absence, he was away when an inspector from Gröss-Rosen arrived and walked through the workshop with *Untersturmführer* Josef Liepold, the new Commandant, who was always happy for a chance to intrude inside the factory. The inspector's orders, originating from Oranienburg, were that the Gröss-Rosen subcamps should be scoured for children to be used in Dr. Josef Mengele's medical experiments in Auschwitz. Olek Rosner and his small cousin Richard Horowitz, who'd believed they had no need of a hiding place here, were spotted racing around the annex, chasing each other upstairs, playing among the abandoned spinning machines. So was the son of Dr. Leon Gross, who had nursed Amon's recently developed diabetes, who had helped Dr. Blancke with the Health *Aktion*, and who had other crimes still to answer for. The inspector remarked to *Untersturmführer* Liepold that these were clearly not essential munitions workers. Liepold – short, dark, not as crazy as Amon – was still a convinced SS officer and did not bother to defend the brats.

Further on in the inspection Roman Ginter's nine-year-old was discovered. Ginter had known Oskar from the time the ghetto was founded, had supplied the metal works at Płaszów with scrap from DEF. But *Untersturmführer* Liepold and the inspector did not recognise any special relationships. The Ginter boy was sent under escort to the gate with the other children. Frances Spira's boy, ten and a half years old, but tall and on the books as fourteen, was working on top of a long ladder that day, polishing the high windows. He survived the raid.

The orders required the rounding up of the children's parents as well, perhaps because this would obviate the risk of parents beginning demented revolutions on the subcamp premises. Therefore Rosner the violinist, Horowitz, and Roman Ginter were arrested. Dr. Leon Gross rushed down from the clinic to negotiate with the SS. He was flushed. The effort was to show this inspector from Gröss-Rosen that he was dealing with a really responsible sort of prisoner, a friend of the system. The effort counted for nothing. An SS *Unterscharführer*, armed with an automatic weapon, was given the mission of escorting them to Auschwitz.

The party of fathers and sons travelled from Zwittau as far as Katowice, in Upper Silesia, by ordinary passenger train. Henry Rosner expected other passengers to be hostile. Instead, one woman walked down the aisle looking defiant and gave Olek and the others a heel of bread and an apple, all the while staring the sergeant in the face, daring him to react. The *Unterscharführer* was polite to her, however, and nodded formally. Later, when the train stopped at Usti, he left the prisoners under the guard of his assistant and went to the station cafeteria, bringing back biscuits and coffee paid for from his own pocket. He and Rosner and Horowitz got talking. The more the *Unterscharführer* chatted, the less he seemed to belong to that same police force as Amon, Hujar, John, and all those others. 'I'm taking you to Auschwitz,' he said, 'and then I have to collect some women and bring them back to Brinnlitz.'

So, ironically, the first Brinnlitz men to discover that the women might be let out of Auschwitz were Rosner and Horowitz, themselves on their way there.

Rosner and Horowitz were ecstatic. They told their sons: This good gentleman is bringing your mother back to Brinnlitz. Rosner asked the *Unterscharführer* if he would give a letter to Manci, and Horowitz pleaded to be able to write to Regina. The two letters were written on pieces of paper the *Unterscharführer* gave them, the same stuff the man used to write to his own wife. In his letter, Rosner made arrangements with Manci to meet at an address in Podgórze if they both survived.

When Rosner and Horowitz had finished writing, the SS man put the letters in his jacket. *Where have you been these past years?* Rosner wondered. *Did you start out as a fanatic? Did you cheer when the gods on the rostrum screamed', 'The Jews are our misfortune'?*

Later in the journey, Olek turned his head in against Henry's arm and began to weep. He would not at first tell Rosner what was wrong. When he did speak at last, it was to say that he was sorry to drag Henry off to Auschwitz. 'To die just because of me,' he said. Henry could have tried to soothe him by telling lies, but it wouldn't have worked. All the children knew about the gas. They grew petulant when you tried to deceive them.

The *Unterscharführer* leaned over. Surely he had not heard, but there were tears in his eyes. Olek seemed astonished by them – the way another child might be astounded by a cycling circus animal. He stared at the man. What was startling was that they looked like fraternal tears, the tears of a fellow prisoner. 'I know what will happen,' said the *Unterscharführer*. 'We've lost the war. You'll get the tattoo. You'll survive.'

Henry got the impression that the man was making promises not to the child but to himself, arming himself with an assurance which – in five years' time perhaps, when he remembered this train journey – he could use to soothe himself.

On the afternoon of her attempt to find the wires, Clara Sternberg heard the calling of names and the sound of women's laughter from the direction of the *Schindlerfrauen* barracks. She crawled from her own damp hut and saw the Schindler women lined up beyond an inner fence of the women's camp. Some of them were dressed only in blouses and long drawers. Skeleton women, without a chance. But they were chattering like girls. Even the blond SS girl seemed delighted, for she too would be liberated from Auschwitz if they were. '*Schindlergruppe*' she called, 'you're going to the sauna and then to the trains.' She seemed to have a sense of the uniqueness of the event.

Doomed women from the barracks all around looked blankly out through the wire at the celebratory girls. They compelled you to watch, those list women, because they were so suddenly out of balance with the rest of the city. It meant nothing, of course. It was an eccentric event; it had no bearing on the majority's life; it did not reverse the process or lighten the smoky air.

But for Clara Sternberg, the sight was intolerable. As it was also for sixty-year-old Mrs. Krumholz, also half-dead in a hut assigned to the older women. Mrs. Krumholz began to argue with the Dutch *Kapo* at the door of her barracks. I'm going out to join them, she said. The Dutch *Kapo* put up a mist of arguments. In the end, she said, you're better off here. If you go, you'll die in the cattle cars. Besides that, I'll have to explain why you aren't here. You can tell them, said Mrs. Krumholz, that it's because I'm on the Schindler list. It's all fixed. The books will balance. There's no question about it.

They argued for five minutes and in the process talked of their families, finding out about each other's origins, perhaps looking for a vulnerable point outside the strict logic of the dispute. It turned out that the Dutch woman's name was also Krumholz. The two of them began discussing the whereabouts of their families. My husband is in Sachsenhausen, I think, said the Dutch Mrs. Krumholz. The Cracow Mrs. Krumholz said, My husband and grown son have gone somewhere. I think Mauthausen. I'm meant to be in the Schindler camp in Moravia. Those women beyond the fence, that's where they're going. They're not going anywhere, said the Dutch Mrs. Krumholz. Believe me. No one goes anywhere, except in one direction. The Cracow Mrs. Krumholz said, They think they're going somewhere. *Please!* For even if the *Schindlerfrauen* were deluded, Mrs. Krumholz from Cracow wanted to share the delusion. The Dutch *Kapo* understood this and at last opened the door of the barracks, for whatever it was worth.

For a fence now stood between Mrs. Krumholz, Mrs. Sternberg, and the rest of the Schindler women. It was not an electrified perimeter fence. It was nonetheless built, according to the rulings of Section D, of at least eighteen strands of wire. The strands ran closest together at the top. Farther down, they were stretched in parallel strands about six inches apart. But between each set of parallels and the next there was a gap of less than a foot. That day, according to the testimony of witnesses and of the women themselves, both Mrs. Krumholz and Mrs. Sternberg somehow tore their way through the fence to rejoin the Schindler women in whatever daydream of rescue they were enjoying. Dragging themselves through the perhaps nine-inch gap, stretching the wire, ripping their clothes off and tearing their flesh on the barbs, they put themselves back on the Schindler list. No one stopped them because no one believed it possible. To the other women of Auschwitz, it was in any case an irrelevant example. For any other escapee, the breaching of that fence brought you only to another, and then another, and so to the outer voltage of the place. Whereas for Sternberg and Krumholz, this fence was the only one. The clothing they'd brought with them from the ghetto and kept in repair in muddy Płaszów hung now on the wire. Naked and streaked with blood, they ran in among the Schindler women.

Mrs. Rachela Korn, condemned to a hospital hut at the age of forty-four, had also been dragged out the window of the place by her daughter, who now held her upright in the Schindler column. For her as for the other two, it was a birthday. Everyone in the line seemed to be congratulating them.

In the washhouse, the Schindler women were barbered. Latvian girls sheared a lice promenade down the length of their skulls and shaved their armpits and pubes. After their shower they were marched naked to the quartermaster's hut, where the clothes of the dead were issued to them. When they saw themselves shaven and in odds and ends of clothing, they broke into laughter – the hilarity of the very young. The sight of little Mila Pfefferberg, down to 70 pounds, occupying garments cut for a fat lady had them reeling with hilarity. Half-dead and dressed in their paint-coded rags, they pranced, modelled, mimed, and giggled like schoolgirls.

'What's Schindler going to do with all the old women?' Clara Sternberg heard an SS girl ask a colleague.

'It's no one's business,' the colleague said. 'Let him open an old people's home if he wants.'

No matter what your expectations, it was always a horrifying thing to go into the trains. Even in cold weather, there was a sense of smothering, compounded by blackness. On entering a car, the children always pushed themselves toward any sliver of light. That morning, Niusia Horowitz did that, positioning herself against the far wall at a place where a slat had come loose. When she looked out through the gap, she could see across the railway lines to the wires of the men's camp. She noticed a straggle of children over there, staring at the train and waving. There seemed to be a very personal insistence to their movements. She thought it strange that one of them resembled her six-year-old brother, who was safe with Schindler. And the boy at his side was a double for their cousin Olek Rosner. Then, of course, she understood. It *was* Richard. It *was* Olek.

She turned and found her mother and pulled at her uniform. Then Regina looked, went through the same cruel cycle of identification, and began to wail. The door of the car had been shut by now; they were all packed close in near darkness, and every gesture, every scent of hope or panic, was contagious. All the others took up the wailing too. Manci Rosner, standing near her sister-in-law, eased her away from the opening, looked, saw her son waving, and began keening too.

The door slid open again and a burly NCO asked who was making all the noise. No one else had any motive to come forward, but Manci and Regina struggled through the crush to the man. 'It's my child over there,' they both said. 'My boy,' said Manci. 'I want to show him that I'm still alive.'

He ordered them down onto the concourse. When they stood before him, they began to wonder what his purpose was. 'Your name?' he asked Regina.

She told him and saw him reach behind his back and fumble

under his leather belt. She expected to see his hand appear holding a pistol. What it held, however, was a letter for her from her husband. He had a similar letter from Henry Rosner, too. He gave a brief summary of the journey he'd made from Brinnlitz with their husbands. Manci suggested he might be willing to let them get down under the car, between the tracks, as if to urinate. It was sometimes permitted if trains were long delayed. He consented.

As soon as Manci was down there under the carriage, she let out the piercing Rosner whistle she had used on the *Appellplatz* of Płaszów to guide Henry and Olek to her. Olek heard it and began waving. He took Richard's head and pointed it toward their mothers, peering out between the wheels of the train.

After wild waving, Olek held his arm aloft and pulled back his sleeve to show a tattoo like a varicose scrawl along the flesh of his upper arm. And of course the women waved, nodded, applauded, young Richard also holding up his tattooed arm for applause. *Look*, the children were saying by their rolled-up sleeves. *We have permanence.*

But between the wheels, the women were in a frenzy. 'What's happened to them?' they asked each other. 'In God's name, what are they doing here?' They understood that there would be a fuller explanation in the letters. They tore them open and read them, then put them away and went on waving.

Next, Olek opened his hand and showed that he had a few pelletlike potatoes in his palm. 'There,' he called, and Manci could hear him distinctly. 'You don't have to worry about me being hungry.'

'Where's your father?' Manci shouted.

'At work,' said Olek. 'He'll be back from work soon. I'm saving these potatoes for him.'

'Oh, God,' Manci murmured to her sister-in-law. So much for the food in his hand. Young Richard told it straighter. '*Mamushka, Mamushka, Mamushka,*' he yelled, 'I'm so hungry!'

But he too held up a few potatoes. He was keeping them for Dolek, he said. Dolek and Rosner the violinist were working at the rock quarry.

Henry Rosner arrived first. He too stood at the wire, his left arm bared and raised. 'The tattoo,' he called in triumph. She could see, though, that he was shivering, sweating and cold at the same time. It had not been a soft life in Płaszów, but he'd been allowed to sleep off in the paint shop the hours of work he'd put in playing Lehar at the villa. Here, in the band which sometimes accompanied the lines marching to the 'bathhouses,' they didn't play Rosner's brand of music.

When Dolek turned up, he was led to the wire by Richard. He could see the pretty, hollow-faced women peering out from the undercarriage. What he and Henry dreaded most was that the women would offer to stay. They could not be with their sons in the male camp. They were in the most hopeful situation in Auschwitz there, hunkered under a train that was certain to move before the day was over. The idea of a clan reunion here was illusory, but the fear of the men at the Birkenau wire was that the women would opt to die for it. Therefore Dolek and Henry talked with false cheer – like peacetime fathers who'd decided to take the kids up to the Baltic that summer so that the girls could go to Carlsbad on their own. 'Look after Niusia,' Dolek kept calling, reminding his wife that they had another child, that she was in the car above Regina's head.

At last some merciful siren sounded in the men's camp. The men and boys now had to leave the wire. Manci and Regina climbed limply back into the train and the door was locked. They were still. Nothing could surprise them anymore.

The train rolled out in the afternoon. There were the usual speculations. Mila Pfefferberg believed that if the destination was not Schindler's place, half the women crammed in the cars would not live another week. She herself expected that she had only days left. The girl Lusia had scarlet fever. Mrs. Dresner, tended by Danka but leached by dysentery, seemed to be dying.

But in Niusia Horowitz' car, the women saw mountains and pine trees through the broken slat. Some of them had come to these mountains in their childhood, and to see the distinctive hills even from the floor of these putrid wagons gave them an unwarranted sense of holiday. They shook the girls who sat in the muck staring. 'Nearly there,' they promised. But where? Another false arrival would finish them all.

At cold dawn on the second day, they were ordered out. The locomotive could be heard hissing somewhere in the mist. Beards of dirty ice hung from the understructures of the train, and the air pierced them. But it was not the heavy, acrid air of Auschwitz. It was a rustic siding, somewhere. They marched, their feet numb in clogs, and everybody coughing. Soon they saw ahead of them a large gate and, behind it, a great bulk of masonry from which chimneys rose; they looked like brothers to the ones left behind in Auschwitz. A party of SS men waited by the gate, clapping their hands in the cold. The group at the gate, the chimneys – it all looked like part of that sickening continuum. A girl beside Mila Pfefferberg began to weep. 'They've brought us all this way to send us up the chimney anyhow.'

'No,' said Mila, 'they wouldn't waste their time. They could have done all that at Auschwitz.'

Her optimism was, however, like that of the girl Lusia – she couldn't tell where it came from.

As they got closer to the gate, they became aware that Herr Schindler was standing in the midst of the SS men. They could tell at first by his memorable height and bulk. Then they could see his features under the Tyrolean hat which he'd been wearing lately to celebrate his return to his home mountains. A short, dark SS officer stood beside him. It was the Commandant of Brinnlitz, *Untersturmführer* Liepold. Oskar had already discovered – the women would discover it soon – that Liepold, unlike his middle-aged garrison, had not yet lost faith in that proposition called 'the Final Solution.' Yet though he was the respected deputy of *Sturmbannführer* Hassebroeck and the supposed incarnation of authority in this place, it was Oskar who stepped forward as the lines of women stopped. They stared at him. A phenomenon in the mist. Only some of them smiled. Mila Pfefferberg, like others of the girls in the column that morning, remembers that it was an instant of the most basic and devout gratitude, and quite unutterable. Years later, one woman from those lines, remembering the morning, would face a German television crew and attempt to explain it. 'He was our father, he was our mother, he was our only faith. He never let us down.'

Then Oskar began to talk. It was another of his outrageous speeches, full of dazzling promises. 'We knew you were coming,' he said. 'They called us from Zwittau. When you go inside the building, you'll find soup and bread waiting for you.' And then, lightly and with pontifical assurance, he said it: 'You have nothing more to worry about. You're with me now.'

It was the sort of address against which the *Untersturmführer* was powerless. Though Liepold was angry at it, Oskar was oblivious. As the *Herr Direktor* moved with the prisoners into the courtyard, there was nothing Liepold could do to break into that certainty.

The men knew. They were on the balcony of their dormitory looking down. Sternberg and his son searching for Mrs. Clara Sternberg, Feigenbaum senior and Lutek Feigenbaum looking out for Nocha Feigenbaum and her delicate daughter. Juda Dresner and his son Janek, old Mr. Jereth, Rabbi Levartov, Ginter, Garde, even Marcel Goldberg all strained for a sight of their women. Mundek Korn looked not only for his mother and sister but for Lusia the optimist, in whom he'd developed an interest. Bau now fell into a melancholy from which he might never fully emerge. He knew definitively, for the first time, that his mother and wife would not arrive in Brinnlitz. But Wulkan the jeweller, seeing Chaja Wulkan below him in the factory courtyard, knew with astonishment now that there *were* individuals who intervened and offered astounding rescue.

Pfefferberg waved at Mila a package he had kept for her arrival – a hank of wool stolen from one of the cases Hoffman had left behind, and a steel needle he had made in the welding department. Frances Spira's ten-year-old son also looked down from the balcony. To stop himself from calling out, he had jammed his fist into his mouth, since there were so many SS men in the yard.

The women staggered across the cobbles in their Auschwitz tatters. Their heads were cropped. Some of them were too ill, too hollowed out to be easily recognised. Yet it was an astounding assembly. It would not surprise anyone to find out later that no such reunion occurred anywhere else in stricken Europe. That there had never been, and would not be, any other Auschwitz rescue like this one.

The women were then led up into their separate dormitory. There was straw on the floor – no bunks yet. From a large DEF tureen, an SS girl served them the soup Oskar had spoken about at the gate. It was rich. There were lumps of nutrient in it. In its fragrance, it was the outward sign of the value of the other imponderable promises. 'You have nothing more to worry about.'

But they could not touch their men. The women's dormitory was for the moment quarantined. Even Oskar, on the advice of his medical staff, was concerned about what they might have brought with them from Auschwitz.

There were, however, three points at which their isolation could be breached. One was the loose brick above young Moshe Bejski's bunk. Men would spend the coming nights kneeling on Bejski's mattress, passing messages through the wall. Likewise, on the factory floor there was a small fanlight which gave into the women's latrines. Pfefferberg stacked crates there, making a cubicle where a man could sit and call messages. Finally, for early morning and late evening, there was a crowded wire barrier between the men's balcony and the women's. The Jereths met there: old Mr. Jereth, from whose wood the first Emalia barracks had been built; his wife, who had needed a refuge from the *Aktions* in the ghetto. Prisoners used to joke about the exchanges between Mr. and Mrs. Jereth. 'Have your bowels moved today, dear?' Mr. Jereth would sombrely ask his wife, who had just come from the dysentery-ridden huts of Birkenau.

On principle, no one wanted to be put in the clinic. In Płaszów it had been a dangerous place where you were made to take Dr. Blancke's terminal benzine treatment. Even here in Brinnlitz, there was always a risk of sudden inspections, of the type that had already taken the boy children. According to the memos of Oranienburg, a labour-camp clinic should not have any patients with serious illnesses. It was not meant to be a mercy home. It was there to offer industrial first aid. But whether they wanted it or not, the clinic at Brinnlitz was full of women. The teen-age Janka Feigenbaum was put in there. She had cancer and might die in any case, even in the best of places. She had at least come to the best of places left to her. Mrs. Dresner was brought in, as were dozens of others who could not eat or keep food in their stomachs. Lusia the optimist and two other girls were suffering from scarlet fever and could not be kept in the clinic. They were put in beds in the cellar, down amid the warmth of the boilers. Even in the haze of her cold fever, Lusia was aware of the prodigious warmth of that cellar ward.

Emilie worked as quiet as a nun in the clinic. Those who were well in Brinnlitz, the men who were disassembling the Hoffman machines and putting them in storehouses down the road, scarcely noticed her. One of them later said that she was just a quiet and submissive wife. For the healthy in Brinnlitz stayed hostage to Oskar's flamboyance, to this great Brinnlitz confidence trick. Even the women who were still standing had their attention taken by the grand, magical, omniprovident Oskar.

Manci Rosner, for example. A little later in Brinnlitz' history, Oskar would come to the lathes where she worked the night shift and hand her Henry's violin. Somehow, during a journey to see Hassebroeck at Gröss-Rosen, he'd got the time to go into the warehouse there and find the fiddle. It had cost him 100 RM. to redeem it. As he handed it to her, he smiled in a way that seemed to promise her the ultimate return of the violinist to go with the violin. 'Same instrument,' he murmured. 'But – for the moment – different tune.'

It was hard for Manci, faced by Oskar and the miraculous

violin, to see behind the *Herr Direktor* to the quiet wife. But to the dying, Emilie was more visible. She fed them semolina, which she got God knows where, prepared in her own kitchen and carried up to the *Krankenstube*. Dr. Alexander Biberstein believed that Mrs. Dresner was finished. Emilie spooned the semolina into her for seven days in a row, and the dysentery abated. Mrs. Dresner's case seemed to verify Mila Pfefferberg's claim that if Oskar had failed to rescue them from Birkenau, most of them would not have lived another week.

Emilie tended Janka Feigenbaum also, the nineteen-year-old with bone cancer. Lutek Feigenbaum, Janka's brother, at work on the factory floor, sometimes noticed Emilie moving out of her ground-floor apartment with a canister of soup boiled up in her own kitchen for the dying Janka. 'She was dominated by Oskar,' Lutek would say. 'As we all were. Yet she was her own woman.'

When Feigenbaum's glasses were broken, she arranged for them to be repaired. The prescription lay in some doctor's office in Cracow, had lain there since before the ghetto days. Emilie arranged for someone who was visiting Cracow to get the prescription and bring back the glasses made up. Young Feigenbaum considered this more than an average kindness, especially in a system which positively desired his myopia, which aimed to take the spectacles off all the Jews of Europe. There are many stories about Oskar providing new glasses for various prisoners. One wonders if some of Emilie's kindnesses in this matter may not have been absorbed into the Oskar legend, the way the deeds of minor heroes have been subsumed by the figure of Arthur or Robin Hood.

34

The doctors in the *Krankenstube* were Doctors Hilfstein, Handler, Lewkowicz, and Biberstein. They were all concerned about the likelihood of a typhus outbreak. For typhus was not only a hazard to health. It was, by edict, a cause to close down Brinnlitz, to put the infested back into cattle cars and ship them to die in the ACHTUNG TYPHUS! barracks of Birkenau. On one of Oskar's morning visits to the clinic, about a week after the women arrived, Biberstein told him that there were two more possible cases among the women. Headache, fever, malaise, general pains throughout the whole body – all that had begun. Biberstein expected the characteristic typhoid rash to appear within a few days. These two would need to be isolated somewhere in the factory.

Biberstein did not have to give Oskar too much home instruction in the facts of typhus. Typhus was carried by louse bite. The prisoners were infested by uncontrollable populations of lice. The disease took perhaps two weeks to incubate. It might be incubating now in a dozen, a hundred prisoners. Even with the new bunks installed, people still lay too close. Lovers passed the virulent lice to each other when they met, fast and secretly, in some hidden corner of the factory. The typhus lice were wildly migratory. It seemed now that *their* energy could checkmate Oskar's.

So that when Oskar ordered a delousing unit – showers, a laundry to boil clothes, a disinfection plant – built upstairs, it was no idle administrative order. The unit was to run on hot steam piped up from the cellars. The welders were to work double shifts on the project. They did it with a will, for willingness characterised the *secret* industries of Brinnlitz. Official industry might be symbolised by the Hilo machines rising from the new-poured workshop floor. It was in the prisoners' interest and in Oskar's, as Moshe Bejski later observed, that these machines be properly erected, since it gave the camp a convincing front. But the uncertified industries of Brinnlitz were the ones that counted. The women knitted clothing with wool looted from Hoffman's left-behind bags. They paused and began to look industrial only when an SS officer or NCO passed through the factory on his way to the *Herr Direktor's* office, or when Fuchs and Schoenbrun, the inept civil engineers ('Not up to the weight of *our* engineers,' a prisoner would later say) came out of their offices.

The Brinnlitz Oskar was still the Oskar old Emalia hands remembered. A *bon vivant*, a man of wild habits. Mandel and Pfefferberg, at the end of their shift and overheated from working on the pipe fittings for the steam, visited a water tank high up near the workshop ceiling. Ladders and a catwalk took them to it. The water was warm up there, and once you climbed in, you could not be seen from the floor. Dragging themselves up, the two welders were amazed to find the tub already taken. Oskar floated, naked and enormous. A blond SS girl, the one Regina Horowitz had bribed with a brooch, her naked breasts buoyant at the surface, shared the water with him. Oskar became aware of them, looked up at them frankly. Sexual shame was, to him, a concept something like existentialism, very worthy but hard to grasp. Stripped, the welders noticed, the girl was delicious.

They apologised and left, shaking their heads, whistling softly, laughing like schoolboys. Above their heads, Oskar dallied like Zeus.

When the epidemic did not develop, Biberstein thanked the Brinnlitz delousing unit. When the dysentery faded, he thanked the food. In a testimony in the archives of the *Yad Vashem*, Biberstein declares that at the beginning of the camp, the daily ration was in excess of 2,000 calories. In all the miserable winter-bound continent, only the Jews of Brinnlitz were fed this living meal. Among the millions, only the soup of the Schindler thousand had body.

There was porridge too. Down the road from the camp, by the stream into which Oskar's mechanics had recently thrown black-market liquor, stood a mill. Armed with a work pass, a prisoner could stroll down there on an errand from one or another department of DEF. Mundek Korn remembers coming back to the camp loaded with food. At the mill you simply tied your trousers at the ankles and loosened your belt. Your friend then shovelled your pants full of oatmeal. You belted up again and returned to the camp – a grand repository, priceless as you walked, a little bandy-legged, past the sentries into the annex. Inside, people loosened your cuffs and let the oatmeal run out into pots.

In the drafting department, young Moshe Bejski and Josef Bau had already begun forging prison passes of the type that allowed people to make the mill run. Oskar wandered in one day and showed Bejski documents stamped with the seal of the rationing authority of the Government General. Oskar's best contacts for black-market food were still in the Cracow area. He could arrange shipments by telephone. But at the Moravian border, you had to show clearance documents from the Food and Agriculture Department of the Government General. Oskar pointed to the stamp on the papers in his hand. Could you make a stamp like that? he asked Bejski.

Bejski was a craftsman. He could work on little sleep. Now he turned out for Oskar the first of the many official stamps he would craft. His tools were razor blades and various small cutting instruments. His stamps became the emblems of Brinnlitz' own outrageous bureaucracy. He cut seals of the Government General, of the Governor of Moravia, seals to adorn false travel permits so that prisoners could drive by truck to Brno or Olomouc to collect loads of bread, of black-market gasoline, of flour or fabric or cigarettes. Leon Salpeter, a Cracow pharmacist, once a member of Marek Biberstein's *Judenrat*, kept the storehouse in Brinnlitz. Here the miserable supplies sent down from Gröss-Rosen by Hassebroeck were kept, together with the supplementary vegetables, flour, cereals bought by Oskar under Bejski's minutely careful rubber stamps, the eagle and the hooked cross of the regime precisely crafted on them.

'You have to remember,' said an inmate of Oskar's camp, 'that Brinnlitz was hard. But beside any other – paradise!' Prisoners seem to have been aware that food was scarce everywhere; even on the outside, few were sated.

And Oskar? Did Oskar cut his rations to the same level as those of the prisoners?

The answer is indulgent laughter. '*Oskar?* Why would Oskar cut his rations? He was the *Herr Direktor*. Who were we to argue with his meals?' And then a frown, in case you think this attitude too serflike. 'You don't understand. We were grateful to be there. There was nowhere else to be.'

As in his early marriage, Oskar was still temperamentally an absentee, was away from Brinnlitz for stretches of time. Sometimes Stern, purveyor of the day's requests, would wait up all night for him. In Oskar's apartment Itzhak and Emilie were the keepers of vigils. The scholarly accountant would always put the most loyal interpretation on Oskar's wanderings around Moravia. In a speech years after, Stern would say, 'He rode day and night, not only to purchase food for the Jews in Brinnlitz camp – by means of forged papers made by one of the prisoners – but to buy us arms and ammunition in case the SS conceived of killing us during their retreats.' The picture of a restlessly provident *Herr Direktor* does credit to Itzhak's love and loyalty. But Emilie would have understood that not all the absences had to do with Oskar's brand of humane racketeering.

During one of Oskar's furloughs, nineteen-year-old Janek Dresner was accused of sabotage. In fact Dresner was ignorant of metalwork. He had spent his time in Płaszów in the delousing works, handing towels to the SS who came for a shower and sauna, and boiling lice-ridden clothes taken from prisoners. (From the bite of a louse he'd suffered typhus, and survived only because his cousin, Dr. Schindel, passed him off in the clinic as an angina case.)

The supposed sabotage occurred because engineer Schoenbrun, the German supervisor, transferred him from his lathe to one of the larger metal presses. It had taken a week for the engineers to set the metrics for this machine, and the first time Dresner pressed the start button and began to use it, he shorted the wiring and cracked one of the plates. Schoenbrun harangued the boy and went into the office to write a damning report. Copies of Schoenbrun's complaint were typed up and addressed to Sections D and W in Oranienburg, to Hassebroeck at Gröss-Rosen, and to *Untersturmführer* Liepold in his office at the factory gate.

In the morning, Oskar had still not come home. So rather than mail the reports, Stern took them out of the office mailbag and hid them. The complaint addressed to Liepold had already been hand-delivered, but Liepold was at least correct in the terms of the organisation he served and could not hang the boy until he had heard from Oranienburg and Hassebroeck. Two days later, Oskar had still not appeared. 'It must be some party!' the whimsical ones on the shop floor told each other. Somehow Schoenbrun discovered that Itzhak was sitting on the letters. He raged through the office, telling Stern that *his* name would be added to the reports. Stern seemed to be a man of limitless calm, and when Schoenbrun finished he told the engineer that he had removed the reports from the mailbag because he thought the *Herr Direktor* should, as a matter of courtesy, be apprised of their contents before they were mailed. The *Herr Direktor*, said Stern, would of course be appalled to find out that a prisoner had done 10,000 R.M. worth of damage to one of his machines. It seemed only just, said Stern, that Herr Schindler be given the chance to add his own remarks to the report.

At last Oskar drove in through the gate. Stern intercepted him and told him about Schoenbrun's charges. *Untersturmführer* Liepold had been waiting to see Schindler too and was eager to push his authority inside the factory, to use the Janek Dresner case as a pretext. I will preside over the hearing, Liepold told Oskar. You, *Herr Direktor*, will supply a signed statement attesting to the extent of the damage.

Wait a minute, Oskar told him. It's my machine that's broken. *I'm* the one who'll preside.

Liepold argued that the prisoner was under the jurisdiction of Section D. But the machine, replied Oskar, came under the authority of the Armaments Inspectorate. Besides, he really couldn't permit a trial on the shop floor. If Brinnlitz had been a garment or chemical factory, then perhaps it wouldn't have much impact on production. But this was a munitions factory engaged in the manufacture of secret components. 'I won't have my work force disturbed,' said Oskar.

It was an argument Oskar won, perhaps because Liepold gave in. The *Untersturmführer* was afraid of Oskar's contacts. So the court was convened at night in the machine-tool section of DEF, and its members were Herr Oskar Schindler as president, Herr Schoenbrun, and Herr Fuchs. A young German girl sat at the side of the judicial table to keep a record, and when young Dresner was brought in, he saw in front of him a solemn and fully constituted court. According to a Section D edict of April 11, 1944, what Janek faced was the first and crucial stage of a process which should, after a report to Hassebroeck and a reply from Oranienburg, end in his hanging on the workshop floor in front of all the Brinnlitz people, his parents and sister among them.

Janek noticed that tonight there was none of that shop-floor familiarity to Oskar. The *Herr Direktor* read aloud Schoenbrun's report of the sabotage. Janek knew about Oskar mainly from the reports of others, particularly from his father, and couldn't tell now what Oskar's straight-faced reading of Schoenbrun's accusations meant. Was Oskar really grieving for the cracked machine? Or was it all just theatrics?

When the reading was finished, the *Herr Direktor* began to ask questions. There was not much Dresner could say in answer. He pleaded that he was unfamiliar with the machine. There had been trouble setting it, he explained. He had been too anxious and had made a mistake. He assured the *Herr Direktor* that he had no reason to wish to sabotage the machinery. If you are not skilled at armaments work, said Schoenbrun, you shouldn't be here. The *Herr Direktor* has assured me that all you prisoners have had experience in the armaments industry. Yet here you are, *Häftling* Dresner, claiming ignorance.

With an angry gesture, Schindler ordered the prisoner to detail exactly what he had done on the night of the offence. Dresner began to talk about the preparations for starting up the machine, the setting of it, the dry run at the controls, the switching on of the power, the sudden racing of the engine, the splitting of the mechanism. Herr Schindler became more and more restless as Dresner talked, and began to pace the floor glowering at the boy. Dresner was describing some alteration he had made to one of the controls when Schindler stopped, ham fists clenched, his eyes glaring.

What did you say? he asked the boy. Dresner repeated what he had said: I adjusted the pressure control, *Herr Direktor*.

Oskar walked up to him and hit him across the side of the jaw. Dresner's head sang, but in triumph, for Oskar – his back to his fellow judges – had winked at Dresner in a way that could not be mistaken. Then he began waving his great arms, dismissing the boy. 'The stupidity of you damned people!' he was bellowing all the while. 'I can't believe it!'

He turned and appealed to Schoenbrun and Fuchs, as if they were his only allies. 'I *wish* they were intelligent enough to sabotage a machine. Then at least I'd have their goddamned hides! But what can you do with these people? They're an utter waste of time.'

Oskar's fist clenched again, and Dresner recoiled at the idea of another roundhouse punch. *'Clear out!'* yelled Oskar.

As Dresner went out through the door, he heard Oskar tell the others that it was better to forget all this. 'I have some good Martell upstairs,' he said.

This deft subversion may not have satisfied Liepold and Schoenbrun. For the sitting had not reached a formal conclusion; it had not ended in a judgment. But they could not complain that Oskar had avoided a hearing, or treated it with levity.

Dresner's account, given later in his life, raises the supposition that Brinnlitz maintained its prisoners' lives by a series of stunts so rapid that they were nearly magical. To tell the strict truth though, Brinnlitz, both as a prison and as a manufacturing enterprise, was itself, of its nature and in a literal sense, the one sustained, dazzling, integral confidence trick.

35

For the factory produced nothing. 'Not a shell,' Brinnlitz prisoners will still say, shaking their heads. Not one 45mm shell manufactured there could be used, not one rocket casing. Oskar himself contrasts the output of DEF in the Cracow years with the Brinnlitz record. In Zablocie, enamelware was manufactured to the value of 16,000,000 RM. During the same time, the munitions section of Emalia produced shells worth 500,000 RM. Oskar explains that at Brinnlitz, however, 'as a consequence of the falling off of the enamel production,' there was no output to speak of. The armaments production, he says, encountered 'start-up difficulties.' But in fact he did manage to ship one truckful of 'ammunition parts,' valued at 35,000 RM., during the Brinnlitz months. 'These parts,' said Oskar later, 'had been transferred to Brinnlitz already half-fabricated. To supply still less [to the war effort] was impossible, and the excuse of "start-up difficulties" became more and more dangerous for me and my Jews, because Armaments Minister Albert Speer raised his demands from month to month.'

The danger of Oskar's policy of nonproduction was not only that it gave him a bad name at the Armaments Ministry. It made other managements angry. For the factory system was fragmented, one workshop producing the shells, another the fuses, a third packing in the high explosives and assembling the components. In this way, it was reasoned, an air raid on any one factory could not substantially destroy the flow of arms. Oskar's shells, dispatched by freight to factories farther down the line, were inspected there by engineers Oskar did not know and could not reach. The Brinnlitz items always failed quality control. Oskar would show the complaining letters to Stern, to Finder, to Pemper or Garde. He would laugh uproariously, as if the men writing the reprimands were comic-opera bureaucrats.

Later in the camp's history one such case occurred. Stern and Mietek Pemper were in Oskar's office on the morning of April 28, 1945, a morning when the prisoners stood at an extremity of danger, having been, as will be seen, all condemned to death by *Sturmbannführer* Hassebroeck. The day was Oskar's thirty-seventh birthday, and a bottle of cognac had already been opened to mark it. And on the desk lay a telegram from the armaments assembly plant near Brno. It said that Oskar's antitank shells were so badly produced that they failed all quality-control tests. They were imprecisely calibrated, and because they had not been tempered at the right heat they split under testing.

Oskar was ecstatic at this telegram, pushing it toward Stern and Pemper, making them read it. Pemper remembers that he made another of his outrageous statements. 'It's the best birthday present I could have got. Because I know now that no poor bastard has been killed by my product.'

This incident says something about two contrasting frenzies. There is some madness in a manufacturer like Oskar who rejoices when he does not manufacture. But there is also a cool lunacy in the German technocrat who, Vienna having fallen, Marshal Koniev's men having embraced the Americans on the Elbe, still takes it for granted that an arms factory up in the hills has time to tidy up its performance and make a condign offering to the grand principles of discipline and output.

But the main question that arises from the birthday telegram is how Oskar lasted those months, the seven months up to the date of his birthday.

The Brinnlitz people remember a whole series of inspections and checks. Men from Section D stalked the factory, checklists in their hands. So did engineers from the Armaments Inspectorate. Oskar always lunched or dined these officials, softened them up with ham and cognac. In the Reich there were no longer so many good lunches and dinners to be had. The prisoners at the lathes, the furnaces, the metal presses would state that the uniformed inspectors reeked of liquor and reeled on the factory floor. There is a story all the inmates tell of an official who boasted, on one of the final inspections of the war, that Schindler would not seduce *him* with camaraderie, with a lunch and liquor. On the stairs leading from the dormitories down to the workshop floor, the legend has it, Oskar tripped the man, sending him to the bottom of the stairs, a journey that split the man's head and broke his leg. The Brinnlitz people are, however, generally unable to say who the SS hard case was. One claims that it was Rasch, SS and police chief of Moravia. Oskar himself never made any recorded claim about it. The anecdote is one of those stories that reflect on people's picture of Oskar as a provider who covers all possibilities. And one has to admit, in natural justice, that the inmates had the right to spread this sort of fable. They were the ones in deepest jeopardy. If the fable let them down, they would pay for it most bitterly.

One reason Brinnlitz passed the inspections was the relentless trickery of Oskar's skilled workers. The furnace gauges were rigged by the electricians. The needle registered the correct temperature when the interior of the furnace was in fact hundreds of degrees cooler. 'I've written to the manufacturers,' Oskar would tell the armaments inspectors. He would play the sombre, baffled manufacturer whose profits were being eroded. He would blame the floor, the inferior German supervisors. He spoke yet again of 'start-up difficulties,' implying future tonnages of munitions once the problems faded.

In the machine-tool departments, as at the furnaces, everything looked normal. Machines seemed perfectly calibrated, but were in fact a micromillimetre off. Most of the arms inspectors who walked through seem to have left not only with a gift of cigarettes and cognac, but with a faint sympathy for the thorny problems this decent fellow was enduring.

Stern would always say in the end that Oskar bought boxes of shells from other Czech manufacturers and passed them off as his own during inspections. Pfefferberg makes the same claim. In any case, Brinnlitz lasted, whatever sleight-of-hand Oskar used.

There were times when, to impress the hostile locals, he invited important officials in for a tour of the factory and a good dinner. But they were always men whose expertise did not run to engineering and munitions production. After the *Herr Direktor's* stay in Pomorska Street, Liepold, Hoffman, and the local Party *Kreisleiter* wrote to every official they could think of – local, provincial, Berlin-based – complaining about him, his morals, his connections, his breaches of race and penal law. Sussmuth let him know about the barrage of letters arriving at Troppau. So Oskar invited Ernst Hahn down to Brinnlitz. Hahn was second in command of the bureau of the Berlin main office devoted to services for SS families. 'He was,' says Oskar with customary reprobate's primness, 'a notorious drunkard.' With him Hahn brought his boyhood friend Franz Bosch. Bosch, as Oskar has already remarked in this narrative, was also 'an impenetrable drunkard.' He was also the murderer of the Gutter family. Oskar, however, swallowing his contempt, welcomed him for his public-relations value.

When Hahn arrived in town, he was wearing exactly the splendid, untarnished uniform Oskar had hoped he would. It was festooned with ribbons and orders, for Hahn was an old-time SS man from the early glory days of the Party. With this dazzling *Standartenführer* came an equally glittering adjutant.

Liepold was invited in, from his rented house outside camp walls, to dine with the visitors. From the start of the evening, he was out of his depth. For Hahn loved Oskar; drunks always did. Later Oskar would describe the men and the uniforms as 'pompous.' But at least Liepold was convinced now that if he wrote complaining letters to distant authorities, they were likely to land on the desk of some old drinking friend of the *Herr Direktor's*, and that this could well be perilous to himself.

In the morning, Oskar was seen driving through Zwittau, laughing with these glamorous men from Berlin. The local Nazis stood on the pavements and saluted all this Reich splendour as it passed.

Hoffman was not as easily quelled as the rest. The three hundred women of Brinnlitz had, in Oskar's own words, 'no employment possibility.' It has already been said that many of them spent their days knitting. In the winter of 1944, for people whose only cover was the striped uniform, knitting was no idle hobby. Hoffman, however, made a formal complaint to the SS about the wool the Schindler women had stolen from the cases in the annex. He thought it scandalous, and that it showed up the true activities of the so-called Schindler munitions works.

When Oskar visited Hoffman, he found the old man in a triumphant mood. 'We've petitioned Berlin to remove you,' said Hoffman. 'This time we've included sworn statements declaring that your factory is running in contravention of economic and race law. We've nominated an invalided *Wehrmacht* engineer from Brno to take over the factory and turn it into something decent.'

Oskar listened to Hoffman, apologised, tried to appear penitent. Then he telephoned Colonel Erich Lange in Berlin and asked him to sit on the petition from the Hoffman clique in Zwittau. The out-of-court settlement still cost Oskar 8,000 RM., and all winter the Zwittau town authorities, civil and Party, plagued him, calling him in to the town hall to acquaint him with the complaints of various citizens about his prisoners, or the state of his drains.

Lusia the optimist had a personal experience of SS inspectors that typifies the Schindler method.

Lusia was still in the cellar – she would be there for the entire winter. The other girls had got better and had moved upstairs to recuperate. But it seemed to Lusia that Birkenau had filled her with a limitless poison. Her fevers recurred again and again. Her joints became inflamed. Carbuncles broke out in her armpits. When one burst and healed, another would form. Dr. Handler, against the advice of Dr. Biberstein, lanced some of them with a kitchen knife. She remained in the cellar, well fed, ghost-white, infectious. In all the great square mileage of Europe, it was the only space in which she could have lived. She was aware of that even then, and hoped that the enormous conflict would roll by above her head.

In that warm hole under the factory, night and day were irrelevant. The time the door at the top of the cellar stairs burst open could have been either. She was used to quieter visits from Emilie Schindler. She heard boots on the stairs and tensed in her bed. It sounded to her like an old-fashioned *Aktion*.

It was in fact the *Herr Direktor* with two officers from Gröss-Rosen. Their boots clattered on the steps as if to stampede over her. Oskar stood with them as they looked around in the gloom at the boilers and at her. It came to Lusia that perhaps she was *it* for today. The sacrificial offering you had to give them so that they would go away satisfied. She was partially hidden by a boiler, but Oskar made no attempt to conceal her, actually came to the foot of her bed. Because the two gentlemen of the SS seemed flushed and unsteady, Oskar had a chance to speak to her. His were words of wonderful banality, and she would never forget them: 'Don't worry. Everything's all right.' He stood close, as if to emphasise to the inspectors that this was not an infectious case.

'This is a Jewish girl,' he said flatly. 'I didn't want to put her in the *Krankenstube*. Inflammation of the joints. She's finished anyway. They don't give her more than thirty-six hours.'

Then he rambled on about the hot water, where it came from, and the steam for the delousing. He pointed to gauges, piping, cylinders. He edged around her bed as if it too were neutral, part of the mechanism. Lusia did not know where to look, whether to open or close her eyes. She tried to appear comatose. It might seem a touch too much, but Lusia did not think so at the time, that as he ushered the SS men back to the base of the stairs, Oskar flashed her a cautious smile. She would stay there for six months and hobble upstairs in the spring to resume her womanhood in an altered world.

*

During the winter, Oskar built up an independent arsenal. Again there are the legends: Some say that the weapons were bought at the end of winter from the Czech underground. But Oskar had been an obvious National Socialist in 1938 and 1939 and may have been wary of dealing with the Czechs. Most of the weapons, in any case, came from a flawless source, from *Obersturmbannführer* Rasch, SS and police chief of Moravia. The small cache included carbines and automatic weapons, some pistols, some hand grenades. Oskar would later describe the transaction offhandedly. He acquired the arms, he would say, 'under the pretence of protecting my factory, for the price of the gift of a brilliant ring to his [Rasch's] wife.'

Oskar does not detail his performance in Rasch's office in Brno's Spilberk Castle. It is not hard to imagine, though. The *Herr Direktor*, concerned about a possible slave uprising as the war grinds on, is willing to die expensively at his desk, automatic weapon in hand, having mercifully dispatched his wife with a bullet to save her from something worse. The *Herr Direktor* also touches on the chance that the Russians might turn up at the gate. My civilian engineers, Fuchs and Schoenbrun, my honest technicians, my German-speaking secretary, all of them deserve to have the means of resistance. It's gloomy talk, of course. I'd rather speak of issues closer to our hearts, *Herr Obersturmbannführer*. I know your passion for good jewellery. May I show you this example I found last week?

And so the ring appeared on the edge of Rasch's blotter, Oskar murmuring, 'As soon as I saw it, I thought of Frau Rasch.'

Once Oskar had the weapons, he appointed Uri Bejski, brother of the rubber-stamp maker, keeper of the arsenal. Uri was small, handsome, lively. People noticed that he wandered into and out of the Schindlers' private quarters like a son. He was a favourite, too, with Emilie, who gave him keys to the apartment. Frau Schindler enjoyed a similar maternal relationship with the surviving Spira boy. She took him regularly into her kitchen and fed him up on slices of bread and margarine.

Having selected the small body of prisoners for training, Uri took one at a time into Salpeter's storehouse to teach them the mechanisms of the *Gewehr* 41 W's. Three commando squads of five men each had been formed. Some of Bejski's trainees were boys like Lutek Feigenbaum. Others were Polish veterans such as Pfefferberg and those other prisoners whom the Schindler prisoners called the 'Budzyn people.'

The Budzyn people were Jewish officers and men of the Polish Army. They had lived through the liquidation of the Budzyn labour camp, which had been under the administration of *Untersturmführer* Liepold. Liepold had brought them into his new command in Brinnlitz. There were about 50 of them, and they worked in Oskar's kitchens. People remember them as very political. They had learned Marxism during their imprisonment in Budzyn, and looked forward to a Communist Poland. It was an irony that in Brinnlitz they lived in the warm kitchens of that most apolitical of capitalists, Herr Oskar Schindler.

Their rapport with the bulk of the prisoners, who, apart from the Zionists, merely followed the politics of survival, was good. A number of them took private lessons on Uri Bejski's automatics, for in the Polish Army of the Thirties they had never held such sophisticated weapons.

If Frau Rasch, in the last and fullest days of her husband's power in Brno, had idly — during a party, say; a musical recital at the castle — gazed into the core of the diamond that had come to her from Oskar Schindler, she would have seen reflected there the worst incubus from her own dreams and her *Führer's*. An armed Marxist Jew.

36

Old drinking friends of Oskar's, Amon and Bosch among them, had sometimes thought of him as the victim of a Jewish virus. It was no metaphor. They believed it in virtually literal terms and attached no blame to the sufferer. They'd seen it happen to other good men. Some area of the brain fell under a thrall that was half-bacterium, half-magic. If they'd been asked whether it was infectious, they would have said, yes, highly. They would have seen the case of *Oberleutnant* Sussmuth as an example of conspicuous contagion.

For Oskar and Sussmuth connived over the winter of 1944-45 to get a further 3,000 women out of Auschwitz in groups of 300 to 500 at a time into small camps in Moravia. Oskar supplied the influence, the sales talk, the palm-greasing for these operations. Sussmuth did the paperwork. In the textile mills of Moravia there was a labour shortage, and not all the owners abhorred the Jewish presence as sharply as Hoffman. At least five German factories in Moravia – at Freudenthal and Jagerndorf, at Liebau, Grulich, and Trautenau – took these drafts of women and supplied a camp on the premises. Any such camp was never paradise, and in its management the SS were permitted to be more dominant than Liepold could ever hope to be. Oskar would later describe these women in the little camps as 'living under endurable treatment.' But the very smallness of the textile camps was an aid to their survival, for the SS garrisons were older, slacker, less fanatical men. There was typhus to be eluded, and hunger to be carried like a weight beneath the ribs. But such tiny, almost countrified establishments would for the most part escape the extermination orders that would come to the bigger camps in the spring.

But if the Jewish sepsis had infected Sussmuth, for Oskar Schindler it galloped. Through Sussmuth, Oskar had applied for another 30 metalworkers. It is simple fact that he had lost interest in production. But he saw, with the detached side of his mind, that if his plant was ever to validate its existence to Section D, he would need more qualified hands. When you look at other events of that mad winter, you can see that Oskar wanted the extra 30 not because they were used to lathes and machine tools, but because they were simply an extra 30. It is not too fantastic to say that he desired them with some of the absolute passion that characterised the exposed and flaming heart of the Jesus which hung on Emilie's wall. Since this narrative has tried to avoid the canonisation of the *Herr Direktor*, the idea of the sensual Oskar as the desirer of souls has to be proved.

One of these 30 metalworkers, a man named Moshe Henigman, left a public account of their unlikely deliverance. A little after Christmas, 10,000 prisoners from the quarries of Auschwitz III – from such establishments as the Krupp Weschel-Union armaments factory and from German Earth and Stone, from the Farben synthetic-petroleum plant and the airplane-dismantling enterprise – were put in a column and marched away toward Gröss-Rosen. Perhaps some planner believed that once they arrived in Lower Silesia, they would be distributed among the area's factory camps. If that was the scheme, it escaped the SS officers and men who marched with the prisoners. It ignored also the devouring cold of the merciless turning of the year, and it did not inquire how the column would be fed. The limpers, the coughers were culled out at the beginning of each stage and executed. Of 10,000, says Henigman, there were within ten days only 1,200 left alive. To the north, Koniev's Russians had burst across the Vistula south of Warsaw and seized all the roads on the column's northwesterly route. The diminished group was therefore put in an SS compound somewhere near Opole. The Commandant of the place had the prisoners interviewed, and lists made of the skilled workers. But each day the weary selections continued, and the rejects were shot.

A man whose name was called out never knew what to expect, a lump of bread or a bullet. When Henigman's name was called, however, he was put in a railway car with 30 others and, under the care of an SS man and a *Kapo*, was shunted south. 'We were given food for the trip,' Henigman recalls. 'Something unheard of.'

Henigman later spoke of the exquisite unreality of arriving at Brinnlitz. 'We could not believe that there was a camp left where men and women worked together, where there were no beatings, no *Kapo*.' His reaction is marked by a little hyperbole, since there *was* segregation in Brinnlitz. Occasionally, too, Oskar's blond girlfriend let fly with an open palm, and once when a boy stole a potato from the kitchen and was reported to Liepold, the Commandant made him stand on a stool all day in the courtyard, the potato clamped in his open mouth, saliva running down his chin, and the placard 'I AM A POTATO THIEF!' hung around his neck.

But to Henigman this sort of thing was not worthy of report. 'How can one describe,' he asks, 'the change from hell to paradise?'

When he met Oskar, he was told to build himself up. Tell the supervisors when you're ready to work, said the *Herr Direktor*. And Henigman, faced with this strange reversal of policy, felt not simply that he'd come to a quiet pasture, but that he had gone through the mirror.

Since 30 tinsmiths were merely a fragment of the 10,000, it must be said again that Oskar was only a minor god of rescue. But like any tutelary spirit, he saved equally Goldberg and Helen Hirsch, and equally he tried to save Dr. Leon Gross and Olek Rosner. With this same gratuitous equality, he made a costly deal with the Gestapo in the Moravia region. We know that the contract was struck, but we do not know how expensive it was. That it cost a fortune is certain.

A prisoner named Benjamin Wrozlawski became one subject of this deal. Wrozlawski was formerly an inmate of the labour camp at Gliwice. Unlike Henigman's camp, Gliwice was not in the

Auschwitz region, but was close enough to be one of the Auschwitz subsidiary camps. By January 12, when Koniev and Zhukov launched their offensive, Höss's awesome realm and all its close satellites were in danger of instant capture. The Gliwice prisoners were put in *Ostbahn* cars and shipped toward Fernwald. Somehow Wrozlawski and a friend named Roman Wilner jumped from the train. One popular form of escape was through loosened ventilators in the cars' ceilings. But prisoners who tried it were often shot by guards stationed on the roofs. Wilner was wounded during this escape, but he was able to travel, and he and his friend Wrozlawski fled through the high quiet towns of the Moravian border. They were at last arrested in one of these villages and taken to the Gestapo offices in Troppau.

As soon as they had arrived and been searched and put in a cell, one of the gentlemen of the Gestapo walked in and told them that nothing bad would happen. They had no reason to believe him. The officer said further that he would not transfer Wilner to a hospital, in spite of the wound, for he would simply be collected and fed back into the system.

Wrozlawski and Wilner were locked away for nearly two weeks. Oskar had to be contacted and a price had to be settled. During that time, the officer kept talking to them as if they were in protective custody, and the prisoners continued to find the idea absurd. When the door was opened and the two of them were taken out, they presumed they were about to be shot. Instead, they were led to the railway station by an SS man who escorted them on a train southeast toward Brno.

For both of them, the arrival at Brinnlitz had that same surreal, delightful and frightening quality it had had for Henigman. Wilner was put in the clinic, under the care of Doctors Handler, Lewkowicz, Hilfstein, Biberstein. Wrozlawski was put in a sort of convalescent area which had been set up – for extraordinary reasons soon to be explained – in a corner of the factory floor downstairs. The *Herr Direktor* visited them and asked how they felt. The preposterous question scared Wrozlawski; so did the surroundings. He feared, as he would put it years later, 'the way from the hospital would lead to execution, as was the case in other camps.' He was fed with the rich Brinnlitz porridge, and saw Schindler frequently. But as he confesses, he was still confused, and found the phenomenon of Brinnlitz hard to grasp.

By the arrangement Oskar had with the provincial Gestapo, 11 escapees were added to the crammed-in camp population. Each one of them had wandered away from a column or jumped from a cattle car. In their stinking stripes, they had tried to stay at large. By rights, they should all have been shot.

In 1963, Dr. Steinberg of Tel Aviv testified to yet another instance of Oskar's wild, contagious, and unquestioning largesse. Steinberg was the physician in a small work camp in the *Sudeten* hills. The Gauleiter in Liberec was less able, as Silesia fell to the Russians, to keep labour camps out of his wholesome province of Moravia. The camp in which Steinberg was imprisoned was one of the many new ones scattered among the mountains. It was a *Luftwaffe* camp devoted to the manufacture of some unspecified aircraft component. Four hundred prisoners lived there. The food was poor, said Steinberg, and the workload savage.

Pursuing a rumor about the Brinnlitz camp, Steinberg managed to get a pass and the loan of a factory truck to go and see Oskar. He described to him the desperate conditions in the *Luftwaffe* camp. He says that Oskar quite lightly agreed to allocate him part of the Brinnlitz stores. The main question that preoccupied Oskar was, On what grounds could Steinberg regularly come to Brinnlitz to pick up supplies? It was arranged that he would use some excuse to do with getting regular medical aid from the doctors in the camp clinic.

Twice a week thereafter, says Steinberg, he visited Brinnlitz and took back to his own camp quantities of bread, semolina, potatoes, and cigarettes. If Schindler was around the storehouse on the day that Steinberg was loading up, he would turn his back and walk away.

Steinberg does not give any exact poundage of food, but he offers it as a medical opinion that if the Brinnlitz supplies had not been available, at least 50 of the prisoners in the *Luftwaffe* camp would have died by the spring.

Apart from the ransoming of the women in Auschwitz, however, the most astounding salvage of all was that of the Goleszów people. Goleszów was a quarry and cement plant inside Auschwitz III itself, home of the SS-owned German Earth and Stone Works. As has been seen with the 30 metalsmiths, throughout January 1945 the dread fiefdoms of Auschwitz were being disbanded, and in mid-month 120 quarry workers from Goleszów were thrown into two cattle cars. Their journey would be as bitter as any, but would end better than most. It is worth remarking that, like the Goleszów men, nearly everyone else in the Auschwitz area was on the move that month. Dolek Horowitz was shipped away to Mauthausen. Young Richard, however, was kept behind with other small children. The Russians would find him later in the month in an Auschwitz abandoned by the SS and would claim quite correctly that he and the others had been detained for medical experiments. Henry Rosner and nine-year-old Olek (apparently no longer considered necessary for the laboratories) were marched away from Auschwitz in a column for thirty miles, and those who fell behind were shot. In Sosnowiec they were packed into freight cars. As a special kindness, an SS guard who was supposed to separate the children let Olek and Henry go into the same car. It was so crowded that everyone had to stand, but as men died of cold and thirst a gentleman whom Henry described as 'a smart Jew' would suspend them in their blankets from horse hooks near the roof. In this way there was more floor space for the living. For the sake of the boy's comfort, Henry got the idea of slinging Olek in his blanket in exactly the same way from the horse hooks. This not only gave the child an easier ride; when the train stopped at stations and sidings, he would call to Germans by the rails to throw snowballs up to the wire gratings. The snow would shatter and spray the interior of the wagon with moisture, and men would struggle for a few ice crystals.

The train took seven days to get to Dachau, and half the population of the Rosners' car died. When it at last arrived and the door was opened, a dead body fell out, and then Olek, who picked himself up in the snow, broke an icicle off the undercarriage and began to lick it ravenously. Such was travel in Europe in January 1945.

For the Goleszów quarry prisoners it was even worse. The bill of lading for their two freight cars, preserved in the archives of the *Yad Vashem*, shows that they were travelling without food for more than ten days and with the doors frozen shut. R, a boy of sixteen, remembers that they scraped ice off the inside walls to quench their thirst. Even in Birkenau they weren't unloaded. The killing process was in its last furious days. It had no time for them. They were abandoned on sidings, reattached to locomotives, dragged for 50 miles, uncoupled again. They were shunted to the gates of camps, whose commandants refused them on the clear ground that by now they lacked industrial value, and because in any case facilities – bunks and rations – were everywhere at the limit.

In the small hours of a morning at the end of January, they were uncoupled and abandoned in the rail yards at Zwittau. Oskar says a friend of his telephoned from the depot to report human scratchings and cries from inside the cars. These pleadings were uttered in many tongues, for the trapped men were, according to the manifest, Slovenes, Poles, Czechs, Germans, Frenchmen, Hungarians, Netherlanders, and Serbians. The friend who made the call was very likely Oskar's brother-in-law. Oskar told him to shunt the two cars up the siding to Brinnlitz.

It was a morning of gruesome cold – minus 30 degrees Celsius (minus 22 degrees Fahrenheit), says Stern. Even the exact Biberstein says that it was at least minus 20 degrees (minus 4 degrees F). Poldek Pfefferberg was summoned from his bunk, fetched his welding gear, and went out to the snowy siding to cut open the doors iced hard as iron. He too heard the unearthly complaints from within.

It is hard to describe what they saw when the doors were at last opened. In each car, a pyramid of frozen corpses, their limbs madly contorted, occupied the centre. The hundred or more still living stank awesomely, were seared black by the cold, were skeletal. Not one of them would be found to weigh more than 75 pounds.

Oskar was not at the siding. He was inside the factory, where a warm corner of the workshop floor was being made ready for the shipment from Goleszów. Prisoners dismantled the last of Hoffman's dumped machinery and carried it to the garages. Straw was brought in and the floor strewn with it. Already Schindler had been out to the Commandant's office to speak to Liepold. The *Untersturmführer* didn't want to take the Goleszów men; in that, he resembled all the other commandants they had met in the past few weeks. Liepold remarked pointedly that no one could pretend that *these* people were munitions workers. Oskar admitted that, but guaranteed to put them on the books, and so to pay 6 RM. a day for each of them. 'I can use them after their recuperation,' said Oskar. Liepold recognised two aspects of the case. First, that Oskar was unstoppable. Second, that an increase in the size of Brinnlitz and the labour fees paid might well please Hassebroeck. Liepold would have them quickly enrolled on the books and the entries back-dated, so that even as the Goleszów men were carried in through the factory gate, Oskar was paying for them.

Inside the workshop, they were wrapped in blankets and laid down on the straw. Emilie came from her apartment, followed by two prisoners toting an enormous bucket of porridge. The doctors noted the frostbite and the need for frost ointments. Dr. Biberstein mentioned to Oskar that the Goleszów people would need vitamins, though he was sure there were none to be had in Moravia.

In the meantime the 16 frozen corpses were placed in a shed. Rabbi Levartov, looking at them, knew that with their limbs twisted by the cold they would be hard to bury in the Orthodox manner, which permitted no breaking of bones. The matter,

Levartov knew, would, however, have to be argued with the Commandant. Liepold had on file from Section D a number of directives urging SS personnel to dispose of the dead by burning. In the boiler rooms were perfect facilities, industrial furnaces capable almost of vaporising a body. Yet Schindler had so far twice refused to permit the burning of the dead.

The first time was when Janka Feigenbaum died in the Brinnlitz clinic. Liepold had at once ordered her body incinerated. Oskar heard through Stern that this was abhorrent to the Feigenbaums and to Levartov, and his resistance to the idea may have been fuelled also by the Catholic residue in his own soul. In those years the Catholic Church was firmly opposed to cremation. As well as refusing Liepold the use of the furnace, Oskar also ordered the carpenters to prepare a coffin, and himself supplied a horse and wagon, allowing Levartov and the family to ride out under guard to bury the girl in the woods. Feigenbaum father and son had walked behind the wagon, counting the steps from the gate so that when the war ended they could reclaim Janka's body.

Witnesses say that Liepold was furious at this sort of pandering to the prisoners. Some Brinnlitz people even comment that Oskar could show toward Levartov and the Feigenbaums a more exacting delicacy and courtesy than he usually managed with Emilie.

The second time Liepold wanted the furnaces used was when old Mrs. Hofstatter died. Oskar, at Stern's request, had another coffin prepared, allowing a metal plaque on which Mrs. Hofstatter's vital statistics were marked to be included in the coffin. Levartov and a *minyan*, the quorum often males who recite *Kaddish* over the dead, were permitted to leave camp and attend the funeral.

Stern says that it was for Mrs. Hofstatter's sake that Oskar established a Jewish cemetery in the Catholic parish of Deutsch-Bielau, a nearby village. According to him, Oskar went to the parish church on the Sunday Mrs. Hofstatter died and made the priest a proposition. A quickly convened parish council agreed to sell him a small parcel of land just beyond the Catholic cemetery. There is nothing surer than that some of the council resisted, for it was an era when Canon Law was interpreted narrowly in its provisions as to who could and who could not be buried in consecrated ground.

Other prisoners of some authority say, however, that the Jewish cemetery plot was bought by Oskar at the time of the arrival of the Goleszów cars with their tithe of twisted dead. In a later report, Oskar himself implies that it was the Goleszów dead who caused him to buy the land. By one account, when the parish priest pointed out the area beyond the church wall reserved for the burial of suicides and suggested that the Goleszów people be buried there, Oskar answered that these weren't suicides. These were victims of a great murder.

The Goleszów deaths and the death of Mrs. Hofstatter must have come close together in any case, and were both marked with full ritual in the unique Jewish cemetery of Deutsch-Bielau.

It is clear from the way all Brinnlitz prisoners spoke of it that this interment had enormous moral force within the camp. The distorted corpses who were unloaded from the freight cars had seemed less than human. Looking at them, you became frightened for your own precarious humanity. The inhuman thing was beyond feeding, washing, warming. The one way left to restore it – as well as yourself – to humanity was through ritual. Levartov's rites, therefore, the exalted plainchant of *Kaddish*, had a far larger gravity for the Brinnlitz prisoners than such ceremonies could ever have had in the relative tranquillity of prewar Cracow.

To keep the Jewish burial ground tidy in case of future deaths, Oskar employed a middle-aged SS *Unterscharführer* and paid him a retainer.

Emilie Schindler had transactions of her own to make. Carrying a clutch of false papers supplied by Bejski, she had two prisoners load up one of the plant trucks with vodka and cigarettes, and ordered them to drive her to the large mining town of Ostrava up near the border of the Government General. At the military hospital she was able to make an arrangement with various of

Oskar's contacts and to bring back frostbite ointments, sulpha, and the vitamins Biberstein had thought beyond procuring. Such journeys now became regular events for Emilie. She was growing to be a traveller, like her husband.

After the first deaths, there were no others. The Goleszów people were *Mussulmen*, and it was a first principle that the condition of *Mussulmen* could not be reversed. But there was some intractability in Emilie which would not accept it. She harried them with her bucketfuls of farina. 'Out of those rescued from Goleszów,' said Dr. Biberstein, 'not one would have stayed alive without her treatment.' The men began to be seen, trying to look useful, on the factory floor. One day a Jewish storeman asked one of them to carry a box out to a machine on the workshop floor. 'The box weighs thirty-five kilos,' said the boy, 'and I weigh thirty-two. How in the hell can I carry it?'

To this factory of ineffective machines, its floor strewn with scarecrows, Herr Amon Goeth came that winter, following his release from prison, to pay his respects to the Schindlers. The SS court had let him out of prison in Breslau because of his diabetes. He was dressed in an old suit that may have been a uniform with the markings stripped off. There are rumors about the meaning of this visit, and they persist to this day. Some thought that Goeth was looking for a handout, others that Oskar was holding something for him — cash or kind from one of Amon's last Cracow deals in which Oskar had perhaps served as Amon's agent. Some who worked close to Oskar's office believe that Amon even asked for a managerial post at Brinnlitz. No one could say that he did not have the experience. In fact, all three versions of Amon's motives in coming down to Brinnlitz are possibly correct, though it is unlikely that Oskar ever acted as Amon's agent.

As Amon stepped through the gate of the camp, it could be seen that prison and tribulation had thinned him down. The fleshiness had vanished from his face. His features were more like those of the Amon who had come to Cracow in the New Year of 1943 to liquidate the ghetto, yet they were different too, for they were jaundice-yellow and prison-grey. And if you had the eyes for it, if you dared to look, you saw a new passivity there. Some prisoners, however, glancing up from their lathes, glimpsed that figure from the pit of their foulest dreams, there unannounced, passing by the doors and windows, proceeding through the factory yard toward Herr Schindler's office. Helen Hirsch sat galvanised, wanting nothing except that he should vanish again. But others hissed him as he passed, and men bent at their machines and spat. More mature women lifted their knitting toward him like a challenge. For that was vengeance – to show that in spite of all his terror, Adam still delved and Eve span.

If Amon wanted a job at Brinnlitz – and there were few other places a *Hauptsturmführer* under suspension could go – Oskar either talked him out of it or bought him off. In that way, this meeting was like all their others. As a courtesy the *Herr Direktor* took Amon on a tour of the plant, and on this circuit of the workshop floor, the reaction against him was stronger still. Back in the office, Amon was overheard demanding that Oskar punish the inmates for their disrespect, and Oskar was heard rumbling away, pledging that he would do something about the pernicious Jews and expressing his own undiminished respect for Herr Goeth.

Though the SS had let him out of prison, the investigation of his affairs was still in progress. A judge of the SS Court had come to Brinnlitz in the past few weeks to question Mietek Pemper again about Amon's managerial procedures. Before the interrogation began, Commandant Liepold had muttered to Pemper that he'd better be careful, that the judge would want to take him to Dachau for execution after he'd been drained of evidence. Wisely, Pemper had done all he could to convince the judge of the unimportance of his work in the main office at Płaszów.

Somehow, Amon had heard that the SS investigators had been pursuing Pemper. Soon after he arrived in Brinnlitz, he cornered his ci-devant typist in Oskar's outer office and wanted to know what questions the judge had asked. Pemper believed, reasonably enough, that he could detect in Amon's eyes resentment that his onetime prisoner was still a breathing source of evidence for the SS Court. Surely Amon was powerless here, thinned down, looking doleful in an old suit, washed up in Oskar's office? But you couldn't be sure. It was still Amon, and he had the habit of authority. Pemper said, 'The judge told me I was not to talk to anyone about my interrogation.' Goeth was outraged and threatened to complain to Herr Schindler. That, if you like, was a measure of Amon's new impotence. He had never had to go to Oskar before to appeal for the chastisement of a prisoner.

By the second night of Amon's visit, the women were feeling more triumphant. He couldn't touch them. They persuaded even Helen Hirsch of this. Yet her sleep was uneasy.

The last time Amon passed within sight of prisoners, it was on his way to be taken by car to the station at Zwittau. He had never in the past made three visits to any space without bringing some poor bastard's world crashing down. It was clear now that he had no power at all. Yet still not everyone could look him in the face as he left. Thirty years later, in the sleep of Płaszów veterans from Buenos Aires to Sydney, from New York to Cracow, from Los Angeles to Jerusalem, Amon would still be rampaging. 'When you saw Goeth,' said Poldek Pfefferberg, 'you saw death.'

So, in his own terms, he was never an utter failure.

37

Oskar's thirty-seventh birthday was celebrated by Oskar himself and all the prisoners. One of the metalworkers had crafted a small box suitable for holding studs or cuff links, and when the *Herr Direktor* appeared on the workshop floor, the twelve-year-old Niusia Horowitz was pushed toward him to make a rehearsed speech in German. '*Herr Direktor*,' she said in a voice he had to stoop to hear. 'All the prisoners wish you the very best for this your birthday.'

It was a *Shabbat*, which was apt, because the Brinnlitz people would always remember it as a festival. Early in the morning, about the time Oskar had begun celebrating with Martell cognac in his office and flourishing that insulting telegram from the engineers at Brno, two truckloads of white bread rolled into the courtyard. Some went to the garrison, even to the hung-over Liepold sleeping late in his house in the village. That much was necessary to stop the SS from grumbling about the way the *Herr Direktor* favoured prisoners. The prisoners themselves were issued three-quarters of a kilo of the bread. They inspected it as they ate and savoured it. There was some speculation about where Oskar had got it. Perhaps it could be partially explained by the goodwill of the local mill manager, Daubek, the one who turned away while Brinnlitz prisoners filled their pants with oatmeal. But that Saturday bread was truly celebrated more in terms of the magic of the event, of the wonder-working.

Though the day is remembered as jubilant, there was in fact not so much cause for festive feeling. Sometime in the past week, a long telegram had been directed from Herr Commandant Hassebroeck of Gröss-Rosen to Liepold of Brinnlitz giving him instructions about the disposal of the population in the event the Russians drew near. There was to be a final selection, said Hassebroeck's telegram. The aged and the halt were to be shot immediately, and the healthy were to be marched out in the direction of Mauthausen.

Though the prisoners on the factory floor knew nothing of this telegram, they still had an unspecified fear of something like it. All that week there had been rumors that Poles had been brought in to dig mass graves in the woods beyond Brinnlitz. The white bread seemed to have come as an antidote to that rumor, a warranty of all their futures. Yet everyone seemed to know that an era of dangers more subtle than those of the past had begun.

If Oskar's factory hands knew nothing of the telegram, neither did Herr Commandant Liepold himself. The cable was delivered first to Mietek Pemper in Liepold's outer office. Pemper had steamed it open and resealed it and taken the news of its contents straight to Oskar. Schindler stood at his desk reading it, then turned to Mietek. 'All right, then,' growled Oskar. 'We have to say goodbye to *Untersturmführer* Liepold.'

For it seemed both to Oskar and to Pemper that Liepold was the only SS man in the garrison capable of obeying such a telegram. The Commandant's deputy was a man in his forties, an SS *Oberscharführer* named Motzek. While Motzek might be capable of some sort of panic slaughter, to administer the cool murder of 1,300 humans was beyond him.

In the days before his birthday, Oskar made a number of confidential complaints to Hassebroeck about the excessive behavior of Herr Commandant Liepold. He visited the influential Brno police chief, Rasch, and lodged the same sort of charges against Liepold. He showed both Hassebroeck and Rasch copies of letters he had written to the office of General Glücks in Oranienburg. Oskar was gambling that Hassebroeck would remember Oskar's past generosities and the promise of future ones, that he would take note of the pressure for Liepold's removal now being built up by Oskar in Oranienburg and Brno, that he would transfer

Liepold without bothering to investigate the *Untersturmführer's* behavior toward the inmates of Brinnlitz.

It was a characteristic Schindler manoeuvre – the Amon-Oskar game of blackjack writ large. All the Brinnlitz men were in the stake, from Hirsch Krischer, Prisoner No. 68821, a forty-eight-year-old auto mechanic, to Jarum Kiaf, Prisoner No. 77196, a twenty-seven-year-old unskilled worker and survivor of the Goleszów carriages. And all the Brinnlitz women were counted in as well, from No. 76201, twenty-nine-year-old metalworker Berta Aftergut, to No. 76500, thirty-six-year-old Jenta Zwetschenstiel.

Oskar got fuel for further complaints about Liepold by inviting the Commandant to dinner at the apartment inside the factory. It was April 27, the eve of Schindler's birthday. About eleven o'clock that night, the prisoners at work on the floor of the plant were startled to see a drunken Commandant reeling across the factory floor, assisted on his way by a steadier *Herr Direktor*. In the course of his passage, Liepold attempted to focus on individual workers. He raged, pointing at the great roof beams above the machinery. The *Herr Direktor* had so far kept him off the factory floor, but here he was, the final and punishing authority. 'You fucking Jews,' he was roaring. 'See that beam, see it! That's what I'll hang you from. Every one of you!'

Oskar eased him along, directing him by the shoulder, murmuring at him, 'That's right, that's right. But not tonight, eh? Some other time.'

The next day Oskar called Hassebroeck and others with predictable accusations. The man rages around the factory drunk, making threats about *immediate* executions. They're not labourers! They're sophisticated technicians engaged in secret-weapons manufacture, and so on. And although Hassebroeck was responsible for the deaths of thousands of quarry workers, although he believed that all Jewish labour should be liquidated when the Russians were close, he did agree that until then Herr Schindler's factory should be treated as a special case.

Liepold, said Oskar, kept stating that he'd like at last to go into combat. He's young, he's healthy, he's willing. Well, Hassebroeck told Oskar, we'll see what can be done. Commandant Liepold himself, meanwhile, spent Oskar's birthday sleeping off the dinner of the night before.

In his absence, Oskar made an astounding birthday speech. He had been celebrating all day, yet no one remembers his delivery being unsteady. We do not have the text of what he said, but there is another speech, made ten days later on the evening of May 8, of which we do have a copy. According to those who listened, both speeches pursued similar lines. Both were, that is, promises of continuing life.

To call either of them a speech, however, is to demean their effect. What Oskar was instinctively attempting was to adjust reality, to alter the self-image of both the prisoners and the SS. Long before, with pertinacious certainty, he'd told a group of shift workers, Edith Liebgold among them, that they would last the war. He'd flourished the same gift for prophecy when he faced the women from Auschwitz, on their morning of arrival the previous November, and told them, 'You're safe now; you're with me.' It can't be ignored that in another age and condition, the *Herr Direktor* could have become a demagogue of the style of Huey Long of Louisiana or John Lang of Australia, whose gift was to convince the listeners that they and he were bonded together to avert by a whisker all the evil devised by other men.

Oskar's birthday speech was delivered in German at night on the workshop floor to the assembled prisoners. An SS detachment had to be brought in to guard a gathering of that size, and the German civilian personnel were present as well. As Oskar began to speak, Poldek Pfefferberg felt the hairs on his lice stand to attention. He looked around at the mute faces of Schoenbrun and Fuchs, and of the SS men with their automatics. *They will kill this man*, he thought. *And then everything will fall apart.*

The speech pursued two main promises. First, the great tyranny was coming to a close. He spoke of the SS men around the walls as if they too were imprisoned and yearned for liberation. Many of them, Oskar explained to the prisoners, had been conscripted from other units and without their consent into the *Waffen* SS. His second promise was that he would stay at Brinnlitz until the end of the hostilities was announced. 'And five minutes longer,' he said. For the prisoners, the speech, like past pronouncements of Oskar's, promised a future. It stated his vigorous intent that they should not go into graves in the woods. It reminded them of his investment in them, and it enlivened them.

One can only guess, however, how it bedeviled the SS men who heard it. He had genially insulted their corps. How they protested, or whether they swallowed it, he would learn from their reaction. He had also warned them that he would stay in Brinnlitz at least as long as they would, and that therefore he was a witness.

But Oskar did not feel as blithe as he sounded. Later he confessed that at the time he was concerned about actions retreating military units in the Zwittau area might take in regard to Brinnlitz. He even says, 'We were in a panic, because we were afraid of the despairing actions of the SS guards.' It must have been a quiet panic, for no prisoner, eating his white bread on Oskar's birthday, seems to have caught a whiff of it. Oskar was also concerned about some Vlasov units which had been stationed on the edges of Brinnlitz. These troops were members of the ROA, the Russian Army of Liberation, formed the year before on the authority of Himmler from the vast ranks of Russian prisoners in the Reich and commanded by General Andrei Vlasov, a former Soviet general captured in front of Moscow three years past. They were a dangerous corps for the Brinnlitz people, for they knew Stalin would want them for a special punishment and feared that the Allies would give them back to him. Vlasov units everywhere were therefore in a state of violent Slavic despair, which they stoked with vodka. When they withdrew, seeking the American lines farther west, they might do anything.

Within two days of Oskar's birthday speech, a set of orders

arrived on Liepold's desk. They announced that *Unterstrumführer* Liepold had been transferred to a *Waffen* SS infantry battalion near Prague. Though Liepold could not have been delighted with them, he seems to have packed quietly and left. He had often said at dinners at Oskar's, particularly after the second bottle of red wine, that he would prefer to be in a combat unit. Lately there had been a number of field-rank officers, *Wehrmacht* and SS, from the retreating forces invited to dinner in the *Herr Direktor's* apartment, and their table talk had always been to stir Liepold's itch to seek combat. He had never been faced with as much evidence as the other guests that the cause was finished.

It is unlikely that he called Hassebroeck's office before packing his bags. Telephone communications were not sound, for the Russians had encircled Breslau and were within a walk of Gröss-Rosen itself. But the transfer would not have surprised anyone in Hassebroeck's office, since Liepold had often made patriotic sounds to them too. So, leaving *Oberscharführer* Motzek in command of Brinnlitz, Josef Liepold drove off to battle, a hard-liner who had got his wish.

With Oskar, there was no mute waiting for the close. During the first days of May, he discovered somehow – perhaps even by telephone calls to Brno, where lines were still operating – that one of the warehouses with which he regularly dealt had been abandoned. With half a dozen prisoners, he drove off by truck to loot it. There were a number of roadblocks on the way south, but at each of them they flashed their dazzling papers, forged, as Oskar would write, with the stamps and signatures 'of the highest SS police authorities in Moravia and Bohemia.' When they arrived at the warehouse, they found it encircled by fire. Military storehouses in the neighborhood had been set alight, and there had been incendiary bombing raids as well. From the direction of the inner city, where the Czechoslovak underground was fighting door to door with the garrison, they could hear firing. Herr Schindler ordered the truck to back into the loading dock of the warehouse, broke the door open, and discovered that the interior was full of a brand of cigarettes called Egipski.

In spite of such lighthearted piracy, Oskar was frightened by rumors from Slovakia that the Russians were uncritically and informally executing German civilians. From listening to the BBC news each night, he was comforted to find that the war might end before any Russian reached the Zwittau area.

The prisoners also had indirect access to the BBC and knew what the realities were. Throughout the history of Brinnlitz the radio technicians, Zenon Szenwich and Artur Rabner, had continually repaired one or another radio of Oskar's. In the welding shop, Zenon listened with an earphone to the 2 P.M. news from the Voice of London. During the night shift, the welders plugged into the 2 A.M. broadcast. An SS man, in the factory one night to take a message to the office, discovered three of them around the radio. 'We've been working on it for the *Herr Direktor*' they told the man, 'and just got it going a minute ago.'

Earlier in the year, prisoners had expected that Moravia would be taken by the Americans. Since Eisenhower had stood fast at the Elbe, they now knew that it would be the Russians. The circle of prisoners closest to Oskar were composing a letter in Hebrew, explaining what Oskar's record was. It might do some good if presented to American forces, which had not only a considerable Jewish component, but field rabbis. Stern and Oskar himself therefore considered it vital that the *Herr Direktor* somehow be got to the Americans. In part Oskar's decision was influenced by the characteristic Central European idea of the Russians as barbarians, men of strange religion and uncertain humanity. But apart from that, if some of the reports from the east could be believed, he had grounds for rational fear.

But he was not debilitated by it. He was awake and in a state of hectic expectation when the news of the German surrender came to him through the BBC in the small hours of May 7. The war in Europe was to cease at midnight on the following night, the night of Tuesday, May 8. Oskar woke Emilie, and the sleepless

Stern was summoned into the office to help the *Herr Direktor* celebrate. Stern could tell that Oskar now felt confident about the SS garrison, but would have been alarmed if he could have guessed how Oskar's certitude would be demonstrated that day.

On the shop floor, the prisoners maintained the usual routines. If anything, they worked better than on other days. Yet about noon, the *Herr Direktor* destroyed the pretence of business as usual by piping Churchill's victory speech by loudspeaker throughout the camp. Lutek Feigenbaum, who understood English, stood by his machine flabbergasted. For others, the honking and grunting voice of Churchill was the first they'd heard in years of a language they would speak in the New World. The idiosyncratic voice, as familiar in its way as that of the dead *Führer*, carried to the gates and assailed the watchtowers, but the SS took it soberly. They were no longer turning inward toward the camp. Their eyes, like Oskar's, were focused – but far more sharply – on the Russians. According to Hassebroeck's earlier telegram, they should have been busy in the rich green woods. Instead, clock-watching for midnight, they looked at the black face of the forest, speculating whether partisans were there. A fretful *Oberscharführer* Motzek kept them at their posts, and duty kept them there also. For duty, as so many of their superiors would claim in court, was the SS genius.

In those uneasy two days, between the declaration of peace and its accomplishment, one of the prisoners, a jeweller named Licht, had been making a present for Oskar, something more expressive than the metal stud box he'd been given on his birthday. Licht was working with a rare quantity of gold. It had been supplied by old Mr. Jereth of the box factory. It was established – even the Budzyn men, devout Marxists, knew it – that Oskar would have to flee after midnight. The urge to mark that flight with a small ceremony was the preoccupation of the group – Stern, Finder, Garde, the Bejskis, Pemper – close to Oskar. It is remarkable, at a time when they were not sure themselves that they would see the peace, that they should worry about going-away presents.

All that was handy to make a gift with, however, was base metals. It was Mr. Jereth who suggested a source of something better. He opened his mouth to show his gold bridgework. Without Oskar, he said, the SS would have the damned stuff anyway. My teeth would be in a heap in some SS warehouse, along with the golden fangs of strangers from Lublin, Lodz, and Lwów.

It was, of course, an appropriate offering, and Jereth was insistent. He had the bridgework dragged out by a prisoner who had once had a dental practice in Cracow. Licht melted the gold down and by noon on May 8 was engraving an inscription on the inner circle in Hebrew. It was a Talmudic verse which Stern had quoted to Oskar in the front office of Buchheister's in October 1939. 'He who saves a single life saves the entire world.'

In one of the factory garages that afternoon, two prisoners were engaged in removing the upholstery from the ceiling and inner doors of Oskar's Mercedes, inserting small sacks of the *Herr Direktor's* diamonds and replacing the leatherwork without, they hoped, leaving any bulges. For them too it was a strange day. When they came out of the garage, the sun was setting behind the towers where the Spandaus sat loaded yet weirdly ineffectual. It was as if all the world were waiting for a decisive word.

Words of that nature seem to have come in the evening. Again, as on his birthday, Oskar instructed the Commandant to gather the prisoners on the factory floor. Again the German engineers and the secretaries, their escape plans already made, were present. Among them stood Ingrid, his old flame. She would not be leaving Brinnlitz in Schindler's company. She would make her escape with her brother, a young war veteran, lame from a wound. Given that Oskar went to so much trouble to provide his prisoners with trade goods, it is unlikely that he would let an old love like Ingrid leave Brinnlitz without anything to barter for survival. Surely they would meet on friendly terms later, somewhere in the West.

As at Oskar's birthday speech, armed guards stood around the great hall. The war had nearly six hours to run, and the SS were sworn never to abandon it in any case. Looking at them, the prisoners tried to gauge their states of soul.

When it was announced that the *Herr Direktor* would make another address, two women prisoners who knew shorthand, Miss Waidmann and Mrs. Berger, had each fetched a pencil and prepared to take down what was said. Because it was an *ex tempore* speech, given by a man who knew he would soon become a fugitive, it was more compelling as spoken than it is on the page in the Waidmann-Berger version. It continued the themes of his birthday address, but it seemed to make them conclusive for both the prisoners and the Germans. It declared the prisoners the inheritors of the new era; it confirmed that everyone else there – the SS, himself, Emilie, Fuchs, Schoenbrun – was now in need of rescue.

'The unconditional surrender of Germany,' he said, 'has just been announced. After six years of the cruel murder of human beings, victims are being mourned, and Europe is now trying to return to peace and order. I would like to turn to you for unconditional order and discipline – to all of you who together with me have worried through many hard years – in order that you can live through the present and within a few days go back to your destroyed and plundered homes, looking for survivors from your families. You will thus prevent panic, whose results cannot be foreseen.'

He did not, of course, mean panic in the prisoners. He meant panic among the garrison, among the men lining the walls. He was inviting the SS to leave, and the prisoners to let them do so. General Montgomery, he said, the commander of the Allied land forces, had proclaimed that one should act in a humane way toward the conquered, and everyone – in judging the Germans – had to distinguish between guilt and duty. 'The soldiers at the front, as well as the little man who has done his duty everywhere, shall not be responsible for what a group calling itself German has done.'

He was uttering a defense of his countrymen which every prisoner who survived the night would hear reiterated a thousand times in the era to come. Yet if anyone had earned the right to make that defense and have it listened to with – at least – tolerance, it was surely Herr Oskar Schindler.

'The fact that millions among you, your parents, children, and brothers, have been liquidated has been disapproved by thousands of Germans, and even today there are millions of them who do not know the extent of these horrors.' The documents and records found in Dachau and Buchenwald earlier in the year, their details broadcast by the BBC, were the first, said Oskar, that many a German had heard of 'this most monstrous destruction.' He therefore begged them once again to act in a humane and just way, to leave justice to those authorised. 'If you have to accuse a person, do it in the right place. Because in the new Europe there *will* be judges, incorruptible judges, who will listen to you.'

Next he began to speak about his association with the prisoners in the past year. In some ways he sounded almost nostalgic, but he feared as well being judged in a lump with the Goeths and the Hassebroecks.

'Many of you know the persecutions, the chicanery and obstacles which, in order to keep my workers, I had to overcome through many years. If it was already difficult to defend the small rights of the Polish worker, to maintain work for him and to prevent him from being sent by force to the Reich, to defend the workers' homes and their modest property, then the struggle to defend the Jewish workers has often seemed insurmountable.'

He described some of the difficulties, and thanked them for their help in satisfying the demands of the armaments authorities. In view of the lack of output from Brinnlitz, the thanks may have sounded ironic. But they were not offered in an ironic way. What the *Herr Direktor* was saying in a quite literal sense was *Thank you for helping me make a fool of the system*.

He went on to appeal for the local people. 'If after a few days here the doors of freedom are opened to you, think of what many of the people in the neighborhood of the factory have done to help you with additional food and clothing. I have done everything and spent every effort in getting you additional food, and I pledge to do the utmost in the future to protect you and safeguard your daily bread. I shall continue doing everything I can for you until five minutes past midnight.

'Don't go into the neighboring houses to rob and plunder. Prove yourselves worthy of the millions of victims among you and refrain from any individual acts of revenge and terror.'

He confessed that the prisoners had never been welcome in the area. 'The Schindler Jews were taboo in Brinnlitz.' But there were higher concerns than local vengeance. 'I entrust your *Kapos* and foremen to continue keeping up order and continued understanding. Therefore tell your people of it, because this is in the interest of your safety. Thank the mill of Daubek, whose help in getting you food went beyond the realms of possibility. On behalf of you, I shall now thank the brave director Daubek, who has done everything to get food for you.

'Don't thank me for your survival. Thank your people who worked day and night to save you from extermination. Thank your fearless Stern and Pemper and a few others who, thinking of you and worrying about you, especially in Cracow, have faced death every moment. The hour of honour makes it our duty to watch and keep order, as long as we stay here together. I beg of you, even among yourselves, to make nothing but humane and just decisions. I wish to thank my personal collaborators for their complete sacrifice in connection with my work.'

His speech, weaving from issue to issue, exhausting some ideas, returning tangentially to others, reached the centre of its temerity. Oskar turned to the SS garrison and thanked *them* for resisting the barbarity of their calling. Some prisoners on the floor thought, He's *asked* us *not to provoke them? What is he doing himself?* For the SS *was* the SS, the corps of Goeth and John and Hujar and Scheidt. There were things an SS man was taught, things he did and saw, which marked the limits of his humanity. Oskar, they felt, was dangerously pushing the limits.

'I would like,' he said, 'to thank the assembled SS guards, who without being asked were ordered from the Army and Navy into this service. As heads of families, they have realised for a long time the contemptibility and senselessness of their task. They have acted here in an extraordinarily humane and correct manner.'

What the prisoners did not see, aghast if a little exalted by the *Herr Direktor's* nerve, was that Oskar was finishing the work he'd begun on the night of his birthday. He was destroying the SS as combatants. For if they stood there and swallowed his version of what was 'humane and correct,' then there was nothing more left to them but to walk away.

'In the end,' he said, 'I request you all to keep a three-minute silence, in memory of the countless victims among you who have died in these cruel years.'

They obeyed him. *Oberscharführer* Motzek and Helen Hirsch; Lusia, who had come up from the cellar only in the past week; and Schoenbrun, Emilie, and Goldberg. Those itching for time to pass, those itching to flee. Keeping silent among the giant Hilo machines at the limit of the noisiest of wars.

When it was over, the SS left the hall quickly. The prisoners remained. They looked around and wondered if they were at last the possessors. As Oskar and Emilie moved toward their apartment to pack, prisoners waylaid them. Licht's ring was presented. Oskar spent some time admiring it; he showed the inscription to Emilie and asked Stern for a translation. When he asked where they had got the gold and discovered it was Jereth's bridge work, they expected him to laugh; Jereth was among the presentation committee, ready to be teased and already flashing the little points of his stripped teeth. But Oskar became very solemn and slowly placed the ring on his finger. Though nobody quite understood it, it was the instant in which they became themselves again, in which Oskar Schindler became dependent on gifts of theirs.

38

In the hours following Oskar's speech the SS garrison began to desert. Inside the factory, the commandos selected from the Budzyn people and from other elements of the prison population had already been issued the weapons Oskar had provided. It was hoped to disarm the SS rather than wage a ritual battle with them. It would not be wise, as Oskar had explained, to attract any retreating and embittered units to the gate. But unless something as outlandish as a treaty was arrived at, the towers would ultimately have to be stormed with grenades.

The truth, however, was that the commandos had only to formalise the disarming described in Oskar's speech. The guards at the main gate gave up their weapons almost gratefully. On the darkened steps leading up to the SS barracks, Poldek Pfefferberg and a prisoner named Jusek Horn disarmed Commandant Motzek, Pfefferberg putting his finger in the man's back and Motzek, like any sane man over forty with a home to go to, begging them to spare him. Pfefferberg took the Commandant's pistol, and Motzek, after a short detention during which he cried out for the *Herr Direktor* to save him, was released and began to walk home.

The towers, about which Uri and the other irregulars must have spent hours of speculation and scheming, were discovered abandoned. Some prisoners, newly armed with the garrison's weapons, were put up there to indicate to anyone passing by that the old order still held sway here.

When midnight came, there were no SS men or women visible in the camp. Oskar called Bankier to the office and gave him the key to a particular storeroom. It was a naval supply store and had been situated, until the Russian offensive into Silesia, somewhere in the Katowice area. It must have existed to supply the crews of river and canal patrol boats, and Oskar had found out that the Armaments Inspectorate wanted to rent storage space for it in some less threatened area. Oskar got the storage contract – 'with the help of some gifts,' he said later. And so eighteen trucks loaded with coat, uniform, and underwear fabric, with worsted yarn and wool, as well as with a half a million reels of thread and a range of shoes, had entered the Brinnlitz gate and been unloaded and stored. Stern and others would declare that Oskar knew the stores would remain with him at the end of the war and that he intended the material to provide a starting stake for his prisoners. In a later document, Oskar claims the same thing. He had sought the storage contract, he says, 'with the intention of supplying my Jewish protégés at the end of the war with clothing . . . . Jewish textile experts estimated the value of my clothing store at more than $150,000 U.S. (peace currency).'

He had in Brinnlitz men capable of making such a judgment – Juda Dresner, for example, who had owned his own textile business in Stradom Street; Itzhak Stern, who had worked in a textile company across the road.

For the rite of passing over this expensive key to Bankier, Oskar was dressed in prisoner's stripes, as was his wife, Emilie. The reversal toward which he'd been working since the early days of DEF was visibly complete. When he appeared in the courtyard to say goodbye, everyone thought it a lightly put on disguise, which would be lightly taken off again once he encountered the Americans. The wearing of the coarse cloth was, however, an act that would never completely be laughed off. He would in a most thorough sense always remain a hostage to Brinnlitz and Emalia.

Eight prisoners had volunteered to travel with Oskar and Emilie. They were all very young, but they included a couple, Richard and Anka Rechen. The oldest was an engineer named Edek Reubinski, but he was still nearly ten years younger than the

Schindlers. Later, he would supply the details of their eccentric journey.

Emilie, Oskar, and a driver were meant to occupy the Mercedes. The others would follow in a truck loaded with food and with cigarettes and liquor for barter. Oskar seemed anxious to be away. One arm of Russian threat, the Vlasovs, was gone. They had marched out in the past few days. But the other, it was presumed, would be in Brinnlitz by the next morning, or even sooner. From the back seat of the Mercedes, where Emilie and Oskar sat in their prison uniforms – not, it had to be admitted, much like prisoners; more like bourgeoisie off to a masquerade ball – Oskar still rumbled out advice for Stern, orders to Bankier and Salpeter. But you could tell he wanted to be off. Yet when the driver, Dolek Grünhaut, tried to start the Mercedes, the engine was dead. Oskar climbed out of the back seat to look under the hood. He was alarmed – a different man from the one who'd given the commanding speech a few hours before. 'What is it?' he kept asking. But it was hard for Grünhaut to say in the shadows. It took him a little time to find the fault, for it was not one he expected. Someone, frightened by the idea of Oskar's departure, had cut the wiring.

Pfefferberg, part of the crowd gathered to wave the *Herr Direktor* off, rushed to the welding shop, brought back his gear, and went to work. He was sweating and his hands seemed clumsy, for he was rattled by the urgency he could sense in Oskar. Schindler kept looking at the gate as if the Russians might at any second materialise. It was not an improbable fear – others in the courtyard were tormented by the same ironic possibility – and Pfefferberg worked too hard and took too long. But at last the engine caught to Grünhaut's frantic turning of the key.

Once the engine turned over, the Mercedes left, the truck following it. Everyone was too unnerved to make formal goodbyes, but a letter, signed by Hilfstein and Stern and Salpeter, attesting to Oskar's and Emilie's record, was handed to the Schindlers. The Schindler convoy rolled out the gate and, at the road by the siding, turned left toward Havlíčkův Brod and toward what was for Oskar the safer end of Europe. There was something nuptial about it, for Oskar, who had come to Brinnlitz with so many women, was leaving with his wife. Stern and the others remained standing in the courtyard. After so many promises, they were their own people. The weight and uncertainty of *that* must now be borne.

The hiatus lasted three days and had its history and its dangers. Once the SS left, the only representative of the killing machine left in Brinnlitz was a German *Kapo* who had come from Gröss-Rosen with the Schindler men. He was a man with a murderous record in Gröss-Rosen itself, but one who had also made enemies in Brinnlitz. A pack of male prisoners now dragged him from his bunk down to the factory hall and enthusiastically and mercilessly hanged him from one of the same beams with which *Untersturmführer* Liepold had recently threatened the prison population. Some inmates tried to intervene, but the executioners were in a rage and could not be stopped.

It was an event, this first homicide of the peace, which many Brinnlitz people would forever abhor. They had seen Amon hang poor engineer Krautwirt on the *Appellplatz* at Płaszów, and this hanging, though for different reasons, sickened them as profoundly. For Amon was Amon and beyond altering. But these hangmen were their brothers.

When the *Kapo* ceased his twitching, he was left suspended above the silenced machines. He perplexed people, though. He was supposed to gladden them, but he threw doubt. At last some men who had not hanged him cut him down and incinerated him. It showed what an eccentric camp Brinnlitz was, that the only body fed into the furnaces which, by decree, should have been employed to burn the Jewish dead was the corpse of an Aryan.

The distribution of the goods in the Navy store went on throughout the next day. Lengths of worsted material had to be cut from the great bolts of fabric. Moshe Bejski said that each prisoner was given three yards, together with a complete set of underwear and some reels of cotton. Some women began that very day to make the suits in which they would travel home. Others kept the fabric intact so that, traded, it would keep them alive in the confused days to come.

A ration of the Egipski cigarettes which Oskar had plundered from burning Brno was also issued, and each prisoner was given a bottle of vodka from Salpeter's storehouse. Few would drink it. It was, of course, simply too precious to drink.

After dark on that second night, a *Panzer* unit came down the road from the direction of Zwittau. Lutek Feigenbaum, behind a bush near the gate and armed with a rifle, had the urge to fire as soon as the first tank passed within sight of the camp. But he considered it rash. The vehicles rattled past. A gunner in one of the rear tanks in the column, understanding that the fence and the watchtowers meant that Jewish criminals might be lying low in there, swivelled his gun and sent two shells into the camp. One exploded in the courtyard, the other on the women's balcony. It was a random exhibition of spite, and through wisdom or astonishment none of the armed prisoners answered it.

When the last tank had vanished, the men of the commandos could hear mourning from the courtyard and from the women's dormitory upstairs. A girl had been wounded by shell fragments. She herself was in shock, but the sight of her injuries had released in the women all the barely expressed grief of the past years. While the women mourned, the Brinnlitz doctors examined the girl and found that her wounds were superficial.

Oskar's party travelled for the first hours of their escape at the tail of a column of *Wehrmacht* trucks. At midnight feats of this nature had become feasible, and no one pestered them. Behind them they could hear German engineers dynamiting installations, and occasionally there was the clamour of a distant ambush arranged by the Czech underground. Near the town of Havlíčkův Brod they must have fallen behind, because they were stopped by Czech partisans who stood in the middle of the road. Oskar went on impersonating a prisoner. 'These good people and I are escapees from a labour camp. The SS fled, and the *Herr Direktor*. This is the *Herr Direktor*'s automobile.'

The Czechs asked them if they had weapons. Reubinski had come from the truck and joined the discussion. He confessed that he had a rifle. All right, said the Czechs, you'd better give us what you have. If the Russians intercepted you and found that you had weapons, they might not understand why. Your defense is your prison uniforms.

In this town, southeast of Prague and on the road to Austria, there was still the likelihood of meeting disgruntled units. The partisans directed Oskar and the others to the Czech Red Cross office in the town square. There they could safely bunk down for the rest of the night.

But when they reached town, the Red Cross officials suggested to them that given the uncertainty of the peace, they would probably be safest in the town jail. The vehicles were left in the square, in sight of the Red Cross office, and Oskar, Emilie, and their eight companions carried their few pieces of baggage and slept in the unlocked cells of the police station.

When they returned to the square in the morning, they found that both vehicles had been stripped. All the upholstery had been torn from the Mercedes, the diamonds were gone, the tires had been taken from the truck, and the engines had been plundered. The Czechs were philosophical about it. *We all have to expect to lose something in times like these.* Perhaps they may even have suspected Oskar, with his fair complexion and his blue eyes, of being a fugitive SS man.

The party were without their own transport, but a train ran south in the direction of Kaplice, and they caught it, dressed still in their stripes. Reubinski says that they took the train 'as far as the forest, and then walked.' Somewhere in that forested border region, well to the north of Linz, they could expect to encounter the Americans.

They were hiking down a wooded road when they met two

young gum-chewing Americans sitting by a machine gun. One of Oskar's prisoners began to speak with them in English. 'Our orders are not to let anyone pass on this road,' one of them said.

'Is it forbidden to circle around through the woods?' asked the prisoner.

The GI chewed. This strange chewing race!

'Guess not,' said the GI at last.

So they swung through the woods and, back on the road half an hour later, ran into an infantry company marching north in double column. Through the English speaker once more, they began to talk to the unit's reconnaissance men. The commanding officer himself drew up in a jeep, dismounted, interrogated them. They were frank with him, telling him that Oskar was the *Herr Direktor*, that they were Jews. They believed they were on safe ground, for they knew from the BBC that the U.S. forces included many Americans of both German and Jewish origins. 'Don't move,' said the captain. He drove away without explanation, leaving them in the half-embarrassed command of the young infantrymen, who offered them cigarettes, the Virginia kind, which had that almost glossy look – like the jeep, the uniforms, the equipment – of coming from a grand, brash, unfettered, and un-*ersatz* manufactory.

Though Emilie and the prisoners were uneasy that Oskar might be arrested, he himself sat on the grass apparently unconcerned and breathed in the spring air in these high woods. He had his Hebrew letter, and New York, he knew, was ethnically a city where Hebrew was not unknown. Half an hour passed and some soldiers appeared, coming down the road in an informal bunch, not strung out in the infantry manner. They were a group of Jewish infantrymen and included a field rabbi. They were very effusive. They embraced all the party, Emilie and Oskar as well. For these, the party was told, were the first concentration-camp survivors the battalion had met.

When the greetings were over, Oskar brought out his Hebrew reference, and the rabbi read it and began to weep. He relayed the details to the other Americans. There was more applause, more hand shaking, more embraces. The young GIs seemed so open, so loud, so childlike. Though one or two generations out of Central Europe, they had been so marked by America that the Schindlers and the prisoners looked at them with as much amazement as was returned.

The result was that the Schindler party spent two days on the Austrian frontier as guests of the regimental commander and the rabbi. They drank excellent coffee, such as the authentic prisoners in the group had not tasted since before the founding of the ghetto. They ate opulently.

After two days, the rabbi presented them with a captured ambulance, in which they drove to the ruined city of Linz in Upper Austria.

On the second day of peace in Brinnlitz, the Russians still had not appeared. The commando group worried about the necessity of hanging on to the camp for longer than they had thought they'd have to. One thing they remembered was that the only time they'd seen the SS show fear – apart from the anxiety of Motzek and his colleagues in the past few days – had been when typhus broke out. So they hung typhus signs all over the wire.

Three Czech partisans turned up at the gate in the afternoon and talked through the fence to the men on sentry duty. It's all over now, they said. You're free to walk out whenever you want.

When the Russians arrive, said the prison commandos. Until then we're keeping everyone in.

Their answer exhibited some of the pathology of the prisoner, the suspicion you got after a time that the world outside the fence was perilous and had to be reentered in stages. It also showed their wisdom. They were not convinced yet that the last German unit had gone.

The Czechs shrugged and went away.

That night, when Poldek Pfefferberg was part of the guard at the main gate, motorcycle engines were heard on the road. They did not pass by, as the *Panzers* had done, but could be heard turning in toward the camp itself. Five cycles marked with the SS death's-head materialised out of the dark and drew up noisily by the front fence. As the SS men – very young, Poldek remembers – switched off their engines, dismounted, and approached the gate, a debate raged among the armed men inside as to whether the visitors ought to be immediately shot.

The NCO in charge of the motorcycle party seemed to understand the risk inherent in the situation. He stood a little way from the wire with his hands extended. They needed gasoline, he said. He presumed that being a factory camp, Brinnlitz would have gasoline.

Pfefferberg advised that it was better to supply them and send them packing than to create problems by opening fire on them. Other elements of their regiment might be in the region, and be drawn by an outburst of gunfire.

So in the end the SS men were let in through the gate, and some of the prisoners went to the garage and drew gasoline. The SS NCO was careful to convey to the camp commandos – who had put on blue coveralls in an attempt to look like informal guards, or at least like German *Kapos* – that he did not find anything peculiar in the idea of armed prisoners' defending their camps from within.

'I hope you realise there's typhus here,' said Pfefferberg in German, pointing to the signs.

The SS men looked at each other.

'We've already lost two dozen people,' said Pfefferberg. 'We have another fifty isolated in the cellar.'

This claim seemed to impress the gentlemen of the death's-head. They were tired. They were fleeing. That was enough for them. They didn't want any bacterial perils on top of the others.

When the gasoline arrived in 5-gallon cans, they expressed their thanks, bowed, and left through the gate. The prisoners watched them fill their tanks and considerately leave by the wire any cans they could not fit into their sidecars. They put on their gloves, started their engines, and left without too much revving of the motors, being too careful to waste their new tankfuls on flourishes. Their roar faded southwest through the village. For the men at the gate, this polite encounter would be their last with anyone wearing the uniform of Heinrich Himmler's foul legion.

When on the third day the camp was liberated, it was by a single Russian officer. Riding a horse, he emerged through the defile through which the road and the railway siding approached the Brinnlitz gate. As he drew closer it became apparent that the horse was a mere pony, the officer's thin feet in the stirrups nearly touching the road and his legs bent in comically underneath the horse's skinny abdomen. He seemed to be bringing to Brinnlitz a personal, hard-won deliverance, for his uniform was worn, the leather strap of his rifle so withered by sweat and winter and campaigning that it had had to be replaced by rope. The reins of the horse were also of rope. The officer was fair-complexioned and, as Russians always look to Poles, immensely alien, immensely familiar.

After a short conversation in hybrid Polish-Russian, the commando at the gate let him in. Around the balconies of the second floor, the rumor of his arrival spread. As he dismounted he was kissed by Mrs. Krumholz. He smiled and called, in two languages, for a chair. One of the younger men brought it.

Standing on it to give himself a height advantage which, in relation to most of the prisoners, he did not need, he made what sounded like a standard liberation speech in Russian. Moshe Bejski could catch its gist. They had been liberated by the glorious Soviets. They were free to go to town, to move in the direction of their choosing. For under the Soviets, as in the mythical heaven, there was neither Jew nor Gentile, male nor female, bond nor free. They were not to take any cheap revenge in the town. Their Allies would find their oppressors, and subject them to solemn and appropriate punishment. The fact of their freedom should, to them, outweigh any other consideration.

He got down from his chair and smiled, as if saying that now he had finished as a spokesman and was prepared to answer questions. Bejski and some of the others began to speak to him, and he pointed to himself and said in creaky Belorussian Yiddish – the sort you pick up from your grandparents rather than your parents – that he was Jewish.

Now the conversation took on a new intimacy.

'Have you been in Poland?' Bejski asked him.

'Yes,' the officer admitted. 'I've come from Poland now.'

'Are there any Jews left up there?'

'I saw none.'

Prisoners were crowding around, translating and relaying the conversation to one another.

'Where are you from?' the officer asked Bejski.

'Cracow.'

'I was in Cracow two weeks ago.'

'Auschwitz? What about Auschwitz?'

'I heard that at Auschwitz there are still a few Jews.'

The prisoners grew thoughtful. The Russian made Poland sound like a vacuum now, and if they returned to Cracow they'd rattle around in it bleakly like dried peas in a jar.

'Is there anything I can do for you?' the officer asked.

There were cries for food. He thought he could get them a cartload of bread, and perhaps some horsemeat. It should arrive before dusk. 'But you should see what they have in town here,' the officer suggested.

It was a radical idea – that they ought to just go out the gate and begin shopping in Brinnlitz. For some of them it was still an unimaginable option.

Young men like Pemper and Bejski pursued the officer as he left. If there were no Jews in Poland, there was nowhere to go. They didn't want him to give them instructions, but felt he ought to discuss their quandary with them. The Russian paused in untying the reins of his pony from a railing.

'I don't know,' he said, looking them in the face. 'I don't know where you ought to go. Don't go east – that much I can tell you. But don't go west either.' His fingers returned to untying the knot. 'They don't like us anywhere.'

As the Russian officer had urged them, the Brinnlitz prisoners moved out the gate at last to make their first tentative contact with the outer world. The young were the first to try it. Danka Schindel went out the day after the liberation and climbed the wooded hill behind the camp. Lilies and anemones were beginning to bud, and migratory birds were arriving from Africa. Danka sat on the hill for a while, savouring the day, then rolled down it and lay in the grass at the bottom, inhaling the fragrances and looking at the sky. She was there for so long that her parents presumed she had come to grief in the village, with either the townspeople or the Russians.

Goldberg left early too, was perhaps the first to go, on his way to pick up his riches in Cracow. He would emigrate, as quickly as he could arrange it, to Brazil.

Most of the older prisoners stayed in camp. The Russians had now moved into Brinnlitz, occupying as an officers' quarters a villa on a hill above the village. They brought to the camp a butchered horse, which the prisoners ate ravenously, some of them finding it too rich after their diet of bread and vegetables and Emilie Schindler's porridge.

Lutek Feigenbaum, Janek Dresner, and young Sternberg went foraging in town. The village was patrolled by the Czech underground, and Brinnlitz folk of German descent were therefore wary of the liberated prisoners. A grocer indicated to the boys that they were welcome to a bag of sugar he'd been keeping in his storeroom. Young Sternberg found the sugar irresistible, lowering his face to it and swallowing it by the handful. It made him cruelly ill. He discovered what the Schindler group were finding in Nuremburg and Ravensburg – that liberty and the day of plenty had to be approached gradually.

The main purpose of this expedition to town had been to get bread. Feigenbaum was armed, as a member of the Brinnlitz commandos, with a pistol and a rifle, and when the baker insisted there was no bread, one of the others said to him, 'Threaten him with the rifle.' The man, after all, was *Sudetendeutsch* and in theory an approver of all their misery. Feigenbaum pointed the weapon at the baker and moved through the shop into the residence beyond, looking for hidden flour. In the parlor, he found the baker's wife and two daughters huddled in shock. They looked so frightened, indistinguishable from any Cracow family during an *Aktion*, that a great shame overwhelmed him. He nodded to the women as if he were on a social visit, and left.

The same shame overtook Mila Pfefferberg on her first visit to the village. As she entered the square, a Czech partisan stopped two *Sudeten* girls and made them take off their shoes so that Mila, who had only clogs, could select the pair that fitted her better. This sort of dominance made her flush, and she sat on the pavement making her embarrassed choice. The partisan gave the clogs to the *Sudeten* girl and passed on. Mila then turned in her tracks, ran up behind the girl, and gave the shoes back. The *Sudetendeutscherin*, Mila remembers, was not even gracious.

In the evenings, the Russians came to the camp looking for women. Pfefferberg had to put a pistol to the head of a soldier who penetrated the women's quarters and grabbed Mrs. Krumholz. (Mrs. Krumholz would for years later chide Pfefferberg, pointing at him and accusing him. 'Whatever chance I had of running off with a younger man, that scoundrel prevented it!') Three girls were taken away – more or less voluntarily – to a Russian party, and came back after three days and, they claimed, a good time.

The hold of Brinnlitz was a negative one, and within a week the prisoners began to move out. Some whose families had been consumed went directly to the West, never wishing to see Poland again. The Bejski boys, using their cloth and vodka to pay their way, travelled to Italy and boarded a Zionist ship to Palestine. The Dresners walked across Moravia and Bohemia and into Germany, where Janek was among the first ten students to enroll in the Bavarian University of Erlangen when it opened later in the year.

Manci Rosner returned to Podgórze, where Henry had agreed to meet her. Henry Rosner himself, liberated from Dachau with Olek, was in a *pissoir* in Munich one day and saw another client of the place wearing prison-camp stripes. He asked the man where he had been imprisoned. 'Brinnlitz,' said the man. Everyone except an old lady, the man told him (inaccurately, as it turned out), had survived Brinnlitz. Manci herself would hear of Henry's survival through a cousin who came to the room in Podgórze where Manci was waiting and waved the Polish paper in which were listed the names of Poles liberated from Dachau. 'Manci,' said the cousin, 'give me a kiss. Henry's alive, and so is Olek.'

Regina Horowitz had a similar rendezvous. It took her three weeks to travel from Brinnlitz to Cracow with her daughter Niusia. She rented a room – the handout from the Navy store made that possible – and waited for Dolek. When he arrived, they sought to make inquiries of Richard, but there was no news. One day that summer Regina saw the film of Auschwitz which the Russians had made and were showing free of charge to the Polish population. She saw the famous frames involving the camp children, who looked out from behind the wire or were escorted by nuns past the electrified fence of Auschwitz I. Being so small and so engaging, Richard figured in most of the frames. Regina got up screaming and left the theatre. The manager and a number of passing citizens tried to soothe her in the street. 'It's my son, it's my son!' she kept screaming. Now that she knew he was alive, she was able to discover that Richard had been released by the Russians into the hands of one of the Jewish rescue organisations. Thinking both his parents dead, the rescue body had had him adopted by some old acquaintances of the Horowitzes', people named Liebling. Regina was given the address, and when she arrived at the Lieblings' apartment could hear Richard inside, banging on a saucepan and calling, 'Today there'll be soup for everyone!' When she knocked on the door, he called to Mrs. Liebling to answer it.

So he was returned to her. But after what he had seen of the scaffolds of Płaszów and Auschwitz, she could never take him to a children's playground without his growing hysterical at the sight of the swing frames.

At Linz, Oskar's group reported to the American authorities, were relieved of their unreliable ambulance, and were taken by truck north to Nuremberg, to a large holding centre for wandering concentration-camp prisoners. They were discovering that, as they had suspected, liberation wasn't a straightforward business.

Richard Rechen had an aunt in Constanz, by the lake on the Swiss border. When the Americans asked the group if there was anywhere they could go, they nominated this aunt. The intent of the eight young prisoners from Brinnlitz was to deliver the Schindlers, if possible, across the Swiss border, in case vengeance against Germany erupted suddenly and, even in the American zone, the Schindlers were unjustly punished. Additionally, all eight of them were potential emigrants and believed that these matters would be easier to arrange from Switzerland.

Reubinski remembers that their relationship with the American commandant in Nuremburg was cordial, but the man would not spare them any transport to take them south to Constanz. They made the journey through the Black Forest as best they could, some of it on foot, some of it by train. Near Ravensburg they went to the local prison camp and spoke to the U.S. commandant. Here again they stayed as guests for some days, resting and living high on Army rations. In return, they sat up late with the commandant, who was of Jewish descent, and told him their stories of Amon and Płaszów, of Gröss-Rosen, Auschwitz, Brinnlitz. They hoped he would give them transport to Constanz, possibly a truck. He could not spare a truck, but gave them a bus instead, together with some provisions for the journey. Though Oskar still carried diamonds worth over 1,000 RM. as well as some currency, the bus does not appear to have been bought but was instead given freely. After his dealings with the German bureaucrats, it must have been difficult for Oskar to adjust to that sort of transaction.

West of Constanz, on the Swiss border and in the French

Occupied zone, they parked the bus in the village of Kreuzlingen. Rechen went to the town hardware store and bought a pair of wire cutters. It seems that the party were still wearing their prison uniforms when the wire cutters were purchased. Perhaps the man behind the counter was influenced by one of two considerations: (a) this was a prisoner, and if thwarted might call his French protectors; (b) this was in fact a German officer escaping in disguise and perhaps should be helped.

The border fence ran through the middle of Kreuzlingen and was guarded on the German side by French sentries of the *Sûreté Militaire*. The group approached this barrier on the edge of the village and, snipping the wires, waited for the sentry to near the end of his beat before slipping through to Switzerland. Unhappily, a woman from the village observed them from a bend of the road and rushed to the border to alert the French and Swiss. In a quiet Swiss village square, a mirror image of the one on the German side, the Swiss police surrounded the party, but Richard and Anka Rechen broke away and had to be chased and apprehended by a patrol car. The party was, within half an hour, passed back to the French, who at once searched their possessions, discovering jewels and currency; drove them to the former German prison; and locked them in separate cells.

It was clear to Reubinski that they were under suspicion of having been concentration-camp guards. In that sense the weight they had put on as guests of the Americans boomeranged, for they did not look as deprived as when they'd first left Brinnlitz. They were interrogated separately about their journey, about the valuables they were carrying. Each of them could tell a plausible story, but did not know if the others were telling the same one. They seem to have been afraid, in a way that had not applied with the Americans, that if the French discovered Oskar's identity and his function in Brinnlitz, they would arraign him as a matter of course.

Prevaricating for Oskar's sake and Emilie's, they remained there a week. The Schindlers themselves now knew enough about

Judaism to pass the obvious cultural tests. But Oskar's manner and physical condition didn't make his posture of recent-prisoner-of-the-SS very credible. Unhappily, his Hebrew letter was over in Linz, in the files of the Americans.

Edek Reubinski, as the leader of the eight, was questioned most regularly, and on the seventh day of his imprisonment was brought into the interrogation room to find a second person there, a man in civilian clothes, a speaker of Polish, brought in to test Reubinski's claim that he came from Cracow. For some reason – because the Pole played a compassionate role in the questioning that followed, or because of the familiarity of the language – Reubinski broke down, began to weep, and told the full story in fluent Polish. The rest were called one by one, were shown Reubinski, were told he had confessed, and then were ordered to recite their version of the truth in Polish. When at the end of the morning the versions matched, the whole group, the Schindlers included, were gathered in the interrogation room and embraced by both interrogators. The Frenchman, says Reubinski, was weeping. Everyone was delighted at that phenomenon – a weeping interrogator. When he managed to compose himself, he called for lunch to be brought in for himself, his colleague, the Schindlers, the eight.

That afternoon he had them transferred to a lakeside hotel in Constanz, where they stayed for some days at the expense of the French military government.

By the time he sat down to dinner that evening at the hotel with Emilie, Reubinski, the Rechens, and the others, Oskar's property had passed to the Soviets, and his last few jewels and currency were lost in the interstices of the liberating bureaucracy. He was as good as penniless, but was eating as well as could be managed in a good hotel with a number of his 'family.' All of which would be the pattern of his future.

Epilogue

Oskar's high season ended now. The peace would never exalt him as had the war. Oskar and Emilie came to Munich. For a time they shared lodgings with the Rosners, for Henry and his brother had been engaged to play at a Munich restaurant and had achieved a modest prosperity. One of his former prisoners, meeting him at the Rosners' small, cramped apartment, was shocked by his torn coat. His property in Cracow and Moravia had, of course, been confiscated by the Russians, and his remaining jewellery had been traded for food and liquor.

When the Feigenbaums arrived in Munich, they met his latest mistress, a Jewish girl, a survivor not of Brinnlitz but of worse camps than that. Many of the visitors to Oskar's rented rooms, as indulgent as they were toward Oskar's heroic weaknesses, felt shamed for Emilie's sake.

He was still a wildly generous friend and a great discoverer of unprocurables. Henry Rosner remembers that he found a source of chickens in the midst of chickenless Munich. He clung to the company of those of his Jews who had come to Germany – the Rosners, the Pfefferbergs, the Dresners, the Feigenbaums, the Sternbergs. Some cynics would later say that at the time it was wise of anyone involved in concentration camps to stay close to Jewish friends as protective colouration. But his dependence went beyond that sort of instinctive cunning. The *Schindlerjuden* had become his family.

In common with them, he heard that Amon Goeth had been captured by Patton's Americans the previous February, while a patient in an SS sanitarium at Bad Tolz; imprisoned in Dachau; and at the close of the war handed over to the new Polish government. Amon was in fact one of the first Germans dispatched to Poland for judgment. A number of former prisoners were invited to attend the trial as witnesses, and among the defense witnesses a deluded Amon considered calling were Helen Hirsch and Oskar Schindler. Oskar himself did not go to Cracow for the trials. Those who did found that Goeth, lean as a result of his diabetes, offered a subdued but unrepentant defense. All the orders for his acts of execution and transportation had been signed by superiors, he claimed, and were therefore *their* crimes, not his. Witnesses who told of murders committed by the Commandant's own hand were, said Amon, maliciously exaggerating. There had been some prisoners executed as saboteurs, but there were always saboteurs in wartime.

Mietek Pemper, waiting in the body of the court to be called to give evidence, sat beside another Płaszów graduate who stared at Amon in the dock and whispered, 'That man still terrifies me.' But Pemper himself, as first witness for the prosecution, delivered an exact catalogue of Amon's crimes. He was followed by others, among them Dr. Biberstein and Helen Hirsch, who had precise and painful memories. Amon was condemned to death and hanged in Cracow on September 13, 1946. It was two years to the day since his arrest by the SS in Vienna on black-marketeering charges. According to the Cracow press, he went to the gallows without remorse and gave the National Socialist salute before dying.

In Munich, Oskar himself identified Liepold, who had been detained by the Americans. A Brinnlitz prisoner accompanied Oskar at the lineup, and says that Oskar asked the protesting Liepold, 'Do you want *me* to do it, or would you rather leave it to the fifty angry Jews who are waiting downstairs in the street?' Liepold would also be hanged – not for his crimes in Brinnlitz, but for earlier murders in Budzyn.

Oskar had probably already conceived the scheme of becoming a farmer in Argentina; a breeder of nutria, the large South American aquatic rodents considered precious for their skins. Oskar presumed that the same excellent commercial instincts which had brought him to Cracow in 1939 were now urging him to cross the Atlantic. He was penniless, but the Joint Distribution Committee, the international Jewish relief organisation to whom Oskar had made reports during the war and to whom his record was known, were willing to help him. In 1949 they made him an *ex gratia* payment of $15,000 and gave a reference ('To Whom It May Concern') signed by M. W. Beckelman, the vice chairman of the 'Joint's' Executive Council. It said:

The American Joint Distribution Committee has thoroughly investigated the wartime and Occupation activities of Mr. Schindler . . . . We recommend wholeheartedly that all organisations and individuals contacted by Mr. Schindler do their utmost to help him, in recognition of his outstanding service . . . .

Under the guise of operating a Nazi labour factory first in Poland and then in the Sudetenland, Mr. Schindler managed to take in as employees and protect Jewish men and women destined for death in Auschwitz or other infamous concentration camps . . . . 'Schindler's camp in Brinnlitz,' witnesses have told the Joint Distribution Committee, 'was the only camp in the Nazi-occupied territories where a Jew was never killed, or even beaten, but was always treated as a human being.'

Now that he is about to begin his life anew, let us help him as once he helped our brethren.

When he sailed for Argentina, he took with him half a dozen families of *Schindlerjuden*, paying the passage for many of them. With Emilie, he settled on a farm in Buenos Aires province and worked it for nearly ten years. Those of Oskar's survivors who did not see him in those years find it hard now to imagine him as a farmer, since he was never a man for steady routine. Some say, and there is some truth to it, that Emalia and Brinnlitz succeeded in their eccentric way because of the acumen of men like Stern and Bankier. In Argentina, Oskar had no such support, apart, of course, from the good sense and rural industriousness of his wife.

The decade in which Oskar farmed nutria, however, was the period in which it was demonstrated that breeding, as distinct from trapping, did not produce pelts of adequate quality. Many other nutria enterprises failed in that time, and in 1957 the Schindlers' farm went bankrupt. Emilie and Oskar moved into a house provided by B'nai B'rith in San Vicente, a southern suburb of Buenos Aires, and for a time Oskar sought work as a sales representative. Within a year, however, he left for Germany. Emilie remained behind.

Living in a small apartment in Frankfurt, he sought capital to buy a cement factory, and pursued the possibility of major compensation from the West German Ministry of Finance for the loss of his Polish and Czechoslovakian properties. Little came of this effort. Some of Oskar's survivors considered that the failure of the German government to pay him his due arose from lingering Hitlerism in the middle ranks of the civil service. But Oskar's claim probably failed for technical reasons, and it is not possible to detect bureaucratic malice in the correspondence addressed to Oskar from the ministry.

The Schindler cement enterprise was launched on capital from the Joint Distribution Committee and 'loans' from a number of Schindler Jews who had done well in postwar Germany. It had a brief history. By 1961, Oskar was bankrupt again. His factory had been hurt by a series of harsh winters in which the construction industry had closed down; but some of the Schindler survivors believe the company's failure was abetted by Oskar's restlessness and low tolerance for routine.

That year, hearing that he was in trouble, the *Schindlerjuden* in Israel invited him to visit them at their expense. An advertisement appeared in Israel's Polish-language press asking that all former inmates of Concentration Camp Brinnlitz who had known 'Oskar Schindler the German' contact the newspaper. In Tel Aviv, Oskar was welcomed ecstatically. The postwar children of his survivors mobbed him. He had grown heavier and his features had thickened. But at the parties and receptions, those who had known him saw that he was the same indomitable Oskar. The growling deft wit, the outrageous Charles Boyer charm, the voracious thirst had all survived his two bankruptcies.

It was the year of the Adolf Eichmann trial, and Oskar's visit to Israel aroused some interest in the international press. On the eve of the opening of Eichmann's trial, the correspondent of the London *Daily Mail* wrote a feature on the contrast between the records of the two men, and quoted the preamble of an appeal the *Schindlerjuden* had opened to assist Oskar. 'We do not forget the sorrows of Egypt, we do not forget Haman, we do not forget Hitler. Thus, among the unjust, we do not forget the just. Remember Oskar Schindler.'

There was some incredulity among Holocaust survivors about the idea of a beneficent labour camp such as Oskar's, and this disbelief found its voice through a journalist at a press conference with Schindler in Jerusalem. 'How do you explain,' he asked, 'that you knew all the senior SS men in the Cracow region and had regular dealings with them?' 'At that stage in history,' Oskar answered, 'it was rather difficult to discuss the fate of Jews with the Chief Rabbi of Jerusalem.'

The Department of Testimonies of the *Yad Vashem* had, near the end of Oskar's Argentine residence, sought and been given by him a general statement of his activities in Cracow and Brinnlitz. Now, on their own initiative and under the influence of Itzhak Stern, Jakob Sternberg, and Moshe Bejski (once Oskar's forger of official stamps, now a respected and scholarly lawyer), the Board of Trustees of *Yad Vashem* began to consider the question of an official tribute to Oskar. The chairman of the board was Justice Landau, the presiding judge at the Eichmann trial. *Yad Vashem* sought and received a mass of testimonies concerning Oskar. Of this large collection of statements, four are critical of him. Though these four witnesses all state that without Oskar they would have perished, they criticise his business methods in the early months of the war. Two of the four disparaging testimonies are written by a father and son, called earlier in this account the Cs. In their enamelware outlet in Cracow, Oskar had installed his mistress Ingrid as *Treuhänder*. A third statement is by the Cs' secretary and repeats the allegations of punching and bullying, rumors of which Stern had reported back to Oskar in 1940. The fourth comes from a man who claims to have had a prewar interest in Oskar's enamel factory under its former name, Rekord – an interest, he claimed, that Oskar had ignored.

Justice Landau and his board must have considered these four statements insignificant when set against the massed testimony of other *Schindlerjuden*, and they made no comment on them. Since all four stated that Oskar was their saviour in any case, it is said to have occurred to the board to ask why, if Oskar had committed crimes against these people, he went to such extravagant pains to save them.

The municipality of Tel Aviv was the first body to honour Oskar. On his fifty-third birthday he unveiled a plaque in the Park of Heroes. The inscription describes him as saviour of 1,200 prisoners of AL Brinnlitz, and though it understates numerically the extent of his rescue, it declares that it has been erected in love and gratitude. Ten days later in Jerusalem, he was declared a Righteous Person, this title being a peculiarly Israeli honour based on an ancient tribal assumption that in the mass of Gentiles, the God of Israel would always provide a leavening of just men. Oskar was invited also to plant a carob tree in the Avenue of the Righteous leading to the *Yad Vashem* Museum. The tree is still there, marked by a plaque, in a grove which contains trees planted in the name of all the other Righteous. A tree for Julius Madritsch, who had illicitly fed and protected his workers in a manner quite unheard of among the Krupps and the Farbens, stands there also, and a tree for Raimund Titsch, the Madritsch supervisor in Płaszów. On that stony ridge, few of the memorial trees have grown to more than 10 feet.

The German press carried stories of Oskar's wartime rescues and of the *Yad Vashem* ceremonies. These reports, always laudatory, did not make his life easier. He was hissed on the streets of Frankfurt, stones were thrown, a group of workmen jeered him and called out that he ought to have been burned with the Jews. In 1963 he punched a factory worker who'd called him a 'Jew-kisser,' and the man lodged a charge of assault. In the local court, the lowest level of the German judiciary, Oskar received a lecture from the judge and was ordered to pay damages. 'I would kill myself,' he wrote to Henry Rosner in Queens, New York, 'if it wouldn't give them so much satisfaction.'

These humiliations increased his dependence on the survivors. They were his only emotional and financial surety. For the rest of his life he would spend some months of every year with them, living honoured and well in Tel Aviv and Jerusalem, eating free of charge at a Rumanian restaurant in Ben Yehudah Street, Tel Aviv, though subject sometimes to Moshe Bejski's filial efforts to limit his drinking to three double cognacs a night. In the end, he would always return to the other half of his soul: the disinherited self; the mean, cramped apartment a few hundred metres from Frankfurt's central railway station. Writing from Los Angeles to other *Schindlerjuden* in the United States that year, Poldek Pfefferberg urged all survivors to donate at least a day's pay a year to Oskar Schindler, whose state he described as 'discouragement, loneliness, disillusion.'

Oskar's contacts with the *Schindlerjuden* continued on a yearly basis. It was a seasonal matter – half the year as the Israeli butterfly, half the year as the Frankfurt grub. He was continually short of money.

A Tel Aviv committee of which Itzhak Stern, Jakob Sternberg, and Moshe Bejski were again members continued to lobby the West German government for an adequate pension for Oskar. The grounds for their appeal were his wartime heroism, the property he had lost, and the by-now-fragile state of his health. The first official reaction from the German government was, however, the award of the Cross of Merit in 1966, in a ceremony at which Konrad Adenauer presided. It was not till July 1, 1968, that the Ministry of Finance was happy to report that from that date it would pay him a pension of 200 marks per month. Three months later, pensioner Schindler received the Papal Knighthood of St. Sylvester from the hands of the Bishop of Limburg.

Oskar was still willing to cooperate with the Federal Justice Department in the pursuit of war criminals. In this matter he seems to have been implacable. On his birthday in 1967, he gave confidential information concerning many of the personnel of KL Płaszów. The transcript of his evidence of that date shows that he does not hesitate to testify, but also that he is a scrupulous witness. If he knows nothing or little of a particular SS man, he says so. He says it of Amthor; of the SS man Zugsburger; of Fraulein Ohnesorge, one of the quick-tempered women supervisors. He does not hesitate, however, to call Bosch a murderer and an exploiter, and says that he recognised Bosch at a railway station in Munich in 1946, approached him, and asked him if – after Płaszów – he could manage to sleep. Bosch, says Oskar, was at that point living under an East German passport. A supervisor named Mohwinkel, representative in Płaszów of the German Armaments Works, is also roundly condemned; 'intelligent but brutal,' Oskar says of him. Of Goeth's bodyguard, Grün, he tells the story of the attempted execution of the Emalia prisoner Lamus, which he himself prevented by a gift of vodka. (It is a story to which a great number of prisoners also testify in their statements in *Yad Vashem*.) Of the NCO Ritschek, Oskar says that he has a bad reputation but that he himself knows nothing of his crimes. He is also uncertain whether the photograph the Justice Department showed him is in fact Ritschek. There is only one person on the Justice Department list for whom Oskar is willing to give an unqualified commendation. That is the engineer Huth, who had helped him during his last arrest. Huth, he says, was highly respected and highly spoken of by the prisoners themselves.

As he entered his sixties, he began working for the German Friends of Hebrew University. This involvement resulted from the urgings of those *Schindlerjuden* who were concerned with restoring some new purpose to Oskar's life. He began to work raising funds in West Germany. His old capacity to inveigle and charm officials and businessmen was exercised once again. He also helped set up a scheme of exchanges between German and Israeli children.

Despite the precariousness of his health, he still lived and drank like a young man. He was in love with a German woman named Annemarie, whom he had met at the King David Hotel in Jerusalem. She would become the emotional linchpin of his later life.

His wife, Emilie, still lived, without any financial help from him, in her little house in San Vicente, south of Buenos Aires. She lives there at the time of the writing of this book. As she was in Brinnlitz, she is a figure of quiet dignity. In a documentary made by German television in 1973, she spoke – without any of the abandoned wife's bitterness or sense of grievance – about Oskar and Brinnlitz, about her own behavior in Brinnlitz. Perceptively, she remarked that Oskar had done nothing astounding before the war and had been unexceptional since. He was fortunate, therefore, that in that short fierce era between 1939 and 1945 he had met people who summoned forth his deeper talents.

In 1972, during a visit by Oskar to the New York executive office of the American Friends of Hebrew University, three *Schindlerjuden*, partners in a large New Jersey construction company, led a group of seventy-five other Schindler prisoners in raising $120,000 to dedicate to Oskar a floor of the Truman Research Centre at Hebrew University. The floor would house a Book of Life, containing an account of Oskar's rescues and a list of the rescued. Two of these partners, Murray Pantirer and Isak Levenstein, had been sixteen years old when Oskar brought them to Brinnlitz. Now Oskar's children had become his parents, his best recourse, his source of honour.

He was very ill. The men who had been physicians in Brinnlitz – Alexander Biberstein, for example – knew it. One of them warned Oskar's close friends, 'The man should not be alive. His heart is working through pure stubbornness.'

In October 1974, he collapsed at his small apartment near the railway station in Frankfurt and died in a hospital on October 9.

His death certificate says that advanced hardening of the arteries of the brain and heart had caused the final seizure. His will declared a wish he had already expressed to a number of *Schindlerjuden* – that he be buried in Jerusalem. Within two weeks the Franciscan parish priest of Jerusalem had given his permission for Herr Oskar Schindler, one of the Church's least observant sons, to be buried in the Latin Cemetery of Jerusalem.

Another month passed before Oskar's body was carried in a leaden casket through the crammed streets of the Old City of Jerusalem to the Catholic cemetery, which looks south over the Valley of Hinnom, called Gehenna in the New Testament. In the press photograph of the procession can be seen – amid a stream of other Schindler Jews – Itzhak Stern, Moshe Bejski, Helen Hirsch, Jakob Sternberg, Juda Dresner.

He was mourned on every continent.

Afterword

Writers do not always have sound instincts when it comes to assessing the impact of a story. If we did, we would write irresistible narratives every time we became obsessed with a particular tale. But it struck me when I first encountered the Schindler story that this was an extraordinary one, engrossing in itself, irrespective of what I might do with it. There were two main reasons for its – dare I say – attractive qualities. One was the paradoxically flawed human being Schindler appeared to be, a man whose virtues and vices seemed to be instinctive to him and not a matter for philosophical weighing and measuring. Thus he was as implausible a hero as most of us are. But unlike other humans whose sophistication might have rendered them hesitant and despairing, he was a joyous, hectic pragmatist.

Second, I saw at once that, as a businessman and *Abwehr* (German Military Intelligence) operative, Schindler had contact with every stage of the process of the destruction of Jewish Europeans. That is, he saw the confiscation of residential and commercial properties of all Jewish people – he occupied a confiscated flat, though he always insisted he acquired his Krakow factory, Emalia, legally. He saw the ghettoisation of the Jews and was part of their exploitation as cheap labour in factories. He saw the unutterably violent liquidation camps, and was a whistle-blower as to the existence of *Vernichtungslageren*, destruction camps, where death was delivered by industrial gas on a production-line scale.

Another reason to write the book was the Holocaust itself. First of all, the Holocaust is a fantastical *reductio ad adsurdum* of a culture of race-hate, and it seems as much akin to sci-fi as to actual history. If it had not happened, it could almost be one of those fables dreamed up by a writer to warn us of many human flaws, not least our capacity to be so enchanted by technology that we use it in the service of our doctrines of ethnicity and social control. We always think of such extreme actions as 'inhuman', but they are all too human. Absurdity again, and the absurd inventiveness that can arise when we are hysterical about race!

What also struck me about the Holocaust was that it is a moral template. One asks oneself, could I have done what Schindler did? I wrote the book in part from a fascinated knowledge that I could not – I am not as talented at risk-taking and as reckless as Oscar was. I like to doubt I could have been as abandoned in murderousness as was the Plaszow commandant Amon Goeth. But the question one asks oneself is this: if I had been raised in the Weimar republic and my family's neediness was blamed upon an international Jewish conspiracy, and I was then inducted into the SS . . .? You can complete the scenario. What would you have done when faced with the obvious humanity of the victims? What would I have done?

And had I been Jewish, would I have served as a member of the *Ordnungsdienst*, the Jewish police, and in that capacity, when the intentions of the SS became clear, what would I have done?

Therefore, for me, as for all students of history, the Holocaust focuses speculation about one's moral fibre, and raises questions that we both cannot help asking and cannot hope to have answered unless we find ourselves in a crisis of such lethal and tyrannous extremes as World War II.

So, the moral question fascinated me. But last of all, as an Australian, a postcolonial descendant of European settlers (and even of convicts), I was always amazed that it was my metropolitan betters in vaunted Northern Europe who had accomplished such a fantastically barbarous thing as the Holocaust. After millennia of race hysteria, it was the Europeans *in Europe* who brought their hatred to this mass-murdering culmination.

I claim no special virtue for Antipodeans. Aboriginals of the more than two hundred and fifty nations who have suffered from dispossession would not permit me to, and that's just to begin with. Yet in that connection, some thirty-four years after the book was first published, I am still frequently asked two questions, the first of which is why an Australian, of all people, would write such a book? It is as if people assume Australians are off hunting crocodiles and have no involvement in the affairs of the world. The truth is that, though at a great global remove and in a nation quickly becoming more and more Asian, I have always felt part of the European equation, an inheritor of the glories, twitches and malice of Europe. I was also in fact only one degree of separation from the Nazi regime. Despite growing up in a bush town and then in the Western Suburbs of Sydney, I had a father who spent nearly three years in the Middle East during World War II, was acquainted with the Nazi *Afrika Korps*, and sent me Nazi memorabilia, posters flare guns, badges of rank and postcards, which I still now store away in my swimming trunk and tie drawer. The cake tins full of mementoes of the Reich he sent me would tease my childhood imagination, which compared these concrete things with what I would see in the newsreels of the war, and in the absurdly propagandistic American, British and Australian films at the Vogue Cinema in Homebush, New South Wales. I was aware that many British and Australian soldiers in the Middle East paid their counterparts in the *Afrika Korps* a certain compliment of respect. I was astounded that these respected men should be parties, however remote, to the extraordinary effort of the regime, its other 'great exercise', to obliterate the Jews of Europe.

I was more than ready to examine that question in my own work when I first met my first *Schindlerjuden*, Leopold Pfefferberg and his gentle wife Ludmila, in their leather goods store in Beverly Hills, California, in October 1980. For reasons already stated I felt attracted to the story and unqualified to write it, but to my cries that I was neither metropolitan European nor Jewish, Leopold Pfefferberg cried enthusiastically, 'That's perfect. You don't have an axe to grind.' (Later, when there were film delays, this remarkable survivor would similarly and improbably harry Steven Spielberg with the battle call, 'An Oscar for Oskar!')

The second thing I am asked is whether I resent the fact that Spielberg changed the title from *Schindler's Ark* to *Schindler's List*. I have to defend Spielberg on this matter. It was the American publishers in 1982 who altered the title for their edition, after much wrangling, and arguments that American Jewry would be offended by the idea whereby animals were saved two by two. We argued that it was the Ark of the Covenant that the title referred to, and that there was a rough covenant between Oskar and his prisoners, as there had been between Yahweh and those and the people of Moses. That argument did not prevail and, in the end, knowing the book was doomed to limited notice, we let it be called *List*.

When Spielberg decided in 1992 that he would proceed with the film, and invited me to visit him at the fabled Amblin Studios, I asked him to call the film *Schindler's Ark*, but he said that he wanted to use lists to visual effect on in the film. And so he did, and who can argue with the filmic efficacy of that.

The story of Oskar Schindler, his imperfections and ambiguous triumph, is now still seen in the light I first saw it, as an exceptional human tale, the sort so encapsulating, dramatic and lustrous that it can only be diminished by the artistic fallibility of the narrator. Knowing well my shortcomings as a story-teller, I chose to employ the narrative methods Truman Capote had used in *In Cold Blood*. I wanted to give the tale a literary quality – such is the vanity of writers – rather than write it as a conventional biography. But of course, the method of faction or the documentary novel meant that I would interview many former prisoners, including survivors settled in Sydney and Melbourne, and indeed from Beverly Hills to Krakow itself, by way of Israel. I was able to contact Emilie Schindler, Oskar's wife, and ask her questions about the operation of Oskar's factory camp and the post-war period. It was understood in all cases that I would relate the stories of former prisoners and witnesses accurately.

Schindler's Ark

As I have said in earlier introductions to Schindler, the survivors were anxious that the overarching events and their meaning should be rendered with historical accuracy, as should the individual stories as well. The reason for this concern was two-fold – former prisoners feared that other survivors, who had not experienced in the Holocaust process any of the generosity that characterised Oskar, would consider this tale to be a fatuous version of 'the good German'. Similarly they did not want denialists to use the Oskar story as a means to undermine the authenticity of what befell European Jewry. Hence, though the tone of this book might in some ways be that of a novel, it is substantively and conscientiously true. A number of former prisoners – including Leopold Pfefferberg, Mila Pfefferberg, Moshe Bejski, reformist Israeli judge, Mieteck Pember and Itzhak Stern's widow, Dr Maria Stern – read and corrected the manuscript in its entirety, and many others examined the sections that referred to them and make corrections of fact.

How does one introduce dialogue into a novel that purports to be factual? I reconstructed an early conversation in the book – between Schindler and various other Nazis regarding the future of the Jews – from what Schindler himself tells us about the characteristic discourses of the day amongst bureaucrats and officials; basically, from what people like that were saying. As for the rest, if two or three former prisoners narrated substantially the same dialogue about an event, or if an individual such as Helen Hirsch recollected with what seemed an acute memory her fear on first seeing Schindler and her subsequent conversations with him, I felt it was within my remit to convey what was said as dialogue. It was an instinctive rather than reasoned choice, and the reader can decide whether, in overall effect and validity and veracity, it works. Otherwise, I cut down entirely upon dialogue, even if I am grateful that European Jews are simply one group amongst the splendid array of *homo sapiens* who like to portray past events in direct speech as well as mere description.

I have written many books but I have never been able to invent a story as morally complex and affecting as the Schindler story. Schindler's rescue, small in terms of the overall numbers, made it possible for readers to visit the experience of the individual prisoners, young and old, and to feel for a second the iron judgement of racial condemnation against them.

It is not an irrelevant experience. At the moment there are sixty million displaced people in the world. The number is not likely to diminish soon. The Schindler story should at least inspire the people of Europe, and my own country Australia, not to call the masses of the dislocated by names that belittle or undermine their humanity. If a former generation was judged by the Holocaust, we should not doubt that we will be judged by this crisis. For the past is neater, and the present is complex. What we are guided by is the realisation that in all human crises we cannot be reduced to the methods of the Third Reich, which began with name-calling and proceeded to destruction.

We must all try to behave in a manner that honours what has become the Oskar inheritance.

Thomas Keneally
New South Wales, 2016